When Is A Pig A Hog?

A GUIDE TO CONFOUNDINGLY RELATED ENGLISH WORDS

Bernice Randall

NEW YORK LONDON TORONTO SYDNEY TOKYO SINGAPORE

PRENTICE HALL

15 Columbus Circle
New York, NY 10023

Prentice Hall and colophons are
registered trademarks of Simon & Schuster, Inc.

Manufactured in the United States of America

1   2   3   4   5   6   7   8   9   10

ISBN 0-13955212-X

Contents

Acknowledgments

I am grateful to many people for helping me turn my "pig / hog" notion into a book. First, to David B. Guralnik, editor in chief emeritus of Webster's New World Dictionaries, who offered encouragement and invaluable advice on the content and linguistic approach. To Victoria Neufeldt, the present editor in chief, who generously opened the Webster's New World cite files to me. To Philip Friedman, who, as associate publisher of Simon & Schuster's Reference Division, shepherded my proposal through the approval process and granted me permission to draw on *Webster's New World Dictionary of American English,* Third College Edition, and to Kate Kelly, senior editor at Prentice Hall Press, who carried the project to completion. To Beverly Cory, Kathi George, Patty Green Holubar, Judith Quinn, and Tralelia Twitty, editors and longtime colleagues who, as an informal focus group, suggested ways to improve the organization of the book. To Elede Hall, a friend and librarian who helped me with the research.

I am indebted also to Beverly Cory, who cast a practiced editorial eye on the manuscript, and to the following experts, who offered guidance and advice on entries in their special fields: Pamela Forbes, editor in chief of *Triptych,* at The Museum Society of San Francisco, and Barbara Jackson, artist; Klaus W. Krause, a technical editor at SRI International; Samuel Matlovsky, musician; Robin A. Rolfe, executive director of The United States Trademark Association; Dr. Melvin S. Rosenthal, associate professor of medicine, Case Western Reserve University; Robert Sager, laboratory chief, and Margaret Stevenson, senior forensic chemist, Western Regional Laboratory, Drug Enforcement Administration, U.S. Department of Justice; and Harry R. Van Cleve, lawyer and civil servant. Their willingness to review parts of the manuscript in no way makes them responsible for my errors in statements of fact.

I appreciate, as well, the kindness of the many individuals and institutions that responded to my requests for information. Though I cannot list them all, I would like to mention Jacuzzi Whirlpool Bath, Walnut Creek, California; the reference librarians at the Menlo Park, California, Library; Leaneta G. Smith, public information specialist at the National Live Stock and Meat Board, Chicago; and Herb Roche, inspector in the Division of Law Enforcement, U.S. Fish & Wildlife Service, Department of the Interior, Burlingame, California.

Preface

When is a pig not a pig? When it's a hog. That is, once a pig tips the scale at 120 pounds, it becomes a hog. But no matter how much weight a salamander puts on, it does not become a lizard. And a polliwog is a tadpole from the moment it hatches.

Whether English is our first language or an acquired one, we are sometimes uneasy in choosing between certain words. That is because we are not sure whether the words have virtually the same meanings and can therefore freely replace one another, have closely related meanings yet are interchangeable only in certain contexts, or have different meanings but are nonetheless linked through frequent association.

Tadpole, polliwog is but one pair of virtual equivalents we might hesitate to use interchangeably for fear of overlooking a distinction our listeners or readers know about. Among the others are *income statement, profit and loss statement; tone poem, symphonic poem;* and *crib death, SIDS, sudden infant death syndrome.* The number is not limitless, of course, because two or more words with precisely the same meaning are a rarity in any language. In fact, even among terms generally considered alike there is room for choice. For example, *Indian, American Indian, Native American, Amerindian,* and *Amerind* are freely substituted for one another, but nowadays many people prefer *Native American,* especially in reference to North American Indians.

The vast English word stock includes countless terms that, without being equivalents, have one or more closely related senses—so closely related as to make us uneasy occasionally. In some contexts, we wonder, is one word more appropriate than another? Even though *hog* refers to a full-grown *pig,* can either word be applied to a domesticated *swine?* Is *normal school* as commonly used as *teachers college?* Should the *QE2* be called a *boat* or a *ship?* What is the connection between *Kampuchea* and *Cambodia?*

And then there are many terms that, though they differ in meaning, somehow spring to mind in pairs or sets. So the question arises as to which term means what. Both a *salamander* and a *lizard* are coldblooded vertebrates, but which is a reptile like a snake and which an amphibian like a frog? Is it the *Peter Principle, Murphy's Law,* or *Parkinson's Law* that says if there is a possibility for something to go wrong it will? Does a *battalion* consist of more than one *brigade,* or is it the other way around? Is a child of one's parent's first cousin a *second cousin* or a *first cousin once removed?* Besides wanting to feel comfortable with such terms when we come across them in our reading and conversation, we often think of words but have trouble recalling others that mean the opposite or at least something quite different. If *zenith* is up, what is down? What is the angle that is greater than a *right angle* but less than a *straight angle?* What do we call a sculpture that is abstract like a *mobile* yet stationary? What, besides *draw,* is a basic form of poker?

In writing *When Is a Pig a Hog?* I had in mind two kinds of reader who, I hoped, would be one and the same person. First, someone who, without being a grammarian or linguist, has a lively interest in the English language. And, second, someone who is curious about people, places, things, human activities, nature, science—whatever his or her experience encompasses and more.

The book is divided into eight main sections:

Human and Not So Human Beings

Here and There

Things

Concepts, Actions, and Other Intangibles

The Arts: Fine and Otherwise

Nature and Science

Our Bodies and Medicine

Organizations and Institutions

In addition, two appendixes give information not easily incorporated in the text:

Gods and Goddesses in Greek and Roman Mythology

Geologic Time Chart

A book nowhere near a dictionary or encyclopedia in size and scope cannot, of course, exhaust such a broad range of subjects. Given the infinite number of possibilities, it was difficult to decide what to include and what to leave out, and not everyone will agree with the choices I finally made.

The short, informal entries deal more with current, everyday terms than with dated or abstruse ones: *couch, sofa, settee, davenport, divan, chesterfield,* say, instead of *cuspidor, spittoon* or *bow-back armchair, banister-back chair, comb-back rocker.* Even the abstractions are likely to be familiar to most readers (*crime, felony, misdemeanor,* for example, rather than *adjure, abjure*). Pairs or sets of words are not included simply because they have similar or identical sounds (*cryogenics, cryonics* and *reign, rein*), any more than those that vary only in spelling are (*advisor, adviser* and *kindergartner, kindergartener*). Nor is the book intended as a compendium of British and American equivalents, such as *elevator* and *lift*. However, British usage is brought up if it is appropriate to a discussion of related terms used in the United States; for instance, the word *chemist* is mentioned in the *pharmacist / druggist* entry in "Human and Not So Human Beings."

Within each subject category the entries are arranged somewhat loosely by subtopic. "Here and There," for example, begins with a number of terms referring to the world at large, among them *nation, state,* and *country,* before discussing others having to do specifically with the Western Hemisphere, Europe, the Middle East, Africa, and Asia. This organization is different from the dictionary-style alphabetical arrangement found in many reference books, especially those concerned with words, for it is intended to invite browsing. Most readers will readily follow the progression from, say, *Near East / Middle East* to *Iran / Persia* without wondering why the sequence is not reversed. For those who want to know whether a particular word is discussed and, if so, where, the index lists not only the two headwords that introduce the entries but virtually all words defined or explained in the text and the appendixes. The *Near East / Middle East* entry, for example, takes up *Far East* as well, besides giving *Mideast* as a variant of *Middle East,* so all four terms appear in the index.

The various subject categories naturally have some give. One reason is so that the information on a certain topic can be rounded out. For example, even though *pants / trousers* and *shirt / blouse* are entries in "Things," *black belt / white belt* follows *jujitsu / judo* among those on sports and games in "Concepts, Actions, and Other Intangibles": black belts neither hold up pants nor keep shirts tucked in. Another reason is simply that language refuses to be squeezed into compartments. The *remainder / residue* entry, for instance, appears in "Concepts, Actions, and Other Intangibles," for both words commonly express qualities thought of as unrelated to a particular or material object ("the remainder of one's life" and "the residue of Grandpa's estate"). Yet, because it includes *remnant,* which often suggests that which can be perceived by the senses ("remnants of cloth from the ends of bolts"), the entry might have been placed in "Things." Indeed, the classic trick image of a vase that becomes a couple about to kiss turns up from time to time in the book. While we are looking at the vase, we cannot for the life of us see the couple—until they drive the vase completely out of sight.

Human and Not So Human Beings

man / male

Man is the standard general term for an adult human being who is not a woman (as in "President Reagan appointed 13 men and no women to his cabinet in 1981").

Male is applied to plants, animals, and human beings as the basic term for members of the sex that is biologically distinguished from the female sex. The male biological symbol is ♂. Both within and beyond the fields of science and technology, the word *male* is appropriate wherever *female* would be in a similar context.

Boy is roughly the equivalent of *girl* ("Two boys and two girls were finalists in the spelling bee"). Once a boy is 18 years old, he is generally referred to as a *man* or a *young man*. *Youth* is also applied to a male who falls somewhere between childhood and adulthood. Although *youths* means "young people" or "young people collectively" (as in "Black TV anchors are positive role models for black youths"), the singular form of the word is associated with a young man, not with a young woman. *Lad* may seem old-fashioned, recalling, say, A. E. Housman's late-nineteenth-century poem *A Shropshire Lad*, but it is sometimes used as the equivalent of *boy, young man,* or *youth*.

woman / female

Woman is the standard general term for an adult human being who is not a man (as in "President Bush appointed 13 men and 1 woman to his cabinet in 1989").

The word may be modified by *young* if the person is no longer a child yet not old enough to be considered an adult ("As a young woman, she spent her summers as a camp counselor"). When used simply as an equivalent of *woman, female* is widely regarded as a contemptuous term. So statements like "FDR's mother was a strong-willed female" and "Sandra Day O'Connor is the first female appointed to the U.S. Supreme Court" occur less often in speech and writing than they used to.

On the other hand, *female* is considered appropriate in biological references, whether to plants, animals, or human beings, if *male* would be expected in similar constructions involving the other sex. (For example: The uterus is a hollow, muscular organ of female mammals. The prostate gland is a partly muscular gland surrounding the urethra at the base of the bladder in most male mammals.) The female biological symbol is ♀. *Female,* like *male,* often appears in statistical tables and other technical contexts, particularly if age is either unknown or irrelevant ("In 1988 the total number of arrests for females was 1,583,426; for males, 7,251,407").

Until recently, *lady* was used in polite or genteel references to any woman ("In case she is in an accident, a lady never leaves home with a safety pin on her underwear"). Nowadays, however, *lady* is frowned upon as a general substitute for *woman* unless *gentleman* would be the corresponding term in place of *man.* That is, "Amelia Earhart was the first lady to make a solo transatlantic flight" would go counter to current usage no less than "Charles Lindbergh was the first gentleman to make a solo, nonstop transatlantic flight" would. Because of the same implied condescension, *lady* is ordinarily avoided as a modifier too. For instance, *lady lawyer* is likely to be replaced by *woman lawyer* or simply *lawyer; cleaning lady,* by *cleaning woman* or simply *cleaner.* Yet *lady* is still used in certain set phrases, such as "ladies and gentlemen"; in poetry (as in Yeats's verse "She was more beautiful than thy first love, / This lady by the trees"); and for a woman of high social position ("Today's economy has compelled more than one English lord and lady to open their manor houses to tourists").

Though appropriate in referring to a female under 18 years of age, *girl* is considered patronizing as a general term for a woman of any age, married or single. So "the girls" in Helen Hokinson's cartoons of yesterday would be women today; women or young women, not girls, attend Mills College; and many executives are careful to say, "My secretary will send you a copy of the memo"—not "My girl," much less "My gal." In keeping with the trend toward nonsexist language, even "The Kelly Girl People" now call themselves "Kelly Temporary Services" in their ads.

Indian / American Indian

Thinking they had reached the subcontinent of India instead of America, European explorers of Columbus's time called the inhabitants they encountered *Indians.* In the eighteenth century, the term *American Indian* took its place alongside *Indian* to designate a member of any of the aboriginal peoples of North America, especially south of the Arctic, or of South America or the West Indies. Nowadays *Native American* is preferred by many, especially in reference to North American Indians. *Amerindian* and *Amerind,* both blends of *American Indian,* are also used, though more often in scientific contexts than in everyday speech and writing.

black / African-American

Over time, a number of terms have been used to designate a dark-skinned American of African descent. Because language does not change overnight, an expressed preference for one of them has not immediately driven out all the others. So, with greater or lesser acceptance, *Negro, colored person, black, Afro-American,* and *African-American* have existed side by side.

Negro, a Latin-derived word meaning "black," which English borrowed from Spanish and Portuguese, has been used continuously in the United States since colonial times. The 1688 "Germantown Mennonite Resolution against Slavery," for instance, advocated the freedom of "negers"; and in his last will and testament (1799), George Washington asked that his slaves, whom he called "Negros," be freed. In 1900, Booker T. Washington founded the National Negro Business League. Title VI of the Civil Rights Act of 1960 refers to the "Negroes' right to vote." And the word *Negro* appears in the names of many active organizations, including the National Council of Negro Women, founded in 1935 by Mary McLeod Bethune, and the United Negro College Fund, founded in 1944.

Originally simply a dialectal variant of *Negro,* the term *nigger* is today acceptable only in Black English. In all other contexts it is now regarded as virtually taboo because of the legacy of racial hatred that underlies the history of its use among whites and because of its continuing use among a minority as a viciously hostile epithet.

The adjective *colored,* too, goes back a long way. A number of organizations such as the Colored National Labor Union were founded in the nineteenth century, and since its establishment in 1909 the National Association for the Advancement of Colored People (NAACP) has played a major role in the civil rights movement. James Weldon Johnson's *Autobiography of an Ex-Colored Man* was published in 1912. Yet in recent years the word *colored* has largely fallen into disuse in the States. In 1970, for instance, the Catholic Board for Mission Work among the Colored People became the Catholic Negro-American Mission Board. In South Africa, however, *colored* (usually written *Coloured*) continues to be applied to a person of racially mixed parentage.

That *black* has for many years been freely interchanged with *Negro* and *colored person* is apparent from publications like David Walker's 1829 antislavery pamphlet, in which all three terms appear. But not until the 1960s did many people, including leaders of the Congress of Racial Equality (CORE) and the Student Nonviolent Coordinating Committee (SNCC), call for the adoption of *black* as a positive term of identification. The concept of "black power" and the slogan "black is beautiful" became assertions of pride and self-awareness. Gradually taken up by the news media and the public at large, *black* is now the most widely used term. Unlike *Negro*, which (together with *Caucasian*) is capitalized as the name of a race, *black* (like *white*) is generally lowercased in designating the pigmentation of one's skin. Yet *black* is of course capitalized in proper names, such as Black English, Black Muslim, Black Panther Party, and Congressional Black Caucus.

Though not as popular as *Negro* or *black*, *Afro-American* (sometimes *Aframerican)* has also been widely used. As early as 1850, an Afro-American Convention was held in Chicago. From the 1960s on, *Afro-American* has, like *black*, replaced *Negro* in the names of many organizations, institutions, and publications. The Association for the Study of Afro-American Life and History, for example, used to be called the Association for the Study of Negro Life and History.

African-American has had its advocates, too. Long before Jesse Jackson and other prominent blacks endorsed the term in 1988, organizations such as the African-American Institute and the African-American Labor Center had been in operation. Although *African-American* is gaining acceptance in speech and print, its detractors point out that the reference to Americans of African ancestry fails to take into account the diversity of black America.

The wide choice of current terms has not gone unnoticed by the Bureau of the Census. In the pamphlet *Your Guide for the 1990 U.S. Census Form,* the instruction for the question on "the race each person considers himself / herself to be" notes: "The Black or Negro category also includes persons who identify as African-American, Afro-American, Haitian, Jamaican, West Indian, Nigerian, and so on."

Hispanic / Latino

Hispanic and *Latino* are freely interchanged in referring to a Spanish-speaking person of Latin American origin who lives in the United States. For example, the Congressional Hispanic Caucus, in Washington, is likely to hear regularly from the National Association of Latino Elected and Appointed Officials. And, reacting strongly to the view expressed in early 1990 by the U.S. Attorney for San Francisco to the effect that the Hispanic community protects drug dealers, several civil rights groups described Joseph Russoniello's statements as "a painful, grave and racist insult to the Hispanic community in the Bay Area and to Latinos everywhere."

Hispanic seems to have a slight edge over *Latino*. This may be because *Latino*, like *Latin-American*, is applied also to a native or inhabitant of Latin America (much the way *Spanish-American* is to a native or inhabitant of Spanish America, especially one of Spanish descent). Those who want a feminine form of *Latino* follow Spanish practice by using *Latina*.

4

Chicano / Mexican-American

Chicano designates a *Mexican-American;* that is, a citizen or inhabitant of the United States who is of Mexican descent. The word drops the first syllable of the Spanish *mexicano,* from which it is derived. It is pronounced with an initial "ch" resembling the "sh" sound of "meshicas," as the *mexicas,* a small but important group of early inhabitants of the Valley of Mexico, were called. The feminine form of *Chicano* is *Chicana.*

mestizo / mulatto

Terms referring to people whose parents are of different ethnic types are generally regarded as offensive, because they are often used contemptuously. Yet these words are part of the language, so distinguishing among the principal ones might be helpful for those who come across them, especially in their reading.

Amerasian denotes a person of both American and Asian descent, especially the child of a U.S. serviceman and an Asian mother.

Creole originally referred to a person of European parentage born in the West Indies, Central America, tropical South America, or the Gulf States of the United States. The term was later applied to a descendant of such people: specifically (1) a person descended from the original French settlers of Louisiana, especially of the New Orleans area; (2) a person descended from the original Spanish settlers in the Gulf States, especially Texas; and (3) a person of mixed Creole and Negro descent.

Eurasian (formerly *half-caste*) designates a person who has one European parent and one Asian parent, or a person who is generally of mixed European and Asian descent.

Half-breed (or sometimes *half-blood*), though it may denote anyone whose parents are of different ethnic types, refers especially to a person who has one North American Indian parent and one parent of European ancestry.

Mestizo, though also often applied to anyone of mixed ancestry, refers especially in the western United States and in Latin America to a person who has one Spanish or Portuguese parent and one American Indian parent.

Mulatto designates a person who has one black parent and one white parent. Technically, the term refers to anyone with mixed Negro and Caucasian ancestry.

nisei / issei

A *nisei* is a native U.S. citizen born of immigrant Japanese parents and educated in America. An *issei* is a Japanese who emigrated to the United States after the Oriental exclusion proclamation of 1907 and was thus ineligible by law, until 1952, to become a U.S. citizen. A *kibei* is a native U.S. citizen born of immigrant Japanese parents but educated largely in Japan. *Nisei* means "second generation" in Japanese; *issei*, "first generation"; and *kibei*, of Sino-Japanese origin, "return to America, U.S.A." All three words are often capitalized

atheist / agnostic

In a religious context, *believers* are people who accept the truth of a particular religion or of the existence of God or gods. Those who are less accepting are generally grouped according to the extent of their uncertainty.

An *atheist* rejects all religious belief and flatly denies the existence of God. The word comes from the Greek: the prefix *a-* (meaning "without") + *theos* ("god").

An *agnostic* believes that the human mind cannot know whether there is a God or an ultimate cause, or anything beyond material phenomena. That is, he or she questions the existence of God, heaven, and other religious tenets in the absence of material proof and in unwillingness to accept supernatural revelation. The term, coined in 1870 by the English biologist Thomas Henry Huxley, attaches the prefix *a-* to *gnostic*, which derives from a Greek word for "knowledge."

A *freethinker* believes in God as a creative, moving force but otherwise rejects formal religion and revelation, divine authority, and other doctrines as incompatible with reason. In other words, he or she forms opinions about religion independently of tradition, authority, or established belief.

Though sometimes considered a person who holds no religious belief, an *infidel* is more often thought to be one who does not believe in a certain religion or the prevailing religion. Specifically, he or she is likely to be a non-Christian among Christians or a non-Muslim among Muslims.

An *unbeliever* is simply a person who does not accept any religious belief. This is a negative term, used without further qualification. An unbeliever is sometimes called a *nonbeliever*.

A *skeptic* (also spelled *sceptic,* especially by the British) is someone who habitually doubts, questions, or suspends judgment on matters that most people accept. Fundamental religious doctrines are but one such matter.

heretic / apostate

Though often used in political or philosophical contexts, the words *heretic, apostate,* and *renegade* have related religious senses as well. A *heretic* is a person who, though a member of a particular church, holds a belief opposed to the orthodox doctrines of that church. The charge of heresy is especially likely if the belief has been specifically denounced by the church. An *apostate,* like a *renegade,* is a person who has turned away from his or her religious faith, often replacing the abandoned religion with a set of opposing beliefs.

Baptist / Methodist

A *Protestant* is a member not of a single church but of any of the various Christian churches established as a result of the sixteenth-century Reformation. Generally speaking, a Protestant is any Christian not belonging either to the Roman Catholic Church or to the Eastern Orthodox Church. This latter community of churches (also called the Orthodox Eastern Church and, very loosely, the Greek Orthodox or Greek Church) is joined in its rejection of the authority of the pope and the Latin Rite.

Protestantism is divided into dozens of denominations, with specific names, structures, and sets of beliefs. Some of these religious bodies, and their members, are mentioned here.

A *Baptist* is a member of the Baptist denomination, which holds that the rite of purification known as baptism should be offered only to believers after confession of faith and that baptism should be by immersion rather than sprinkling.

A *Christian Scientist* is a member of the Church of Christ, Scientist, whose system of healing is based on an interpretation of the Scriptures asserting that disease, sin, and death may be overcome by understanding and applying the divine principles of Christian teachings. This religious movement was founded in the nineteenth century by the American Mary Baker Eddy.

A *Congregationalist* is a member of the Congregational denomination, in which each member church, or congregation, is self-governing. This organization stems from the belief that the local congregations have Jesus Christ alone as their head and that the members are joined in one common family of God. Prominent in early New England, Congregationalism was later marked by union with other Protestant denominations.

An *Episcopalian* is a member of the Protestant Episcopal Church, which in the United States grew out of the Church of England. Authority to govern the church rests in a body of bishops, and worship is based largely on the Book of Common Prayer, the official book of services and prayers for the Anglican Communion (the informal organization of the Church of England and derived churches with closely related beliefs and practices). Besides the U.S. church, the Anglican Communion includes such other churches as the Anglican Church of Canada and the Episcopal Church of Scotland.

A *Jehovah's Witness* is a member of the proselytizing American sect known as Jehovah's Witnesses, established in the late nineteenth century and named after Isaiah 43:10 ("Ye are my witnesses"). The Witnesses, each of whom is considered a minister of the gospel, believe in the second coming of Christ, the imminent battle of Armageddon, and the potential salvation of mortal souls during the millennium.

A *Lutheran* is a member of the Protestant denomination founded by Martin Luther, who, in the sixteenth century, broke with the Roman Catholic Church and led the Protestant Reformation in Germany. According to Lutheranism, the Bible is the only necessary guide to truth, the sacraments are no more than aids to faith, and salvation comes through faith, this being available through the redeeming work of Christ.

A *Mennonite* is a member of a Christian sect founded in the sixteenth century and existing in the United States since the seventeenth. Like the Anabaptists of Switzerland, with whom they got their start, Mennonites oppose the taking of oaths, infant baptism (though they favor baptism of adult believers), military service, and the holding of public office. The

Amish, a conservative group who separated from the Mennonites in the seventeenth century, share many of the Mennonites' beliefs. Some, even among those who live in the States, rely as little as possible on modern conveniences, preferring plain dress and plain living in their chiefly agrarian society.

A *Methodist* is a member of any branch of the Methodist Church, so named because its eighteenth-century evangelistic English founders stressed methodical religious study and worship. Personal and social responsibility and the ideal of Christian perfection are widely held beliefs and practices. The doctrinal and liturgical standards of Methodism, however, vary among the many groups into which the church has been divided.

A *Mormon* is a member of the Church of Jesus Christ of Latter-Day Saints (commonly called the Mormon Church). Faith is based mainly on the Bible and the sacred Book of Mormon, which Joseph Smith, who founded the church in 1830, represented as his translation of an account of some ancient American peoples by a prophet among them named Mormon. Revelation through the connection of spiritual and physical worlds is a central doctrine of the church, whose members are encouraged to win converts to their faith.

A *Pentecostalist* is a member of any of various Pentecostal churches named after the Pentecost, which celebrates the descent of the Holy Spirit upon the Apostles. This Christian festival, held on the seventh Sunday after Easter, is also called Whitsunday. The various fundamentalist Pentecostal sects, of which the Assemblies of God is the largest, generally stress direct inspiration by the Holy Spirit, as in glossolalia (speaking in tongues), faith healing, and the second coming of Christ.

A *Presbyterian* is a member of the Presbyterian Church, founded in Scotland in the sixteenth century and brought to America early in the eighteenth. Presbyterianism, in which presbyters, or elders, play an important role in church government, grew out of the Christian doctrines of John Calvin and his followers, including predestination and salvation of the elect solely by God's grace. Presbyterians believe in the prime authority of the Bible and accept the sacraments of baptism and the Eucharist (the consecrated bread or wine, or both, used in Holy Communion).

A *Quaker* (also called a *Friend*) is a member of the Society of Friends, a Christian denomination established in England about 1650 by George

Fox. The Friends have no formal creed, rites, liturgy, or priesthood, and reject violence in human relations, including war. Their religious meetings (called Quaker meetings) are marked by long periods of silent meditation and prayer. Although the word *Quaker* was originally a term of derision, said to come from Fox's admonition to "quake" at the word of the Lord, it no longer has that negative connotation.

A *Unitarian* is, traditionally, a member of the Unitarian denomination, which is characterized by congregational autonomy, tolerance of differing religious views, and absence of creed. Unitarians deny the doctrine of the Trinity, accepting the moral teachings but rejecting the divinity of Jesus, and hold that God exists as one person or being. Nowadays Unitarians are often called *Unitarian Universalists,* the American Unitarian Association and the Universalist Church of America having merged in the early 1960s.

Buddhist / Confucian

Of the world's major religions, five were either established or given their basic form in ancient India, China, or Japan. Today these religious faiths have adherents beyond the boundaries of the three countries.

A *Buddhist* is a follower of Buddhism, a religious and philosophic system founded by Siddhartha Gautama, an Indian religious philosopher and teacher better known as Buddha ("Enlightened One"). An outgrowth of Hinduism, Buddhism teaches that right thinking and self-denial will enable the soul to reach Nirvana, a divine state of release from misdirected desire.

A *Confucian* is a follower of Confucianism, the body of ethical principles formulated by the Chinese philosopher and teacher K'ung Fu-tzu, commonly known by the Latinized name of Confucius. The sayings and dialogues of Confucius, which were introduced into Chinese religion, emphasize devotion to parents, family, and friends; cultivation of the mind; self-control; and just social activity.

A *Hindu* is a follower of Hinduism, a complex body of religious, cultural, and social beliefs and practices. Though not confined to India and the Indian subcontinent, Hindus are largely identified with those areas. The doctrines of Hinduism, which incorporates elements of several other ancient religions, include reincarnation; karma (the totality of a person's actions in any one of the successive states of his or her existence, thought of as determining the fate of the next stage); and the mystic and ascetic

10

discipline known as yoga, by means of which it is possible to seek liberation of the self and union with the supreme spirit or universal soul. Among the other features of Hinduism is acceptance of the caste system, which divides all people into distinct, hereditary social classes, each traditionally, but no longer officially, excluded from social dealings with the others.

A *Shintoist* is a follower of Shinto (or Shintoism), an ancient native religion of Japan. Influenced by both Buddhism and Confucianism, Shinto emphasizes the worship of nature and of ancestors and ancient heroes. Until 1945, it was the state religion of Japan, the emperor being regarded as a direct descendant of the sun goddess and most important deity. The Japanese word *shintō* or *shindō* combines the Sino-Japanese *shin* (meaning "god") with *tō* or *dō* (meaning "way").

A *Taoist* is a follower of Taoism, which, like Confucianism, is a native Chinese religion and philosophy. Based on the doctrines of Laotzu, Taoism holds that an ever-changing universe follows the Tao, or path (*tao* means "the way" in Chinese), and that simplicity, selflessness, meditation, and a close relationship with nature can lead to the Tao.

Muslim / Mohammedan

A *Muslim* (or *Moslem*) is an adherent of Islam, a monotheistic religion in which the supreme deity is Allah and the chief prophet and founder is Mohammed. In Arabic the word *Islam* means "submission to God's will." The terms *Mohammedanism* (or *Muhammadanism*), for the religion, and *Mohammedan* (or *Muhammadan*), for one of its followers, are less commonly used, even by non-Muslims, than they once were.

The Koran, the sacred book of Islam, contains revelations made to Mohammed by Allah in A.D. 610. Besides being the standard of religious faith, the Koran underlies Muslim law and practices. These include prayer conducted five times each day while the believer faces Mecca; at least one pilgrimage, if possible, to this holy city (the birthplace of Mohammed); almsgiving; and daily fasting during Ramadan, the ninth month of the Muslim year.

The two great sects of Muslims are the *Sunnites* (or *Sunni*) and the *Shiites*, whose differences center mainly on two issues. The first is whether the Sunna, or Muslim law based on the teachings and practices of Mohammed, should be accepted as an authoritative supplement to the Koran: the orthodox Sunnites believe it should; the Shiites believe it should not. The second is whether the line of succession should begin with abu-Bakr, one of the first of Mohammed's followers whom the Sunnites proclaimed the caliph (supreme ruler) upon the prophet's death in 632, or with Ali, Mohammed's son-in-law, whom, according to the Shiites, the prophet had designated as his rightful successor.

Orthodox Jew / Reform Jew

A *Jew* is a person of either sex whose religion is Judaism (a Jewish woman or girl is now rarely called a *Jewess*). Judaism is a monotheistic religion based on the Holy Scripture, especially the Pentateuch or Torah, as the first five books of the Old Testament are sometimes called, and on the Talmud, the collection of writings that constitutes the Jewish civil and religious law.

Judaism is commonly divided into three main groups or movements, whose names are applied to the members as well.

An *Orthodox Jew* belongs to the group known as Orthodox Judaism. This group strictly conforms to the rites and traditions of Judaism, as formulated by the Torah and the Talmud. Among these rites and traditions are observance of the Sabbath and adherence to the kosher dietary laws prescribed in Leviticus 11.

A *Conservative Jew* belongs to the group known as Conservative Judaism. This group subscribes to most of the laws and ordinances on which the religion is based. Yet it accepts moderate adaptation of religious ritual and traditional forms to the framework of modern life. It has, for example, accepted women into the rabbinate, even though the ordination of women as rabbis is not countenanced in Orthodox Judaism.

A *Reform Jew* belongs to the group known as Reform Judaism. This group goes further than Conservative Judaism in seeking to bring historical Judaism into conformity with rational thought and present-day life. That is, it emphasizes the ethical aspects of the religion without requiring strict observance of traditional Orthodox ritual.

Another movement in Judaism is Reconstructionism, which originated in the United States. Focusing on the needs of this world rather than on the hereafter, *Reconstructionists* seek a dynamic creativity in adjusting to modern times. This means, for example, the adaptation and reinterpretation of traditional Jewish observances within a continuously evolving Judaism.

extrovert / introvert

One whose interest is directed to things outside oneself and to other people rather than to oneself or one's experiences is sometimes said to be an *extrovert* or *extroverted*. On the other hand, one whose interest is more in oneself than in external objects or other people may be said to be an *introvert* or *introverted*. Both of these terms are related to the attitudes known in psychology as *extroversion* and *introversion*.

Extroversion is an altered form of the German *extraversion*, in which the Latin prefix *extra-* ("outside" or "beyond") is combined with *versus*, from a Latin verb meaning "to turn." In *introversion* the prefix is *intro-* ("within" or "inward").

egoist / egotist

Egoist and *egotist* are often used interchangeably to describe a conceited, self-centered, or selfish person. Both words have as their root *ego*—from which the first-person singular pronoun *I* is derived. Yet *egotist* generally conveys a stronger note of disapproval than *egoist*.

A *narcissist*, too, is excessively interested in his or her own appearance, comfort, importance, abilities, and other qualities. This word for someone filled with self-love comes from Narcissus, a beautiful youth in Greek mythology. After the death of the nymph Echo, whose love he did not return, Narcissus is made to pine away for love of his own reflection in a spring, until he eventually changes into the narcissus plant.

cynic / misanthrope

According to the commonest present-day meaning of the word, a *cynic* is someone who sees people as being motivated in all their actions only by selfishness. For example, a cynic is probably convinced that anyone charged with a white-collar crime can buy off someone in the criminal justice system. This contemptuous disbelief in human goodness and sincerity leads some cynics to deny the value of living.

Without going so far, a *skeptic* is someone who customarily doubts, questions, or suspends judgment on matters (including religious beliefs) that are generally accepted. For example, a skeptic probably doubts that the public is concerned about white-collar crime. Some people, especially Britons, prefer the spelling *sceptic*.

A *pessimist* is someone whose attitude, often habitual, is one of expecting the worst to happen. For example, a pessimist probably believes that for every case of white-collar crime brought to trial, two new crimes will be committed.

A *misanthrope* is someone with a deep-seated hatred or distrust of people in general. For example, a misanthrope would probably like to see a mandatory death sentence for anyone convicted of any kind of crime.

zealot / fanatic

A *zealot* is a person who is extremely—excessively, some would say—devoted to a cause and vehemently active in its support (as in "Zealots bombed a library whose collection included *Huckleberry Finn* and other so-called subversive books"). A *fanatic* is one who, out of overzealousness, goes to any length to uphold or put into practice his or her beliefs ("an anti-smoking fanatic"). A *bigot* is one who holds blindly and intolerantly to a creed or opinion ("a religious bigot"). An *enthusiast* is one who is animated by an intense and eager interest in a cause, activity, pastime, or the like ("a fresh-air enthusiast"). Other names for such a person include *devotee* ("a devotee of ballet"), *fan* ("a hockey fan"), *buff* ("a jazz buff"), and *aficionado* ("a soap-opera aficionado").

aesthete / dilettante

An *aesthete* is someone who has a well-developed sensitivity to art and beauty. When used in a belittling way, the word suggests that the person cultivates artistic sensitivity in an artificial way or makes a cult of art and beauty.

A *dilettante* was once considered to be simply a person who loves the fine arts, but the word (which comes from a Latin verb meaning "to charm, delight") is rarely used in that neutral sense anymore. Nowadays a dilettante is thought to be one who follows an art or science only for amusement and in a superficial way—that is, a dabbler.

Like *cognition* and *cognoscente*, *connoisseur* comes from a Latin word meaning "to know." A *connoisseur*, then, is someone who has expert knowledge and keen discrimination in some field, especially in the fine arts, and, by extension, in any matters of taste. One might, for example, be a connoisseur of pre-Columbian sculpture, a wine connoisseur, or a connoisseur of Oriental rugs.

In this comparison, a *virtuoso* is a collector or connoisseur of art objects, perhaps with a tendency toward faddishness. *Virtuoso* is of course more widely applied to a person who displays great technical skill in some fine art, especially in the performance of music.

epicure / gourmet

A person whose taste in food and drink is highly refined and who greatly enjoys indulging that taste is likely to be known as an *epicure* or *gourmet*. Those who see a slight difference in meaning between the two words are apt to think of the gourmet as taking particular pride in his or her ability to appreciate subtle differences in flavor and quality. A *bon vivant*, too, is interested in good food and drink but considers them, along with all the other luxuries of life, best shared with like-minded companions. A *gastronome* (sometimes called a *gastronomer* or *gastronomist*) goes beyond enjoying and having a discriminating taste for food and drink: he or she is an expert in all phases of the art or science of good eating.

Though sometimes thought of as being the same as a gourmet, a *gourmand* is more inclined to eat to excess out of a liking for good food. A *glutton* is a greedy, voracious eater and drinker, more concerned with quantity than quality. The term comes from a Latin verb meaning "to devour" and is related to a word for "gullet." Another hearty eater is a *trencherman* or *trencherwoman,* the word *trencher* being used here in the sense of "a serving board or platter" or "a supply of food." Once *trencherman* designated a person who frequents a patron's table—someone who today might be called a parasite, a hanger-on, or a sponger—but this meaning has fallen into disuse.

heterosexual / homosexual

Among the many combining forms that English borrowed from Greek are *hetero-* (meaning "other, different") and *homo-* ("same, equal, like"). A *heterosexual* is therefore a person characterized by sexual desire for those of the opposite sex; a *homosexual,* for those of the same sex. Widely accepted slang terms for a *heterosexual* include *straight* and the clipped form *hetero.* Yet the slang clipping *homo,* for a homosexual, is considered disparaging. A homosexual man is often called, and calls himself, a *gay.* This word is sometimes applied to a homosexual woman, too, as in the title of Allan Berube's book *Coming Out under Fire: The History of Gay Men and Women in World War II.* However, the more common term is *lesbian* (from the island of Lesbos, where, in the sixth century B.C., the Greek lyric poet Sappho lived, so the story goes, with a band of homosexual followers). The name of an organization like the Gay and Lesbian Alliance against Defamation illustrates current usage.

Several related words begin with prefixes that came into English from Latin. A *bisexual* (*bi-* meaning "two") is a person who is sexually attracted by both sexes. A *transsexual* (*trans-,* "across, over") is a person who is predisposed to identify with the opposite sex, sometimes so strongly as to undergo surgery and hormone injections to effect a change of sex. A *transvestite* is a person who derives sexual pleasure from cross-dressing, that is, dressing in the clothes of the opposite sex.

nymphomaniac / satyr

When we see or hear *nymph* we usually think either of a beautiful young Greek or Roman goddess living in a river or tree or on a mountain, or of a lovely young woman. But when *-maniac* is attached to the word, the picture that springs to mind is of a woman with an abnormal and uncontrollable desire for sexual intercourse. Though the words *satyr* and *satyriasis* come up less often in literature and everyday conversation, they are the male counterparts of *nymphomaniac* and *nymphomania*. In Greek mythology, the woodland god called a *satyr* is known for a fondness for merriment and lechery.

bull / bear

We might expect to see bulls and bears in the wild, but not on the phone to their stockbrokers. Yet a *bull* is a person who buys stocks or securities in the expectation that their prices will rise, or who seeks to bring about such a rise, in order to sell them at a profit. A market which tends to rise, and thus to fulfill that expectation, is called *bullish* or a *bull market*. Conversely, a *bear* is a person who believes that prices on the stock or commodity markets are going to decline, especially one who sells shares in the expectation of buying them later at a lower price. A market with falling prices is called *bearish* or a *bear market*. Some people who have trouble keeping the terms straight use this mnemonic device: Bulls charge fearlessly about the bullring; bears retreat to their dens in winter.

cardsharp / card shark

Over the years, a person who swindles, cheats, or otherwise victimizes others has been called both a *sharp* (or *sharper*) and a *shark*. In informal American English, the terms *cardsharp* (or *cardsharper*) and *card shark* are applied interchangeably to someone, especially a professional gambler, who cheats at card games. But *card shark* refers also to an expert, though not necessarily dishonest, card player.

quack / charlatan

Both *quack* and *charlatan* apply to a person who unscrupulously pretends to knowledge or skill he or she does not possess. However, *quack* almost always is used for a fraudulent or incompetent practitioner of medicine. One might say, for example, "Charlatans often dazzle party guests with astrological predictions," but "Quacks are cashing in on the AIDS epidemic."

Nowadays *mountebank* designates a person who resorts to cheap and degrading methods in his or her work (as in "In most universities, a mountebank or two manage to publish articles written by their teaching assistants"). The word was originally applied to someone who mounted a bench, or platform, in a public place and sold quack medicines, usually attracting an audience by stories and tricks. *Faker* is also used for a person who practices deception or misrepresentation.

Impostor, like *fraud,* refers especially to a person who pretends to be someone or something he or she is not ("Beware of impostors in the service departments of computer stores"). More generally, both words apply to anyone who is a *hypocrite;* that is, one who pretends to be better than he or she really is, or who gives the impression of being pious, virtuous, and so on, without really being so.

hippie / yippie

Hippie refers to any of the young people of the 1960s who, in their alienation from conventional society, turned variously to mysticism, psychedelic drugs, communal living, and avant-garde arts. The Americanism comes from *hip,* in the American slang sense of "sophisticated; knowing; aware," + the suffix *-ie,* meaning "one connected with." Hippies are often called *flower children.*

Their forerunners were the *beatniks,* or the *beat generation,* a group of young people who, in the 1950s, rebelled against middle-class attitudes, dress, and speech, largely out of disillusionment with society and the cold war. Writers like Jack Kerouac, Allen Ginsberg, Lawrence Ferlinghetti, and Kenneth Rexroth brought beat values and lifestyles to the attention not only of the United States but of the whole world.

A *yippie* is any of a group of young people in the United States who, about the time of the 1968 Democratic Convention in Chicago, were loosely organized as radical activists. Free speech and opposition to the Vietnam War became their rallying cries. Patterned after *hippie, yippie* begins with a blend of the first letters of *Youth International Party* (a supposed but nonexistent group).

yuppie / preppy

Around the mid-1980s, the term *yuppie* was applied to any of a group of young, well-educated, relatively affluent city-dwelling Americans who were regarded variously as upscale, ambitious, materialistic, and faddish. The informal Americanism is a blend of the first letters of *young, urban,* and *professional,* with the additon of another *p* and the *hippie*-type suffix *-ie.*

It did not take long for a number of variations to be spun from *yuppie.*

Yumpie, for example (from *young, upwardly mobile professional* or *person*), adds to the qualities ascribed to a yuppie a desire to move up in the world socially as well as financially. And *huppie,* according to Rose Del Castillo Guilbault (*San Francisco Chronicle*), denotes a Hispanic who has been successful in following the yuppie route.

These with-it people might or might not be preppies and trendies as well. A *preppy* is someone whose lifestyle, especially taste in clothes, is associated with what are generally considered to be the standards of preparatory school students or graduates. Preppies dress conservatively and casually, making sure that the right labels are on their button-down shirts and Shetland sweaters. Also a very fashionable person, a *trendy* works hard at not being caught taking up the second-to-latest fad or style.

vagrant / tramp

Vagrant refers to a person without a fixed home who wanders about from place to place, getting along mainly by begging. In legal usage, the term designates an idle or disorderly person whose way of living makes him or her liable to arrest and detention. *Vagabond* originally implied shiftlessness or roguishness but now often connotes no more than a carefree, roaming existence.

Tramp, drifter, derelict, and the Americanisms *bum* and *hobo* are sometimes used as informal substitutes for *vagrant* and *vagabond.* Bum, however, suggests an idle, dissolute, often alcoholic person who lives either by begging or by doing odd jobs. *Hobo* is also applied to a migratory worker.

The homeless refers to a group of destitute individuals and families, often recently poor or mentally ill, who lack the financial resources to have a home. These people, largely rejected by society, can be seen especially in large urban centers.

Bag lady is a 1970s slang term for a homeless, destitute, usually elderly woman who wanders the streets of a city. The name comes from the fact that she carries her few possessions with her, usually in shopping bags. Such a hapless man is likely to be called a bum or a drifter—not a *bagman,* for this slang term denotes a go-between in offering bribes, collecting money for the numbers racket, or engaging in similar shady activities.

bass / baritone

Given the variability of the musical instrument that is the human voice, the groups into which singers are usually classified nowadays are not narrowly defined. With some overlap and some subvarieties, the three main categories of adult male operatic singers are *bass, baritone,* and *tenor.*

The voice of a *bass* is in the lowest range (roughly from low E, an octave and a half below middle C, to middle C). Such a voice calls to mind the dark timbre of the string instrument known as a double bass. Among well-known basses (or, as they are often called, *bassos,* from the Italian) are Fyodor Chaliapin, Paul Robeson, and Samuel Ramey.

The voice of a *baritone* is in the middle natural register (roughly from low G, an octave and a half below middle C, to the E above middle C). Lawrence Tibbett, Leonard Warren, Robert Merrill, and Sherrill Milnes are famous operatic baritones. By bringing the deep bass resonance into a higher register, the voice of a *bass baritone* like Ezio Pinza achieves a rich, dramatic, ringing sound somewhat like that produced by a cello.

The voice of a *tenor* is in the highest range (roughly from the second B below middle C to the G above middle C). Tenors familiar to opera lovers include Enrico Caruso, Jussi Björling, Jan Peerce, and Luciano Pavarotti. Two others, Lauritz Melchior and Plácido Domingo, illustrate the fact that voices sometimes move upward or downward, from one register to another, for both were baritones before becoming tenors. (For nearly 25 years, Melchoir was the Metropolitan Opera's leading Wagnerian tenor.)

contralto / soprano

Like male singers, adult female singers are grouped somewhat loosely according to their voice range. The three main classifications are *contralto, mezzo-soprano,* and *soprano.*

The voice of a *contralto* (or *alto*) is in the lowest range (roughly from the F below middle C to the second D above middle C). In its full, enveloping warmth, such a voice resembles a viola. World-famous operatic contraltos include Ernestine Schuman-Heink, Marian Anderson, and Kathleen Ferrier.

The voice of a *mezzo-soprano* is in the middle range (roughly from the A below middle C to the second F or G above middle C). That such a register is about midway between a contralto's and a soprano's is not surprising, for the word *mezzo-soprano* (or *mezzo* for short) means "middle soprano." Jennie Tourel, Risë Stevens, Tatiana Troyanos, and Frederica von Stade are among the mezzo-sopranos who have won international acclaim. Marilyn Horne, a soprano before becoming a mezzo, is one of a number of singers whose voices have changed from one range to another.

The voice of a *soprano* is in the highest range (roughly from middle C to high C). There are many well-known sopranos, including Maria Callas, Victoria de los Angeles, Leontyne Price, Beverly Sills, and Kiri Te Kanawa. The voice of a *coloratura soprano* (or *coloratura*) such as Lily Pons, Joan Sutherland, or Kathleen Battle is capable of singing compositions or passages marked by brilliant runs, trills, and other ornamentation, with a flexibility resembling that of a flute.

prima donna / diva

To describe the principal female singer in an opera, English borrowed two terms from Italian: *prima donna* (meaning "first lady") and *diva* (meaning "goddess"). *Diva* is used especially in references to grand opera. Because of some opera stars' reputation for being temperamental, vain, or arrogant, *prima donna* has taken on this extended informal sense as well (as in "The school board needs team players, not prima donnas").

The equivalents for the leading male singer in an opera are *primo uomo* ("first man") and *divo* ("god"), but neither of these terms occurs often in speech or print. The title of Helena Matheopoulos's book *Divo: Great Tenors, Baritones and Basses Discuss Their Roles* is therefore an eye-catcher.

gaffer / best boy

A film, whether shown in a movie house or on television, ordinarily acknowledges the work of the many people who helped produce it. As we watch the credits roll, we immediately recognize the titles of some of those people, like the producer, the director, the script supervisor, and the hairdresser. And we can imagine what the casting director, the audio mixer, the special-effects coordinator, and most of the others do. But what about the technicians whose titles evoke a mysterious past without giving a clue to their duties on a present-day motion picture or TV production set?

A *gaffer* is the chief electrician in charge of lighting. A sixteenth-century alteration of *godfather*, the word was originally applied respectfully or affectionately to an old man, especially one from the country. Nowadays anyone calling an old man a *gaffer* outside the world of film or television is probably being either funny or contemptuous. (The seldom used feminine equivalent of *gaffer*, in the sense of an old person, is *gammer*, from *godmother* or *grandmother*.)

The *key grip* (or *first grip* or *head grip*) is responsible for all sorts of work, including carpentry, moving scenery, and seeing that lights are set up for filming a particular shot or series of shots. Several *grips* (sometimes still called *stagehands*) report to the key grip. A *dolly grip*, for instance, moves the wheeled platform known as a dolly along the dolly tracks, so that the mounted camera can be positioned for the filming of an action shot.

A *best boy* is a chief assistant either to the gaffer or to the key grip. Credits often distinguish between the two by listing *best boy electric* and *best boy grip*.

A *boom operator* handles the microphone boom—an upright, movable device like a crane, with a long beam from which a microphone is suspended. A nautical term, *boom* originally designated a spar extending from the ship's mast to hold the bottom of the sail outstretched.

Most people who work backstage in the theater have titles that are more straightforward than those of their counterparts in film or television. *Flyman* is perhaps the only title that is not self-explanatory. During a production the flymen handle the ropes from which overhead lights and scenery flats are suspended in the fly, or space behind and above the proscenium arch. But neither their work nor that of other stagehands is likely to be publicly acknowledged. Indeed, the only backstage staff mentioned in some play-bills are *production* (or *house*) *manager; master* (or *house*) *carpenter, electrician,* and *prop man; wardrobe steward;* and *stage door.*

interior designer / interior decorator

An *interior designer* is concerned with the overall shaping and organizing of the space within a house, room, office, or other architectural environment. This often involves everything from initial planning to selecting and even providing the furniture, draperies, wall and floor coverings, and furnishings. An *interior decorator,* though sometimes said to be the same as an interior designer, is mainly concerned with completing the decoration and furnishing of a planned interior.

Interior decoration is an older term than *interior design.* When the American Society of Interior Designers was established in 1931, for example, it was called the American Institute of Interior Decorators.

judge / arbiter

The word *judge* is not limited to an elected or appointed official with authority to hear and decide cases in a court of law. One of its other meanings applies to a person whose expert knowledge in a certain field gives him or her the authority to settle a controversy or determine the winner of a contest. One can be a judge at many events, including a Miss Universe Pageant, a hog-calling contest at a state fair, and an international music competition.

Arbiter, as applied to a person fully authorized or qualified to judge or decide something, suggests indisputable influence in a particular matter (as in "Emily Post became America's arbiter of etiquette in the early 1920s"). *Arbitrator*, often used interchangeably with *arbiter*, is now the more likely word in connection with labor-management or legal disputes. Here it refers to an impartial person who is appointed with the consent of both sides and whose decision is considered binding. (A *mediator* may also be a third party in such disputes, but, without authority to compel a settlement, he or she usually seeks conciliation by suggesting ways of resolving the differences between the two sides.)

Referee and *umpire* are frequently used interchangeably too. Both often designate a person to whom anything is referred for decision or settlement, as in certain legal proceedings. In sports, the particular game largely determines which title is applied to an official who rules on the plays and in other ways is charged with regulating the contest. For example, in boxing and basketball this responsibility is assigned to a referee; in baseball and tennis, to an umpire. Football has both a referee, who is primarily responsible for running the game and for interpreting the rules, and an umpire, who is one of the officials who mainly rule on the players' actions on the line of scrimmage.

middleweight / heavyweight

When Sugar Ray Robinson died in 1989, the media reminded us that the phrase "the greatest fighter, pound for pound" had been coined in his honor. Robinson's record of five world titles as a middleweight and one as a welterweight transcended the usual divisions into which *boxers* (also called *prizefighters, fighters,* or, more formally, *pugilists*) are grouped on the basis of weight.

Here, with maximum weights, are the terms by which professional boxers are known:

flyweight: 112 pounds (50.80 kilograms)
bantamweight: 118 pounds (53.52 kg)
featherweight: 126 pounds (57.15 kg)
junior lightweight: 130 pounds (58.97 kg)
lightweight: 135 pounds (61.24 kg)
junior welterweight: 140 pounds (63.50 kg)
welterweight: 147 pounds (66.68 kg)
junior middleweight: 154 pounds (69.85 kg)
middleweight: 160 pounds (72.58 kg)
light heavyweight: 175 pounds (79.38 kg)
heavyweight: any weight, but typically more than 190 pounds (86.18 kg)

slugger / batter

In baseball, the Americanism *slugger* denotes a player who has a high percentage of extra-base hits, especially home runs. So a slugger is not the same as a *batter*, who is simply the player at bat or whose turn it is to bat. (A batter may also be called a *batsman*, though this word is more likely to be applied to a cricket player whose turn it is to bat.) Nor is a slugger the same as a *hitter*, who is a player who gets a base hit; that is, who hits a fair ball and reaches base without benefit of an opponent's error and without forcing a runner already on base. The slugger hits a fair ball hard enough and far enough to get past first base many of the times he or she is at bat.

astronaut / cosmonaut

A *cosmonaut*, like an *astronaut*, is a person trained to make rocket flights in outer space, but he or she is likely to be stationed in the Soviet Union. Both words, which English borrowed from other languages, have as their root *naut*—from *nautēs*, the Greek word for "sailor." The Russian *kosmonaut* adds the combining form *kosmo-* (or *cosmo-*), meaning "world, universe." The derivation of the French *astronaute* is slightly more complicated. This word dates back to the 1927 coinage *astronautique*, in which *astro-* ("of a star, or stars") is blended with *aeronautique* ("the science, art, or work of designing, making, and operating aircraft"). But in *aeronautics* itself *aero-*, whose senses include "of aircraft or flying," is attached to the Greek-derived *nautical*, which means "of or having to do with sailors, ships, or navigation."

blue-collar worker / white-collar worker

The colors of the shirts typically worn by certain groups of workers on the job have given rise to an informal classification of the work force. According to this color coding, which now reflects neither actual payment for services nor clothing preferences, a *blue-collar worker* is an industrial worker, especially one who is unskilled or semiskilled, whereas a *white-collar worker* is a person employed in clerical, professional, or other work that is usually salaried and is not essentially manual.

Pink being the customary color for baby girls (just as blue is for baby boys), a *pink-collar worker* is, by extension, a woman employed as a secretary or salesclerk, or in other work for which women have traditionally been hired. *Steel-collar worker* is the nickname given the latest addition to the work force: the industrial robot.

lawyer / attorney

> Bette Davis, the two-time Oscar winner whose toughness, huge eyes and haughty, cigaret-smoking style made her a movie industry legend, died yesterday of cancer at age 81, her longtime lawyer said today.
>
> Davis died in a Paris hospital after returning there from the San Sebastian film festival in Spain, said her longtime attorney Harold Schiff.

In two short paragraphs the writer of this AP story (October 1989) shows a commendable familiarity with house style, for, according to *The Associated Press Stylebook,* "in common usage" the words *attorney* and *lawyer* "are interchangeable." Whether the shift from one synonym to another in consecutive sentences is good writing is another matter.

In the United States a person who is trained in the law and is licensed to give legal advice and to handle the legal affairs of clients, appearing on their behalf, if necessary, in civil, criminal, or administrative proceedings, is likely to be called a *lawyer, attorney, counsel,* or *counselor.* One who specializes in representing clients in lawsuits may be called a *trial counsel* or *advocate.* *Counsel* is applied to a team of lawyers, as well as to an individual one. Of all the terms for a member of the legal profession, only *counselor* is used in direct address (as in "Your witness, counselor").

In England some people connected with lawyering go by the same names as in the United States but do different things; some go by different names but do largely the same things; and some go by different names and do different things. Although any member of the English legal profession may be called a *lawyer,* this general term is applied especially to a *solicitor,* who advises clients on matters of law, draws up legal documents, pleads cases in certain lower courts, and engages and prepares cases for barristers. (In the States a solicitor is a lawyer who serves as chief law officer for a town, city, or other governmental body.) A *barrister* tries cases but, unlike an American trial counselor, is retained by a solicitor, not directly by the client, and pleads only in the higher courts. As in the States, an *advocate* pleads a client's case in a court of law. The terms *attorney* and *counselor* (even when spelled *counsellor*) are not widely used in England; yet *counsel* is, in the sense of a barrister or group of barristers engaged in conducting cases in court and advising on legal matters.

In everyday, nonlegal American speech and writing, the choice is between *lawyer* and *attorney.* Which word is used in reference to a member of the legal profession depends mainly on how formal, and sometimes how pretentious, the person doing the referring is. The front page of a newspaper may carry an account of the murder of "a Seattle lawyer," while the society page reports the marriage of "a prominent attorney." In the Yellow Pages for some cities "Attorneys" appears as the main heading, with a cross-reference from "Lawyers," while in those for other cities the main listing and cross-reference are the other way around. And in the index to Dilys Winn's *Murder Ink: The Mystery Reader's Companion,* "Attorneys" is not even an entry, though both "Lawyers" and "Barristers" are.

Some, but by no means all, American lawyers refer to themselves as attorneys—not only on their business cards but also in conversation ("What do I do? I'm an attorney"). Among the lawyers who call themselves lawyers, those who live in Philadelphia probably take care in saying so, for *Philadelphia lawyer* describes a shrewd or tricky attorney, especially one skilled in taking advantage of technicalities. This informal term was first applied to Andrew Hamilton of Philadelphia, who, in 1735, obtained acquittal of Peter Zenger, a German-born American journalist and publisher, from libel charges.

stockbroker / financial planner

A *broker* is someone who acts as an intermediary between a buyer and a seller, usually charging a commission. In the world of securities, a *stockbroker* ordinarily handles stocks, bonds, commodities, and mutual funds, although someone who specializes in, say, bonds may be called a *bond broker.* Besides handling the actual purchase and sale of securities, a *full-service broker* provides clients with a wide range of services, including, for example, investment consultation and custodial services for special accounts. A *discount broker* typically charges a smaller commission for buying and selling securities already decided on by investors and offers limited consultative and other services.

A *financial planner* helps clients plan and prepare some or all of their personal or business finances, ordinarily providing advice not only on the management of assets and liabilities but also on insurance and taxes. Financial planners may either be paid consulting fees by their clients or receive commissions on the sale of securities (for example, stocks, bonds, bills, money market funds, and real estate). A *portfolio manager* (sometimes called an *investment manager*) principally invests pools of money on behalf of a group of individual clients, usually with a specific objective, such as matching the Standard and Poor's Index (a popular index of market performance). The fees are based on the funds so managed.

A *securities analyst,* who is likely to be employed by a brokerage house, bank, or investment institution, studies the financial condition of a company or group of companies in an entire industry or segment of an industry, within the context of the securities market. Many analysts make recommendations on the purchase and sale of securities within their specialty.

publisher / printer

The word *publish* goes back to a Latin verb meaning "to make public." A *publisher*, then, is a person, or a firm usually headed by that person, whose business is to bring books, newspapers, magazines, sheet music, and other material before the public. The word *print* also goes back to a Latin verb, this one meaning "to press." So a *printer* is a person, or a firm probably headed by that person, whose business is to produce material on presses that use inked type, plates, or rolls. Publishers and printers need each other to survive, although some do both publishing and printing under one roof.

Besides being mistaken for a publisher, a printer is often confused with a *compositor* or *typesetter*. Both of these names are applied to a person, or, again, a firm generally headed by that person, who prepares material in a form suitable for printing or for making printing plates. The material is typically pages produced either by metal-type characters (whether set by hand or by machine) or by machine composition (mainly typewriters or phototypesetting equipment). Computers, lasers, and other electronic devices play an ever-greater role in machine composition or typesetting.

proofreader / editor

In book publishing, a proofreader's work does not begin until an editor's work is finished. The larger the company, the more editors are involved in every manuscript accepted for publication. Leaving aside the *editor in chief, executive editor, managing editor*, and others responsible for the day-to-day operations and editorial direction of the company, an in-house *editor* sees the book through the initial stages of production, working with the author on its content and overall shape. Depending on the type of publishing house, this staff member may be given any of a number of titles, including *acquisitions editor, procurement editor, sponsoring editor, project editor*, and *senior editor*. In seeing that the manuscript is ready for composition, a *copyeditor* is concerned for the most part with clarity, consistency, and editorial style. Finally, a *production editor* may mark the manuscript with instructions to the compositor. Then, after the manuscript has been set in type, a *proofreader* reads the proofs for misspelled words, omissions, transposed lines, wrong typefaces, and other errors.

Magazines and newspapers have their own hierarchies of editors. A number of titles, such as *editor in chief, executive editor, managing editor, editor*, and *senior editor*, are the same as those adopted by book publishers. Magazine mastheads typically include, as well, *corporate editor, editor at large, picture editor*, and *research editor;* a *contributing editor* is a regular writer. At a newspaper, the title of *editor* is sometimes held by the chief operating officer, sometimes by the person in charge of the editorial staff, and sometimes by the staff member responsible for a single department (*foreign editor, national editor, metropolitan editor, editor of the editorial page, business editor, book editor, sports editor, food editor,* and so on). The *assignment editor* assigns reporters and photographers to cover certain events. A proofreader at a newspaper or magazine does much the same work as a book publisher's proofreader. The tighter the publishing deadline, of course, the less time allowed for detecting and correcting errors.

In filmmaking and television, an *editor* makes a coherent whole of the various audio and visual components. This usually involves cutting, splicing, and reassembling film or videotape.

translator / interpreter

Both a *translator* and an *interpreter* are concerned with making one language intelligible to speakers of another language. Traditionally, a *translator* renders the foreign words into the second language by either speech or writing, whereas an interpreter works orally. More and more, however, as in international organizations, a *translator* deals only with printed words, and an *interpreter*—sometimes wearing earphones and using a microphone—turns a speaker's remarks into another language sentence by sentence. This procedure is called *simultaneous interpretation.* Waiting until a speaker finishes part or all of a statement before repeating what has been said for the benefit of the listeners is called *consecutive interpretation.*

linguist / polyglot

Linguist, like *language,* is derived from the Latin *lingua,* meaning "tongue." For centuries, the word has referred to a person who commands several languages. In this sense, it has been used as the equivalent of *polyglot,* which comes from the Greek *polyglōttos* (*poly-,* meaning "many," + *glōtta,* "tongue"). An American tourist, for example, might have said, "Being a linguist (polyglot) would make travel in Europe a lot easier." Nowadays, however, *linguist* is applied less to a person who speaks, writes, or understands more than one language than to a specialist in *linguistics,* or the science of language.

physician / doctor

A person licensed to practice medicine and surgery is a *physician.* Because the course of study typically leads to a degree of doctor of medicine or doctor of osteopathy, a graduate is commonly called a *doctor.* This term invites ambiguity, however, for it can be applied to anyone who holds a doctorate in any field. For instance, a university professor who has earned a PhD (doctor of philosophy) in sociology is often addressed as "doctor." This is also the title by which many PhDs refer to themselves.

family doctor / general practitioner

A *family doctor* is a physician who looks after the health and keeps the medical records of an entire family. Without specializing in any particular field of medicine, such as cardiology or pediatrics, he or she diagnoses the family members' illnesses and either treats the patients or refers them to specialists. Other names for this kind of primary-care doctor include *family physician* and *family practice physician. General practitioner* (*GP*) is not commonly used anymore.

intern / resident

On graduating from medical school, a doctor takes further training in a hospital. The official organizations responsible for this period of advanced, specialized medical or surgical training use the term *residency* and call all the trainees *residents*. Traditionally, however, a first-year trainee is known as an *intern* and a trainee in subsequent years as a *resident* or *house officer*.

psychiatrist / psychoanalyst

A *psychiatrist* is a physician concerned with the study, treatment, and prevention of disorders of the mind, including psychoses, behavioral disturbances, emotional maladjustments, and other problems. This medical specialty requires a four-year residency in psychiatry after graduation from medical school. Treatment may include medication, counseling, or any of the various forms of communication between therapist and patient that are known as psychotherapy (or, informally, "talking cures").

A *psychoanalyst,* using methods developed by Freud and others, investigates mental processes and treats behavioral problems and certain other disorders of the mind. A basic assumption of psychoanalysis is that conflicts caused by repressed instinctual forces in the unconscious can be resolved or diminished by discovering and analyzing the repressions and bringing them into consciousness through free association, dream analysis, and other techniques. Most psychoanalysts are psychiatrists (and therefore doctors of medicine) who have had advanced training at a special institute and have themselves undergone psychoanalysis to deal with their own emotional problems.

A *psychotherapist* is a person, with or without formal medical training, who treats mental and emotional problems by psychotherapy. The idea is that, in a climate of warmth and trust, the therapist can help the patient work through immediate behavioral problems and, insofar as possible, come to understand his or her own conflicts and feelings.

A *psychologist* is a nonmedical specialist in psychology, the science that deals with the mind and with mental and emotional processes. Psychologists, particularly clinical psychologists, are qualified to test patients and to treat their mental and emotional problems through counseling or psychotherapy.

obstetrician / gynecologist

An *obstetrician* is a physician who specializes in the care and treatment of women during pregnancy, childbirth, and the period immediately following. A *gynecologist* is a physician who specializes in the diagnosis and treatment of female diseases, especially of the reproductive system. Many obstetricians are also gynecologists. Indeed, these two branches of medicine are so closely related as to give rise to a third: obstetrics-gynecology. The abbreviation *OB-GYN* is applied both to the medical field and to a practitioner (*obstetrician-gynecologist*).

A *pediatrician* (sometimes *pediatrist*) is a physician who specializes in the development and care of infants and children. He or she is especially concerned with the prevention and treatment of childhood diseases.

podiatrist / chiropodist

In American medicine, a *podiatrist* is a specialist in the examination, diagnosis, treatment, and prevention of disorders of the feet. College graduates pursuing this specialty take a four- year course at an accredited college of podiatric medicine, and most complete a postgraduate residency of a year or more. *Chiropodist,* an earlier name for a podiatrist, has largely fallen into disuse in the United States. In 1970, for example, the American Association of Colleges of Chiropody became the American Association of Colleges of Podiatric Medicine.

optometrist / ophthalmologist

An *optometrist* is a specialist trained in examining the eyes and in prescribing and supplying glasses or contact lenses to correct defects in the eyes' ability to focus and see. He or she is not licensed to prescribe drugs or perform surgery. This is done by an *ophthalmologist,* a physician who specializes in the structure, functions, and diseases of the eye. In conducting examinations to determine the quality of a patient's vision, an ophthalmologist (formerly called an *oculist*) also checks for the presence of glaucoma, cataracts, and any other eye disorders. An *optician* is a person who makes or deals in optical instruments, especially one who prepares and sells eyeglasses and contact lenses.

pharmacist / druggist

In the United States a person authorized to fill medical prescriptions is called either a *pharmacist* or a *druggist.* A *pharmacy* is a place where drugs and medicines are prepared and sold. So is a *drugstore,* but nowadays most drugstores sell a wide variety of merchandise as well, from T-shirts to lawn furniture. In Britain a person licensed to practice pharmacy is called a *chemist.* A *chemist,* or *chemist's shop,* is likely to sell cosmetics and other items, along with medicines—though not nearly on the scale of an American drugstore.

Apothecary is no longer widely used as a synonym of *pharmacist, druggist,* or, in Britain, *chemist.* It still appears, though, in terms like *apothecaries' measure* (a system of liquid measure used in pharmacy); *apothecaries' weight* (a system of weights used in pharmacy); and *apothecary jar* (a wide-mouthed covered jar, either plain or decorated, which is generally used for medicines, herbs, or bathroom supplies like cotton balls).

funeral director / mortician

For centuries, the English word for a person who prepares the dead for burial or cremation and conducts funerals has been *undertaker.* However, it leaves too little doubt about what it means. So Americans, with their fondness for euphemism, have added at least two new words to the language. One sounds reassuringly like *physician: mortician* (*mors,* from a Latin word meaning "death," + *-ician,* a suffix meaning "a person engaged in, skilled in, or specializing in"). The other is *funeral director.*

truant officer / attendance officer

State laws require students to attend schools up to a specified age. A student who plays hooky—that is, who stays away from school without parental permission or another valid excuse—is a *truant.* In a public school system, the official who deals with cases of truancy used to be called a *truant officer;* however, this old-fashioned term has been all but replaced by *attendance officer.*

citizen / subject

Citizen refers to a member of a state or nation, especially one with a republican form of government, who owes it allegiance and, whether by birth or naturalization, is entitled to full civil rights (as in "a U.S. citizen"). *Subject* is the term used when the government is headed by a monarch or other sovereign ("a British subject"). *National* is applied to a person residing away from the country in which he or she is, or once was, a citizen or subject ("Wherever they find themselves on July 14, most French nationals celebrate Bastille Day"). People from the same country who are living abroad are especially likely to use this term of one another. *Native* refers to a person who was born in a given country ("a native Italian"). The word is applied particularly to an original or indigenous inhabitant of a region, as distinguished from an invader, explorer, colonist, or other newcomer ("a Native American").

emigrant / immigrant

The word *migrate* conveys the notion of moving from one place to another. With the change in seasons, many birds and some fishes migrate, or move from one region to another. People migrate, or move from one place to another, too. The prefix *ex-* (*e-* when followed by the initial sound of *migrate*) adds the sense of "away from" or "out of," so an *emigrant* is someone who leaves one country or region to settle in another. An *émigré* is a citizen of one country who has left it to take political refuge in another (English borrowed the word from French). The prefix *in-* (*im-* when followed by the initial sound of *migrate*) adds the sense of "in," "into," or "toward" to *migrate,* so an *immigrant* is a person who comes to a new country or region to settle. Because the prefix *trans-* means "across," a *transmigrant* is an emigrant passing through a country or place on the way to the country in which he or she will be an immigrant. And a *migrant* is a farm laborer who moves from place to place to harvest seasonal crops.

Several other related words enter into the picture. An *expatriate* (*ex-* meaning "out of" + *patria,* "fatherland") is an exile; that is, someone who has either been driven from his or her native land or has chosen to leave it. An *alien* is someone born in one country and living in another country in which he or she has not become a naturalized citizen. So is a *foreigner,* but the country from which this person comes is likely to have a different language and cultural pattern. A *stranger* is someone who comes from another region and is unfamiliar with local people, customs, and the like. An *outsider* is someone who is not a member of or in sympathy with a given group. The senses of all these words are included in *auslander,* which English borrowed from German.

31

coterie / circle

A *coterie* is a small, intimate, somewhat select group of people associated for social purposes or other reasons (as in "the coterie of writers, artists, and musicians drawn to the Manhattan townhouses and Long Island estates of the Averill Harrimans and Jock Whitneys"). Though the word, which English borrowed from French, calls to mind wealth, fashion, talent, and leisure, it originally referred to an organization of peasants holding land from a feudal lord.

A *circle* is any group of people having in common some particular interest or pursuit. The word is equally applicable to Gertrude Stein's literary and artistic circle in the Paris of the 1920s, to the financial circles of New York and Tokyo, and to a sewing circle in Keokuk, Iowa.

A *set* is a group of people having a common background, habits, and interests. It is likely to be larger and therefore less exclusive than a coterie. For example: the sporting set, the thirty-something set, the smart set (sophisticated, fashionable people, collectively).

A *clique* is a small, highly exclusive group, often within a larger one. The French word, derived from the onomatopoeic verb *cliquer,* meaning "to make a noise," suggests snobbery, selfishness, and perhaps even intrigue. Wherever people get together—an office, a factory, an apartment house, a school—one or more cliques usually form. Though it seems to mean just the opposite, the word *crowd* is sometimes used as the equivalent of *clique.* For example: the Silicon Valley crowd, the Sardi's crowd, and "Our Crowd" (the interwoven Jewish banking families of New York, described in Stephen Birmingham's book of that name).

crowd / throng

Crowd, though sometimes interchanged with *clique,* ordinarily refers to an assembly of people so densely packed as to lose their personal identity (as in "A cheering crowd greeted the President's motorcade"). *Mob* suggests a disorderly or lawless crowd ("An angry mob rushed onto the playing field"). When used to describe the masses or any specific group of people, *mob* is considered an abusive term. *Throng* refers to a moving crowd of people pushing one another ("a throng of New Year's Eve revelers"). *Swarm,* too, implies continuous movement in a large group ("a swarm of sightseers").

Multitude stresses greatness in number ("a multitude arrayed against him"). *Host,* though it may be used generally of any sizable group considered collectively, often suggests a large, organized body marshaled together ("a host of well-wishers"). *Horde* refers to any large predatory band ("a horde of office seekers in pursuit of their newly elected senator").

intelligentsia / cognoscenti

The people who are regarded as, or who regard themselves as, the educated and enlightened class of a nation—that is, intellectuals collectively—are known as the *intelligentsia*. Historians, for example, point out that from the time of Peter the Great until the revolution of 1917, the growing Russian intelligentsia acquired Western humanitarian ideals. The relationship between *intelligentsia* and *intelligence* did not escape the notice of wits in a branch of computer science: specialists concerned with developing machines or programs capable of humanlike thought processes have been nicknamed the *artificial intelligentsia*.

A group of scholarly or learned people, especially but not exclusively those whose work is in the field of literature, are often referred to as the *literati*. For instance, one might say that America's literati hosted an international conference on the relationship between technology and culture. The word *literati*, whose Latin origin is shared by *literate* as well as *literature*, is sometimes used interchangeably with *intelligentsia*. And, like *intelligentsia*, it has no English singular form. Nor does *glitterati*, a blend of *glitter* and *literati*, which denotes people who are wealthy, chic, and famous (as in "The glitterati were represented at the White House dinner for the winners of the Kennedy Center Honors").

A group of people who either have or are thought to have special knowledge in a certain field, such as art, literature, or fashion, may be called the *cognoscenti*. One might say, for example, that the references to Picasso in certain drawings of Jasper Johns are apparent only to the cognoscenti. Or that every year the Paris dress salons are filled with the cognoscenti from all parts of the world. Like *cognizance, cognition,* and *connoisseur*, the word *cognoscenti* and its singular form, *cognoscente*, go back to a Latin verb meaning "to know."

associate / colleague

Associate refers to a person who is frequently in another's company, usually because of some shared work or project (as in "a business associate"). *Colleague* denotes a co-worker, especially in one of the professions, and may or may not imply a close, personal relationship ("her colleagues at the university"). *Companion* always refers to a person who actually accompanies another and usually implies a close, personal relationship ("a dinner companion"). *Comrade* designates a close associate and implies a sharing in activities and fortunes ("comrades in arms"). *Ally* now usually refers not to a person but to a government joined with another or others in a common pursuit, especially war ("the Allies in World War II"). *Confederate* is applied to a person who joins with another or others for some common purpose, specifically in some unlawful act ("confederates in a drug ring"). *Accomplice* refers to a person who unites with others, as either a principal or a subordinate, with criminal intent ("an accomplice in a bank robbery").

follower / supporter

Follower is the general term for a person who follows or believes in another's teachings or theories ("a follower of Keynes," for example). *Supporter* applies to someone who endorses a person, an opinion, or a theory, especially if any of these is disputed or under attack ("a supporter of transcendental meditation"). *Adherent* refers to a close, active follower of some theory, cause, or the like ("an adherent of free trade"). *Partisan*, in this comparison, designates an unswerving, often blindly devoted, adherent of some person or cause ("a partisan of white supremacy"). *Disciple* implies a personal, devoted relationship to the teacher of some doctrine or leader of some movement ("Martin Luther King, Jr., was a disciple of Gandhi").

sponsor / patron

Whether as proponent, advisor, underwriter, or something else, a *sponsor* is a person who assumes a certain degree of responsibility for another person or project (as in "a sponsor of a foreign exchange student"). A *patron* is a person who assumes the role of protector or benefactor, now usually in a financial capacity, in supporting the work of an artist, a museum, an orchestra, a ballet company, or other institution. A *backer* is a person who lends support, again, usually financial, to an individual or to an undertaking but does not necessarily take on any responsibilities. Many magazines, for instance, could not get started without backers. An *angel* is, in informal usage, generally an investor in a play or other theatrical enterprise.

client / customer

Customers and certain kinds of *clients*, *patrons*, and *guests* have one thing in common: their wallets or checkbooks are likely to be open once they receive the goods or services they are after. Yet, even in this related sense, the words describing such people are not exact equivalents.

As the word itself suggests, a *customer* is generally someone who is in the habit of buying from or frequenting an establishment such as a restaurant, shop, department store, hairdresser's, or movie house (as in "Kim is always the last customer to leave the bookstore").

A *client* does the same. But a client, not a customer, may also arrange for the professional advice or services of a lawyer, architect, accountant, advertising agency, or other person or company. Someone who receives care or treatment from a physician, family counselor, electrologist, or the like is called a *client* or, perhaps more often, a *patient.*

A *patron* is a steady and regular visitor to a store, hotel, theater, or similar establishment. However, those who consider this word either too formal or too pretentious are apt to use *customer* or *client* instead. Or they might substitute *shopper, guest* (for a paying customer of a hotel or restaurant), *theatergoer, moviegoer,* and so on.

opponent / enemy

An unemotional word, *opponent* refers to anyone who is opposed to someone else or to "the other side," especially in a fight, game, political race, or debate. *Antagonist* implies more active opposition, especially in a struggle for control or power. *Adversary* usually suggests outright hostility in the conflict. *Enemy* may imply actual hatred in the opponent and a desire to injure, or it may simply refer to any member of the opposing group, nation, or the like, whether or not there is personal animosity or hostility involved. *Foe,* now a somewhat literary synonym for *enemy,* connotes more active hostility.

plaintiff / defendant

Two parties are involved in every civil lawsuit—that is, every court action relating to rights and injuries. The party who initiates the suit is called the *plaintiff* or *complainant.* (At first glance, these two words may not seem to be related. Yet, both having in their development a form of the Latin verb *plangere,* which means "to beat the breast," they share the sense of giving expression to one's grievance. That is why we talk about a plaintive song, the plaintive sound of an oboe, and the like.) The party defending or denying—that is, the one sued or accused in the suit—is called the *defendant.*

The adversarial roles of the opponents can be seen in the way the cases are referred to, the Latin word *versus* (usually abbreviated as *v.* or *vs.*) meaning "in contest against." As the following case titles show, the plaintiff or the defendant, or both, can be one or more individuals, companies, or federal, state, or local agencies: *Hellman* v. *McCarthy, Namath* v. *Sports Illustrated, Westmoreland* v. *CBS, United States* v. *Louisiana,* and *Dawson* v. *Mayor and City Council of Baltimore.* In saying a case title, some people pronounce the *v.* as "vee"; some give the full form, *versus;* and some substitute the word *against.*

35

In the case title of the original suit, the plaintiff is listed first. However, if the losing party in a suit in a federal court appeals the case, this party's name appears first; in other words, the case title in the appellate procedure gives *appellant* versus *appellee*. If the appeal goes all the way to the U.S. Supreme Court, the party seeking the review is called the *petitioner* and the party responding to the petition is called the *respondent*. For example, when James J. Hill sued Time, Inc., for invasion of privacy, the case was titled *Hill* v. *Time, Inc.*, but on appeal the title became *Time, Inc.* v. *Hill*.

Every criminal case—that is, every court action taken to redress a public wrong—also has a defendant, but here the initiator of the proceedings is called the *prosecution*. The *prosecutor*, or *prosecuting attorney*, who is a public official such as a district attorney, conducts the criminal suit on behalf of the state or the people.

Criminal actions are referred to much the same way as civil ones. In the original case title the prosecution (the name of the federal, state, or local entity) precedes the name of the defendant; but in any appellate procedure whoever seeks the review is listed first. For example, by the time *Illinois* v. *Gacy* reached the U.S. Supreme Court for review, it was called *Gacy* v. *Illinois*, John Wayne Gacy having appealed his conviction and death sentence for murder.

criminal / felon

A *criminal* or *offender* is a person guilty, or legally convicted, of a crime. Although a *culprit* can be a person only accused of or charged with the commission of a crime, the word also commonly refers to someone who has been found guilty. If the crime is serious enough to be classified as a felony, the person might be referred to by the legal term *felon*. A *convict* is a person who not only has been found guilty of a crime but, as a result of that conviction, is serving a sentence in a jail, prison, or penitentiary. A person who is confined in prison following conviction of a crime might be called a *prisoner*, as might someone who, having been accused of a crime, is held in custody or released on bail while on or awaiting trial.

pupil / student

In an educational context, a *student* is anyone receiving instruction—whatever the level and whether at school or another educational institution, through a correspondence course, in jail, or by some other means. Therefore, although a *pupil* is generally considered to be a child in elementary school (typically, from kindergarten through sixth grade), the word *student* is no less appropriate. In their wider usage, *student* refers to anyone who is making a study of a particular subject ("Pogo is a perceptive student of human behavior"), and *pupil* to anyone who is under the supervision of a teacher ("Schoenberg is Zemlinsky's best-known pupil"). Though originally equivalent to *pupil, scholar* is now usually applied to someone who has general erudition or who is highly versed in a particular branch of learning ("Of all Shakespearean scholars, Kittredge is perhaps best known in the United States").

salutatorian / valedictorian

Long before it had anything to do with raising the right hand to the forehead as a mark of military, naval, or official respect, the Latin-derived word *salute* referred to a friendly greeting or welcome. Not surprisingly, then, the graduating student (usually the second highest in scholastic rank) who gives the opening or welcoming address at a school or college commencement exercise is the *salutatorian.* The *valedictorian* (ordinarily the highest- ranking student) gives the *valedictory,* or farewell speech. Like the seldom-used *valediction,* both *valedictorian* and *valedictory* go back to a Latin verb meaning "to say farewell"—and even further back to the imperative form of one meaning "to be well."

nuclear family / extended family

A *family* is a basic social unit consisting of parents and the children they bring up. In a *nuclear family* the parents and children live in one household. In an *extended family* a group of relatives by blood, marriage, or adoption, often including a nuclear family, live in close proximity or together; the term is most likely to be used if three generations are involved. A *family circle* includes immediate family members and intimate friends.

stepparent / adoptive parent

A *stepparent* (that is, a *stepfather* or *stepmother*) is a person who has married one of a child's parents after the other parent has died or divorced. An *adoptive parent* is a person who has chosen to take a child into his or her family by legal process and to raise the child as his or her own. A *foster parent* is a person other than a child's natural or adoptive parent who generally cares for the child on a full-time, though temporary, basis. In some cases the foster child may return to his or her natural parents; in others, the child may be adopted by the foster parent or by someone else.

stepbrother / half brother

One's *stepbrother* is the son one's stepparent had by a former marriage. That is, though a member of one's family, he is not what is sometimes called a blood relation (or blood relative). On the other hand, one's *half brother* is a blood relation, for he is the son of either one's mother or one's father. Not of both parents, for then he would be a *brother*.

One's *stepsister, half sister,* and *sister* are of course related in the same way.

great-aunt / grandaunt

Once past the grandparent-grandchild stage, the combining form *great-* is used interchangeably with *grand-* to indicate one generation removed; that is, a relative who is older or younger by one generation. A sister of any of one's grandparents, or—put another way—the aunt of one's parent, is one's *great-aunt* (or *grandaunt*). Conversely, a grandson of one's brother or sister is one's *great-nephew* (or *grandnephew*). A *great-uncle* (or *granduncle*) and a *great-niece* (or *grandniece*) are related the same way.

Each additional *great-* or *grand-* indicates one further degree of removal in the relationship. So a sister of any of one's great-grandparents—that is, the great-aunt (or grandaunt) of one's parent—is one's *great-great-aunt* (or *grand-grandaunt*). Conversely, a great-grandson of one's brother or sister is one's *great-great-nephew* (or *grand-grandnephew*). A *great-great-uncle* (or *grand-granduncle*) and a *great-great-niece* (or *grand-grandniece*) are of course related the same way. When the two combining forms are mixed, *great-* is likely to precede *grand-,* as in *great-grandaunt* or *great-grandfather*.

second cousin / first cousin once removed

Originally, a *cousin* was any collateral relative more distant than a brother or sister, descended from a common ancestor. Over time, however, cousinly relationships have been sorted out. The term *cousin* is now applied to a child of one's uncle or aunt, as is *first cousin, full cousin,* or *cousin-german* (the adjective *german* meaning "closely related"). One's *second cousin* is a child of one's parent's first cousin. One's *first cousin once removed* is either a child of one's own first cousin or a first cousin of one's parent.

Anthropologists refine cousin relationships even further. A *cross cousin* is a child of one's father's sister or one's mother's brother. A *parallel cousin,* on the other hand, is a child of one's father's brother or one's mother's sister.

In loose usage, a *cousin* is any relative by blood or marriage. A *kissing cousin,* in informal speech and writing, need not be a cousin at all. Instead, he or she is probably a distant relative known well enough to greet with a friendly kiss.

fairy / elf

The folklore of virtually all parts of the world is populated with *little people*, imaginary beings that are usually of human or partly human form and are supposed to have magical powers. Such a supernatural creature, especially one who is tiny, graceful, delicate, and good, is commonly known as a *fairy*. A special kind of fairy, a *tooth fairy* puts money under a child's pillow in exchange for a fallen-out tooth placed there by the child.

A number of other words are often used in place of *fairy*, but the little people they describe have their own personalities, characteristics, and forms of behavior—not necessarily good. For instance:

A *brownie* may misbehave occasionally, but ordinarily this small brown creature appears during the night to do helpful tasks for people. *Brownie* has come to designate a level within the Girl Scouts as well.

An *elf*, usually found haunting woods and hills, is likely to be prankish.

A *gnome* is a misshapen, dwarflike being who dwells within the earth and guards its treasures.

A *goblin* is a mischievous or evil spirit, often depicted as having a human-like, ugly, or misshapen form.

A *gremlin* is a mischievous invisible being created more recently than most other mythical little people. The word is a humorous World War II coinage for an elf or goblin who is responsible for the faulty operation of airplanes. By extension, it refers to any unaccountable disruption of an operation or procedure (as in "Gremlins got into the computer last night").

A *hobgoblin* is often regarded as the equivalent of a goblin. *Hob,* whose origin is no more sinister than a familiar form of Robin or Robert, suggests mischief, trouble, or disorder in the expression *play* (or *raise*) *hob with* (as in "Television plays hob with conversation"). Both *Hob* and *Hobgoblin* are other names for the impish sprite known as Robin Goodfellow or Puck. (The character in Shakespeare's *A Midsummer Night's Dream* is called Puck.) Nowadays, *hobgoblin* often replaces *bogy, bogeyman,* or *bugbear* in designating an imaginary evil being who is enlisted to frighten children into good behavior.

A *pixie* is especially puckish, or full of mischief.

A *spirit* is thought of in various ways, sometimes as an angel, demon, fairy, or elf who inhabits a certain region or displays either a good or evil character, and sometimes as a ghost who haunts or possesses a person, house, or the like.

A *sprite* is generally considered to be the same as a spirit, fairy, elf, or goblin. A water sprite, as might be expected, dwells in or haunts a body of water. The word *sprite,* which shares a common origin with *spirit,* was once applied to a ghost.

Some supernatural imaginary creatures are identified with specific countries or cultures. For example:

An *afreet* is, in Arabian mythology, a strong, evil demon or jinni.

A *banshee* is, in Celtic folklore, a female spirit believed to wail outside a house as warning that a death will occur soon in the family.

A *barghest* is, in English folklore, a doglike goblin whose appearance supposedly foreshadows death or bad luck.

A *jinni* is, in Muslim folklore, a supernatural being that can take human or animal form and influence human affairs. (The plural form, *jinn,* is popularly regarded as a singular, with *jinns* as its plural.) The word *genie,* first used to translate *jinni* in *The Arabian Nights,* sometimes appears in folk stories and fairy tales to designate a servant whose magical powers can make a person's wishes come true.

A *kachina* is, in Pueblo folklore, a beneficent spirit, either a minor deity or the spirit of an ancestor.

A *kobold* is, in Germanic folklore, a household spirit rather like a brownie in being helpful sometimes and mischievous at other times.

A *leprechaun* is, in Irish folklore, a fairy in the form of a little old man who can reveal a buried crock of gold to anyone who catches him.

A *nix* is, in Germanic folklore, a water sprite, usually small and of human or partly human form.

A *pooka* (sometimes written *phooka*) is, in Irish folklore, a mischievous or malignant sprite. The word may have the same origin as *Puck*, who also goes by the names Hob, Hobgoblin, and Robin Goodfellow.

A *troll* is, in Scandinavian folklore, a supernatural being, sometimes conceived of as a giant and at other times a dwarf, living underground or in caves. Trolls are usually considered cunning and dangerous.

ghost / poltergeist

Ghost refers to the supposed disembodied spirit of a dead person, conceived of as appearing to the living as a pale, shadowy apparition. *Specter, spirit, wraith, phantom, phantasm,* and the informal Americanism *spook* are often used instead. However, *wraith* is applied not only to a ghost in the sense of a supernatural being haunting or possessing a person, house, or the like, but also to the spectral figure of a person supposedly seen as a premonition just before that person's death. *Spook,* too, has an extended meaning; it conveys the notion of any person who appears unexpectedly or in an extraordinary way, including a spy (as in "a CIA spook").

Poltergeist is not always interchangeable with *ghost,* because the word designates a ghost that is supposed to be responsible for mysterious noisy disturbances. Poltergeists are what go bump in the night.

centaur / griffin

Among the fabulous beings created through myth, legend, and other forms of folklore, a number are part human and part animal. For example:

A *centaur* is, in Greek mythology, any of a race of monsters with the head, trunk, and arms of a man and the body and legs of a horse.

A *faun* is any of a class of minor Roman deities, usually represented as having the body of a man and the horns, pointed ears, tail, and hind legs of a goat.

A *Gorgon* is, in Greek mythology, any of three sisters, including Medusa, with snakes for hair and an appearance so horrible as to turn the beholder to stone.

The *Minotaur* is, in Greek mythology, a monster with the body of a man and the head of a bull (or, in some versions, with the body of a bull and the head of a man).

A *satyr* is, in Greek mythology, any of a class of minor woodland deities, usually represented as having pointed ears, short horns, the head and body of a man, and the legs of a goat. The word *satyr* has come to mean "a lustful or lecherous man," whose female counterpart is a nymphomaniac.

A *siren* is, in Greek and Roman mythology, any of several sea nymphs with the head and sometimes the breast and arms of a woman but the rest of the body in the form of a bird. Because the sirens' seductive singing lures sailors to their death on rocky coasts, the word *siren* is applied nowadays to a woman who uses her sexual attractiveness to entice or allure men. At one time *mermaid* was used as the equivalent of *siren*, and there is indeed a similarity between the classical siren and the fabled sea creature with the head and upper body of a beautiful woman and the tail of a fish. Though less commonly used, the term *merman* designates the male counterpart.

A *sphinx* is, in Greek mythology, a winged monster with the body of a lion and the head and breasts of a woman. The combining form *andro-* meaning "man, male, masculine," an *androsphinx* is like a sphinx except that the body of the lion has a man's head. The word *sphinx* refers also to any ancient Egyptian statue or figure having, typically, the body of a lion and the head of man, ram, or hawk.

Some of the wildly imaginary creatures of folklore do not resemble humans at all. Instead they combine parts of various animals. For instance:

A *basilisk* (also called a *cockatrice*) is a mythical lizardlike monster supposedly hatched by a serpent from a cock's egg and having power to kill by a glance.

The *chimera* is, in Greek mythology, a fire-breathing monster, usually represented as having the head of a lion, the body of a goat, and the tail of a serpent.

A *griffin* is a mythical monster with the body and hind legs of a lion and the head, wings, and claws of an eagle.

A *hippocampus* is, in Greek and Roman mythology, a sea monster with the head and hindquarters of a horse and the tail of a dolphin or fish.

A *hippogriff* is a mythical monster with the hindquarters of a horse and the head and wings of a griffin.

Devil / Satan

The *Devil* is the chief evil spirit in Jewish and Christian theology. He is a supernatural being subordinate to, and the foe of, God and the tempter of human beings. His other names include *Satan, Prince of Darkness, Lucifer, Beelzebub,* and *Belial.*

In medieval legend and later in a number of literary and operatic works, *Mephistopheles* is a devil to whom an old philosopher named Faust (or Faustus) sells his soul in exchange for knowledge and power. This demonic character appears, for example, in plays by Goethe and Christopher Marlowe (the former titled *Faust* and the latter *The Tragical History of Dr. Faustus*) and in Gounod's opera *Faust.*

Typically depicted as a man with horns, a tail, and cloven feet, the Devil is firmly established in everyday speech and writing as well. Among his many informal names are the *Deuce, Harry, Old Boy, Old Nick,* and *Foul Fiend.*

incubus / succubus

A kind of diabolic Bobbsey Twins of medieval times, *incubus* and *succubus* are evil spirits or demons thought to descend upon and have sexual intercourse with sleeping people—the incubus with women and the succubus with men. *Incubus* shares a common Latin origin with *incubate* (*incubare*, "to lie in or upon"). *Succubus* also came into English from the Latin: first the verb *succubare* ("to lie under"), then *succuba* ("strumpet"), and, finally, the present form of the word by association with *incubus.* In Medieval Latin *incubus* conveyed the related sense of a demon supposed to cause nightmares. By extension, the word is now used in the sense of both a nightmare and anything that is oppressive or burdensome. In Gilbert and Sullivan's *Trial by Jury,* for example, the Judge sings:

> At length I became as rich as the Gurneys—
> An incubus then I thought her,
> So I threw over that rich attorney's
> Elderly, ugly daughter.

Succubus has not found a comparable place in modern English usage.

Here and There

utopia / never-never land

Any idealized place, state, or situation is sometimes called *utopia*, after an imaginary island described in Sir Thomas More's book of the same name, published in 1516. Yet *utopia*—which comes from two Greek words: *ou* (meaning "not") and *topos* ("a place")—is not the only name for somewhere perfect though nonexistent (or perfect because nonexistent).

Arcadia is any place of rural peace and simplicity. A city in southwestern California (a suburb of Los Angeles) took this name in allusion to a relatively isolated pastoral region in ancient Greece.

Camelot is any place or time idealized as having excitement, purpose, a high level of culture, and other positive qualities. In Arthurian legend, which centers on the partly mythical, partly historical figure of King Arthur, Camelot is the English town where Arthur has his court and Round Table. *The Once and Future King,* published in 1958 by the English writer T. H. White, draws on that large body of literature. Alan Jay Lerner and Frederick Loewe, in turn, based their musical *Camelot* on White's series of four related novels. And admirers of President John F. Kennedy applied the name *Camelot* to his brief administration (1961–1963).

Cloudland is any region of dreams, imagination, or impractical speculation. This visionary realm is so named because anyone who is "in the clouds" is not only high up in the sky but fanciful and impractical. By adding a reference to a bird whose name means "crazy; foolish; silly" in slang, *cloud-cuckooland* reinforces the notion of utopian impracticality. The Greek equivalent of *cloud-cuckooland* is the name that, in his comedy *The Birds*, Aristophanes gave his version of a city in the clouds, far removed from the pettiness of everyday Athenian life.

Dreamland, as the word suggests, is any lovely but imaginary place, as one seen in a dream.

Eden is any delightful place or state—in other words, a paradise. In the Bible (Genesis 2:8), Eden was indeed Paradise, the garden where Adam and Eve first lived.

El Dorado is any place that is, or is supposed to be, rich in gold, opportunity, and other good things. It started out as a legendary country in South America, believed to be rich in gold and precious stones and therefore sought by early Spanish explorers. The name means "that which is gilded."

Goshen is a land of plenty. In the Bible (Genesis 45:10), it is the fertile land assigned to the Israelites in Egypt.

Lotus land has come to designate any fabulous, dreamlike setting. In slang, it refers to Hollywood and its film industry, thought of as glittery and alluring, not like the real world. These extended senses are derived from Homeric legend, for in the *Odyssey* the lotus-eaters are a people who, after eating the fruit of the lotus plant, became indolent, dreamy, and forgetful of duty.

Never-never land is any unreal or unrealistic place or situation. In J. M. Barrie's dramatic fantasy *Peter Pan* (1902), Peter runs away to Never-Never-Land to escape growing up.

Oz is a happy land where dreams can come true. The original Oz appears in Frank Baum's *The Wonderful Wizard of Oz* (1900). This classic fairy tale and its many sequels have been made into a number of musicals and motion pictures. In one film, called *The Wizard of Oz,* Judy Garland played the part of little Dorothy, who, with her dog, Toto, is swept up by a cyclone and transported from Kansas to the magical world of Oz, "somewhere over the rainbow."

Paradise is a perfect place or state of beauty, contentment, satisfaction, happiness, or delight. Originally, it was the garden of Eden; then the abode of the righteous after death, the abode of God and the blessed: that is, heaven.

A *promised land* is a place where one expects to have a better life. In the Bible (Genesis 17:8), the Promised Land is Canaan, promised by God to Abraham and his descendants. The night before he was assassinated in 1968, Martin Luther King, Jr., said, in his "Mountaintop" speech: "And I've seen the Promised Land. And I may not get there with you. But I want you to know tonight that we as a people will get to the Promised Land. . . . With this faith, we will be able to achieve this new day, when all of God's children—black men and white men, Jews and Gentiles,

Protestants and Catholics—will be able to join hands and sing with the Negroes in the spiritual of old, 'Free at last! Free at last! Thank God almighty we are free at last.'"

Seventh heaven is a condition of perfect happiness. The name was applied to the outermost of concentric spheres in certain ancient cosmological systems. The seventh sphere, or heaven, where God and his angels are, was viewed as enclosing the earth.

Shangri-La is any imaginary, idyllic utopia or hidden paradise. The name comes from the mythical Himalayan setting of *Lost Horizon*, a novel by the English writer James Hilton (1933).

earth / world

Earth refers to the fifth-largest planet of the solar system, the one we live on. The word is often capitalized as the proper name of the planet but lowercased when preceded by the definite article. (For example: Venus and Mars are Earth's closest neighbors. The diameter of the earth is about 12,760 kilometers, or about 7,930 miles.)

Globe designates, generally, any round, ball-shaped thing and, specifically, the earth (as in "Is there a part of the globe on which a Coca-Cola bottle has not yet been tossed?"). The word applies, as well, to a spherical model of the earth, showing the continents, seas, and other features, and to a similar model of the heavens, showing the celestial bodies.

Universe denotes the whole system of planets, stars, space, and so on, and everything that exists in it. For years scientists have debated the question, "How did the universe begin and how will it end?" In *Leaves of Grass* Walt Whitman brings all of creation down to a personal level: "The whole theory of the universe is directed unerringly to one single individual— namely to You."

Cosmos refers to a universe considered as a harmonious and orderly system. Indeed, cosmology is the scientific study of the form, content, organization, and evolution of the universe. In *Pragmatism* William James says that each person's philosophy comes only partly from books; "it is our individual way of just seeing and feeling the total push and pressure of the cosmos." Had he chosen to, he might have said "the total push and pressure of the universe."

World is sometimes a generalized synonym for *universe* and sometimes the designation of any heavenly body thought of hypothetically as inhabited. H. G. Wells's *The War of the Worlds*, for instance, describes an invasion of England by Martians. More often, however, *world* is equivalent to *earth*, especially in connection with human activities. In "The Second Coming"

William Butler Yeats says, "Things fall apart; the centre cannot hold; / Mere anarchy is loosed upon the world."

motherland / fatherland

One's native land or country can be called either one's *motherland* or one's *fatherland* (as in "Many immigrants continue to feel affection for their motherland [fatherland]"). Yet, in this sense, *motherland* is customarily applied to certain countries, such as England, and *fatherland* to others, such as Germany. *Mother country* is used interchangeably with *motherland,* but English has no *father country.*

Fatherland and sometimes *motherland* refer also to the land of one's ancestors. Another sense of *motherland,* not generally shared with *fatherland,* is a country thought of as an originator or source ("Italy is the motherland of opera").

nation / state

In referring to the independent political units into which the world is divided, many people use the words *nation, state,* and *country* interchangeably. They are not far wrong.

Nation calls attention to the people who, whatever their origin, belong to a particular territory that is united under a single government. After all, the word *nation,* like *nationality,* comes from a Latin verb meaning "born." Allowing for some diversity, a nation is generally thought to be a stable, historically developed community of people with a territory, economic life, culture, and language in common. Even if *United States* had not already been claimed as the name of one of its members, the largest international organization in the world might well have have preferred to call itself the *United Nations* when it was formed in 1945.

State emphasizes political organization and structure. That is, a state is usually regarded as the power or authority represented by a body of people politically organized under one government, especially an independent government, within a territory or territories having definite boundaries (as in "Organization of American States"). The notion of independence is reinforced by the term *sovereign state,* meaning "independent of all others." For example, the Commonwealth, or Commonwealth of Nations, is an association of sovereign states, all former components of the British Empire, united for purposes of consultation and mutual assistance.

Country is the broadest of the three terms. Indeed, a country is usually taken to be the whole land or territory of a nation or state, together with its people. So, for example, a *New York Times* article on an election in Greece in April 1990 begins like this: "Greek voters tried again on Sunday to pull their country from its political rut, turning out boisterously at the polls for the third time in 10 months in search of a government to lead the nation out of political paralysis."

village / town

The places where people live are not universally defined in terms of area, population, number of houses, legal powers, or services provided. So when most of us think of, say, a hamlet, village, town, or city, we loosely compare that kind of settlement to the others.

The starting point is likely to be a *village*, which is generally considered to be a group of houses in the country. A *hamlet* is a very small village (a "wide spot in the road"), less commonly found in the United States than in Great Britain, where it is considered to be too small to have its own church. A *town* is a more or less concentrated group of houses and private and public buildings, larger than a village but smaller than a city. A *city* is a population center that is larger or more important than a town or village.

city / metropolis

Like villages and towns, cities and large urban centers are usually defined in terms of each other. Besides being larger or more important than a town or village, a *city* is, in the United States, an incorporated municipality whose boundaries and powers of self-government are defined by a charter granted by the state in which it is located.

A *metropolis* is any large city or center of population, culture, finance, industry, or the like. It may be not only the main city but also the capital of a country, state, or region.

A *megalopolis* is an extensive, heavily populated, continuously urban area. One such agglomeration of gradually merging metropolises and cities, the "BosWash Corridor," extends along the eastern coast of the United States from Boston, Massachusetts, to Washington, D.C.

capital / capitol

A *capital* is, among other things, a city or town that is the official seat of government of a state, nation, or the like. Rome, then, is the capital of Italy. And Washington, D.C., is the capital of the United States, just as

Pierre is the capital of the state of South Dakota. A *capitol* is a building where a legislative body meets. In written or printed reference to the building in Washington where the U.S. Congress holds its sessions, *Capitol* is used, but this word is ordinarily lowercased when it designates the building where a state legislature meets.

Americas / Western Hemisphere

America, the Americas, and *the Western Hemisphere* are often applied interchangeably to that half of the earth which includes North America, South America, and the West Indies, considered together. *America* is sometimes used also for *North America* alone and as a shortened form of *United States of America.*

North America / South America

The continents of *North America* and *South America* are located in the Western Hemisphere.

North America is generally considered to be bounded by the Atlantic Ocean on the east, the Arctic Ocean on the north, the Pacific Ocean on the west, and the Isthmus of Panama on the south. It includes Canada, the United States, Mexico, the seven countries in *Central America* (Belize, Costa Rica, El Salvador, Guatemala, Honduras, Nicaragua, and Panama), and the islands of the West Indies. Greenland, to the northeast of Canada, is sometimes regarded as part of North America as well.

South America occupies the land south of Panama to Cape Horn. This continent includes the countries of Argentina, Bolivia, Brazil, Chile, Colombia, Ecuador, Guyana, Paraguay, Peru, Suriname, Uruguay, and Venezuela, and also the French department of French Guiana.

United States / the States

United States of America is the official name of the country that is made up of the North American area extending from the Atlantic Ocean to the Pacific Ocean between Canada and Mexico, together with Alaska and Hawaii. The name is commonly shortened to *United States* and, if clear in context, *the States.* English-speakers outside the country, especially in Britain, often use *America,* even though this word has a broader geographic sense. *United States of America* is abbreviated *U.S.A.* (or *USA*); *United States* as *U.S.* (or *US*).

Washington / District of Columbia

Named after Christopher Columbus, the *District of Columbia* is a federal district of the United States, on the northern bank of the Potomac River. It occupies the same 69 square miles (179 square kilometers) as the city of *Washington*. The name of the nation's capital, *Washington, D.C.,* therefore attaches to the city name the abbreviation *D.C.* (or *DC*), which stands for *District of Columbia.*

Alaska Highway / Alcan Highway

The *Alaska Highway* extends from Dawson Creek, British Columbia, to Fairbanks, Alaska. It is also called by its earlier name, the *Alcan Highway* (*Alcan* being a blend of the first letters of *Alaska* and *Canada*).

Inside Passage / Inland Passage

The protected sea route along the western coast of North America, from Seattle, Washington, to the northern part of Alaska, is known as either the *Inside Passage* or the *Inland Passage.* The route, which uses channels and straits between islands and the mainland, is about 950 miles (1,528 kilometers) long.

Continental Divide / Great Divide

In the United States, the *Continental Divide* is a ridge of the Rocky Mountains that forms a watershed separating eastward-flowing rivers from westward-flowing ones. It is sometimes called the *Great Divide,* although this term can refer as well to any principal watershed and, by extension, to any important dividing line.

Corn Belt / Snow Belt

The notion of encircling a person's waist with a *belt* to hold his or her pants up has led to several metaphoric uses of the word. A *beltway,* for example, is an expressway that passes around an urban area. And a *belt* is an area or zone that is distinguished from others in a certain way. Some of these areas in the United States are known for the crops or domestic animals raised there. The *Farm Belt,* which stretches across the north-central plains, is the site of large-scale and extremely varied commercial farming. Within it, the *Corn Belt,* extending from western Ohio to eastern Nebraska and northeastern Kansas, is particularly noted for corn and cornfed livestock. Corn, together with wheat, soybeans, and other cereals, is a staple crop in the

Grain Belt, which encompasses a dozen states from North Dakota to Texas. Covering much of the southern and southeastern part of the country, from Texas to the Carolinas, the *Cotton Belt* produces more of the world's cotton crop than does any other area.

Other regions reflect weather and economic conditions. The *Snow Belt,* or, as it is also called, the *Frost Belt,* is characterized by cold, snowy winters; it comprises states of the Midwest and Northeast. The *Sun Belt,* on the other hand, is characterized by a warm, sunny climate; it includes most of the states of the South and Southwest, and is regarded as an area of rapid population and economic growth. The *Rust Belt* encompasses those parts of the Midwest and Northeast where many heavy manufacturing industries, such as steel, chemicals, and shipbuilding, fell on hard times in the last half of the twentieth century.

The American writer, editor, and critic H. L. Mencken coined *Bible Belt* in 1925 to describe those regions of the United States, particularly in the South, where fundamentalist beliefs prevail and Christian clergy are especially influential.

Cape Canaveral / Cape Kennedy

Cape Canaveral, on the eastern coast of Florida, is a proving ground for U.S. missiles and spacecraft. The name comes from the Spanish word *cañaveral,* meaning "canebrake," a dense growth of cane plants. From 1963 to 1973 the cape was called *Cape Kennedy,* after President John F. Kennedy. The memorial to the assassinated President at this site is now the *Kennedy Space Center,* operated by NASA (National Aeronautics and Space Administration).

Hoover Dam / Boulder Dam

When it was completed in 1936, the large dam on the Colorado River, on the Arizona-Nevada border, was called *Boulder Dam.* In 1947 it was re-named *Hoover Dam,* after Herbert Clark Hoover, the 31st President of the United States (1929–1933).

Latin America / Spanish America

Latin America refers to the region of the Western Hemisphere south of the United States, in Mexico, Central America, the West Indies, and South America, where Spanish, Portuguese, and French are the official languages. *Spanish America,* a narrower term, is applied only to that part of Latin America where Spanish is the chief language. *Hispanic America* and *Ibero-America* encompass Spanish America plus Brazil, whose official language is

Portuguese, for both *Hispanic* and *Ibero-* often refer to the Iberian Peninsula, in Europe, where both Spain and Portugal are located.

Canal Zone / Panama Canal Zone

In the Central American country of Panama a strip of land extends five miles on either side of the Panama Canal, excluding the cities of Panamá and Colón. This area is called either the *Canal Zone* or the *Panama Canal Zone.*

Belize / British Honduras

Belize, a country in Central America, on the Caribbean Sea, was called *British Honduras* as a colony and territory of Great Britain. It became independent in 1981.

Guyana / Guiana

Guyana (officially the *Cooperative Republic of Guyana*), on the northern coast of South America, east of Venezuela, was called *British Guiana* as a colony of Great Britain. In 1966 the country became independent, resuming its traditional name. The Guyana jungle was the site of one of the most bizarre incidents in modern history: the mass murder-suicide of some 900 members of a U.S. sect known as the People's Temple and their leader, the Reverend Jim Jones, in 1978.

Another republic in South America also used to have *Guiana* in its English name, and a European overseas department in the same Guiana region still does. Called *Dutch Guiana* as a territory of the Netherlands, *Suriname* (officially the *Republic of Suriname*) became independent in 1975. It lies to the east of Guyana, and to its east is *French Guiana,* which has been under French authority for some 400 years and an overseas department of France since 1946. One of the islands off the coast is Devil's Island, once the site of an infamous French penal colony.

West Indies / East Indies

The *West Indies* is an archipelago between southeastern North America and northern South America. It is bounded by the Atlantic Ocean, to the east; the Gulf of Mexico, to the northwest; and the Caribbean Sea, to the south. The three main island groups are the Bahamas; the Greater Antilles (Cuba, Hispaniola, Jamaica, and Puerto Rico); and the Lesser Antilles (the Leeward and Windward Islands, Barbados, Trinidad and Tobago, and the islands off the northern coast of Venezuela).

As it was in the past, the term *East Indies* (or *East India*) is sometimes still loosely applied to India, Indochina, and the Malay Archipelago, in Southeast Asia. In somewhat more precise usage, it refers to the Malay Archipelago, especially the islands of Indonesia.

Dominican Republic / Santo Domingo

The *Dominican Republic* is a country occupying the eastern part of the island of *Hispaniola,* in the West Indies (Haiti occupies the western part). In 1961 the capital reclaimed its former name, *Santo Domingo,* having been known as *Ciudad Trujillo* during the long dictatorship of Rafael Leonidas Trujillo. Both the country now known as the *Dominican Republic* and the island now known as *Hispaniola* (which Columbus discovered in 1492 and named *La Española*) were once called *Santo Domingo,* after Saint Dominic, the Spanish priest who founded the Dominican order.

Leeward Islands / Windward Islands

The nautical terms *leeward* (meaning "in the direction toward which the wind blows," or "away from the wind") and *windward* (meaning "in the direction from which the wind blows," or "toward the wind") are incorporated into the names of two groups of islands in the Lesser Antilles of the West Indies. The Leeward Islands, more sheltered from the prevailing northeasterly winds than the Windwards, lie mainly to the east and south of Puerto Rico. They include the Virgin Islands, St. Kitts–Nevis, Antigua and Barbuda, and Guadeloupe. The Windward Islands, continuing southward, include Dominica, Martinique, and Grenada.

El Salvador / San Salvador

The Central American country that lies southwest of Honduras, on the Pacific, is *El Salvador,* which means "The Savior" in Spanish. Its capital is *San Salvador,* which can be translated as "Holy Savior."

United Kingdom / Great Britain

The island country in western Europe known officially as the *United Kingdom of Great Britain and Northern Ireland* is often referred to as the *United Kingdom* for short and the *U.K.* (or *UK*) for even shorter. It consists of England, Scotland, Wales, and Northern Ireland.

Great Britain, the principal island in the United Kingdom, comprises England, Scotland, and Wales. Administratively it includes the adjacent islands except the Isle of Man and the Channel Islands, which, though possessions of the British Crown, have their own legislatures and laws. In popular usage, *Great Britain,* or *Britain,* often replaces *United Kingdom of Great Britain and Northern Ireland.* Another widely used term, *British Isles,* refers to the group of islands consisting of Great Britain, Ireland, and adjacent islands.

Ireland / Eire

Eire, the Gaelic name for *Ireland,* was the official name of the country from 1937 to 1949, when the Republic of Ireland was proclaimed. *Erin,* an old poetic name for Ireland, shares its Old Irish origin with *Eire*—indeed, grammarians may be interested to know that it is the dative case, or form, of this word. *Hibernia,* the Roman name for the country, has also been used poetically from time to time. This Latin word can be traced to the same Old Irish source as *Eire* and *Erin.*

Ulster / Northern Ireland

In informal usage, *Ulster* sometimes refers to *Northern Ireland.* However, it more strictly applies to a former province in the country of *Ireland,* divided in 1920 to form Northern Ireland (a division of the United Kingdom) and a province in the Republic of Ireland. This province in the northern part of the Republic of Ireland, comprising the counties Donegal, Cavan, and Monaghan, is still called Ulster.

Netherlands / Holland

A country in western Europe, on the North Sea, the *Netherlands* (officially the *Kingdom of the Netherlands*) has its capital in Amsterdam but its seat of government in The Hague. The country is popularly known as *Holland.* This was once the name of a medieval country of the Holy Roman Empire and now is part of the names of two provinces of the Netherlands (*North Holland* and *South Holland*). The adjective referring to the country's people, language, culture, and so on is *Dutch.*

West Germany / East Germany

In 1945, after World War II, Germany was divided into four zones of occupation, administered by France, Great Britain, the Soviet Union, and the United States. In 1949 it was partitioned into the *Federal Republic of Germany* (FRG), also called *West Germany,* with its capital in Bonn, and the *German Democratic Republic* (GDR), also called *East Germany,* with its capital in East Berlin. The 45 years of division ended on October 3, 1990, when the two Germanys were united in the Federal Republic of Germany. A unified Berlin was chosen to be the new German capital, as it had been before the war.

Russia / Union of Soviet Socialist Republics

The word *Russia* has several political meanings. First, it refers to an empire (the *Russian Empire*) which existed in eastern Europe and northern Asia from 1547 until 1917, was ruled by the czars, and had its capital in St. Petersburg. Second, it is applied loosely to the *Union of Soviet Socialist Republics* (ordinarily shortened to *USSR, the Soviet Union,* or *Soviet Russia*). Third, it refers to all or, especially, the European part of the *Russian Soviet Federated Socialist Republic (RSFSR)*, the largest of the constituent republics in the USSR. With its capital in Moscow, like that of the country itself, the RSFSR stretches from the Baltic Sea to the Pacific and from the Arctic Ocean to the Chinese border.

Leningrad / St. Petersburg

Many Russian place names were changed after the revolution of 1917, but none evokes stronger memories of the past than *St. Petersburg,* now *Leningrad.* Built in 1712 by Peter the Great, St. Petersburg was the capital of the Russian Empire for more than two centuries. Peter's "window to the West," on the Gulf of Finland, was renamed *Petrograd* in 1914. It was given its present name in 1924, after the death of Vladimir Ilyich Lenin, a leader of the Communist revolution and the first premier of the Soviet Union. By then, however, the capital had been moved to Moscow.

Near East / Middle East

Near East, Middle East, and *Far East* are as imprecise in defining present-day geographic regions as they are pervasive in everyday speech and writing. For one thing, few reference books agree on the limits of each region. For another, *near, far,* and the in-between *middle* are relative terms, deriving what little meaning they have from their distance from, say, the Houses of Parliament in London.

Near East once designated the vast Ottoman Empire of the Turks, which lasted from about 1300 to 1918 and which included at its peak much of southeastern Europe, southwestern Asia, and northeastern Africa. The term is fast falling into disuse, having been all but replaced by *Middle East.* For example, *The Associated Press Stylebook and Libel Manual* says of *Near East:* "There is no longer a substantial distinction between this term and

Middle East." And *The New York Times Manual of Style and Usage* says of *Near East:* "Do not use. See *Middle East.*" When *Near East* is used today, it is generally as a somewhat vague reference to countries near the eastern end of the Mediterranean Sea, including those of southwestern Asia, the Arabian Peninsula, and northeastern Africa.

Middle East (or *Mideast*) is now ordinarily taken to mean the large region encompassing the Arabian Peninsula (Bahrain, Kuwait, Oman, Qatar, Saudi Arabia, the United Arab Emirates, Yemen); Cyprus; Egypt; Iran; Iraq; Israel; Jordan; Lebanon; Libya; Sudan; Syria; and Turkey (the Asian part). At one time, Afghanistan, Burma (or Myanmar), India, and Pakistan were included.

In its narrowest sense, *Far East* usually designates China, Japan, Hong Kong, Mongolia, North Korea, South Korea, Taiwan, and eastern Siberia (in the Soviet Union). In a broader sense, it also includes the countries of Southeast Asia (mainly Burma, Cambodia, Indonesia, Laos, Malaysia, the Philippines, Singapore, Thailand, and Vietnam).

Iran / Persia

Iran, a country in southwestern Asia, between the Caspian Sea and the Persian Gulf, was called *Persia* until 1935. The empire was abolished and an Islamic republic established in 1979. The words *Persia* and *Persian* are still widely used, both in reference to Iran and its people and language and in established compounds like *Persian cat, Persian blinds,* and *Persian rug.*

Istanbul / Constantinople

The largest seaport in Turkey is *Istanbul,* but its two former names live on in history and romantic literature. From A.D. 330 to 1930 the city was called *Constantinople.* At the time of its founding, about 600 B.C., it was known as *Byzantium.*

United Arab Emirates / Trucial States

The *United Arab Emirates,* a country in eastern Arabia, on the Persian Gulf, consists of seven Arab sheikdoms: Abu Dhabi, Ajman, Dubai, Fujairah,

Ras al-Khaimah, Sharjah, and Umm al-Qaiwain. The federation was established in 1971 (the word *emirate* designating a state of jurisdiction of an *emir*, who, in certain Muslim countries, is a ruler, prince, or commander). Earlier the group of sheikdoms had been known as the *Trucial States*, in a region called *Trucial Oman*, on the *Trucial Coast* of the Persian Gulf. The unusual word *trucial* refers to a maritime truce made in 1835 between the British government and several Arab states on the Gulf of Oman.

Yemen / Southern Yemen

In May 1990, two countries on the southern Arabian Peninsula proclaimed a merger as the *Republic of Yemen*. The *Yemen Arab Republic* (usually called *Yemen*) had been an independent republic since 1962. Bordering on the Red Sea, it had the inland city of San'a as its capital. The *People's Democratic Republic of Yemen*, on the Gulf of Aden, had been formed in 1967 from the former Federation of South Arabia. For a time it was called *Southern Yemen* (or *South Yemen*). Its capital, the coastal city of Aden, became the capital of the new republic.

Palestine / Holy Land

Palestine and *Holy Land* are used interchangeably for the historical region in southwestern Asia, at the eastern end of the Mediterranean, that comprises parts of modern Israel, Jordan, and Egypt. In its political sense, *Palestine* refers to the territory in this region, west of the Jordan River, that was a British mandate from 1923 until 1948, when the United Nations established the state of Israel.

Ethiopia / Abyssinia

Ethiopia is officially known as the *People's Democratic Republic of Ethiopia*. This ancient country in northeastern Africa, on the Red Sea, has been widely, though never officially, called *Abyssinia*. Yet the name *Ethiopia* was reclaimed, not invented, for, along with *Abyssinia*, it was used from the earliest times to designate an empire that possibly dates to the tenth century B.C.

African Countries Whose Names Were Changed
between 1900 and 1990

Present Name	Other Name(s)	Year of Independence	Country Granting Independence
Angola	Portuguese West Africa	1975	Portugal
Benin	Dahomey	1960	France
Botswana	Bechuanaland	1966	Great Britain
Burkina Faso	Upper Volta	1960	France
Burundi	Ruanda-Urundi	1962	Belgian-administered UN trust
Central African Republic	Ubangi-Shari, Central African Empire	1960	France
Congo	Middle Congo	1960	France
Djibouti	French Somaliland, French Territory of the Afars and Issas	1977	France
Equatorial Guinea	Spanish Guinea	1968	Spain
Ghana	Gold Coast	1957	Great Britain
Guinea	French Guinea	1958	France
Guinea-Bissau	Portuguese Guinea	1974	Portugal
Kenya	British East Africa	1963	Great Britain
Lesotho	Basutoland	1966	Great Britain
Madagascar	Malagasy Republic	1960	France
Malawi	British Central African Protectorate, Nyasaland	1964	Great Britain

Present Name	Other Name(s)	Year of Independence	Country Granting Independence
Mali	French Sudan, Sudanese Republic	1960	France
Morocco	French Morocco and Spanish Morocco	1956	France, Spain
Mozambique	Portuguese East Africa	1975	Portugal
Namibia	South West Africa	1990	South Africa
Somalia	British Somaliland and Italian Somaliland	1960	Great Britain, Italy
South Africa	Union of South Africa	1961	Great Britain
Sudan	Anglo-Egyptian Sudan	1956	Great Britain, Egypt
Tanzania	Tanganyika (1961) and Zanzibar (1963)	1964 (merger)	Great Britain
Togo	Togoland, French Togo	1960	France
Zaire	Congo Free State, Belgian Congo	1960	Belgium
Zambia	Northern Rhodesia	1964	Great Britain
Zimbabwe	Southern Rhodesia, Rhodesia	1980	Great Britain

Pacific Rim / Pacific Basin

The *Pacific Rim* is defined very broadly as a region that includes every country whose coastline touches the Pacific Ocean. This means all the countries in North America, South America, and Asia that border the Pacific, as well as Australia, New Zealand, and the smaller Pacific islands. According to a narrower definition, not only do the Pacific Rim countries have coastlines bordering the Pacific Ocean but they are constantly divided and subdivided into groups pursuing specific economic, political, or cultural purposes.

A newer term, *Pacific Basin* is sometimes used as the equivalent of *Pacific Rim*. It is also applied more specifically to the newly industrialized "Four Tigers" of Asia: Hong Kong, Singapore, South Korea, and Taiwan.

Taiwan / Formosa

In 1949, when the People's Republic of China was proclaimed in Beijing, with the Communist Mao Tse-Tung as chairman, the defeated Nationalists, under Chiang Kai-shek, fled to an island 100 miles (about 160 kilometers) off the coast. This island is now known as Taiwan, though its original Portuguese name was *Formosa*. Together with the Pescadores and the Matsu and Quemoy islands, it forms the Republic of China, with Taipei as its capital. The *Taiwan Strait* (formerly the *Formosa Strait*) separates Taiwan from mainland China.

Malaysia / Malaya

Malaysia is a country in Southeast Asia. In 1963 it was formed of a union of former British territories: the Federation of Malaya, at the southern end of the Malay Peninsula; Sabah and Sarawak, both on the island of Borneo; and Singapore, an island off the southern tip of the Malay Peninsula (which seceded in 1965 to become an independent nation). The largest part of Malaysia, the *Federation of Malaya* was renamed *Peninsular Malaysia*. The word *Malaysia* is, as well, equivalent to *Malay Archipelago*, designating a large group of islands between Southeast Asia and Australia, including Indonesia, the Philippines, and sometimes New Guinea.

Malaya is another name for the *Malay Peninsula*, which, extending from Singapore to the Isthmus of Kra, includes Peninsular Malaysia and part of Thailand. As noted above, *Peninsular Malaysia* is the present name for what was once the *Federation of Malaya*.

Indonesia / Netherlands Indies

Indonesia (officially the *Republic of Indonesia*) is a country in the Malay Archipelago. It consists of Java, Sumatra, most of Borneo, West Irian (on the island of New Guinea), Celebes, and many smaller nearby islands. For many years the group of islands, known as the *Netherlands Indies,* the *Netherlands East Indies,* or *Dutch East Indies,* was either under Dutch control or in various forms of union with the Netherlands. In 1950 it established a unitary republic and was admitted to the United Nations.

Thailand / Siam

Thailand (officially the *Kingdom of Thailand*) is a constitutional monarchy on the Indochinese Peninsula. The country was known as *Siam* until 1939. It is the only nation in Southeast Asia that has never been ruled by a Western power.

Cambodia / Kampuchea

Cambodia, an ancient country in the southeastern part of the Indochinese Peninsula, has been known by various other names in modern times. Following its independence from France in 1954, it was called the *Kingdom of Cambodia.* In 1970, it became the *Khmer Republic* (*Khmer* being the name not only of the Cambodian people and language but also of the empire to which Cambodia belonged between the sixth and fifteenth centuries). In 1976, a year after the Communist Khmer Rouge guerrilla forces had gained control of the government, the country was renamed *Democratic Kampuchea.* Its name was changed again—to the *People's Republic of Kampuchea*—in 1979, when Vietnamese invaders installed a new communist regime. In 1989 the country adopted still another name: the *State of Cambodia.*

Even when *Democratic Kampuchea* or the *People's Republic of Kampuchea* was the official name of the government, many American publications preferred *Cambodia.* "Use this name rather than *Kampuchea* in datelines," said *The Associated Press Stylebook and Libel Manual,* "since the country continues to be known more widely by this name. In the body of stories *Kampuchea* may be used as long as it is identified as another name for *Cambodia.*"

Saigon / Ho Chi Minh City

In 1945, Vietnam was partitioned into two republics, with *Saigon* the capital of South Vietnam and *Hanoi* the capital of North Vietnam. In 1976, after the Vietnam War, Saigon's name was changed to *Ho Chi Minh City,* in honor of the Vietnamese nationalist leader who served as president of

North Vietnam from 1954 until his death in 1969. *Hanoi* became the capital of the reunified country, whose official name is *Socialist Republic of Vietnam.*

Myanmar / Burma

A country in Southeast Asia, on the Indochinese Peninsula, *Burma* was officially a federation of states called the *Union of Burma.* In 1989 the names became *Myanmar* and *Union of Myanmar.* This change has been slow to catch on in the United States, and those Americans who have accepted it usually say or write "Myanmar, formerly Burma." In any case, *Burmese* continues to be the adjective form of the country name ("the Burmese people").

The name of the capital has been changed too: from *Rangoon* to *Yangon.* Again, Americans generally prefer the older, more familiar name.

Pakistan / India

Pakistan (officially the *Islamic Republic of Pakistan*) is a country in southern Asia, on the Arabian Sea. In 1947 it became one of the two successor states to British *India* (the other being the country of India). It was proclaimed a republic in 1956.

Bangladesh / East Pakistan

Bangladesh (officially the *People's Republic of Bangladesh*) is a country in southern Asia, at the head of the Bay of Bengal. From 1955 until 1971, when it became independent, it made up the province of *East Pakistan* in the country of Pakistan.

Sri Lanka / Ceylon

An island nation off the southeastern tip of India, *Sri Lanka* was a British crown colony known for more than a century as *Ceylon.* In 1948, Ceylon became an independent member of the Commonwealth. In 1972, a new constitution established the *Republic of Sri Lanka,* whose official name is the *Democratic Socialist Republic of Sri Lanka.*

Vanuatu / New Hebrides

Vanuatu (officially the *Republic of Vanuatu*) is an archipelago in the southwestern Pacific Ocean, west of Fiji. It gained its independence in 1980, having been under joint British and French control since 1906 as the *New Hebrides.*

Things

street / avenue

A public thoroughfare in a village, town, or city is generally known as a *street*, particularly if it is paved and has sidewalks and buildings along one or both sides. A broad, principal street is often called an *avenue*. In many American towns and cities, avenues run at right angles to streets. As broad and well-constructed as an avenue, a *boulevard* is typically more parklike, with areas along the side or in the center for grass, trees, shrubbery, and flowers. A *drive*, too, is generally scenic, perhaps winding through a park or along a lake. As applied to a private road leading from a street to a house or other building, the word is interchangeable with *driveway*.

A *road* is sometimes considered the same as a street, especially by municipal officials who indiscriminately attach the two words to proper names (though they apparently draw the line at numbers: a city might have either a "Charleston Street" or a "Charleston Road," but seldom an "Eighth Road"). Yet a road is more like a highway in that it is likely to be a paved stretch for motoring between distant places.

highway / freeway

A *highway* is a main road, especially one between towns or cities. To ensure the rapid, safe movement of a great many vehicles, some highways have grade separations; that is, an overpass or underpass is built at the point where two or more roadways intersect, usually by means of a cloverleaf or similar type of interchange. Under full control of access, through traffic is given preference by providing access connections only with selected public roads and by prohibiting both crossings at grade and direct private driveway connections. Under partial control of access, through traffic is, again, given preference by access connections only with selected public roads, but some crossings at grade and some private driveway connections are permitted.

An *expressway* (also called a *thruway* or *superhighway*) is a multilane divided highway designed for high-speed through traffic. Full or partial control of access is ensured, and there are generally grade separations at major intersections.

A *freeway* is an expressway with full control of access. As the name suggests, vehicles may travel on it at no charge.

A *turnpike,* though now constructed much like an expressway, is a *toll road* (or *tollway*). Drivers ordinarily pass through a tollgate, or turnpike, on entering the highway and may be stopped at certain points to pay additional tolls.

A *parkway* is an expressway for noncommercial traffic, with full or partial control of access. Some parkways are broad thoroughfares located within a park or series of parklike developments; they may be bordered and divided with plantings of trees, bushes, and grass.

chuckhole / pothole

Chuckhole designates a rough hole in a paved street or road, made by wear and weathering. This is one sense of the word *pothole,* too. An Americanism, *chuckhole* comes from the dialectal *chock,* meaning "a bump in a road" but, originally, "a stump or block"—as, for example, a tree trunk wedged under a wheel to keep it from rolling. *Pothole,* clearly, suggests that the hollowed-out place is deep and round like a pot.

wharf / pier

Ships that load or unload cargo or passengers at the shore of a harbor, river, or other body of water may lie alongside a structure that is made of wood, stone, or cement and is sometimes roofed over. Such a structure is generally known as a *wharf, pier* (or *landing pier*), or *dock.* Piers are usually built out over the water and supported by pillars or piles; besides being a landing place for ships and boats, they are often used as entertainment pavilions (for example, the Million Dollar Pier and Steeplechase Pier in Atlantic City, New Jersey). A dock, too, may have more than one purpose. One that is an excavated basin equipped with gates to keep water in or out is used for the repair and even building of ships. A dock may also be the area of water between two landing piers.

A number of other words are equivalents or near-equivalents of *wharf, pier,* and *dock.* For instance, if the place for loading or unloading ships is made of stone or concrete, it might be called a *quay* (pronounced *key*). Besides a landing pier, *jetty* (which, like the related word *jet,* suggests an outward movement) designates a kind of wall built out into the water to restrain currents and to protect a harbor or pier. *Slip* refers to a pier or platform sloping into the water and perhaps used for repairing or building, as well as landing, ships; in another sense (this one an Americanism), it refers to a water channel between piers or wharves, used for docking ships. *Berth* conveys this latter sense too, usually referring specifically to a ship's place of anchorage. The word *levee* (which, like *lever*, conveys the notion of raising something) was given two nautical meanings in the United States: first, an embankment built alongside a river to prevent high water from flooding bordering land, and, second, a landing place, such as a pier, on the bank of a river. Another word sometimes used in place of *wharf* is *embarcadero*, American English having borrowed from Spanish this form of a verb meaning "embark."

well / aquifer

A *well* is a hole or shaft sunk into the earth to tap an underground supply of water, gas, oil, or other liquid. An *aquifer* is an underground layer of porous rock, sand, or similar material which contains water and into which wells can be sunk.

garbage / trash

Garbage and *trash* both convey the sense of unwanted, discarded material. But *garbage* is mainly spoiled or waste food, as from a market or kitchen, that is wrapped (usually in plastic bags nowadays) for garbage collectors to cart away. *Trash*, also called *rubbish* or *refuse*, is mainly broken, worthless, or discarded things, such as electrical appliances too expensive to repair, old clothes, old newspapers, and empty bottles and cans, some of which may be salvageable for recycling or re-use. *Litter* is things lying about in disorder, especially bits or scraps of rubbish that are scattered but not necessarily thrown away (as in "How can you find the door with so much litter in your room?").

Though often considered the equivalent of *trash*, the word *waste* is applied also to such useless, superfluous, or discarded material as ashes and sewage, as well as garbage. *Sewage*, a blend of *sewer* + the suffix *-age* (here meaning "the result of"), refers to the liquid or water-borne waste matter carried off by sewers or drains. In one sense, *sewerage* means the same as *sewage*, but it designates, as well, both a system of sewers and the removal of surface water and waste matter by sewers.

house / home

In the sense of a building for people to live in, *house* and *home* are freely interchanged. One might say, for example, "Most of the houses in this part of town are new" or "Most of the homes in this part of town are new." To some people, *house* more strongly implies a physical structure that serves as a dwelling place, whereas *home* has a more sentimental connotation, suggesting a pleasant, restful, congenial place where one likes to be ("I wouldn't trade a day in my home for a month at the Paris Ritz"). Others consider *home* the more elegant word. That is, instead of "We bought our house five years ago," they would say "We bought our home five years ago"—probably replacing *bought* with *purchased* for good measure.

motor home / trailer

Movable places to live or work in are by no means all alike. Besides size, purpose, and degree of comfort, they differ in their ability to move under their own power.

A *motor home* is a motor vehicle—that is, a vehicle that runs on wheels, has its own motor, and is used on streets or highways—with a van or trucklike chassis. It is outfitted as a traveling home, usually with self-contained electrical and plumbing facilities.

A *trailer* (sometimes called a *house trailer*) is a closed vehicle that has wheels but no motor, and is therefore designed to be pulled by a car or truck. With beds, cooking facilities, and the like, it serves as either a dwelling or a place of business.

A *mobile home,* too, is ordinarily pulled by a car or truck. Even though it lacks a permanent foundation, it is connected to utility lines so it can be set more or less indefinitely at one location.

A *camper* can be either a motor vehicle or a trailer equipped for camping out.

Recreational vehicles, or, as they are more commonly called, *RVs,* are campers, trailers, motor homes, and similar vehicles designed as living places during casual travel, camping, and other recreational activities.

master key / skeleton key

A *master key* is a key that is designed to open a number of slightly different locks. The cleaning staff of a hotel, for example, usually carry master keys. A *skeleton key* is a key that can be used to open any of various simple locks, because a large part of the bit (the part of a key that actually turns the lock) has been filed away. The word *passkey*, besides being used in place of either *master key* or *skeleton key,* designates any private key.

andiron / firedog

In many fireplaces the wood rests on a pair of metal supports with ornamented front uprights. Either support in the pair is called an *andiron* or a *firedog*. Though they may not seem to, both words probably incorporate the names of animals. In the extinct Celtic language of ancient Gaul, *andera* is believed to have meant "heifer" and to have been used in references to andirons because these were decorated with a bull's head. Later on, the Old French *andier* became *aundiren* in Middle English, the ending having been altered by association with *iron*. As for *firedog*, English borrowed the sense but not the actual word from French, in which *chenet*, the diminutive of *chien* ("dog"), means "andiron."

mothball / camphor ball

Whether made of camphor or, more likely, of naphthalene, the small ball whose fumes repel moths in furs and woolen clothes, blankets, and other articles is called either a *mothball* or a *camphor ball*.

soap / detergent

In describing a product that is used with water to produce suds for washing or cleaning, *soap* and *detergent* are freely, though somewhat loosely, interchanged. Whether in solid form, as liquids, as powders, or as flakes, soaps and detergents are very much alike in that they both trap dirt or grease and then hold it in suspension until it is washed away. Yet they are unlike in their manufacturing process and chemical composition.

Soap is an organic compound produced by the action of a heated alkali on a fat or oil. The name itself goes back to the Latin word *sebum*, meaning "tallow" or "grease." If the alkali is a caustic soda like sodium hydroxide, the result is ordinary hard soap; if the alkali is a caustic potash like potassium hydroxide, the result is soft soap. Besides referring to actual soap in liquid or semifluid form, *soft soap* has come to be used informally to mean either "flattery or smooth talk" or "to persuade with flattery" (as in "Don't try to soft-soap me into doing your algebra lesson").

A *detergent* is a synthetic surface-active cleansing agent, nowadays made mostly from petroleum byproducts. English adopted the word from a Latin verb in the seventeenth century, but at that time to *deterge* mainly had to do with cleansing a wound. Today's detergents are far more than medicinal, being designed to attack grease or dirt almost anywhere, including skin, dishes, and fabrics. However much it resembles soap, a detergent is different in an important way. By not reacting with the salts in hard water, it does not separate out insoluble gray or whitish clots. In other words, it leaves no ring inside a bathtub.

faucet / tap

Many Americans use the word *faucet* to describe the valve they turn to regulate the flow of a liquid from a pipe, say, the water in a kitchen sink. Others, like most Britons, call the device a *tap*. And still others prefer *spigot* or *cock*, although these words are perhaps more likely to be applied to a plug or peg used to stop the small hole or opening in a barrel or keg.

rug / carpet

Anyone wanting to buy either a *rug* or a *carpet* in an American department store would probably be directed to "floor coverings." The main difference between the two is that whereas a carpet is intended to cover the entire floor, a rug is a smaller single piece of definite shape. *Wall-to-wall carpeting* may cover not only the floors in every room of a house but the halls and stairs as well. The limited portion of a floor for which rugs are made can be seen in words like *area rug* and *scatter rug* (or *throw rug*).

Most rugs and carpets are now mass-produced of wool, cotton, or synthetic fibers woven into a thick, heavy, often napped fabric. Some rugs are made of woven strips of rag, animal skins, and other materials. *Oriental rugs*, with rich, soft colors in intricate, frequently floral, patterns, are handwoven in various countries. Though they are sometimes called *Oriental carpets*, their definite single-piece shape makes the word *rug* more appropriate. An Oriental carpet made in Persia (Iran) is in fact known as a *Persian rug*.

dish / plate

There is no clear-cut distinction between the porcelain, earthenware, glass, or plastic vessels in which food is held and served and those from which it is eaten. In the most general terms, a shallow, concave container used for holding or serving food is called a *dish*, and a shallow, circular dish used for eating food is called a *plate*. So a set of dishes, for example, might have six dinner plates. Yet a dessert can be both served in and eaten from a dessert dish.

Some serving dishes have special names, depending on their function. One that is large, quite flat, and oval, and is often used for meat or fish, is called a *platter*. One that is large and deep, has a lid, and is used for soups, stews, and the like, is called a *tureen*. One that is boat-shaped, for serving gravy, is called a *gravy boat*. One that is large, deep, rounded, and open at the top, and is used for serving various foods, including fruit, is likely to be called a *bowl*. During a meal one might transfer, say, an apple from a bowl to one's plate. Yet cereal is usually eaten from a bowl, not easily from a plate. So bowls are not limited to serving.

silverware / flatware

Though traditionally applied to articles of tableware that are made of or plated with silver, *silverware* has come to mean any metal tableware. *Flatware* refers to relatively flat tableware; that is, plates, platters, and the like, as well as knives, forks, and spoons. *Flat silver* designates silver knives, forks, and spoons, as distinguished from silver trays, teapots, bowls, and so on. Serving dishes and table accessories, especially of silver, that are relatively hollow or concave are called *holloware*.

frying pan / skillet

A shallow pan with a handle, for frying food, is usually called a *frying pan*, though often *frypan* or *skillet*. In some parts of the United States a cast-iron frying pan is known as a *spider*, because it originally had legs for use on a hearth.

couch / sofa

An upholstered piece of furniture that has a fixed back and armrests and is used for sitting or lying on is commonly called either a *couch* or a *sofa*. If it is large and low, with neither armrests nor back, it is likely to be called a *divan*. A *settee* can be a small or medium-sized couch or else a long bench with a back, for seating several people. A *love seat* is a small couch or double chair that seats two people. To most Americans, a *chesterfield* is a heavily stuffed couch, perhaps upholstered in leather, with upright arms as high as the back; to most Canadians, it is any kind of couch.

A *davenport* is a large upholstered couch that can often be opened into a bed. A *sofa bed* always can. With its two mattresses on separate frames, one below the other, a *hi-riser* is a couch that can be turned into a double bed or two single beds. Nowadays, a *daybed* —despite its name—is a couch by day and a bed by night. It might even be a single bed which, with a floor-length cover and cushions, is placed against the wall of a living room or den. In past centuries, however, a daybed was indeed used for reclining or sleeping during the day. It typically had a low head and foot, giving it the appearance of an elongated, usually armless, chair. It thus resembled the *chaise longue*, a couchlike chair with two, one, or no armrests and with both a support for the sitter's back and a seat long enough to support his or her outstretched legs.

chest of drawers / dresser

A *chest of drawers* is a piece of furniture that consists almost solely of a frame containing a set of drawers; it is often placed in a bedroom, for keeping articles of clothing. A *dresser* is a chest of drawers that ordinarily has a mirror, and both a *bureau* and the narrow, high chest of drawers known as a *chiffonier* often do, too. A *highboy* is a high chest of drawers mounted on tall legs, whereas a *lowboy* is mounted on short legs to about table height. A *chest-on-chest* is a chest of drawers placed on another, somewhat larger one.

escalator / moving staircase

An *escalator* is a moving staircase with treads linked in an endless belt.It is used mainly in department stores, hotels, airports, subway stations, and other public places. The word was coined in 1895 as a trademark of the Otis Elevator Company. By the middle of the twentieth century—partly because of the manufacturer's own advertising practices—the consuming public had come to treat *escalator* as the name for a type of product, rather than as the designation for one particular brand of the product. The U.S. Patent Office therefore canceled the registration. Now, instead of being a trademark protected as the exclusive property of its owner, *escalator* is a generic term available for anyone to use. Besides *moving staircase*, the word is now interchangeable with *moving stairway*.

cot / stretcher

Cot (sometimes *camp bed*) refers to a narrow bed that is collapsible because the frame on which canvas or plastic sheeting is stretched can be folded up. Both *stretcher* and *litter* designate a light frame that is covered with canvas or a similar material and is used for carrying the sick, injured, or dead. *Gurney* applies to a cot or stretcher on wheels, used in ambulances and hospitals to move patients.

lectern / podium

Lectern and *podium* are used interchangeably for a stand a speaker might use for holding notes, a book, or other material. But *lectern*, not *podium*, refers as well to a reading desk in a church, particularly such a desk from which a part of the Scriptures is read in a church service. And *podium*, not *lectern*, refers as well to a low platform, especially one a conductor of an orchestra stands on. Although *dais* sometimes replaces *podium* in this sense, it often designates a platform raised above the floor at one end of a hall or room to support a throne, seats of honor, or a speaker's stand (that is, a lectern or podium).

bag / sack

A *bag* is a nonrigid container made of paper, plastic, fabric, leather, or some other material, with an opening at the top (a garbage bag, a book bag, a tote bag, for instance). A *sack* is a bag, especially a large one of coarse cloth, for holding grain, foodstuffs, and the like (a sack of grain, a flour sack, a sack of potatoes). Many people use the words interchangeably, calling a paper or plastic container filled with groceries either "a bag of groceries" or "a sack of groceries." Although in this context *bag* has been more commonly used in the northern part of the United States and *sack* in the southern, the mass media and Americans' propensity for moving from one place to another have blurred this distinction.

Poke, meaning "a sack or bag," remains a dialectal word. This is the poke referred to in the expression *buy a pig in a poke*, which has to do with buying, getting, or agreeing to something without seeing or knowing about it in advance.

pail / bucket

Both a *pail* and a *bucket* are more or less cylindrical containers for holding and carrying liquids and solids. They are generally made of metal, wood, or plastic and have a hoop-shaped handle. Some are open-topped and others have a removable cover.

Although some say that *pail* is somewhat more old-fashioned than *bucket*, the two words are still often interchangeable, as in "a milk pail (bucket)" and "a pail (bucket) of milk." Yet context sometimes favors one word over the other. For example, either "bucket of ice" or "pail of ice" can designate a container filled with ice, perhaps to be carried from one place to another. But "ice bucket," not "ice pail," describes a small, lidded container for holding ice cubes or ice chips to be used in cooling drinks. In fact, sometimes a word more precise than either is called for. The kind of wide-lipped bucket or pail that is used for pouring coal on a fire, for instance, is known as either a *coal scuttle* (or simply *scuttle*) or a *hod*.

box / carton

A *box* is any of various kinds of containers made of cardboard, wood, or other stiff material. Typically rectangular and lidded, it is used for holding or carrying nonliquid things like shoes, money, jewelry, breakfast cereal, and small gifts.

A *carton* can be a boxlike container made of light, waxed cardboard and used for keeping and pouring liquids like milk and fresh-squeezed orange juice. It can also be a boxlike container, either rectangular or square, that is made of sturdy cardboard and is closed with flaps at the top. If large, such a carton may be used, say, for packing clothes, books, and home furnishings for a move. If relatively small, it may be filled with almost anything nonliquid and enclosed in a larger, stronger box for shipping.

A *crate* is a box usually made of slats of wood, for packing large or fragile items to be shipped or stored (furniture, a hi-fi system, dishes, and oranges, for example). Instead of having a certain shape, it may be a framework built around its contents, whatever they may be.

In this context, a *case* is a boxlike container used for holding items or for carrying them easily and safely. Some specific uses are suggested by words with which *case* is combined, including *eyeglass case*, *cigarette case*, *suitcase*, *briefcase*, *attaché case*, and *violin case*. Besides, a case may be a full box or its contents (as in "a case of wine").

bottle / jar

Bottles, jars, jugs, and similar containers come in various sizes and shapes, have various purposes, and are made of various materials, including glass, stone, earthenware, and plastic.

A *bottle* has a round and relatively narrow neck that can be closed with a screw-top cap, a cork, or a stopper. It is used mainly for liquids, such as wine, soft drinks, and perfume.

A *jar* is likely to be cylindrical, with no spout and with a large opening that is ordinarily closed with a screw-top cap or a flat lid. It is used for many things, including jam, pickles, cold cream, and cotton balls.

A *jug* is large and deep, with a small opening and a handle. It is used to hold liquids, such as water, cider, and molasses.

A *crock* is any jar, pot, or similar container, especially one made of coarse earthenware. Today Americans are less likely to use the word in, say, "Let's open the crock of pickles in the cellar" than in "That's a crock!" This slang clipping of "a crock of slops" (a euphemism) can refer to any absurd, insincere, or exaggerated action or attitude.

A *demijohn* has a narrow neck, a wicker casing, and one or two wicker handles. It is very large, holding up to 10 gallons (37.85 liters) of a liquid. With *demi-* as its prefix, the word sounds as though it should mean "half of" or "somewhat less than" something else, just as *demivolt* means "half a volt" and *demigod* often means "a lesser god." Instead, it comes from the French *dame-jeanne,* which probably started out as a fanciful name for the container and which in English means, literally, "Dame Jean," or perhaps "Lady Jane."

A *pitcher* generally has a wide mouth, a broad lip or spout, and a handle. It is used for holding and pouring liquids, such as water, milk, and fruit juices.

A *carafe* is a glass bottle with a spherical body and a narrow neck. It is used for serving wine, water, or coffee.

There are two main kinds of *flask*. One, for laboratory and similar uses, is small and bottle-shaped and usually has a stopper, cap, or other closure. The Erlenmeyer flask, for instance, is a conical laboratory flask with a flat bottom and a short, straight neck. The other kind of flask is a small, flattened or curved container, sometimes made of metal. It is used for carrying liquor, medicine, or other liquids in the pocket.

A *flagon,* whose name shares a common origin with *flask,* has a handle and spout, and sometimes a lid. It is used mainly for serving wine and other liquids during a meal.

A *decanter* is a decorative glass bottle, generally with a stopper. It is used for holding and serving a liquid, especially wine, after it has been decanted; that is, after it has been gently poured from the original bottle without stirring up the sediment.

A *thermos* is a bottle, flask, or jug for keeping liquids at almost their original temperature for several hours. It has two walls enclosing a vacuum and is fitted in a metal outer case. Other names for this once-trademarked container include *thermos bottle, thermos flask, thermos jug,* and *thermos carafe.*

A *canteen* is a small metal or plastic flask, usually encased in canvas. It is used, especially by soldiers, campers, and hikers, for carrying drinking water.

magnum / jeroboam

Over the years bottles of wines, especially champagne, were given distinctive names, depending on their size. For example, an ordinary *bottle* contained 26 fluid ounces; because this amount equals a fifth of a gallon, Americans used *fifth* and *bottle* interchangeably. Besides being twice as large as a *half bottle,* a bottle held four times as much as a *split,* half as much as a *magnum,* and an eighth as much as a *methuselah* (named after the patriarch who, according to Genesis 5:27, lived 969 years). Other bottle names inspired by the Bible include the 104-ounce *jeroboam,* named after the first king of the northern kingdom of Israel (1 Kings 11:26–14:20) and the 520-ounce *nebuchadnezzar,* named after the Babylonian king who conquered Jerusalem (2 Kings 24; Daniel 1).

All this changed on January 1, 1979, when the American wine industry officially went metric. Wine buyers may, for example, still think of a bottle as containing a fifth of a gallon, but the label tells them it contains a little less: 750 instead of 757 milliliters. (One U.S. gallon is the equivalent of 3.7854 liters, and there are 1,000 milliliters in a liter.) Yet, whether falling into disuse or not, traditional names can be applied—give or take a little wine—to the seven bottle sizes for which the U.S. Bureau of Alcohol, Tobacco, and Firearms has established metric capacities. These metric units, not their fluid-ounce equivalents, are shown on the bottles themselves.

A *miniature* holds 100 milliliters (3.4 ounces). Wine is seldom sold in a bottle this small.

A *split* holds 187 milliliters (6.3 ounces). This is still about half as much as a half bottle.

A *half bottle* holds 375 milliliters (12.7 ounces).

A *bottle* holds 750 milliliters (25.4 ounces).

A *quart* holds about the same as a *liter* (33.8 ounces).

A *magnum* still holds twice as much as the usual bottle: 1.5 liters (50.7 ounces).

A *jeroboam* still holds twice as much as a magnum: 3 liters (101.4 ounces).

appetizer / hors d'oeuvre

An *appetizer* is a small portion of tasty and attractive food, usually served with drinks, that was originally supposed to stimulate the appetite before a meal but is now used for many occasions, from weddings to after-bowling get-togethers. A *finger food* is any food intended to be eaten with the fingers. It might be a potato chip served at a cocktail party or fried chicken served at a picnic.

To get away from the idea that a meal is likely to follow, *hors d'oeuvre,* a French word meaning literally "outside of work" but taken in the broader sense of "outside the regular menu," is often used instead of *appetizer.* Hors d'oeuvres, some hot and some cold, may range from a cucumber sandwich to lobster thermidor and caviar (the salted roe, or eggs, of the sturgeon and other large fish). Raw vegetables cut up and served as hors d'oeuvres, generally with a dip, are sometimes called *crudités,* another French loanword meaning literally "raw things."

Though sometimes applied to any appetizer or hors d'oeuvre, *canapé* is apt to refer specifically to a small piece of bread or toast or a cracker, spread with spiced meat, fish, cheese, and other tidbits. For example, pâté de foie gras, a paste made of the livers of fattened geese, is traditionally served on rectangles of bread that have been deep-fried, sautéed, or toasted. *Canapé,* which English borrowed from French, is related to *canopy,* meaning, in the original Greek, "couch with mosquito curtains." The image is quite apt, for a savory atop a cracker or piece of bread does resemble a person seated on an upholstered couch.

Antipasto is an assortment of foods, such as anchovies and other salted fish, marinated vegetables, meats, cheese, and olives, often garnished with radishes and strips of pimento. The Latin-derived word, which English borrowed from Italian, means simply "before food."

Smorgasbord may originally have meant no more than "buttered bread on a table" in Swedish, but it describes a wide variety of appetizers served buffet style. Indeed, the smoked and pickled fish, seasoned meat dishes (such as meatballs in a sauce), cheeses, salads, and even desserts often take the place of a whole meal.

broth / bouillon

Broth, bouillon, and *consommé* are alike in that all three are clear soups, all three are prepared much the same way, and all three are considered basic by most cooks.

Broth is made by simmering meat, poultry, game, fish, or shellfish in water, often with vegetables or herbs. Once the fat is removed, the liquid is strained.

Bouillon is clear, seasoned broth or stock, usually made from browned beef. (*Stock,* used as the basis of soups and sauces, is a richly flavored broth made of fish, meat, or poultry with vegetables or sometimes vegetables alone.) A *bouillon cube* is a small cube of concentrated chicken, meat, or vegetable stock that makes a broth when combined with boiling water.

Consommé, too, is a clear, strong broth or stock. It is typically made from a combination of two or more kinds of meat, such as beef, veal, and poultry, plus some vegetables. Well seasoned and strained, it is served either as a hot soup or a cold jelly.

English borrowed *bouillon* and *consommé* from French, but *broth* is a native English word.

mutton / beef

The flesh of animals that is used as food is commonly called *meat*, particularly if it comes from mammals and, sometimes, from fowl, but not from fish. *Mutton* is the flesh of a full-grown or more mature sheep, while *lamb* is the flesh of a young sheep. *Beef* is the flesh of a full-grown ox, cow, bull, or steer, while *veal* is the flesh of a calf (a young cow or bull). *Pork* is the flesh of a pig or hog, especially when used fresh, or uncured. *Ham* is a cut of pork, from the upper part of a hog's hind leg, sometimes fresh but more often salted, dried, or smoked.

steak / chop

A *steak* is generally a slice of meat (especially beef) or of a large fish, cut thick for broiling or frying. It may also be ground beef cooked the same way. A *fillet* is a boneless, lean piece of meat or fish. If meat, it is likely to be the beef tenderloin. A thick, round cut of lean beef tenderloin that is broiled, often with a bacon strip wrapped around it, is called *filet mignon*. This term, which means literally "tiny fillet" in French, is almost always written with the single-*l* variant spelling of *filet*.

A *chop* is an individual slice, usually of mutton, veal, lamb, or pork, that is cut (or chopped), along with a piece of bone, from the rib, loin, or shoulder. A *cutlet* is usually considered to be a small slice of meat, especially of veal or mutton, cut from the ribs or leg. It is broiled or fried, in the latter case often served breaded. In another sense, a cutlet is a small, flat croquette of chopped meat or fish.

frankfurter / hot dog

A *frankfurter* is a smoked sausage, usually of beef or beef and pork, that is made in cylindrical links a few inches long. It, together with *frankforter*, *frankfurt*, *frankfort*, and the informal *frank*, were named after the German city Frankfurt am Main, where it might or might not have been introduced centuries ago.

This type of sausage goes by several other names in the United States. *Wiener,* short for *wienerwurst,* the German word for "Vienna sausage," is in turn often shortened in casual speech to *wienie.* Another informal term, *hot dog* typically describes a frankfurter served hot in a long, soft roll, with mustard, relish, and "the works." It is believed to have been coined about 1900 by the American cartoonist T. A. Dorgan ("Tad"), whose drawing of a dachshund on a bun probably furthered the popular notion that the sausage was made of dog meat. Fastidious eaters will be glad to know not only that frankfurters, by whatever name, are not made of dog meat, but also that the membranous casings, whether of cellulose or the cleaned intestines of slaughtered animals, are now usually removed before packaging.

hero sandwich / submarine sandwich

A sandwich made of a large roll or small loaf of bread sliced lengthwise and filled with various hot or cold meats, cheeses, vegetables, and relishes is called several different things in the United States, including *hero, hoagie, grinder, submarine, torpedo, poor boy, Coney Island,* and *Italian sandwich.* All these words or their special senses originated in American slang or informal usage.

Two of the names imply that the sandwich is a lot to handle: *hero* and *hoagie* (or *hoagy*), the latter being perhaps an altered form of *hoggie. Grinder* suggests a machine for crushing, and teeth are known informally as *grinders. Submarine* (or *sub*) and *torpedo* call to mind the cigar shape of some hard-crusted rolls. *Poor boy* conveys the notion of a whole meal packed into a relatively inexpensive sandwich; indeed, some poor boys are said to contain all the courses of a full meal, from appetizer to dessert. *Italian sandwich* (or *Italian hero*) calls to mind the peppers, spiced meats, and other foods served in many Italian restaurants. *Coney Island* came about by association with the Brooklyn, New York, amusement park that is almost as famous for its eateries as for its rides.

A *Dagwood sandwich,* named after Dagwood Bumstead, a character in the comic strip "Blondie," is somewhat different from these long, overstuffed sandwiches. It is tall, with various fillings often made from apparently incompatible foods and stacked in layers between ordinary slices of bread.

fettuccine / linguine

Years ago, most Americans ate only three kinds of pasta—spaghetti, macaroni, and noodles—and they called them *spaghetti, macaroni,* and *noodles,* not *pasta.* These three forms of thin flour paste or dough, made principally from semolina wheat, are still popular today. But anyone who shops in a grocery store or eats in a restaurant featuring Italian food comes across pasta varieties in a bewildering range of shapes, colors, and sizes. For example:

Alphabets: tiny letters of the alphabet, used in alphabet soup.

Bow ties (also called *bows* and *farfalle,* which means "butterflies" in Italian): mainly egg noodles in the shape of a bowknot, used in casseroles and soups or served with sauces.

Capellini ("fine hair" in Italian): very thin rods, generally served with delicate sauces but also in soups. *Capellini d'angeli* ("angel hair") are even finer.

Fettuccine ("little ribbons" in Italian): flat, narrow noodles (sometimes green from spinach added to the paste), particularly suited to cream sauces, though also used in casseroles, stews, and soups.

Gnocchi: shells, used in casseroles and salads or served with sauces. This dried pasta, one of several shell-shaped ones, is not the same as the Italian dish gnocchi, which consists of small, variously shaped dumplings of flour, and sometimes potato, served with a sauce. *Gnocchi,* meaning "dumplings" in Italian, is an altered form of *nocchio* (a "nob" or "knot in wood").

Lasagna (or *lasagne,* the plural in Italian): flat, wide strips, usually with ruffled edges, used mainly in a dish of the same name, in which the pasta is baked with alternating layers of, typically, tomato sauce, ground meat, and cheese.

Linguine ("little tongues" in Italian): thin, narrow strips or rods, sometimes used in place of spaghetti but often served with seafood sauces, such as a light clam sauce.

Macaroni: hollow rods, sometimes bent (as in *elbow macaroni*), often baked with cheese or ground meat, or tossed in a salad. The Italian word *maccaroni* goes back to a Greek reference to a "blessed cake."

Manicotti ("little muffs" or "little sleeves" in Italian): long, broad tubes, smooth or ridged, usually stuffed with cheese and baked.

Noodles (from the German *nudel*): flat, narrow strips, typically made with egg, used in casseroles, stroganoff, stews, and soups or served buttered.

Ravioli ("little turnips" in an Italian dialect): square casings, usually filled with seasoned ground meat or cheese and boiled, served either in broth, with butter and grated cheese, or in a savory tomato sauce.

Rigatoni (from an Italian verb meaning "to mark with lines"): short, thick, ridged tubes, served with sauces.

Rotelle ("little wheels" in Italian): more like corkscrews or spirals than their name suggests, used in salads, soups, and casseroles or served with sauces. *Rainbow rotelle,* a combination of tomato, spinach, and regular twirl-shaped pasta, is green, white, and red (the colors of the Italian flag).

Spaghetti ("small cords" in Italian): long, thin strings, served with sauces, especially thick meat sauces, or with butter and cheese.

Spaghettini (the diminutive form of *spaghetti*): rods thinner than spaghetti but thicker than vermicelli, usually served with light, oil-based sauces.

Tagliatelle (from an Italian verb meaning "to cut"): noodles cut in long, flat strips, often used in place of fettuccine. *Tagliarini* are narrower than tagliatelle.

Tortellini ("little twisted loaves of bread" in Italian): small, ring-shaped casings which, like ravioli, are filled and served in a soup or with a sauce.

Vermicelli (better-tasting when not associated with the Italian word for "little worms"): rods, either straight or coiled, thinner than spaghetti but slightly thicker than capellini, usually served with light, oil-based sauces.

Wagon wheels (also called *wheels* and, in Italian, *route*): with rims and spokes fitting their name, used in casseroles, soups, and salads or served with sauces.

Ziti: tubes of medium width, with a smooth or ridged outer surface, served with various meat and tomato sauces. The origin of this word is uncertain.

omelet / frittata

An *omelet* is a dish made of eggs beaten up, often with milk or water, and cooked as a pancake in a frying pan. A filling, such as jelly, cheese, or mushrooms, may be added just before the omelet is folded over for serving. A *frittata* is an omelet that ordinarily has vegetables or meat in the egg mixture, is cooked slowly until fluffy, and is served without folding. *Omelet* (also spelled *omelette*), which English borrowed from French, comes from a Latin word meaning "small plate." *Frittata* is an Italian borrowing. Derived from a word meaning "fried," it is what Italians generally call an omelet.

griddlecake / pancake

A thin, flat batter cake cooked on a griddle (a heavy, flat metal plate or pan) has various names, including *griddlecake, hot cake, flapjack,* and, in one sense of the word, *pancake.*

tofu / bean curd

Bean curd is another name for *tofu,* a bland, cheeselike, protein-rich food that is coagulated from an extract of soybeans. The widespread use of tofu in soups and various other cooked dishes is apparently unrelated to the Sino-Japanese origin of the word: *tō,* meaning "bean," + *fu,* meaning "rot."

cotton candy / spun sugar

Fairs and circuses attract people who, in turn, are drawn to a cottony confection that consists of threadlike fibers of melted sugar spun into a fluffy mass around a stick or paper cone. This sweet, sticky preparation, which comes in various colors, is called either *cotton candy* or *spun sugar.*

espresso / cappuccino

Even though they have not driven out the traditional watery brew that passes for coffee in many parts of the United States, European-style (especially Italian) drinks prepared with darkly roasted coffee are gaining in popularity. The ingredients and the order in which they are combined vary somewhat, but the following drinks are typical of those served at American coffeehouses and in more and more homes:

Espresso is prepared in a special machine that forces steam, under pressure, through finely ground coffee beans. To the dismay of self-proclaimed purists, some people change the first *s* to an *x.* Yet this is an apt variant, because both *espresso* and *expresso* come from a Latin verb meaning "to press out, express," the way juice is pressed or squeezed out of fruit. The strong, smooth black coffee is served in a demitasse, or very small cup, often with a twist of lemon.

Espresso macchiato (or simply *macchiato,* which means "spotted" in Italian) is espresso served in the usual small cup but topped with a bit of foamy steamed milk. An ingredient in many of these espresso drinks, the milk is placed directly under a steam spout next to the one through which the coffee whooshes.

Cappuccino is espresso to which foamy steamed milk is added. Often topped with a sprinkle of cinnamon or cocoa, it is served in a cappuccino cup, which is about the size of a teacup. The Italian word *cappuccino,* some say, is an indirect reference to the brown habit worn by the Capuchin friars of the Franciscan order.

Caffè latte (literally "coffee-milk") is espresso poured into steamed milk. It is served in a *latte glass,* a tall muglike glass with a handle. Not all English-speakers spell the Italian word for *coffee* the way Italians do: with two *f*s and a grave accent on the *e.* Some adopt the French or Spanish spelling, *café,* though they may drop the acute accent.

Café au lait, a French import, is much like the Italian *caffè latte,* except that equal parts of steamed milk and strong brewed coffee (not espresso) are combined in either a cup, a latte glass, or a bowllike mug without a handle. Like *lait,* the Spanish word *leche* means "milk," so *café con leche,* like *café au lait,* means "coffee with milk."

Caffè mocha is steamed chocolate with espresso poured into it. Topped with a sprinkle of cocoa, it is served in a latte glass.

Caffè Borgia is a mixture of steamed chocolate and orange rind with espresso poured into it. Like *caffè mocha,* it is topped with a sprinkle of cocoa and served in a latte glass.

jam / jelly

Various kinds of foods are made by boiling fruit with a large amount of sugar or, nowadays, with artificial sweeteners. *Jam* is a thick mixture resulting from the boiling of fruit pulp and sugar. *Jelly,* made by cooling fruit juice that has been boiled with sugar, is soft, resilient, partially transparent, semisolid, and gelatinous. *Preserves* are, as the name suggests, any fruit preserved whole or in large pieces as it is cooked with sugar. *Marmalade* is a jamlike preserve made by boiling the pulp, and usually the sliced-up rinds, of oranges or some other fruits, together with sugar. *Conserves* are a kind of jam made of two or more fruits, often with nuts or raisins added.

spice / herb

Many people use *spice* and *herb* interchangeably for a substance whose distinctive flavor and aroma make it suitable for seasoning food. Some, however, make this distinction: A *spice* can be any part of a plant (the roots, bark, stems, leaves, seeds, or fruit) that generally grows in the tropics. An *herb*, on the other hand, is the leaf of a soft-stemmed or grassy plant that is likely to be found in the temperate zone. So cinnamon, clove, ginger, nutmeg, pepper, and saffron are among the commonly used spices, most of which are dried and many of which can be used either whole or in powdered form. And basil, dill, marjoram, rosemary, tarragon, and thyme are some of the herbs, whose leaves can be used fresh or dried.

baking soda / baking powder

Baking soda, also called *sodium bicarbonate* or *bicarbonate of soda,* is a white powder with many uses. For example: as a chemical in fire extinguishers, as a deodorizer in refrigerators, as an antacid, as a mouthwash, and as a leavening agent (that is, it makes baked goods rise by forming gas in batter or dough). It is also a principal ingredient in *baking powder,* which is even more widely used as a leavening agent. Here the baking soda is combined with either starch or flour, to keep the mixture dry, and with cream of tartar or some other acid-forming substance, to form a chemical reaction when the powder becomes wet.

dough / batter

What sets *dough* and *batter* apart is their consistency, and this is determined by the proportion of their two main ingredients: flour and liquid. *Batter,* as used in pancakes, waffles, muffins, and cakes, is typically thin enough to be poured, easily dropped from a spoon, or squeezed through a pastry bag. *Dough,* as used in breads, rolls, pie crusts, and most cookies, is typically thick enough to be rolled, kneaded, or pushed from a spoon with the finger.

icing / frosting

Icing refers to a preparation that, combining such ingredients as confectioner's sugar, butter, vanilla, water or other liquid, and egg whites, is spread on cakes for both decoration and taste. In this sense, the word *frosting* is often used instead—though generally not by the people who favor *icing.* For example, *The Joy of Cooking,* by Irma S. Rombauer and Marion Rombauer Becker, gives only *icing* in its recipes, while *The New York Times Cook Book,* edited by Craig Claiborne, stays with *frosting.*

glucose / sucrose

Scores of substances are described as *sugar*, a sweet, crystalline, easily dissolved carbohydrate that accounts for a large number of calories in the typical American's daily diet. All sugars have the same nutritional value: none. That is why many people think of "empty" before "calories" in the sugar industry's slogan "only 16 calories per teaspoon." Health workers say that high sugar intake tends to be associated with low intake of vitamins and minerals, weight problems, and dental problems. But no tooth is harder to pull than a sweet one.

Sugars are generally divided into two groups, the *monosaccharides* and the *disaccharides*, whose differences are best grasped by those with a chemical bent. To such people it is immediately clear that: (1) any word with a form of *saccharo-* in it (*saccharin*, for instance) has something to do with sugar; (2) the prefix *mono-* means "one," so a *monosaccharide* is a simple sugar that cannot be further broken down; and (3) the prefix *di-* means "two," so a *disaccharide* yields two monosaccharides.

The most common simple sugar, or monosaccharide, is *glucose* (also called *grape sugar*), which occurs naturally in fruits, honey, and the blood of mammals, where it provides the cells with energy. *Dextrose* is a form of glucose found in plants and animals and in the human blood; it can also be produced chemically. *Fructose* (or *fruit sugar*), found in sweet fruits and in honey, is an abundant naturally occurring monosaccharide.

As combinations of monosaccharides, disaccharides are similar to the simple sugars. The most important one is *sucrose*, of which table sugar is made. Consisting of both glucose and fructose, sucrose is extracted from sugar cane or sugar beets. Other disaccharides include *lactose* (or *milk sugar*), which is prepared from milk and is used in infant foods and medicine, and *maltose* (or *malt sugar*), which is produced by the action of an enzyme of malt on starch and is used in brewing beer.

granulated sugar / powdered sugar

Anyone preparing a grocery-shopping list is likely to write simply *sugar* for the white crystallized substance made of beet or cane and used to sweeten coffee and many other foods. Yet the box itself carries the name *granulated sugar*, because the last step in processing this kind of sugar is sending it through a granulator, where it is dried and formed into tiny grains. *Powdered sugar* (also called *superfine sugar*) is granulated sugar that has been finely ground. When sprinkled over fruits and added to cold drinks, it dissolves more quickly than granulated sugar. By far the most finely powdered of the solid sugars, *confectioner's sugar* closely resembles cake flour; in fact, a little cornstarch is added to keep it from caking or lumping.

Confectioner's sugar is used in candies, cakes, and icings and for dusting baked products.

Brown sugar is a soft sugar prepared in such a way that the crystals retain a thin, brown coating of dark syrup. That is, whereas all the molasses is boiled away in the refinement of white sugar, some is left in brown sugar. The darker the variety of brown sugar, the stronger the molasses flavor. For example, *turbinado sugar* (*turbinado* for short) is a partially refined, granulated, pale-brown sugar obtained by washing raw sugar in a centrifuge until most of the molasses is removed. American English borrowed the term from Cuban Spanish: *turbina* (here designating a turbine used as a sugar-processing centrifuge) + *-ado* (corresponding to the English suffix *-ate*). Besides being used in candies, cookies, cakes, and icings, brown sugar often serves as a glaze for baked ham and a sweetener for breakfast cereals.

Maple sugar, a hard sugar formed by a further boiling down of maple syrup, is highly prized for its distinctive flavor. Because it is in short supply and therefore expensive, it is used mainly for flavoring candies, icings, and desserts.

saturated fat / unsaturated fat

Some of the fats found in foods or used in cooking are considered unhealthful, while others get high marks from the medical profession. The difference has to do with the chemical structure of most fats—that is, the molecules of beadlike strings of carbon atoms to which hydrogen atoms are attached. Because *saturated fats* tend to make it more difficult for the body to clear excessive cholesterol from the blood, they are often associated with increased risk of heart disease. *Unsaturated fats,* on the other hand, tend to help the body rid itself of excessive, newly formed cholesterol in the blood.

A *saturated fat,* whose molecules contain as many hydrogen atoms as they can hold, is hard at room temperature. Saturated animal fats are found in meats such as beef, pork, and lamb, and in butter, cream, whole milk, cheeses, and lard. Saturated vegetable fats are found mainly in the so-called tropical oils, including coconut oil and palm oil, which are used in many processed foods.

There are two kinds of unsaturated fats—*polyunsaturated fat* and *monounsaturated fat*—both usually liquid at room temperature. *Poly-* meaning "many" and *mono-* meaning "one," the first part of these names shows that one or more pairs of hydrogen atoms are missing in each molecule. Corn, safflower, sesame, and soybean oils are among the foods of vegetable origin that are high in polyunsaturates. Olive, peanut, and avocado oils are among those high in monounsaturates.

A *hydrogenated fat* is a polyunsaturated fat or oil that has been artificially changed from its natural liquid form to a more solid one. Most margarines and shortenings fall into this category. Although this process extends the shelf life of a product, it also increases the saturated fat content.

butter / margarine

Butter is the solid, yellowish, edible fat that results from churning cream or whole milk. *Margarine* (for a time called *oleomargarine*) is made largely of fats and oils processed to the consistency of butter. It is often churned with skim milk and other ingredients, including vitamins A and D, and color is added to give it the appearance of the "higher-priced spread." Some people say that, when spread on bread, added to vegetables and other foods, or used as shortening in baking, each product has a distinctive texture and flavor; others find no difference between them.

Butter and margarine have the same number of calories (100 per tablespoon). They also have the same amount of fat (80 percent), but for the most part not the same kind. Contrary to popular belief, not all margarines are made entirely of unsaturated vegetable fat and are therefore more healthful than butter. Some contain rendered animal fat that is no less saturated than the milk fat from which butter is made; besides, the hydrogenated oil added to most margarines to extend their shelf life increases the saturated fat content. To be sure they are buying a cholesterol-free margarine, careful shoppers check the label.

whole milk / nonfat milk

Milk is not only a nutritious food in itself but also the basis for making butter, cheese, and other dairy products. In the United States, cows are the chief source of milk, which is available in a number of forms. For example:

Whole milk is milk that, according to federal standards, contains not less than 3.25 percent fat and not less than 8.25 percent nonfat milk solids. If it is left standing, a collar of cream rises to the top.

Pasteurized milk is milk that has been heated to a prescribed temperature for a specified period of time in order to destroy disease-producing bacteria and to check the activity of fermentative bacteria. The pasteurization process is named for its developer, the French chemist and bacteriologist Louis Pasteur (1822–1895).

Homogenized milk is whole milk that has been processed so that the fat particles are too finely divided and emulsified for the cream to separate on standing.

Skim (or *skimmed*) *milk* is, like *nonfat milk,* whole milk from which almost all fat has been removed. *Powdered* (or *dried*) *milk* is skim milk from which virtually all moisture has been removed as well.

Low-fat milk is milk from which all but 2 percent of the fat has been removed. In *extra-light milk* all but 1 percent has been removed.

Evaporated milk is unsweetened whole milk thickened by evaporation to about half its weight. It is homogenized and pasteurized before canning. If diluted with an equal amount of water, it can be used like fresh milk and has the same nutritive value.

Condensed milk (also called *sweetened condensed milk*) is a mixture of whole milk and sugar from which more than half of the water is removed before canning.

Buttermilk is, traditionally, the liquid left after whole milk or cream has been churned into butter. It has been largely replaced by commercial, or cultured, buttermilk, which is made by adding certain organisms or bacteria to milk.

Acidophilus milk is milk (usually low-fat or skim) that has been fermented with bacteria cultures. Tart and similar to buttermilk, it is sometimes prescribed in cases of intestinal disorder.

light cream / half-and-half

Cream, the oily, yellowish part of whole milk that naturally rises to the top, is available in a number of forms. For example:

Light cream (also called *coffee cream* or *table cream*) is cream with a fat content of not less than 18 percent (the minimum for cream, according to federal standards) or more than 30 percent. Besides being added to coffee, it is poured on cereals and used in preparing sauces, candies, frostings, and other foods.

Half-and-half is a mixture of equal parts of milk and cream. It is used much the way light cream is, but, with from 10.5 to 18 percent fat, it is lower in calories.

Light whipping cream (or simply *whipping cream*) is cream with between 30 and 36 percent fat. *Heavy cream* has at least 36 percent fat. Because they both can be whipped until stiff, they are often used in desserts.

Sour cream is cream that has been soured and thickened either naturally or by adding a lactobacillus culture. It is used in dressings, dips, and other dishes.

Crème fraîche is high-fat cream (with about 35 percent fat) that, though slightly fermented, is milder than sour cream. It is served with fresh fruit or other desserts and used in sauces. The French gave it this name, which means "fresh cream," probably to distinguish it from buttermilk, butter, and other milk products.

A *creamer* is not cream at all. Instead it is nondairy substance that many people use, especially in coffee and dry cereals, to cut down on cholesterol and saturated fat in their diet.

curds / whey

> Little Miss Muffet
> Sat on a tuffet,
> Eating her curds and whey;
> Along came a big spider,
> And sat down beside her,
> And frightened Miss Muffet away.

In this English nursery rhyme, Miss Muffet is eating two forms of milk as she sits on a low stool. The *curds* are the soft, semisolid part that is formed when milk sours and is used to make cheese. The *whey* is the thin, watery part that separates from the curds after clotting, as in cheese making. The soft, white cheese known as *cottage cheese* is, in fact, made by straining and salting the curds of slightly soured skim milk and, often, adding cream.

beer / ale

Beer is one of the world's oldest alcoholic beverages. The English word originally distinguished such a drink flavored with hops from an older one (*ale*), then brewed without hops. Besides getting their bitter flavor from flowers of the hop vine, beer and ale are alike in that both are made mainly from grain, especially malted barley, and fermented with yeast. Yet, because of differences in the two brewing processes—for one thing, beer is produced by slow fermentation at a relatively low temperature, whereas ale is produced by rapid fermentation at a higher temperature—most ales are darker than beer and have a higher alcoholic content.

While Americans generally use *beer* as the generic term for all malt beverages, many Britons call almost any beer *ale*. Either way, these are some malt beverages of the beer and ale families:

Lager beer is a light-bodied, effervescent beer that is aged at a low temperature for several months after brewing. The term is usually shortened to *lager,* which means "storehouse" in German. Most beers produced and sold in the United States are of this type.

Pilsener (also spelled *Pilsner*) is a light lager beer first made in Pilsen, the German name for a city in Czechoslovakia. It is traditionally served in a tall, conical, footed glass known as a *Pilsener glass.*

Porter (short for *porter's ale*) is a bittersweet, dark-brown ale made from charred or browned malt.

Stout is, like porter, a dark-brown ale, but it is slightly more bitter and its alcoholic content is higher.

Bock (or *bock beer*) is a special kind of beer first made in Einbeck, Prussia. Heavy and dark, it is traditionally brewed in the winter and drunk in early spring.

Scotch whisky / bourbon

In 1988 the British Parliament passed a law making *Scotch whisky* a protected trademark. Under the measure, whisky cannot be called *Scotch* simply because it is distilled in Scotland from malted barley. In conforming to the standards set by the Scotch Whisky Association, it must, for example, have been matured for at least three years in charred oak casks, and all its ingredients, including water from the Highlands, must be Scottish.

Scotch is, of course, not the world's only strong alcoholic liquor distilled from a fermented mash of assorted grains, especially rye, wheat, corn, and barley. And *whisky*, though generally favored in Britain and Canada, is not the only spelling. The United States and Ireland, for instance, ordinarily prefer *whiskey*. However, in a spirit of independence, the U.S. Bureau of Alcohol, Tobacco, and Firearms consistently drops the *e* in its regulations on distilled spirits.

Most American *straight whiskeys* are alcoholic distillates from a fermented mash of grain produced at no more than 160 proof; stored in charred new oak containers for at least two years; and bottled at not less than 80 proof. (*Proof* is an arbitrary standard for measuring the relative strength of an alcoholic liquor. In the States, a spirit of 100 proof contains 50 percent alcohol by volume at 16°C, or 60°F.) *Straight bourbon* (named after Bourbon County, Kentucky) is distilled from a fermented mash containing not less than 51 percent corn, and *straight rye* is distilled from a fermented mash containing not less than 51 percent rye.

Blended whiskeys (or *blends*) are also very popular in the States. Under federal regulations, at least 20 percent of a blend must consist of one or more straight whiskeys, to which neutral spirits and other substances are added.

brandy / cognac

Brandy used to be called *brandywine* (from a Dutch word meaning "burnt wine"). The strong alcoholic liquor is in fact traditionally distilled from wine, although the fermented juice of fruits is often used instead (as in "cherry brandy"). Strictly speaking, *cognac* applies only to a French brandy distilled from wine in the Cognac district of southwestern France. However, in loose usage, the word has come to refer to any French brandy or, for that matter, any brandy.

Armagnac, another well-known French brandy, is distilled from wine in the Armagnac district, in the historical region of Gascony, in southwest France. *Calvados,* the favorite drink of Inspector Maigret in Georges Simenon's detective novels, is apple brandy, distilled from cider in the department of Calvados, in the historical region of Normandy, in northwest France. Brandies from other countries include the American *applejack,* which is distilled from fermented cider, and the Italian *grappa* and the Peruvian *pisco,* which are distilled from the skins, pulp, and seeds left after grapes are pressed to make wine.

liqueur / cordial

Liqueur refers to any of a number of sweet, syrupy alcoholic beverages that are infused with the flavor and aroma of spices, herbs, fruits, or other substances and are usually served after dinner. Though considered somewhat old-fashioned by some, the word *cordial* is often used as the equivalent of *liqueur.*

Instead of being served after dinner, an *aperitif* is taken before a meal to stimulate the appetite. Some aperitifs are light alcoholic drinks served alone, while others (vermouth, for example) are fortified wines flavored with herbs and other substances and used as a cocktail ingredient.

black tie / white tie

Black tie and *white tie* mean more than a black bow tie and a white bow tie worn by men, and even more than the fact that a black bow tie is customarily worn with a tuxedo and a white tie with "tails." They also signify the degree of formality of the occasions at which certain men's attire is considered appropriate. *Black tie* is shorthand for "semiformal evening dress"; *white tie,* for "formal evening dress."

The *tuxedo* (often called a *dinner jacket* or simply shortened to *tux*) is named after a country club at Tuxedo Park, near Tuxedo Lake, New York. This jacket, cut like the jacket of an ordinary suit, is traditionally black, with satin facing on the lapels. The word *tuxedo* refers, as well, to the complete outfit prescribed for semiformal evening dress, including a white shirt (usually with a pleated front); a black silk or satin bow tie; a black satin cummerbund or vest; black trousers with a satin stripe down the side of each leg; and gray suede gloves. Present-day etiquette accepts tuxedo jackets, cummerbunds, vests, and ties in various patterns and colors, especially in warm weather.

Formal parties and balls—the kind for which the invitation says "white tie"—are largely a thing of the past. Men who want to dress properly for such occasions wear what is known, in casual speech and writing, as *tails*. *Swallow-tailed coat, tailcoat,* and *dress coat* are other names for this black coat, which is cut away over the hips; has a long, tapering skirt slit to the waist at the back; and is worn unbuttoned. (It is not the same as the single- or double-breasted *frock coat*, which, with its full skirt reaching to the knees in both front and back, was worn chiefly in the nineteenth century.) Today's "white tie" includes matching black trousers with a silk stripe down the outside of each leg; a white vest; a highly starched white shirt with a wing collar; a white bow tie; and white kid gloves. To give this full-dress attire an even more elegant "Fred Astaire" look, some men add a high silk hat, a cape, and a cane.

A *cutaway*, also known as a *cutaway coat* or a *morning coat*, is a single-buttoned black or Oxford gray coat with the front of the skirt cut so as to curve back to the tails. *Morning dress* also includes gray-and-black striped trousers, a pearl-gray vest, and a gray tie, either striped or plain. Nowadays it is usually worn only at formal or semiformal morning weddings—and then only by the groom, the best man, the ushers, and the father of the bride. Mario Cuomo refused to wear it at his son's wedding in 1990 to Kerry Kennedy, a daughter of Robert F. and Ethel Kennedy. The governor of New York is reported (*New York Times*) to have said: "Tails are the ultimate expression in form over substance. Who likes them? Probably three people in the country, and I would neither vote for those people nor appoint them to any office."

pants / trousers

In the United States, *pants, trousers,* and *slacks* all refer to an outer garment that, divided into a separate covering for each leg, ordinarily extends from the waist to the ankles. The Americanism *pants* (an abbreviation of *pantaloons*) was introduced around the middle of the nineteenth century as a less formal equivalent of *trousers*. Both pants and slacks are worn by women as well as men, whereas trousers are more often worn by men. Slacks are generally not part of a suit; pants may or may not be; trousers almost always are.

In Britain, *pants* has a very different meaning. It does not refer to an outergarment at all, but to a man's or woman's undergarment that reaches from the waist to the thighs—what Americans call *underpants* or *drawers.*

shirt / blouse

A *shirt* is a sleeved garment that is worn on the upper part of the body and typically has a collar and a buttoned opening down the front. Although shirts are ordinarily worn by men, often under a coat or jacket, many women wear them, too. Such unisexism, however, does not extend to a *blouse,* for this garment, which is similar to a shirt but looser, is generally worn only by women. Traditionally, women's shirts and blouses button the opposite way from men's shirts; that is, the buttons are on the left side of the front opening and the buttonholes are on the right. This left-right distinction applies to jackets and coats as well.

handbag / pocketbook

When it does not refer to a small piece of luggage, *handbag* generally designates an article of clothing in which a woman carries money, keys, cosmetics, and the like. Handbags come in various shapes and colors. Most are made of leather, cloth, or vinyl, and they can either be held in the hand or hung from the arm or shoulder.

Many people freely substitute the words *bag, pocketbook,* and *purse* for *handbag.* Some prefer *pocketbook* if the bag has no straps (if it is small and has no handle either, they may call it a *clutch*). Some use *purse* if the bag fits inside a pocket or a larger bag. Some specify *shoulderbag* if the bag is designed only to be hung from the shoulder. And some call a large, open . handbag made of cloth, straw, raffia, or a similar material a *tote bag* (or *tote*).

Bags, or purses, are made for men, too. They are generally envelope-shaped, with a flap, and have either a wrist strap or a shoulder strap.

wallet / billfold

Many Americans, like most Britons, use the word *wallet* for a flat folding case, made of leather or a similar material, with compartments for such small things as paper money, credit cards, and business cards. Others prefer *billfold,* which came into the language through American English.

briefcase / attaché case

Many men and women use the words *briefcase, attaché case* (often shortened to *case* or even *attaché*), and *portfolio* interchangeably in referring to a small case for carrying papers, business cards, pens, a calculator, and the like. Others make a distinction according to what they see as differences in design and manufacture. First, they say, while all three cases are typically made of leather or a leather substitute, attaché cases sometimes use wood, wicker, canvas, cloth, and other materials. Second, attaché cases are rigid, whereas both briefcases and portfolios are flexible. Third, portfolios are generally quite thin, so that even with accordion folds for holding loose sheets of paper, they can fit inside some attaché cases and briefcases. Fourth, attaché cases have a hinged lid with one or two locks, whereas most briefcases and portfolios are closed with a clasp or zipper. And fifth, portfolios have no handle but are carried under the arm, whereas attaché cases and envelope-type briefcases ordinarily have a handle at the top; some briefcases, however, have two handles that retract into the side pockets and an optional shoulder strap.

The origins of the three words suggest the purpose and thus the size and design of the various cases. *Portfolio* is an altered form of *porto folio,* which in turn comes from the earlier Italian *portafoglio* (*portare* meaning "to carry" and *foglio* meaning "leaf" or "sheet"). *Briefcase* is made up of two words: *brief,* in the sense of a concise statement of the main points of a law case, usually filed by counsel for the information of the court, and *case,* as applied to a container, such as folder, for holding or carrying something. As for *attaché case,* the person carrying a small piece of hand luggage filled with important documents was originally an *attaché;* that is, someone with special duties on the diplomatic staff of an ambassador or minister to another country.

luggage / baggage

The trunks, bags, and other equipment of a traveler are known collectively as either *luggage* or *baggage.* A small piece of hand luggage for holding a few articles of clothing and books is called a *grip* (short for *gripsack*) or, especially if it has a shoulder strap, a *satchel.* Both words, along with *valise* and *portmanteau* (from the French *porter,* "to carry," + *manteau,* "cloak"), have been largely replaced by the all-purpose *bag* (as when an agent at an airline check-in counter asks, "How many bags?"). *Suitcase* is also widely used, especially for a rectangular piece of luggage that opens into two hinged compartments.

The names of some pieces of luggage, such as *overnighter, weekender,* and *two-suiter,* suggest how long the traveler will be away. Others call to mind the means of travel. For instance, a *steamer trunk,* a broad, low rectangular trunk, was originally designed to fit under a bunk on shipboard. And a *Pullman case* (or *Pullman*), a suitcase that opens flat and has a hinged divider inside, recalls the luxury train travel that began in the United States around 1860, when sleeping cars named after their inventor, G. M. Pullman, were put into service.

Plane travel demands a new kind of luggage. Today's suitcase, though often still called a Pullman, is likely to be lightweight and have wheels for covering the long distances within airports. Traditionally used to carry the clothing and personal possessions of soldiers and campers, a *duffel* (or *duffle*) *bag*— a large, cylindrical cloth bag, especially of waterproof canvas or duck—is gaining popularity with the signature set. Most matched luggage sets also include a *carry-on,* small enough to fit under an airplane seat or in an overhead compartment. Together with a *garment bag,* for suits or dresses, this flight bag may be all a frequent flier leaves home with.

Whether traveling by train, plane, ship, or car, many women pack cosmetics and incidentals into a *traincase* (occasionally still called a *vanity case*) or a *tote bag* (or *tote*). Or, like many men, they squeeze small travel articles into an *attaché case,* along with papers, books, and the like.

gem / jewel

Any mineral or petrified substance, such as a diamond or turquoise, that can be cut and polished for setting into a piece of jewelry is called a *gemstone. Gem* can be used instead (as in "a fortune in uncut gems"); however, the word typically refers to a gemstone that has already been cut and polished or to a pearl, used for ornamentation. *Gem* is also interchangeable with *jewel* in the general sense of a precious stone, though not in another sense of *jewel:* a valuable ring, pin, or necklace, because such a piece of ornamentation is itself likely to be set with a gem or gems.

Gem and *jewel* share an extended sense, too. Both words are often applied to a person or thing prized for beauty and value, especially if a small and perfect example of its kind—like a poem by Emily Dickinson.

deodorant / antiperspirant

A *deodorant* is a preparation that has the power of preventing, destroying, or masking undesired odors; as a liquid or semisolid substance, it is generally applied to the armpits to neutralize the odor of perspiration. Though sometimes considered the same as a deodorant, a *deodorizer* is more likely to be a spray or other device used for masking odors in a room. An *antiperspirant* is an astringent substance that, when applied to the skin (again, generally the armpits), reduces perspiration.

Products designed to deal with excessive perspiration and the odor it can cause are labeled in various ways: one perhaps as a "deodorant," another as an "antiperspirant," and still another as an "antiperspirant deodorant." The packaging of deodorizers seems to call for less directness and more delicacy. A spray designed to mask room odors, for instance, is apt to be packaged as an "air freshener."

perfume / cologne

Perfume, a substance intended to produce a fragrant or pleasing odor, is a volatile, or quickly evaporating, oil such as that extracted from flowers, or a similar substance prepared synthetically. *Rose water,* which is used as a perfume, is a preparation consisting of water and attar of roses (a concentrated extract made from the petals of damask roses). *Toilet water* is a lightly scented liquid with a high alcohol content, usually applied to the skin after bathing or added to bath water. *Cologne* is a perfumed toilet water consisting of alcohol and aromatic oils. It is often called *eau de Cologne* (literally "water of Cologne"), Cologne being the French name of Köln, the German city where the product was first made.

Perfume, cologne, and toilet water are ranked in this order according to their strength, or concentration. The fragrance of perfume is therefore likely to linger for hours, whereas that of toilet water generally dissipates quickly. The difference in staying power of course affects price.

car / automobile

As its two parts suggest, the word *automobile* refers to something that is able to move (*mobile*) on its own (*auto-*). The word, first used in the United States around 1890, does in fact designate a vehicle which is usually four-wheeled and propelled by an internal-combustion engine built into it, and which is intended to carry passengers on streets or roads. It and its shortened form, *auto,* are still used in the States, but mainly in technical contexts, such as statistical reports on the American automobile (auto) industry. In everyday speech and writing, most Americans, like most Britons, now call such a vehicle a *car* (from the more formal *motorcar*).

speedometer / odometer

Several instruments on the dashboard of a car, bus, truck, or motorcycle give information about speed or distance.

A *speedometer,* whose main purpose is to show how fast the vehicle is moving, is connected to a point on the transmission that rotates at a speed directly proportional to road speed. A pointer on a circular or semicircular scale, or a colored bar on a horizontal or vertical scale, indicates speed, whether in miles per hour, kilometers per hour, or both. Some cars now have speedometers with digital readouts.

An *odometer,* usually integrated with the speedometer, is a total-distance counter; that is, it automatically indicates the number of miles or kilometers traveled by the vehicle. Nowadays this rectangular device, with a readout in numbers, is likely to be accompanied by a *trip counter,* which can be reset to zero at the start of a trip to show the distance traveled between any two points or times.

A *tachometer* is concerned not with the speed or distance traveled by the vehicle but with engine speed. Operated either magnetically, like a speedometer, or electronically, this device measures the rate of rotation of a revolving shaft in the vehicle's engine—in other words, the number of revolutions the engine crankshaft makes in a minute. A red zone at the upper end of the scale indicates the range of speeds at which the engine should not be run for any length of time. Not all vehicles have tachometers; in those that do, the device is ordinarily placed alongside the speedometer.

jumper cables / booster cables

When the battery in a car dies, the live battery in another car can often give it a quick start. Large, sharp, clamplike terminals connect the two batteries by means of a color-coded pair of long, thick, insulated electrical wires. These wires are called either *jumper cables* or *booster cables.*

boat / ship

A *boat* is a small, open vessel propelled by oars, sails, or an engine, whereas a *ship* is a larger vessel, always powered by an engine, and navigating deep water. People who consider themselves seafarers are disturbed to see or hear *boat* when *ship* is meant. To them, only a landlubber would call the *QE2* a boat.

flotsam / jetsam

The phrase *flotsam and jetsam* is often used nowadays to mean either "odds and ends" or "unemployed people who drift from one place to another." In the marine sense of the two nouns, *flotsam* is the wreckage of a ship or its cargo found floating at sea, and *jetsam* is that part of the cargo or equipment of a ship which is intentionally thrown overboard to lighten the load in a storm or other emergency and which either sinks or is washed ashore. *Jetsam,* of course, hardly applies to today's containerized cargo ships.

In maritime law there is a third, related term: *lagan,* or *ligan.* It refers to goods thrown into the sea with a buoy attached so they can be found again by the owner.

helicopter / chopper

A certain kind of aircraft is lifted vertically and then is either moved in any horizontal direction or is kept hovering by large, motor-driven rotary blades mounted horizontally. It is known as a *helicopter* or, in informal speech and writing, a *chopper* or *whirlybird.* The use of *copter,* a clipped form of *helicopter,* originated in the United States. So did the slang term *eggbeater.*

engine / motor

An *engine* is a machine that uses any of various forms of energy to develop mechanical power, especially a machine for transmitting motion to some other machine. This notion is apparent in the word itself, which is related to a Latin verb meaning "to beget." A *motor* is a special kind of engine, particularly an internal-combustion engine for propelling a vehicle. Here again, the Latin origin of the word (meaning, literally, "a mover") conveys the purpose of the machine.

So one might say either "Cold mornings are hard on my car's engine" or "Cold mornings are hard on my car's motor." Yet the two words are not interchangeable in every context. *Engine,* not *motor,* is ordinarily used in compounds like *steam engine, diesel engine,* and *internal-combustion engine.* Yet *motor,* not *engine,* generally appears in the names of vehicles propelled by an internal-combustion engine: *motorcar, motorbike, motorcycle, motorboat,* and the like. And *motor,* not *engine,* is likely to refer to a device that produces or imparts motion to a relatively small appliance; for instance, the motor that runs a slide projector or the one that turns the blades of an electric shaver.

implement / tool

An *implement* is any article or device used to carry on some work or to fulfill some purpose (agricultural implements, for example). A *tool* is ordinarily held in the hand and used in carpentry, plumbing, shoemaking, and similar trades (a saw, a hammer, a screwdriver, an awl, and so on). An *instrument* is specifically designed for delicate work or for scientific or artistic purposes (surgical instruments, a telescope, a thermometer, a stylus). An *appliance* is a mechanical or power-driven device, especially one for household use (an iron, a toaster, a dishwasher). A *utensil* is any implement or container for domestic use, particularly in the kitchen (cooking utensils, pots, pans).

By extension, the words *implement, tool,* and *instrument* are applied to a thing or person serving as a means to an end.

pay phone / public phone

Not that it makes a difference to them, but people who push coins into the slots of a telephone may be using a *pay phone* instead of a *public phone.* Although both kinds of coin phones are operated by telephone companies, *pay phones* are "semipublic" phones installed at the request of businesses, which pay a monthly charge to have them inside their shops, restaurants, theaters, and the like. *Public phones,* on the other hand, are provided by the telephone companies themselves, on street corners and in gas stations, shopping centers, highway rest stops, and other places where they are accessible to the public.

cordless phone / cellular phone

More and more telephone users want to be free of a phone cord. With a *cordless phone* they can talk as they roam about their houses or sit on their patios, and with a *cellular phone* they can talk as they drive their cars from one traffic jam to another. Though both kinds of phones permit freedom of movement, they are technologically different. A *cordless phone* is a mobile receiver which, operated only or optionally by batteries, transmits calls across, say, a residence, to the primary, wired telephone. A *cellular car phone* (or a *cellular phone* or sometimes simply a *cellular*) is part of a computer-controlled communication system that connects the telephone system to a network of mobile radiotelephones. Its name comes from the cell, or local area, whose low-power transmitter picks up a call from a car and passes it along to a switching station. From there, the call goes out over regular phone lines.

polygraph / lie detector

An early device for making copies of writings or drawings was called a *polygraph.* This word is made up of two Greek-derived combining forms: *poly-,* in the sense of "many," and *-graph,* in the sense of "something that writes or records." It was later applied to an instrument for recording simultaneously changes in such bodily activities as blood pressure, respiration, and pulse rate. Carrying this meaning of *polygraph* one step further, the Americanism *lie detector* refers to such a recording instrument used on people suspected of lying, for, it is assumed, certain bodily changes occur when a subject lies. In the United States, *polygraph* and *lie detector* are used interchangeably.

tweeter / woofer

Two high-fidelity speakers are often used in sound reproduction. One, a small speaker for high-frequency sounds, is called a *tweeter* (from the thin, chirping sound, or tweet, of some birds). The other, a large speaker for low-frequency sounds, is called a *woofer* (from the gruff barking sound, or woof, of a dog).

second hand / sweep hand

Some clocks and watches have what is called a *second hand*, a *sweep hand*, or a *sweep second hand*. All three terms are apt descriptions of the pointer that indicates the seconds as it moves around the clock or watch face once every minute.

beeper / pager

Among the devices that send or receive an electronic signal, small, portable receivers used to contact people for messages are especially popular nowadays. Any such electronic device is called either a *beeper* (from the *beep*, or brief, high-pitched electronic signal) or a *pager* (from the sense of the verb *page* that has to do with trying to find, summoning, or notifying someone).

cement / concrete

Cement is a powdered substance made of burned lime and clay. When mixed with water, sand, and gravel, it becomes *concrete*. Today the terms are often used interchangeably in the sense of a hard, compact building material, as in "a *cement* (or *concrete*) sidewalk." Some people, however, still consider this a loose usage.

leather / Naugahyde

Leather is a material consisting of animal skin prepared for use by removing the hair and tanning. But no nauga gave up its hide for *Naugahyde*, a trademarked vinyl-coated fabric that sometimes takes the place of leather in upholstery, luggage, and other things. *Leatherette* is a trademark for a product made chiefly of paper, cloth, or vinyl and colored, finished, and embossed to look like leather.

parchment / vellum

Before paper was readily available, artists and writers used *parchment,* the processed skin of an animal, especially a sheep or goat. *Vellum* is a fine parchment prepared from calfskin, lambskin, or kidskin. Because of their smooth surface and durability, both materials continued to be popular with scribes, painters, and bookbinders for centuries. Today, however, they have been virtually replaced by high-grade paper that resembles the originals in name, finish, and surface qualities and is commonly found in stationery, certificates, and diplomas.

earthenware / porcelain

Earthenware is any ceramic ware, such as dishes, containers, and utensils, made of low-fired clay that is opaque, somewhat coarse, and slightly porous. If a glaze is used, the piece is likely to be nonporous.

Porcelain is a hard, white, nonporous, usually translucent variety of ceramic ware, made of high-fired clay, feldspar, and quartz or flint. Besides fine table and ornamental ware, it is used for such heavy-duty products as laboratory ware and electrical insulators.

Stoneware, a dense, opaque, glazed or unglazed pottery made of high-fired clay, silica, and feldspar, is about halfway between earthenware and porcelain in quality and durability. It is used for large storage vessels and factory utensils, as well as for dishes and ornamental wares.

The term *china* (a shortened form of *china ware*) is applied both to porcelain or any ceramic ware like porcelain and to any earthenware dishes or crockery. It was not until the middle of the sixteenth century that *China* entered the English language as the name of the country in Asia. In the following century, the Persian word *chīnī* was adopted for the fine, semitransparent earthenware manufactured in China. For a time, however, the English spelled it in a number of different ways, including *chiny, cheny,* and *chenea.*

wicker / rattan

Wicker is a thin, flexible twig. When woven together, the long, woody strips are used in making durable, lightweight furniture, baskets, and other objects, known collectively as *wickerwork.* While the willow tree is the usual source of wicker, certain kinds of cane, including rattan and bamboo, and even synthetic fibers are often used instead.

Several varieties of tall climbing palms found mainly in tropical Asia are called *rattan.* So are their tough, flexible, extremely long vinelike stems, which, when split, are generally used for baskets, furniture, and other wickerwork and, when left whole, are often made into umbrella handles and walking sticks such as the lightweight, typically mottled brown Malacca cane.

Bamboo is any of a number of treelike semitropical or tropical grasses known to grow to about 120 feet (about 36 meters). Their jointed stems, which are woody, hard, springy, and often hollow, are used in light construction and, like rattan, in making baskets, furniture, and other wickerwork, and also walking sticks and the like. The young shoots of some species are eaten—by people as well as cuddly pandas.

Raffia is a strong, flexible fiber obtained mainly from the leaves of a palm tree that grows in Madagascar. It is used, among other things, for weaving mats, women's handbags, hats, and, as countless American schoolchildren know, baskets.

Several other natural fibers are still widely used, despite the inroads being made by synthetics. *Hemp,* from which rope, sailcloth, and twine are made, is obtained from the tough fiber of a plant that is native to Asia and has been grown in many temperate and tropical regions throughout the world. Cultivation of hemp is restricted in the United States, because the illegal drugs marijuana and hashish can be made from its leaves and flowers. *Sisal* (also called *sisal hemp*), used for making products such as rope, sacking, and insulation, is obtained from the leaves of an agave plant native to southern Mexico and now cultivated throughout the tropics. *Henequen* is a related agave also native to Mexico; its leaves yield a hard fiber used for making rope, binding twine, stuffing for furniture, rugs, and the like.

oil / grease

Oil is a smooth, slippery, combustible substance obtained from animal, vegetable, or mineral sources. It is a liquid at room temperature, and though it cannot be dissolved in water, it can be in certain organic solvents, such as ether. Various kinds of oil are used for many purposes. For example: as fuel (the words *oil* and *petroleum* being virtual equivalents in the sense of the liquid that occurs naturally under the surface of the earth or the ocean floor); as a lubricant (that is, a film inserted between the moving parts of engines and other machines to cut down on friction and abrasive wear); as food; in cooking; and in the manufacture of soap, candles, and other products.

In form and purpose, *grease* is quite similar to oil. Indeed, as a lubricant grease is typically an oil that has been thickened and made more viscous, not only to withstand the heavy pressure caused by moving surfaces that are in close contact but also to remain in place even when not sealed in. At a service station, for instance, a mechanic pours oil into the engine of a car to coat the moving parts with a thin film but, during a "lube job," pumps grease into the bearings on the axles on which the wheels turn. In cooking, too, grease, as melted animal fat, serves some of the same purposes as oil of vegetable or animal origin, as in lubricating pans so food will not stick.

In fact, it is virtually impossible to describe grease and oil except in terms of each other. That is, grease is generally said to be "a thick, oily substance," just as oil is generally said to be "a greasy, combustible substance." Yet idiomatic usage distinguishes between the two. For example: When we settle a quarrel by calm, soothing methods, we "pour oil (not grease) on troubled waters." When we study or work very late at night, we "burn the midnight oil (not grease)." And to suggest that waiting silently is not the best way to get results, we say "The squeaky wheel gets the grease (not oil)."

Fat is similar to oil and grease in some ways. In references to food— French fries, for instance—the adjectives *fatty, oily,* and *greasy* are often interchangeable. The noun *fat* commonly refers to any of various mixtures of solid or semisolid substances found in the tissue of certain animals or in the seeds of plants. Like oil, fat of this kind can be dissolved in organic solvents but not in water, and, like oil, it is frequently used in cooking. The dietary fats that receive particular attention nowadays are the saturated fats, which are hard at room temperature, and the unsaturated fats (both polyunsaturated and monounsaturated), which, because they remain liquid at room temperature, may be called oils.

Shortening, which is used to make pastry crisp or flaky, comes in several forms, including vegetable oils, butter, margarine, and lard (melted-down hog fat). So they will keep better, some of these products are hydrogenated—that is, saturated and solidified.

varnish / shellac

Varnish is a transparent liquid that, when applied to the surface of wood, metal, and other materials, dries to a hard, glossy protective film. In a *spirit varnish* the resin is dissolved in alcohol or another quickly evaporating solvent; in an *oil varnish* the resin, combined with a drying oil, is dissolved in turpentine or a petroleum product.

Shellac is a spirit varnish, ordinarily yellow, orange, or reddish in color but sometimes bleached white. Besides giving a hard, glossy finish to furniture and floors, it is used as a stiffener and in the manufacture of printing inks and many other products.

Lacquer is the name sometimes given to a quick-drying spirit varnish produced by various chemical processes. A form of lacquer is obtained naturally from certain Chinese and Japanese trees, especially of the cashew family. Because it gives a hard, smooth, highly polished finish to wood, metal, and porcelain, lacquer is widely used in the manufacture of such products as furniture, paper, cars, and china. Pigments are often added for a full range of colors.

sauna / hot tub

As the ancient Romans knew, hot baths do more than keep people clean: they go a long way toward promoting health, relaxation, and sociability. Today's fitness enthusiasts may not be surrounded by the mosaic floors, marble columns, painted ceilings, and statues of, say, the Stabian Baths at Pompeii, but many of them go through similar routines with similar purposes in mind.

In a *Turkish bath,* the best-known of the *steam baths,* the bathers sweat heavily, first in a room with dry heat and then in one with wet steam. After their skin is washed and their muscles massaged, they take a cold shower or a swim and rest until their body temperature returns to normal. Unlike a Turkish bath, a *Russian bath* uses only steam, without the dry heat.

The *sauna* is a system of dry-heat bathing used in Finland for centuries and now popular in many parts of the world. Sitting or lying on wooden benches in a wood-paneled room (wood being effective in absorbing moisture), the bathers produce vapor by throwing small amounts of water on stones that are constantly heated on a stove. To stimulate circulation, they may lightly beat their skin or that of their companions with birch boughs before taking a brief plunge into cold water. As in a steam bath, rest is prescribed until the body temperature returns to normal.

Over the years, the word *spa* has been associated not only with the celebrated health resort of that name in Belgium, but with fashionable resorts boasting mineral springs throughout the world. Today it refers, as well, both to any commercial establishment with steam baths, saunas, and exercise rooms, and to a large vessel in which the water is chemically treated so as not to require draining and refilling after each use.

A *whirlpool bath* is a bath in which an agitating device propels a current of warm water with a swirling motion. By combining air and water in an action that massages the body, whirlpool baths play an important part in *hydrotherapy,* the treatment of various diseases and injuries. *Jacuzzi,* a trademark of Jacuzzi, Inc., is applied to a whirlpool bath specially designed to provide hydromassage for pleasure and relaxation, as well as for health purposes. Unlike spas, whirlpool baths are drained after each use.

A *hot tub* is a large wooden tub, usually of redwood, in which people can soak in water that is heated, filtered, circulated, and drained periodically, as in a spa. Many hot tubs are equipped with a hydrotherapy system. From the 1970s on, this kind of bathing has enjoyed enormous popularity in the

United States. Indeed, the term *hot tub* has come to symbolize leisure for suburbanites, especially in California.

merry-go-round / carousel

Anyone who has been to a carnival or amusement park has probably seen a circular, revolving platform that has wooden animals and seats and is turned by machinery, usually to recorded music. In their central meanings, *merry-go-round* and *carousel* refer to this playful mechanical device, which is sometimes called a *whirligig* as well.

A smaller, simpler merry-go-round might be found on a children's playground. It is likely to be a circular, revolving frame with bars the children grasp as they push the device or jump on it for a ride.

seesaw / teeter-totter

New words are sometimes formed by doubling a root syllable or other element in an existing word (*tomtom,* for example). Slight changes may be made, often in the vowel (*chitchat*). *Seesaw* is an example of the second kind of reduplication. Drawing on *saw* and the sawing-like action it suggests, *seesaw* refers, in one sense, to a plank that is balanced on a support at the middle and is used by children at play. Several other equally descriptive words are also used for this device. Both *teeter-totter* (sometimes shortened to *teeter*) and the Americanism *teeterboard* convey the notion of teetering, tottering, wobbling, or wavering as the plank goes up and down in the air.

puppet / marionette

The word *puppet* originally meant "doll." It now describes a small figure that the puppeteer moves usually by placing the hands inside the body or by pulling strings or wires attached to it. A *marionette* is a puppet controlled from above by strings or wires. Both are generally made to look like people or animals performing on stage, and both are likely to be jointed, for ease of movement.

periodical / newspaper

A *periodical* is a *serial;* that is, a publication issued in successive parts, ordinarily at regular intervals and with the intention of being continued indefinitely. The parts or numbers of a periodical, which contain articles, stories, or other writings by several contributors, generally appear more often than once a year. An *annual* —another kind of serial, which might be a yearbook, a corporate annual report, or a similar time-sensitive publication—is, however, on a 12-month schedule.

Most libraries agree that magazines are periodicals, but not necessarily that newspapers are. Originally a monthly summary of news with a selection of miscellaneous items from daily and weekly publications, a *magazine* has come to be a publication for general reading, with stories and articles by various writers and, usually, advertisements. It typically appears at regular intervals, is paperbound, and carries illustrations. The notion of a storehouse of information is close to the original meaning of *magazine,* for the name comes from an Arabic word for "storehouse" or "granary."

A *newspaper,* whether or not a periodical under strict library rules for cataloguing, is indeed a serial publication, for it is issued at stated and frequent intervals, usually daily, weekly, or semiweekly. Most newspapers, which contain news, opinions, advertisements, and other items of general interest, are printed on large sheets of paper (called *newsprint*) and are unbound.

A *journal* is, among other things, a daily newspaper—in fact, the word is often part of a newspaper's title (*The Wall Street Journal,* for example). In this sense the word probably came from the Italian *giornale,* which, like the other meanings of *journal,* derives from a Latin word for "day." By extension, any newspaper or other serial, especially one dealing with scientific or professional matters, can be considered a journal. Some, like *The Journal of the American Medical Association,* include the word in the title.

book / pamphlet

Almost everyone considers a *book* to be a number of sheets of paper, parchment, or similar material with writing or printing on them, fastened along one edge, usually with protective covers. Beyond that, agreement is hard to come by. UNESCO (United Nations Educational, Scientific and Cultural Organization) has defined a book as "a non-periodical literary publication containing 49 or more pages, not counting covers." According to the U.S. Postal Service, to qualify for the "special fourth-class rates" (formerly "book rates"), a book must have "at least eight printed pages, consisting wholly of reading matter or scholarly bibliography, or reading matter with incidental blank spaces for notations and containing no advertising matter other than incidental announcements of books."

A *pamphlet,* as defined by UNESCO, is "a complete, unbound non-periodical publication of not fewer than five nor more than 48 pages, exclusive of covers." By "unbound," paperbound is usually meant, with the sheets stitched or stapled together. When it comes to the number of pages in a pamphlet, most libraries are more flexible than UNESCO; some say no more than 80, while others consider about 100 sufficient restriction.

A *booklet* is a small book or pamphlet, ordinarily paperbound. So is a *brochure*, but it is more likely to advertise or promote something. A *leaflet* is a booklet or a sheet of printed matter that is folded but not stitched, sewn, or otherwise bound. The term *fly sheet*, like its earlier name, *flying sheet*, is synonymous with *pamphlet*, though less widely used. The current word *flier* (often spelled *flyer*) is interchangeable with *handbill;* both refer to a small printed notice, advertisement, or announcement, for mass distribution by hand. A *broadside* (or *broadsheet*) is a sheet of paper that is usually printed on only one side, for posting or wide distribution; it often carries advertising.

paperback / softbound

Books are sometimes described by the kind and flexibility of their bindings. A book bound in paper instead of, say, cloth, leather, or vinyl is called a *paperback* or a *softcover*. The adjectives *paperbacked* and *paperbound*, as well as *softcover*, are often applied to such a book.

A book bound in a flexible cover, such as vinyl or imitation leather, is called either a *softbound book* or a *softcover book*. On the other hand, one bound in a relatively stiff cover, such as cloth-covered cardboard, is called either a *hardcover book* or a *hardback book*. The clipped forms of all four terms are commonly used: *softbound, softcover, hardcover,* and *hardback. Softcover*, then, indicates both that the cover is flexible and that it is made of paper. *Cloth book* is sometimes used in place of *hardcover* or *hardback*.

foreword / preface

Not all books include the following preliminary sections, and even those that do may order them differently. Yet, over time, these distinctions and this sequence have come to be generally accepted:

The *foreword*, written by someone other than the author, is a brief statement commending the book or the author, or both, to the reader. If the writer is well known, his or her name may appear on the book jacket and title page, as well as at the end of the foreword.

The *preface*, written by the author or editor, explains the purpose, plan, or preparation of the book. It may thank others for their help, and if there is no separate acknowledgments section it may give credit for permission to use previously published material. A preface need not be signed, the assumption being that the reader will know that the author or editor named on the title page wrote this preliminary section, too.

The *introduction* is also written by the author or editor, but it is ordinarily somewhat longer than the preface. In leading the reader into the text proper, it goes more fully into the background of the book. Indeed, an introduction that is directly related to the subject matter may be moved from the preliminaries to the body of the book. Wherever it appears, an introduction is not likely to be signed.

By and large, a *prologue* introduces only a published play or long poem. In a play it is frequently spoken by one of the characters. Authors of other kinds of works occasionally include a prologue as well. In *The Hero with a Thousand Faces,* for instance, Joseph Campbell inserts a prologue subtitled "The Monomyth" before part I.

Though not a standard preliminary section of a book, a *preamble* may of course appear in print—as the formal, but usually brief, introduction to a constitution, treaty, or similar document.

abridgment / abstract

A number of closely related words describe material that, though reduced in compass, attempts to convey the essential information given in the original. Some of these shorter versions can stand alone, whereas others are not intended as substitutes for the original.

An *abridgment* (often spelled *abridgement,* especially in Britain) is a work condensed from a larger work by omitting the less important parts but keeping the main contents and literary style more or less unaltered. "Reader's Digest Condensed Books," for example, is a series of abridgments of works of fiction.

A *compendium* is a brief but comprehensive treatise that reduces and condenses the subject matter of a larger work. Arnold Toynbee's 12-volume *A Study of History,* for instance, has been published in a single-volume compendium.

An *abstract* is a short statement of the essential contents of a book, article, speech, court record, or the like. Indeed, it is frequently the abstract of a journal article that determines whether a browser will go on to read the entire article. Abstracts are also an important means of locating and retrieving widely dispersed material. The *Cambridge Scientific Abstracts* (Bethesda, Maryland), for example, provides comprehensive coverage of literature published throughout the world in microbiology, biochemistry, zoology, the environment, and other scientific and technical fields.

A *summary*, a *brief*, and an *epitome* are all restatements of the essence of a report, incident, or other matter in the shortest possible form. A brief, however, usually presents the main points of a law case, such as one filed by counsel for the information of the court.

A *synopsis* is a condensed, orderly treatment, as of the plot of a novel or play, that permits a quick general view of the whole. Series such as "Monarch Notes" keep high school and college students stocked with synopses of and commentaries on books that are required reading in literature courses.

A *digest* is a concise, systematic treatment, generally broader in scope than a synopsis and often arranged under titles for quick reference. Many libraries keep up-to-date editions of, say, Wilson's *Book Review Digest*, which contains shortened versions of selected reviews, both favorable and unfavorable, from general magazines.

dictionary / encyclopedia

Whether or not they appear side by side on library shelves, dictionaries and encyclopedias are very different kinds of reference books. In general, a *dictionary* is a book or set of books of alphabetically listed words, with definitions, etymologies (word histories), pronunciations, and other facts about the words. And, in general, an *encyclopedia* is a book or set of books that provides information on all or many branches of knowledge, usually in alphabetically arranged articles. Some dictionaries and encyclopedias deal with a particular subject, such as American history, science and technology, business, or sports. *Dictionary*, like *diction*, comes from the Latin *dictio*, meaning "a speaking" or "word." *Encyclopedia* goes back to a Greek word having to do with educating a child.

A *thesaurus* is similar to a dictionary in that it too contains a store of words. Indeed, the term itself comes from the Greek *thēsauros*, meaning "a treasure." But this kind of book is designed for readers who cannot think of the precise word to express an idea—the elusive word at the tip of the tongue. In a thesaurus all words are grouped according to meaning, mainly as *synonyms* (words with the same or nearly the same meaning in one or more senses) and secondarily as *antonyms* (words with opposite meanings). If the body of the book is arranged alphabetically (*motion, motionless, motion picture*, and so on), each entry word is followed by a list of synonyms. If the arrangement is conceptual, the words are clustered under selected headings (*motion, mourn, mutual*, for example). An alphabetical thesaurus has no need of an index, but a good conceptual one is fully indexed. Neither kind is likely to include definitions, etymologies, or pronunciations; however, both often discriminate among the various senses of the words. Antonyms may be presented either in a separate section of a thesaurus or as labeled entries in the main synonym section.

monolingual dictionary / bilingual dictionary

One sense of *lingual* has to do with language, and *mono-* means "one" or "single." A *monolingual dictionary* is therefore a dictionary concerned with only one language. *The Oxford English Dictionary* and *Webster's New World Dictionary of American English* are among the monolingual dictionaries that are not only written entirely in English but contain definitions, etymologies, pronunciations, and other kinds of information intended as a guide for those whose first or acquired language is English.

On the other hand, *bi-* means "having two," so a *bilingual dictionary* is a dictionary that gives words in one language and their equivalents in another. These equivalents, which generally take the place of the definitions found in a monolingual dictionary, are often accompanied by parts of speech, sense discriminations, examples, pronunciations, and other information. Some bilingual dictionaries go in only one direction. *Sanseido's English-Japanese Dictionary*, for example, is designed mainly for Japanese-speakers who want to know the meaning of English words they encounter in speech or writing, although it can of course be used by English-speakers who want to know how to translate words from their own language into Japanese. By going in both directions, other bilingual dictionaries, such as *Simon and Schuster's International Dictionary: English-Spanish, Spanish-English,* are really two dictionaries in one.

Few dictionaries deal with more than two languages, but any that does is called a *multilingual dictionary* or a *polyglot dictionary.* R. Sube's *Dictionary of Radiation Protection, Radiobiology, and Nuclear Medicine: In English, German, French, and Russian* is an example. The greater the number of languages, of course, the more limited the coverage. Most multilingual dictionaries are therefore no more than lists of equivalents, useful mainly for travelers and professionals who want immediate, bare-bones translations.

atlas / gazetteer

A book of maps is known as an *atlas,* a reference to the godlike giant of Greek mythology who supported the earth on his shoulders. It is believed that the first of countless map collections to open with a picture of Atlas was a work begun by the sixteenth-century Flemish geographer Gerhardus Mercator. Present-day atlases provide detailed coverage of countries and their political subdivisions, parts or all of the world, and, indeed, the solar system. Country and regional atlases usually include physical features such as rivers, mountains, natural resources, rainfall, and temperature, and perhaps graphic representations of population centers, transportation systems, economic activities, and the like. Historical atlases may contain special maps dealing with the development of a country or area; a certain time period, such as the Middle Ages; or a specific subject, such as explorations.

Another reference work concerned with geography is a *gazetteer,* but instead of presenting a collection of maps it gives an alphabetical list of geographic names, with brief descriptions. It is therefore more like a dictionary or index than an atlas; in fact, some gazetteers are called *geographic* (or *geographical) dictionaries.* The first use of the word *gazetteer* in this sense is believed to date from around 1700. Besides countries, cities, and towns, modern gazetteers usually include pertinent facts about bodies of water, mountains, and other places of interest throughout the world.

thesis / dissertation

Thesis and *dissertation* are sometimes used interchangeably, because both words can refer to a formal and lengthy discourse or treatise on some subject, especially one based on original research. However, a *thesis* is written in partial fulfillment of the requirements for a master's degree; a *dissertation,* for a doctorate. A *term paper*—a long paper or report that is assigned to be written by a student in a course during a school or college term—is not directly related to any advanced degree.

table / chart

Publications include tables and other graphics for two main reasons: to cut down on the text and to present quantitative information in a form that the reader can readily grasp.

A *table* is a compact arrangement of related facts, figures, values, and other data in orderly sequence, usually in vertical columns and horizontal rows. For example, a table of weights and measures, the multiplication table, and a weather table all allow the reader to assimilate many specific facts at a glance.

A diagram that represents the relationship between variables for easy comparison is usually called either a *graph* or a *chart* (although *chart* is often applied, as well, to a tablelike assembly of facts, as in the IRS's "Standard Deduction Charts"). These are the most widely used graphs and charts:

A *bar graph* is a set of parallel bars whose lengths permit a comparison of statistical frequencies, quantities, and other data. The horizontal and vertical axes are labeled, ordinarily with the horizontal axis showing the variable that expresses time or distance and the vertical axis showing the variable that expresses quantity. For example, successively longer vertical bars would show the amounts by which the cost of mailing a first-class letter has increased over a given period.

A *line graph* is a set of points connected by line segments, usually to show a trend. With the horizontal and vertical axes labeled as in a bar graph, a line graph might represent, say, the volatility of gold prices in a certain span of years.

A *pictograph*, or *picture graph*, is a diagram that conveys information through pictured objects instead of bars or lines. For example, the coffee consumed by Americans in certain years might be represented by cups of various sizes.

A *circle graph*, commonly called a *pie chart*, is a circle divided into sectors whose proportionately different sizes indicate relative quantities. It is particularly useful in showing the relationship of parts to a whole at a given time, in contrast to a bar graph or a line graph, which generally deals with successive time periods. Because they can show at a glance how funds are distributed, circle graphs often appear in business and financial reports.

A *flowchart* is a diagram that typically uses geometric symbols in showing the steps in a sequence of operations. This visual device might, for instance, depict a manufacturing process or a computer program. It is therefore more likely to appear in a technical publication than in one intended for a general audience.

bankbook / passbook

Bankbook and *passbook* are used interchangeably for a book in which a bank enters a record of a depositor's account. The book is held by the depositor.

passport / visa

Generally speaking, a *passport* is a government document issued to a citizen for travel abroad, certifying identity and citizenship. Although a passport entitles the bearer to the protection of his of her country and also that of the countries visited, it is subject to visa requirements. A *visa* is an endorsement on a passport, showing that the passport has been examined by the proper officials of a country and granting entry into or passage through that country. Some countries require travelers to obtain visas before their arrival, while others grant visas at the port of entry.

copy / reproduction

To describe one thing made like another, *copy* is the broadest of several terms. It refers to any imitation, often only approximate, of an original (as in "a carbon copy" or "a copy of a designer's dress"). *Reproduction* implies a close imitation of the original; yet, as in reproductions of paintings, there are often differences in material, size, or quality. A *replica* is an exact reproduction of a work of art; in strict usage, it is one made by the original artist. A *duplicate* is a double, or counterpart, of something, serving all the purposes of the original; for example, all the books of a single printing are duplicates. *Facsimile* refers to an exact reproduction in appearance, though sometimes with variation in scale; a Photostated facsimile of a document, for instance, may be larger or smaller than the original. Nowadays, thanks to the *facsimile machine* (usually shortened to *fax machine* or simply *fax*), text and graphic matter can be transmitted throughout the world as quickly and easily as making a telephone call, with virtually no change in the original size.

Concepts, Actions, and Other Intangibles

wit / humor

Some remarks cause laughter, others a smile, and still others a wince. The message itself and how it is expressed have a lot to do with the listener's or reader's reaction. So does perceived intent.

Wit refers to the ability to perceive the incongruous and to express it in quick, sharp, spontaneous, often sarcastic remarks that delight or entertain. As Lady Sneerwell says, in Richard Brinsley Sheridan's *The School for Scandal,* "Psha! there's no possibility of being witty without a little ill-nature: the malice of a good thing is the barb that makes it stick."

Humor denotes the ability to perceive and express that which is comical, ludicrous, or downright absurd. Medieval court jesters had this ability. So did Mark Twain, Will Rogers, and James Thurber. And so do some of today's stand-up comics, who deliver monologues and tell jokes about what they read in the morning's newspaper or saw on the way to the nightclub, theater, or studio. Behind humor at its best lie kindliness, geniality, sometimes even pathos, both in the humorous remark and in the audience's reaction of sympathetic amusement. But pain, not gentleness, is found in *gallows humor* and *black humor.* Morbid or cynical, *gallows humor* centers on the feelings of one facing disaster, particularly death. *Black humor* is an essentially ironic, pessimistic view of human suffering (*black* being used here in the sense of "sad, dismal, gloomy").

Irony refers, in everyday usage, to the humor implicit in the contradiction between literal expression and intended meaning. Subtle sarcasm often enters into it. For instance, on being thanked by a departing gate-crasher, the host of a cocktail party might say, "Remind me to invite you next time." In a play, irony (often called *dramatic irony*) is the contrast between what a character thinks the truth is, as revealed in a speech or action, and what an audience knows the truth to be.

Satire applies to the use, especially in literature, of ridicule, sarcasm, and irony in exposing and attacking vices or follies. Lady Mary Wortley Montagu said, in *To the Imitator of the First Satire of Horace*, "Satire should, like a polished razor keen, / Wound with a touch, that's scarcely felt or seen."

Repartee implies the ability to return a critical remark with quick, skillful wit or humor. For example, in *George S. Kaufman: An Intimate Biography*, Howard Teichmann describes the playwright's silent horror at the atrocious playing of a fellow member of a bridge club. Sensing disapproval, the bungler asked Kaufman how he would have played the hand. Kaufman's answer: "Under an assumed name."

saying / proverb

A *saying* is the simple, direct term for any pithy expression of wisdom or truth. For instance, one might comment on "the sayings of Chairman Mao" or observe that a cynical friend "knows the price of everything and, as the saying goes, the value of nothing." Several other words are often used in place of *saying*, yet shades of meaning set them somewhat apart.

An *adage* is a saying that has been popularly accepted over a long period of time. For example: "Where there's smoke, there's fire."

An *aphorism* is a terse saying that embodies a general, more or less profound truth or principle. For example: "If you came unbidden you depart unthanked."

An *epigram* is a terse, witty, pointed statement that often has a clever twist of thought. For example: "The only way to get rid of a temptation is to yield to it." (This is not the same as an *epigraph*, which is either an inscription on a monument or building or a brief quotation placed at the beginning of a book or chapter to suggest its theme.)

A *maxim* is a general principle drawn from practical experience and serving as a rule of conduct. For example: "Practice what you preach."

A *motto* is a maxim accepted as a guiding principle or as an ideal of behavior. For example: "Honesty is the best policy."

A *proverb* is a piece of practical wisdom expressed in homely, concrete terms. For example: "A closed mouth catches no flies."

A *saw* is an old, homely saying that is well worn by repetition. For example: "A stitch in time saves nine."

Peter Principle / Murphy's Law

In recent years a number of facetious or satirical propositions have been put forward to explain how things work and why people behave the way they do. For example: According to the *Peter Principle*, formulated by L. J. Peter and R. Hull, each employee in an organization tends to be promoted until reaching his or her level of incompetence. *Murphy's Law*, enunciated by E. A. Murphy, Jr., states that if there is a possibility for something to go wrong, it will. And *Parkinson's Law*, propounded by C. Parkinson, declares that work expands to fill the time available for its completion.

speech / lecture

Speech is the general word for a discourse, whether prepared or impromptu, that is delivered to an audience. A harangue by a street-corner orator fits this description no less than Winston Churchill's "iron curtain" speech. *Lecture* refers to a carefully prepared speech intended to inform or instruct the audience (as in "a lecture to a college class"). If the speaker is a stern parent and the audience consists only of a child, the lecture is likely to be a lengthy rebuke or scolding. *Address* implies a formal, also carefully prepared speech, generally attributing importance to the speaker or the speech ("an address to a joint session of Congress"). *Talk* suggests informality and is applied either to an impromptu speech or to an address or lecture in which the speaker deliberately uses a simple, conversational approach ("the governor's long, rambling talk with reporters"). *Oration* suggests an eloquent, sometimes merely bombastic speech ("Fourth of July orations"). *Sermon* denotes a speech, usually based on Scriptural text and intended to give religious or moral instruction, that a member of the clergy delivers to a congregation.

answer / reply

An *answer* is something said, written, or done in return, as called for by the situation or by courtesy (as in "an answer to your letter" or "in answer to their argument"). A *reply* is, in the strict sense of the word, an answer that satisfies in detail a question asked, a charge made, or the like ("a reply to the accusation"). A *response* is an appropriate reaction made voluntarily or spontaneously to something that serves as a stimulus ("a moving response to the audience's applause"). A *retort* is a reply, especially one that is sharp or witty, provoked by a charge or criticism ("the barbs and retorts, interspersed with food and drink, at the Algonquin Hotel's Round Table"). A *rejoinder* is an answer, originally to a previous reply but now often to an objection ("the mayor's rejoinder to the board's strong statement").

certified mail / registered mail

For a fee, the U.S. Postal Service records the sending and delivery of a piece of first-class mail. It does just that for *certified mail,* which cannot be insured. However, it pays more attention to *registered mail,* which generally has a high monetary value and can be insured. Not only does the post office record the sending of such mail but, in addition to the addressee, each postal employee who handles the piece signs for it.

information / knowledge

Information refers to data that are gathered in any way, such as by reading, observation, or hearsay; it does not necessarily connote validity (as in "information on the sleeping habits of puppies"). *Knowledge* applies to any body of facts gathered by study, observation, and other forms of investigation, and to the ideas inferred from these facts; it connotes an understanding of what is known ("present-day knowledge of the universe"). *Learning* implies knowledge acquired by study, especially in languages, literature, philosophy, and similar fields ("book learning tempered by experience"). *Erudition* implies profound or abstruse learning beyond the comprehension of most people ("Thomas Jefferson was both a statesman and a man of great erudition"). *Wisdom,* in this comparison, implies superior judgment and understanding based on broad knowledge ("the wisdom of a Solomon").

theory / hypothesis

In everyday usage *theory* commonly suggests a mere conjecture or guess (as in "What's your theory about why the Cubs lost the playoffs?"). In a scientific or technical context the word implies a formulation of apparent relationships or underlying principles of certain observed phenomena that have been verified to some degree ("Darwin's theory of evolution"). *Hypothesis* implies an inadequacy of evidence in support of an explanation that is tentatively inferred, often as a basis for further experimentation ("the nebular hypothesis"). In this comparison, *thesis* is a somewhat less formal word that also suggests an unproved statement assumed as a premise ("the thesis that all data, processes, or statements can be reduced to equivalents that are less complex or developed"). *Law* implies an exact formulation of the principle operating in a sequence of events in nature, observed to occur with unvarying uniformity under the same conditions ("the law of the conservation of energy").

inductive method / deductive method

In logic *induction,* or the *inductive method,* is the process of reasoning from the specific to the general. That is, starting from an examination of particular facts or individual cases, one arrives at logically valid generalizations. For example, after studying a large number of high schools, some with a comprehensive school and community drug prevention program and an equal number without, health officials found that students exposed to such a program were half as likely to use cocaine as those who were not so exposed. *Induce, induction,* and *inductive* all come from a Latin verb meaning "to lead."

Deduction, or the *deductive method,* on the other hand, is the process of reasoning from the general to the specific. Starting from basic premises or general principles, one arrives at particular conclusions. Researchers might, for example, assume that high school students exposed to a comprehensive school and community drug prevention program would be less likely to use cocaine than those who were not. So they might carry out a large-scale study of high schools, some with and some without such a program, to determine whether their findings would confirm their initial assumption and, if so, to what extent. *Deduce, deduction,* and *deductive* all come from a Latin verb meaning "to lead down, bring away."

prediction / forecast

A *prediction* and a *prophecy* are both statements about what one believes will happen in the future (as in "Another prediction [prophecy] about the world going to hell in a handbasket?"). *Prophecy,* however, may convey the notion of the divinely inspired utterance of a prophet ("Word of Mohammed's prophecies spread throughout Islam"). And *prediction* often implies an advance estimate based on available signs or indications ("a weather prediction" or "predictions about an upturn in the economy"). *Forecast, projection,* and *prognostication* are also used in this sense of hypothesizing from known data or observation.

A related term in medicine is *prognosis,* which has to do with predicting the probable course of a disease.

opinion / belief

An *opinion* is a conclusion or judgment which, though it remains open to dispute, seems true or probable to one's own mind ("my opinion is that prices will come down"). A *belief* is the mental acceptance of an idea or conclusion, often a doctrine or dogma proposed to one for acceptance ("religious beliefs"). A *view* is an opinion affected by one's own way of looking at things ("his views about human nature"). A *conviction* is a strong belief whose truth one does not doubt ("the lawyer's conviction of her client's innocence"). A *sentiment* is an opinion that results from deliberation but is colored by emotion ("a growing sentiment in favor of bilingual education"). A *persuasion* is a strong belief that is unshakable because one wants to believe in its truth ("the investment community's persuasion that an end to the recession is in sight"). This noun, however, is more often applied to a particular religious belief or system ("various Protestant persuasions").

prejudice / discrimination

Prejudice is just what the Latin origin of the word indicates: *pre-* (meaning "before") + *judicum* ("judgment"). Such a judgment or opinion formed before the facts are known may be favorable, but more often it takes the form of unreasonable suspicion, intolerance, or hatred of races, religions, places, occupations, and the sex other than one's own. The media provide daily reminders of race prejudice, religious prejudice, prejudice against women, prejudice against foreigners, prejudice against the disabled, prejudice against people with AIDS, and other kinds of prejudice somewhere in the world.

Discrimination, too, has both a positive or neutral sense and a negative one. Derived from a Latin verb meaning "to divide, distinguish," the word often denotes perception or discernment; that is, the ability to make or perceive distinctions. For example: discrimination between right and wrong, discrimination in sorting eggs by size and quality, and discrimination in selecting works from Picasso's "blue period" for a particular exhibition. The negative sense of the word comes into play when distinctions lead to the unfair treatment of certain groups of people by denying them rights and privileges enjoyed by others, whether in employment, housing, education, or other areas of daily life. That is, once actions or policies are directed against the welfare of a given group, prejudice turns into discrimination.

error / mistake

Error, the broadest term for something incorrectly done through ignorance or carelessness, implies deviation from truth, accuracy, or right (as in "a computational error" or "an error in judgment"). *Mistake,* in suggesting an error that is the result of carelessness, inattention, or misunderstanding, does not in itself carry a strong implication of criticism ("a mistake in reading a blueprint"). *Blunder,* however, implies stupidity, clumsiness, or inefficiency, so it does carry a suggestion of more severe criticism ("a tactical blunder that nearly cost them the war"). *Slip* refers to a mistake, usually slight, that is made in speaking or writing ("Addressing the governor as 'senator' was a slip"). *Faux pas* and *gaffe* imply a social blunder or error in etiquette that causes embarrassment ("Leaving the party before the ambassador did was a faux pas [gaffe]"). In informal usage, *boner, goof,* and *howler* suggest a silly or ridiculous blunder.

alibi / excuse

As a legal term, *alibi* has to do with a plea made by the defense to prove that the accused was somewhere other than at the scene of the crime and therefore could not have committed it. In informal usage, however, *alibi* is simply another word for *excuse;* that is, a reason given for some action or behavior (as in "What's your alibi for being late?").

envy / jealousy

Envy is generally considered to be one thing and *jealousy* another. *Envy* is a desire to have some thing, advantage, or quality that another has (as in "Every time Jo goes up to the executive suite, envy gets out of the elevator with her"). And *jealousy* is resentful suspicion of a rival or a rival's influence ("Othello strangles Desdemona out of jealousy toward Cassio").

Yet *jealousy* is often used in place of *envy* to convey the notion of ill will at another's possessing something that one keenly wants to have or achieve oneself. For example: "Jo tried to conceal her jealousy over Mike's promotion."

advertisement / commercial

An *advertisement* is a public notice or announcement of things for sale or rent, services, needs, and the like. It usually appears in print and is usually paid for. In informal usage the word is often shortened to *ad* (in Britain, to *advert* as well). A *classified advertisement* is compactly arranged, as in newspaper columns, under such subject headings as "Job Opportunities," "Real Estate Wanted," and "Lost and Found." An informal clipping of this term, which originated in the United States, is *classified* (as in "Have you read the classifieds in this morning's paper?").

A *commercial* is an advertisement, usually for a product or a political candidate or issue, which is aired on the radio or television and is paid for by its sponsor. A musical commercial is called a *jingle.* A *public-service an-*

nouncement (or *community-service announcement*) is a statement which is broadcast in the public interest and for which the radio or television station donates the time.

résumé / curriculum vitae

To describe a summing up or summary, as of events, English borrowed the French *résumé* (now also written *resume* or *resumé*). In time, American English gave that word another sense: a statement of a job applicant's previous employment experience, skills, education, and so on. Such a summary of a person's career and qualifications is also called a *curriculum vitae* (meaning "course of life" in Latin), or simply a *vita* (Latin for "life").

Protestant work ethic / Puritan work ethic

A *work ethic* is a system of values in which central importance is given to work, or purposeful activity, and to qualities of character believed to be promoted by work. Nowhere has the "gospel of work" been more staunchly proclaimed than among the Protestant sects, particularly the Puritans, who were determined to build a new society in the American colonies. Regardless of how much the work ethic has changed over the years, the terms *Protestant work ethic, Protestant ethic, Puritan work ethic,* and *Puritan ethic* are still applied to an attitude that regards idleness as improper, if not downright sinful. One who engages in purposeful activity because he or she subscribes to such a belief is not the same as a *workaholic,* for this is a person whose need to work stems not from conviction but from compulsion.

talent / aptitude

Talent implies a natural ability to do a certain thing and suggests that the ability has been or can be developed through training or practice (as in "a talent for drawing"). *Gift* suggests a special ability thought of as having been given, as by nature, rather than acquired through effort ("a gift for making friends"). *Aptitude* implies a natural inclination that makes it likely that one can do a certain kind of work easily and well ("an aptitude for math"). *Faculty* implies a special ability, whether natural or acquired, as well as a ready ease in exercising it ("a faculty for explaining difficult concepts"). *Knack* implies an ability, acquired through practice or experience, for doing something easily and cleverly ("the knack of solving crossword puzzles"). Though *genius* may imply any great natural ability ("a genius for settling disputes"), it more often suggests an extraordinary natural power to do creative, original work in the arts or sciences ("the genius of Einstein").

occupation / profession

Occupation, profession, vocation, trade, craft, and *business* all have to do with a personal career; that is, permanent work in a given field for which one takes special training and in which one engages as the principal means of earning a living.

Occupation is the most general term for such a pursuit (as in "the occupation of librarian" or "occupations in land management").

Profession implies a career that not only requires advanced education and training but also involves intellectual skills; for example, medicine, law, theology, engineering, architecture, and teaching.

Trade and *craft* both suggest a career involving skilled work ("the carpenter's trade" or "the craft of bookbinding").

Vocation suggests a career for which one feels particularly suited ("Veterinary medicine is clearly her vocation"). Besides describing a vocation, trade, or occupation generally, the adjective *vocational* is often applied to education or training intended to prepare people for an occupation, sometimes specifically in a trade. *Vocational guidance* refers to the work of testing and interviewing people so as to guide them toward the choice of a suitable vocation or toward training for such a vocation.

Business may generally apply to a pursuit that is more commercial or industrial than the others, but the notion of education and training is present here as well ("a real estate agent's business" or "the business of an art auctioneer").

job / position

Job is now the common, comprehensive term for regular remunerative employment of any kind (as in "the job of court reporter," "a teaching job," or "a job as computer programmer"). *Position* refers to any specific employment for salary or wages, but often connotes white-collar or professional employment ("the position of marketing manager"). *Situation* is generally considered an old-fashioned equivalent of *position* ("Mary Poppins brought unusual talents to the situation of governess"). However, it frequently appears in advertisements about positions that are either open or desired ("situation wanted in accounts payable"). *Office* refers to a position of authority or trust, particularly in government or a corporation ("the office of treasurer"). *Post* applies to a position or office that carries heavy responsibilities, especially one to which a person is appointed ("the post of undersecretary of the Department of the Interior").

task / chore

Task refers to a piece of work assigned to or demanded of someone, as by another person or by duty, and usually implies that the work is difficult or arduous (as in "the task of balancing the books"). *Chore* applies to any of the routine domestic activities for which one is responsible ("the daily chore of taking out the garbage"). *Stint* applies to a task that is one's share of the work done by a group and usually connotes a minimum to be done in the time allowed ("his morning stint in the laundry room"). *Assignment* designates a specific, prescribed task allotted by someone in authority ("homework assignments"). *Job,* in this comparison, refers to a specific piece of work, as in one's trade or voluntarily undertaken for pay. Some jobs, though, are done without pay ("Cleaning the attic is one big job").

wage / salary

Wage (also often *wages*) applies to money paid to an employee at relatively short intervals, often daily, especially for manual or physical labor. *Salary* applies to fixed compensation usually paid at longer intervals, often once or twice a month, especially to clerical or professional workers. When not a somewhat lofty substitute for *salary, stipend* is applied to a pension or similar fixed payment. *Fee* applies to the payment requested or given for professional services, as of a doctor, lawyer, architect, or artist. *Pay,* though a general term equivalent to any of these words, specifically denotes compensation to members of the armed forces. *Emolument* is an elevated, now somewhat humorous, substitute for *salary* or *wages.*

golden handshake / golden parachute

A *golden handshake* is payment offered to induce any employee to retire early. A *golden parachute* is a large sum of money or other compensation given as severance pay to a top executive who is dismissed from a corporation as a result of its being acquired by another company. Both terms are informal.

present / gift

Present and *gift* both refer to something given as an expression of friendship, affection, or esteem. However, in current use *gift* more often suggests formal bestowal. So while we speak of "a birthday present," we are likely to say "the painting was a gift to the museum." *Donation* applies to a gift of money or articles for a philanthropic, charitable, or religious purpose, especially as solicited in a public fund-raising drive (as in "a donation to the Red Cross"). *Gratuity* denotes a gift of money to a waiter or waitress, concierge, skycap, or someone else who renders a service; that is, it is a fancy word for *tip.*

reward / prize

Reward once conveyed the idea of recompense both for wrongdoing (as in "Burning was the reward for witchcraft") and for good ("He received a reward for saving the child"). Nowadays, however, the word almost always implies something given in return for a good deed or for service or merit. In having its positive sense prevail, *reward* is like *luck,* which is assumed to be good unless qualified as bad.

Prize refers to something won either in competition ("She garnered first prize in the golf tournament") or in a lottery or game of chance ("Two lucky people split the big prize in the Massachusetts lottery"). *Award* implies a decision by judges but does not connote overt competition in an organized contest ("Herbert L. Block, better known as Herblock, has won many awards for his editorial cartoons"). *Premium* has two related senses: a reward offered as an inducement to greater effort or production ("We paid a premium for overnight delivery"), and a prize offered free or at a low price as an added inducement to buy or do something ("Some banks offer toasters as premiums for opening new bank accounts"). *Bonus,* though it generally designates an extra payment over and above salary that is given to an employee as an incentive or reward ("a Christmas bonus"), sometimes conveys either sense of *premium.*

refund / rebate

A *refund* is a sum of money paid as reimbursement or restitution, typically as repayment for purchased goods or services judged to be unsatisfactory or defective. On December 26, for instance, department stores are besieged with requests for refunds. Tax-collecting agencies also issue refunds, in this case for the overpayment of taxes. A *rebate* is a partial refund or discount, commonly offered during a promotional campaign. For example, a manufacturer might reimburse consumers for a certain portion of the money already spent on a product, and a car dealer might deduct a certain amount from the total purchase price at the time of sale.

socialism / communism

Socialism is far from a single theory or system. Yet its guiding principle is that society or the community, rather than private individuals, should own and operate the means of production and distribution. All members of society or the community, then, would share both in the work and in the products (that is, the capital goods). The word *socialism* refers also to the political movement, with its doctrines, methods, and parties, for establishing and maintaining such an economic system. According to Marxist doctrine, socialism is the stage of society between the capitalist stage and the communist stage, in which private ownership of the means of production and distribution has been eliminated.

Communism is any economic theory or system based on the ownership of all property by the community as a whole. The political movement, with its doctrines, methods, and parties, for establishing and maintaining such an economic system is also encompassed by the word *communism.* Marx, Engels, Lenin, and others envisaged communism as a hypothetical stage of socialism, in which society would be classless and stateless, and all economic goods would be distributed equitably. Such a society would come about not gradually but through revolution. For decades *communism* has designated the form of government in the Soviet Union, China, and other socialist states that profess to be working toward that stage of society through state planning and control of the economy, a one-party political structure, and an emphasis on the requirements of the state rather than on individual liberties. In loose usage, the word is applied to any political ideas or activity thought of as being leftist or subversive.

free enterprise / private enterprise

Both *free enterprise* and *private enterprise* describe the economic doctrine or practice of permitting private industry to operate under freely competitive conditions with a minimum of governmental control.

stock / bond

Both *stocks* and *bonds* are common means of raising capital funds. A *bond* is an interest-bearing certificate issued by a government or business, promising to pay the holder a specified sum on a specified date and to repay the principal amount of the loan at maturity. An *investment-grade bond* is one that rating services like Standard & Poor's Corporation classify as suitable for purchase by prudent investors. A *junk bond* is, in informal usage, one that pays a higher yield but is more speculative; such a bond is sometimes issued to finance the takeover of a corporation.

A *stock certificate,* usually shortened to *stock,* is written evidence of capital invested in a company or corporation. *Capital stock* is divided into negotiable shares, each of which entitles the buyer to a share in the ownership and certain rights and privileges. *Common stock* is ordinary capital stock. It guarantees no definite dividend rate but, by usually allowing the stockholder to vote on the selection of directors and other important matters, it grants a degree of control over the company. Most stocks traded today are common stocks. *Preferred stock,* even though it ordinarily carries no voting rights, has preference over common stock in the payment both of dividends (normally at a specific rate) and of the assets of the company, should it be dissolved.

treasury bill / treasury note

As a pledge against its indebtedness, the U.S. Treasury issues several kinds of securities. The public is especially familiar with three negotiable debt obligations, or, as they are sometimes called, *treasuries.*

A *treasury bill* (or *T-bill*) is a short-term obligation, maturing in a year or less. Treasury bills are sold periodically on the open market at a discount from the face value, and they yield no interest.

A *treasury note* matures between 1 and 10 years. The yield on treasury notes is based on the purchase price, and interest is paid at a fixed rate twice a year.

A *treasury bond* matures over a long period, usually between 10 and 30 years. Treasury bonds are like treasury notes in that the yield is based on the purchase price, and interest is paid at a fixed rate twice a year.

Keogh plan / IRA

To encourage working people to set aside money for their retirement, the U.S. government has established several pension plans with tax incentives. The *Keogh plan* (named after E. J. Keogh, the U.S. congressman who introduced it) allows the self-employed to contribute a certain percentage of their annual earned income to their own pension accounts and requires them to contribute to the pension plans of their eligible employees. Not only might these deposits qualify as deductions from income earned in a given year, but earnings on the investments (in stocks, bonds, money market funds, mutual funds, and the like) grow, tax-deferred, until the account holders withdraw their capital.

The *Individual Retirement Account* (*IRA*) is a similar retirement plan. It allows people whose earnings are from salaries or wages, fees, or self-employment to save or invest a certain amount of their annual income in special accounts, with taxes on the earnings deferred until retirement. The 1986 tax law severely restricted the deduction of IRA contributions from income, basically allowing it only for people not covered by any other retirement plan.

The *Simplified Employee Pension* (*SEP*) *plan* allows both an employee and the employer to contribute to an Individual Retirement Account. Under a *SEP-IRA,* an employee pays no taxes on the employer's contributions. Moreover, both the contributions and all earnings on funds in the plan are tax-deferred until they are withdrawn.

inflation / deflation

Inflation describes an economic condition in which the general price level rises because the amount of money in circulation is large compared to the supply of goods and services available. As a result, the purchasing power of the currency declines quite sharply and rapidly. In a period of *deflation* just the opposite happens: the general price level falls because the amount of money is small compared to the supply of goods and services, and the purchasing power of the currency therefore increases.

The word *stagflation* was coined as an informal blend: *stag(nation)* + *(in)flation.* It describes an economic condition marked by a continuing inflation, together with a decline in business activity and an increase in unemployment.

Disinflation is a planned reduction in the general price level, so as to benefit the economy. That is, the government tries to curb an inflationary trend without inviting a deflationary spiral. The steps taken to increase the purchasing power of the currency might include cutting government spending and raising interest rates and taxes.

depression / recession

In economics, both a *depression* and a *recession* are downward movements. But whereas a *depression* is a prolonged period marked by slackening of business activity, widespread unemployment, and falling prices and wages, a *recession* is a temporary falling off of business activity during a period when such activity has been generally on the rise.

simple interest / compound interest

Those who lend money are often paid for its use. The cost of the loan, expressed as a percentage per unit of time, is known as *interest*. If the unit of time is a year, as it usually is, the percentage is called an *annual rate of interest* (or *annual interest rate*). Interest computed only on the principal, or original amount of the loan, is called *simple interest*. *Compound interest* is a better deal, for it is interest paid on both the principal and the accumulated unpaid interest.

balance of payments / balance of trade

A *balance of payments* (or *balance of international payments*) is a balance estimated for a given time period showing an excess or deficit in total payments of all kinds between one country and another country or countries, including exports and imports, grants, and debt payments. One of the items taken into account in calculating a particular country's balance of payments is its *balance of trade*. This is the difference in value between all the merchandise imports and exports. If a country imports more than it exports over a period of time, it is said to have an unfavorable balance of trade; if it exports more than it imports, it is said to have a favorable balance of trade.

consumer goods / capital goods

Consumer goods are commodities—from chewing gum to jumbo jets—that are used directly in satisfying people's needs. *Durable goods* (or *hardgoods*), including cars, furniture, and household appliances, are expected to last three years or more. *Nondurable goods* (or *softgoods*), including food, clothing, and tobacco, are expected to be replaced in less time. Because of their once-traditional color, household linens, such as sheets and towels, and "big-ticket" household appliances, such as refrigerators and stoves, are often called *white goods*.

Capital goods are commodities, such as raw materials, factories, and machinery, that are used in producing other goods and services. They are also called *producer goods*.

income statement / profit and loss statement

A summary of the various transactions of a business during a specified period, with an indication of the net profit or loss, is called either an *income statement* or a *profit and loss statement* (*P & L*). A *balance sheet* also sheds light on the financial state of a business, but it differs from an income or P & L statement in that it summarizes the assets, liabilities, and net worth at a given date, not over a certain period of time. The *balance sheet* is so called because the sum of the assets equals the total of the liabilities plus the net worth.

invoice / voucher

An itemized list of goods shipped or services rendered, with prices, fees, quantities, shipping charges, and other costs shown, can be called a *bill*, an *invoice*, or a *statement*. A statement or receipt attesting to the expenditure or receipt of money is known as a *voucher* (from the verb *vouch*, as in "Can you vouch for his honesty?"). So in seeking payment for services performed, an architect might send a client not only an invoice recording the time spent and the corresponding fee but also a voucher detailing out-of-pocket expenditures related to travel, long-distance telephone calls, courier services, and the like, for which reimbursement is expected.

inheritance tax / estate tax

An *inheritance tax* is a state tax levied on the individual shares of a deceased person's estate after that estate has been divided. An *estate tax* is a federal tax levied on a deceased person's gross estate before that estate is divided.

law / statute

"There oughta be a law against . . . " And there probably is. Every nation defines the obligations as well as the rights of its members. A number of terms for these prescriptions for behavior are so closely related that each is almost always defined in the context of one or more of the others.

The origins of *law* suggest something laid down or settled. In its broadest sense, the word refers to a body of rules of action or conduct established and enforced by a controlling authority (as in "the law of the land" or "state law"). According to *The Guide to American Law: Everyone's Legal Encyclopedia,* "the term can encompass rules promulgated by government; statutes or enactments of legislative bodies; county or municipal ordinances; constitutions or constitutional provisions; administrative agency rules and regulations; judicial decisions—judgments—or the decrees and rules of a court."

Though commonly referred to as "a law," a formal, written expression of the will of a legislative body, when signed by the proper executive officer, is officially called an *act* or a *statute.* For example, in June 1990, newspapers reported that the Supreme Court had declared "the 1989 federal law against flag burning" unconstitutional, but the majority opinion of the Court itself referred to "the Flag Protection Act of 1989." The American lawmaking process, both federal and state, starts with a *bill* introduced by one or more members of the legislature. If passed, the bill goes to the President or governor for signature. Ordinarily, only when the bill is signed (or, if the bill is vetoed, when the veto is overriden by the legislature) does it become written law—and, in the process, an *act* or *statute*. The President, on receiving a bill from Congress within 10 days of its adjournment, can exercise an indirect veto (called a *pocket veto*) by failing to sign and return the bill before Congress adjourns.

Yet the word *law* has a place in official as well as everyday usage. California, for instance, has a Corporate Securities Law, which, like similar laws in other states, is known informally as a "blue-sky law." (Such legislation, designed to regulate the sale of stocks, bonds, and other securities for the protection of the public from fraud, is said to have got its name from the comment made by an early proponent, to the effect that certain business groups were trying to "capitalize the blue skies.") Moreover, at the end of a state legislative session, all bills that made their way through the process are collected and published in a volume typically bearing the title "Laws of (name of the state)."

An *ordinance* is a law adopted by a town, city, or county legislature. Local ordinances usually deal with matters not already covered by federal or state legislation; for example, zoning, waste disposal, and noise.

A *regulation* is a rule or order by which certain conduct is controlled or directed. Often it is a set of rules prescribed by a governmental administrative agency in the public interest. For example, under authority granted it by the Communications Act of 1934, the Federal Communications Commission has issued regulations on the construction and operation of radio and television stations.

A *rule* is a standard, guide, or regulating principle established by a court or administrative agency for governing its practices and procedures. Even without binding legal force, rules are usually observed in the interests of order and uniformity.

A *ruling*, though it too generally originates in a court or administrative agency, is not the same as a rule. It is a judicial or administrative interpretation of a provision of a statute, order, regulation, ordinance, or other court decision. Yet a ruling, such as one issued by a court, is a form of law in itself. It has the force of law and will persist forever unless reversed by a court or modified by statute.

felony / misdemeanor

A *crime* is an act either committed in violation of a law prohibiting it or omitted in violation of a law ordering it. A *felony* is a major crime, such as murder, arson, rape, robbery, or kidnapping, for which the usual penalty is more than a year's imprisonment in a penitentiary, with or without a fine, or even death. A *misdemeanor* is a less serious crime, such as breaking a municipal ordinance, for which the penalty is usually a fine, a jail sentence of less than a year, or both.

Because a misdemeanor *is* a crime, it may seem odd to title a film *Crimes and Misdemeanors,* as Woody Allen did. But *Black's Law Dictionary* offers an explanation: "'Crime' and 'misdemeanor,' properly speaking, are synonymous terms; though in common usage 'crime' is made to denote such offenses as are of a more serious nature." In archaic usage, the U.S. Constitution (article II, section 4) provides for the removal from office of the President, Vice President, and all civil officers "on impeachment for, and conviction of, treason, bribery, or other high crimes and misdemeanors."

homicide / murder

The killing of one human being by another is *homicide.* Although homicide is a necessary ingredient in both murder and manslaughter, it is not necessarily a crime in itself. That is, it may be committed without criminal intent and without criminal consequences, as in the lawful execution of a judicial sentence, in self-defense when one's life is endangered, or as the only way to arrest an escaping felon. According to *Black's Law Dictionary,* "the term 'homicide' is neutral; while it describes the act, it pronounces no judgment on its moral or legal quality."

Both *murder* and *manslaughter,* however, are crimes. In most states, a person faces the charge of *murder in the first degree* (or *first-degree murder*) if he or she kills another unlawfully and maliciously or with premeditation; with atrocity or cruelty (as by poison, starvation, mayhem, or torture); by lying in wait for the victim; or while committing or attempting to commit a serious felony such as arson, rape, robbery, or burglary. All other kinds of murder are considered *murder in the second degree* (or *second-degree murder*).

Manslaughter is also the unlawful killing of another, but without malice aforethought, either expressed or implied. There are two kinds of manslaughter: *voluntary* (resulting from a sudden quarrel or heat of passion) and *involuntary* (resulting from the failure to exercise due caution or circumspection in the performance of a lawful act, so as to safeguard human life, or from the commission of an unlawful but not felonious act).

Still another unlawful killing is *assassination,* in which the victim is likely to be a politically important person. This kind of murder is committed by surprise attack, usually for payment or from zealous belief.

matricide / fratricide

Just as *-cide* can convey the notion of an agent or substance that kills things (an insecticide, say, kills insects), the suffix is often attached to certain words or parts of words to describe the killing of a person or group of people. For instance:

Homicide (from the Latin *homo,* meaning "a man" or "a human being") is the killing of one person by another.

Suicide (from the Latin *sui,* "of oneself") is the taking of one's own life intentionally.

Infanticide is the murder of a baby.

Regicide (related to *rex,* the Latin for "king") is the assassination of a monarch, especially of one's own country.

Genocide (from the Greek *genos,* "race" or "kind") is the systematic killing of, or a program of action intended to destroy, a whole national or ethnic group. The word was first applied to the attempted extermination of the Jews by Nazi Germany.

Sometimes the victims are family members, the specific type of murder being designated by the Latin root in the word. For example:

Matricide (from *mater*) is the murder of one's mother.

Patricide (from *pater*) is the murder of one's father.

Fratricide (from *frater,* "brother," as in *fraternity*) is the murder of one's brother or sister. There is also a special though less often used word for the murder of one's sister: *sororicide* (from *soror,* as in *sorority*).

burglary / robbery

It is a crime to take another's property without his or her consent and with the intention of depriving the person of it. The general term for such a criminal act is *theft;* the legal term is *larceny.* Two related legal terms that are used in everyday speech and writing are *burglary* and *robbery*. *Burglary* once implied breaking into a dwelling at night with intent to commit a crime; however, in its broader current definitions, entry need not be gained by breaking in, the structure need not be a dwelling, and the act can be carried out at any time. *Robbery* implies the unlawful taking of money, personal property, or any other article of value from another person, against his or her will and by force or intimidation. That is, the victim need not be home when a burglar enters, but of course is present when he or she is forcibly stopped and robbed.

assault / battery

Assault is one kind of unlawful act, *battery* is another, and *assault and battery* is still another. *Assault* is any attempt or threat to do physical harm to another person when the aggressor appears able to inflict such harm. That is, someone may commit an assault without physical contact, for the intentional display of force may be enough to give the victim reason to fear or expect immediate bodily harm. *Battery* is the unjustified application of force to another person, resulting in either bodily injury to, or an offensive touching of, the victim. *Assault and battery,* then, is the carrying out of threatened physical harm or violence.

slander / libel

Both *slander* and *libel* are false and malicious statements that are made about a living person and that tend to bring the subject into public hatred, ridicule, or contempt, or to injure the subject in his or her business or occupation. But the methods of such defamation are different. *Slander* is spoken in the presence of a third person. *Libel,* on the other hand, is expressed in print, writing, pictures, or signs, or, with the advent of radio and television, broadcast.

This, at least, is the traditional distinction between the two legal terms. In popular use, however, libel encompasses slander. Noting that, since the early seventeenth century, the word *libel* has been applied to "any false and defamatory statement in conversation or otherwise," *The Oxford English Dictionary* includes, among its citations, this line in Richard Brinsley Sheridan's play *The School for Scandal* (1777): "His whole conversation is a perpetual libel on all his acquaintance."

More recent evidence that *libel* and *slander* are freely interchanged appeared in 1990 in a *National Review* article by Robert C. McFarlane, national security adviser to President Reagan. Refuting the criticism of his foreign-policy role as expressed in *Fighting for Peace,* a book by Caspar Weinberger (Reagan's secretary of defense), McFarlane wrote that "it takes a second reading to absorb that the defamations are only tactical devices, libelous provocations put forth to distract the reader." He then gave examples of Weinberger's "consistent use of slander as a device for evading responsibility."

copyright / trademark

The federal government seeks to encourage literature and the arts, manufacturing, and new and useful inventions in a number of ways.

A *copyright* is a form of protection granted by law, for a limited period, to the "authors" of "original works of authorship," including literary, dramatic, musical, artistic, and certain other intellectual works. This protection, which applies to both published and unpublished works, invests the copyright owner with the exclusive right to do and to authorize others to do the following, among other things: to display and perform the work and to reproduce, distribute, and sell copies of it. A work created on or after January 1, 1978, when the Copyright Act of 1976 came into effect, is ordinarily protected for the author's (or surviving joint author's) lifetime, plus an additional 50 years. Registration is handled by the U.S. Copyright Office, in the Library of Congress.

A *trademark* is a word, name, symbol or device, or a combination of them, used by a manufacturer or merchant to identify his or her goods and services and to distinguish them from others. Among the trademarks are a *brand name*, such as "Reebok footwear," and a *service mark*, such as "American Express Card Baggage Insurance Plan." A *trade name* identifies a business, such as "The Procter & Gamble Company" (as opposed to, say, a Procter & Gamble trademark like "Tide laundry detergent" or "Ivory soap"). Although rights arise automatically through use of a trademark, the mark is usually registered with the U.S. Patent and Trademark Office. Indeed, applications to register a trademark may now be filed on the basis of an intention to use the mark in commerce. When bona fide use in commerce is made and the trademark registration is granted, all ownership rights in the mark constructively date back to the date the application was filed. The original term of registration runs for 10 years and may be renewed every 10 years thereafter.

A *patent* is a document granting the exclusive right to produce, sell, or derive profit from an invention, process, or the like. Through the U.S. Patent and Trademark Office, the government issues such a grant for a limited time (ordinarily 17 years, with no renewal) in return for the disclosure of the invention to the public. Once a patent has expired, anyone, not just the patent holder or his or her licensee, can legally make, use, and sell any device embodying the invention.

guarantee / warranty

Guarantee and *warranty* both convey the notion of a promise of quality (as in "Does this bagel slicer come with a written guarantee [warranty]?"). However, in this sense as well as several others, *guarantee* is a general term and *warranty* a legal one. Specifically, a warranty is a guarantee or an assurance, explicit or implied, of something having to do with a contract of sale. It deals especially with the seller's assurance to the purchaser that the goods or property is or will be as represented and, if not, will be replaced or repaired.

obscenity / indecency

Over the years, lawmakers, public officials, civil rights organizations, private citizens, and the courts have weighed the protection of freedom of speech and liberty of artistic creation against what many people consider to be offenses against propriety and public morals The debate has centered largely on three elusive terms: *obscenity, indecency,* and *pornography.*

In its 1973 definition of *obscenity* (*Miller* v. *California*), the U.S. Supreme Court prescribed these three tests for a work "taken as a whole": It must appeal to "prurient interest"; contain "patently offensive depictions or descriptions of specific sexual conduct"; and lack "serious literary, artistic, political, or scientific value." Rejecting the notion of a national standard of obscenity, the Court left to local juries applying "community standards" the decisions about whether specific works meet those criteria.

Without having directly defined *indecency,* the Supreme Court indicated in subsequent decisions that speech which is "patently offensive" according to contemporary community standards but which falls short of the three obscenity tests can be considered "indecent." The distinction between obscenity and indecency was blurred even further when, in 1989, the U.S. Senate approved an amendment to an appropriations bill proposed by Senator Jesse Helms, of North Carolina, to bar the National Endowment for the Arts (NEA) from using federal funds for the "dissemination, promotion, or production of obscene or indecent materials or materials denigrating a particular religion."

Pornography came into that legislative debate as well, for Helms described as the purpose of his amendment "to ensure that the American taxpayers' money will never be used again to pay for pornography or attacks on religion." Although pornography has no fixed legal meaning, it is generally considered to be a depiction, in a publication, film, painting, or other work, that is intended primarily to arouse sexual desire or excitement. "Dirt for dirt's sake" is a much-quoted phrase used by U.S. District Court Judge John Woolsey in his celebrated judgment of 1933 (*United States* v. *One Book Called "Ulysses"*). In his landmark decision clearing James Joyce's novel of the obscenity charge that had led to its seizure by the Customs Service, Woolsey referred to the link between obscenity and pornography: "In any case where a book is claimed to be obscene it must first be determined whether the intent with which it was written was what is called, according to the usual phrase, pornographic—that is, written for the purpose of exploiting obscenity." The judge found the work neither pornographic in its intent nor obscene in its effect. That decision, like all other court findings, has of course not ended the controversy over what is fit and what is unfit for the general public to read, see, and hear.

malfeasance / misfeasance

Malfeasance, misfeasance, and *nonfeasance* describe three kinds of wrongdoing, especially by a public official. *Malfeasance* is the commission of an act that is positively unlawful. *Misfeasance* is the commission of a lawful act in an improper manner. *Nonfeasance* is the failure to perform a required duty. In other words, as *Black's Law Dictionary* notes, *malfeasance* is doing something that ought not to be done at all; *misfeasance* is doing something that is all right to do but not doing it right; and *nonfeasance* is not doing what ought to be done.

morality / ethics

As applied to principles of right and wrong viewed as a system or code, *morality* and *ethics* are often interchanged (as in "declining standards of morality [ethics]"). Yet *morality* is more apt to be used when the conduct of all or a large part of society is under discussion ("twentieth-century morality"), and ethics when a particular person, religion, group, or profession is ("Nelson Mandela's code of ethics" or "medical ethics in the AIDS era").

Immaculate Conception / Virgin Birth

According to the Roman Catholic Church, *Immaculate Conception* is the doctrine that the Virgin Mary, though conceived naturally, was from the moment of her conception free from any original sin. *Virgin Birth* is the doctrine that Jesus was born to Mary without violating her virginity and that she was his only human parent.

mortal sin / venial sin

The Roman Catholic Church distinguishes between *mortal sin* and *venial sin*. *Mortal sin* is a willfully committed transgression against the law of God that is so serious as to deprive the soul of divine grace. *Venial sin*, however, does not deprive the soul of divine grace, because it is either not an extremely serious transgression against the law of God or, if serious, is not committed with full consent of one's will.

magic / witchcraft

Magic is the general term for any of the supposed arts of producing marvelous effects by supernatural or occult power (as in "Merlin's feats of magic"). By extension, the word is applied to any extraordinary, seemingly inexplicable power ("the magic of television"). *Black magic* refers to magic with an evil or sinister purpose (*black* being used here in its centuries-old sense of "malignant, baleful, deadly").

Sorcery also suggests the supposed use of an evil supernatural power over people and their affairs, typically by means of charms, fetishes, curses, and spells. *Voodoo*, though not itself magic, is a primitive religion based on a belief in sorcery. It originated in Africa as a form of ancestor worship and is now practiced mainly in the West Indies.

Witchcraft and *wizardry* imply the possession of supernatural power by compact with the devil or other evil spirits. Witchcraft is generally considered to be the province of women; wizardry of men. A woman engaged in such activities is ordinarily called a *witch*. A man used to be too, but in time the male counterpart of *witch* became *warlock*. Nowadays this word is apt to be replaced by *wizard* (especially in fairy tales) or *sorcerer*, a gender-blind term. In a paradoxical extension of the notion of a witch as an ugly and ill-tempered old woman, *witchcraft*, like *bewitch*, suggests irresistible charm, especially the use of womanly wiles. *Wizardry* also has an extended sense, suggesting remarkable skill or cleverness (as in "financial wizardry"). The slang *whiz*, though unrelated to *wizardry* in its origin, is applied to a person of either sex who is very quick, adroit, or skilled at something ("a whiz at computer programming" or "a whiz at eight ball").

yin / yang

Among the words that English borrowed from Chinese, two have to do with traditional Chinese philosophy or cosmology. *Yin*, which means "female, night, lunar" in Mandarin, refers to the passive, negative, feminine force or principle in the universe, the source of darkness and cold. *Yang*, which means "male, daylight, solar" in Mandarin, refers to the active, positive, masculine force or principle in the universe, the source of light and heat. Each term is always both contrasted with and complementary to the other. That is, the interaction of the yin and yang is believed to maintain the harmony of the universe.

hara-kiri / seppuku

Hara-kiri (or *hari-kari*) is a ritual suicide performed by cutting the abdomen. It was carried out by high-ranking Japanese of the military class to avoid execution or disgrace. English borrowed the word from the Japanese (*hara,* "belly," + *kiri,* "a cutting or cut"). Another Japanese loanword with the same meaning is *seppuku* (derived from the Sino-Japanese *setsu,* "cut," + *huku,* "belly").

macrocosm / microcosm

Macrocosm means "the great world or the universe." The word commonly refers to an entity so large and complex as to be considered a world in itself (as in "the macrocosm of the welfare state"). *Microcosm,* on the other hand, means "a little world or a miniature universe." This word is often applied to a community, society, or activity regarded as a miniature or epitome of a larger one. The sociologists Robert and Helen Lynd, for example, portrayed a Middle Western city they called Middletown (really Muncie, Indiana) as a microcosm of American society of the 1920s and 1930s.

The combining forms *macro-* and *micro-* are found in many other words, *macro-* conveying the notion of largeness or length, and *micro-* the notion of smallness. *Macroeconomics* and *microeconomics,* for instance, are both branches of economics: macroeconomics deals with all the forces at work in an economy or with the interrelationship of large sectors, as in employment and income, while microeconomics deals with certain specific factors that affect an economy, such as the behavior of individual consumers and the marketing of particular products.

part / portion

A *part* is, in general, any of the components of a whole (as in "a part of one's life"). A *portion* is specifically a part allotted to someone ("your portion of the inheritance"). A *piece* is either a part separated from the whole ("a piece of pie") or a single standardized unit of a collection ("a piece of statuary"). A *division* is a part formed by cutting, partitioning, classifying, and so on ("the fine arts division of a library"). So is a *section,* but it is usually a smaller part ("a section of the bookcase"). A *segment* is a part separated along natural lines of division ("a segment of a tangerine"). A *fraction* is strictly a part—usually an insignificant one—contained by the whole an integral number of times ("only a fraction of the benefits"). A *fragment* is a relatively small part separated by breaking or by a similar means ("a fragment of rock").

remainder / residue

What is left when a part is taken away can be described in several ways. The most general word is *remainder* (as in "the remainder of a meal" or "the remainder of one's life"). Both *residue* and *residuum* apply to what remains at the end of a process; for example, after the evaporation or combustion of matter or after the settlement of claims in the estate of someone who has died. *Remnant* applies to a fragment, trace, or any small part left after the greater part has been removed ("remnants of cloth from the ends of bolts"). *Balance* is sometimes used in place of *remainder,* but, strictly speaking, it implies the amount remaining on the credit or debit side of an account.

period / era

Period refers to any portion of time, whether the interval betwen certain happenings (as in "a five-year period of peace") or an indefinite period characterized by certain events, processes, or conditions ("a period of dramatic industrial growth"). *Epoch* and *era* are often used interchangeably, but, more precisely, *epoch* applies to the beginning of a new period marked by radical changes, new developments, and the like ("the epoch in rapid transportation ushered in by the steam engine"), whereas *era* applies to the entire period ("an era of progress"). *Age* denotes a period identified with some dominant personality or distinctive characteristic ("the Elizabethan Age" or "the Space Age"). *Eon* (also spelled *aeon*) commonly refers to an extremely long, indefinite period ("I haven't seen you in eons").

In scientific fields such as geology and astronomy, several of these words have special meanings as measurements of time.

Middle Ages / Dark Ages

The period of European history between ancient and modern times is known as the *Middle Ages* (or the *medieval period*). Although no precise dates can be assigned, some historians place the beginning of the Middle Ages at about A.D. 500, following the collapse of the Western Roman Empire, and its ending at about 1500, when Europe was gradually moving into the Renaissance era.

The entire Middle Ages used to be referred to as the *Dark Ages,* but this term more properly applies only to the years roughly between A.D. 500 and the end of the tenth century. The term grew out of the view that this early period of the Middle Ages was characterized by intellectual stagnation, widespread ignorance and poverty, and cultural decline.

calendar year / fiscal year

To most people "a year" is a *calendar year* (also called a *civil year*), which is the period from January 1 through December 31. A *fiscal year,* however, is any 12-month period between settlements of financial accounts. The fiscal year for the U.S. government, for example, runs from October 1 through September 30.

backdate / postdate

It's February 10 and there is no way out of paying a bill that was due on January 15. One might *backdate* (or *predate*) a check by writing a date on it that is earlier than the actual date. Now it's March 31 and too early to make a tax payment that is due on April 15. So one might *postdate* a check mailed early by writing a date on it that is later than the actual date.

Memorial Day / Decoration Day

Memorial Day, which honors the men and women who died in the armed services, is a legal holiday in the United States. Also called *Decoration Day* (though not as commonly as in the past), it falls on the last Monday in May in most states. In the South, *Confederate Memorial Day* is observed on any of several dates, including April 26, May 10, and June 3.

Veterans Day / Armistice Day

Word War I ended on November 11, 1918. For years November 11 was known as *Armistice Day* in observance of the anniversary of that armistice. In the United States the legal holiday, called *Veterans Day* since 1954, honors all veterans of the armed forces. In Britain, too, Armistice Day was renamed. There *Remembrance Sunday,* or *Remembrance Day,* is observed on the second Sunday in November, to commemorate the dead of World Wars I and II.

majority / plurality

In the sense of "the greater part or larger number; more than half of the total," *plurality* is often used as the equivalent of *majority*. Yet in connection with voting results, as in the election of one of several candidates, American English has introduced a distinction between the two words.

Majority denotes the number by which the votes cast for the candidate receiving more than half the votes exceed the remaining votes. For example: If candidate A gets 100 votes, candidate B gets 50, and candidate C gets 30, candidate A has a majority of 20.

Plurality denotes the number of votes cast for the leading candidate over those cast for the next-highest of two or more candidates. For example: If candidate A gets 100 votes, candidate B gets 50, and candidate C gets 30, candidate A has a plurality of 50.

rebellion / revolution

Rebellion implies organized, open resistance to the authority or government in power and, when applied to a historical event, suggests that the resistance failed (as in "Shays' Rebellion"). *Revolution* refers to a rebellion that succeeds in overthrowing an old government and establishing a new one ("the American Revolution"). This word applies also to any movement that brings about a drastic change in society ("the Industrial Revolution"). *Revolt* stresses a casting off of allegiance or a refusal to submit to established authority ("the Peasants' Revolt in sixteenth-century Germany"). *Coup d'état* (often shortened to *coup*) designates the sudden, forcible overthrow, as of a ruler, accomplished deftly and by surprise ("the coup d'état [coup] that toppled the government of President Salvador Allende of Chile"). *Insurrection* and *insurgence* both suggest an outbreak that is smaller in scope and not as well organized as a rebellion or revolt ("the Eritrean insurrection [insurgence] against the Ethiopian government"). *Mutiny* applies to a forcible revolt of soldiers or, especially, sailors against their officers ("the mutiny on HMS *Bounty*"). *Uprising*, a simple, direct term for any outbreak against a government, refers specifically to a small, limited action or to the beginning of a general rebellion ("local uprisings against the Stamp Act").

armistice / truce

A temporary stopping of warfare by agreement between the belligerents, as the first step toward signing a peace treaty, is known as an *armistice*, a *truce*, or a *cease-fire*. *Armistice* is likely to be the word of choice when the warring parties are countries, as they were, for example, in World War I.

Cease-fire and *truce* are freely interchanged in the sense of a temporary cessation of warfare. Indeed, a 1989 *New York Times* caption is headed "Angolan Cease-Fire Seen As First Step toward a Settlement," yet the text under the photo of African government leaders and Angolan guerrilla forces refers to both a *truce* and a *cease-fire*. An accompanying news story uses *cease-fire* throughout, but an editorial uses both words.

obverse / reverse

The side of a coin or medal that bears the main design and the date is the *obverse*. The other side—that is, the side without the main design—is the *reverse*. Another name for *obverse* is *head* (or, often, *heads*); for *reverse*, *tail* (or *tails*). So, before flipping a coin, someone willing to leave a decision to chance might say, "Heads I win; tails I lose." A flimflammer, though, would probably say, "Heads I win; tails you lose."

image / mirror image

The word *image* often refers to a visual impression of someone or something produced by reflection from a mirror (as in "Some men talk to the image they see every morning while shaving"). It seems logical, then, to assume that *mirror image* is simply an emphatic way of describing an exact equivalent ("Some men talk to the mirror image they see every morning while shaving"). Yet, as a visual impression of someone or something actually seen in a mirror, a mirror image shows the right side as though it were the left and the left side as though it were the right. So a man who runs a razor down his right cheek sees the shaver in the mirror do the same on his left cheek.

Yet there is a sense of *image* that *mirror image* shares, at least in loose usage. Either word is sometimes applied to a person or thing that is very much like another; that is, a copy, counterpart, or likeness. One might say, for example, "Liza Minnelli is the mirror image of Judy Garland." But here, unless the informality of the phrase got in the way, *spit and image* (or *spitting image*) would be more apt.

vicious circle / vicious cycle

Sometimes solving one problem leads to another, but the solution of this, or of other problems rising out of it, brings back the first, often made worse in the process. Such a situation is called either a *vicious circle* or a *vicious cycle*. Here *vicious* conveys the notion not of ferociousness ("a vicious dog") or of vice (as in "a vicious politician") but, instead, of defects, flaws, or errors.

zenith / nadir

The point directly overhead in the sky or on the celestial sphere is called the *zenith*. The point directly opposite to the zenith, and therefore directly below the observer, is called the *nadir*. Each term is often used in an extended sense, *zenith* meaning "culmination" or "pinnacle" and *nadir* meaning "the lowest point" or "depths." One might say, for example, that Spanish literature reached its zenith in the sixteenth century, with the writings of Cervantes and Lope de Vega. And that Cordelia's hanging plunges Lear into a nadir of despair.

starboard / port

As one faces forward on a ship, boat, or airplane, the *starboard* is the right-hand side and the *port* is the left-hand side. Anyone who has trouble keeping the two words straight might recall that *port*, like *left*, has four letters, whereas *starboard*, like *right*, has more than four.

sex / gender

Sex means, among other things: (1) either of the two divisions, male and female, into which persons, animals, and plants are divided, with reference to their reproductive functions; and (2) the character of being male or female; that is, all the attributes by which males and females are distinguished. We therefore speak of "a full partnership between the sexes," "the war between the sexes," "discrimination on the basis of sex," and so on.

As a delicate way of referring to maleness or femaleness without using the word *sex*, some people substitute *gender*. Others, perhaps hoping that this use of *gender* will go away, insist that it is limited to informal or humorous speech and writing. Meanwhile, the word turns up in many phrases such as "regardless of race, religion, or gender," "the male and female genders," and "gender reidentification" (a therapeutic process following a sex change). Certain terms in which *gender* is a part are well established, especially in the social sciences. For instance, *gender gap* refers to the apparent disparity between men and women in values, attitudes, voting patterns, and the like, and *gender-specific* has to do with something limited to either sex ("In a study of newborns, hand-arm-eye movements were found to be gender-specific").

But it is grammar, not sex, with which gender is likely to be associated. Gender determines that certain words are changed in form according to their classification as masculine, feminine, or neuter. In an inflected language like Spanish, for instance, the noun *pluma* ("pen") is feminine, so any word that replaces or modifies it takes a feminine ending; similarly, the noun *lapiz* ("pencil") is masculine and the pronoun *ello* ("it") is neuter. For centuries, gender has not been a formal feature of English grammar. Even so, some English words, mainly nouns and pronouns, are distinguished as masculine, feminine, and neuter according to the sex or sexlessness of what the words actually represent. *Man, buck,* and *he,* then, are masculine; *woman, doe,* and *she,* feminine; and *pen, pencil,* and *it,* neuter.

grammar / rhetoric

Grammar is the system of a given language at a given time. It is this set of complex patterns which, having developed over the years, makes English, say, different from Russian. Grammar is also regarded as a body of rules imposed on a given language for speaking and writing it, based on the study of that larger system. And, by extension, grammar is viewed as the way one writes or speaks as judged by those rules (as in "She would get a better job if she used correct grammar").

Grammar is, moreover, an older term for the present-day science of language known as *linguistics,* which comprises several branches. *Morphology* deals with the internal structures and forms of words (for example, *went* as the past tense of *go* and the combination of *pin* and *point* in *pinpoint*). *Syntax* is concerned with the arrangement of and relationships among words, phrases, and clauses forming sentences (for example, the customary placement of adjectives before the nouns they modify and the use of plural verbs with plural subjects). Grammar is now often said to include *phonology,* which has to do with speech sounds (for example, the difference between the "th" sound in *thin* and the "th" sound in *then*), and *semantics,* which is concerned with the nature and development of word meanings (for example, the broadening of the meaning of *manuscript* to include a typewritten or computer-generated document, along with one written by hand).

Being able to speak and write a language well takes more, of course, than knowing the rules of grammar. It takes *style*—the particular manner of expressing oneself, as distinct from the ideas expressed. Whether "proper words in proper places" (Jonathan Swift's definition) or "the mind skating circles round itself as it moves forward" (Robert Frost's), style is essentially *rhetoric,* or the art of prose composition. Derived from a Greek word meaning "orator," *rhetoric* once specifically designated the art of using words effectively through the skillful use of established patterns for the ordering of ideas. One of these patterns follows the structure of the classical oration, with its prescribed introduction, narration, confirmation, refutation, and conclusion. Today, besides referring more broadly to the art of prose composition, *rhetoric* is applied, usually disapprovingly, to artificial eloquence, or language that is showy and elaborate but largely empty of ideas or sincere emotion ("the ritualistic rhetoric of political debates").

142

Diction, usually considered a part of rhetoric, has to do with the selection and use of of words. This is not surprising, for, like *dictionary*, *diction* comes from the Latin *dictio*, meaning "word." Diction is not only a matter of deciding which of a pair or set of words most accurately conveys the writer's or speaker's intended meaning; it often involves choosing an entirely different word that the reader or listener would be more likely to understand and therefore be more comfortable with. *Diction* is commonly used, as well, as the equivalent of *enunciation*, or one's manner of pronouncing words ("Olivier's diction is a model for English actors").

denotation / connotation

The direct, explicit meaning of a word is its *denotation*. The most familiar denotation of *odor*, for instance, is "that characteristic of a substance which makes it perceptible to the sense of smell." So a writing assignment for an English class might be "Odors at a farmers' market."

Besides its explicit meaning, or denotation, a word may have a *connotation*—an idea or notion suggested by or associated with it. For example, a number of nouns have to do with a quality perceived through the sense of smell, but each of them has a slightly different connotation. *Aroma*, say, connotes a pervasive, pleasant, often spicy smell ("the aroma of fine tobacco"), whereas *odor* connotes a smell heavy enough to be clearly recognizable even by someone without a sensitive nose ("the odor of a chemical plant").

homonym / homograph

The first step in keeping *homograph*, *homophone*, and *homonym* straight is to separate the combining form *homo-* (from the Greek *homos*, meaning "same, equal, like") from the other (also Greek-derived) part of each word.

When *homo-* is joined to *-graph* (in the sense of "something written, drawn, or recorded"), we get *homograph:* a word with the same spelling as another but with a different meaning, origin, and, sometimes, pronunciation. The words *bat* (a club), *bat* (the animal), and *bat* (to wink) are homographs, all pronounced alike. The words *bow* (the front part of a ship), *bow* (to bend), and *bow* (a decorative knot) are also homographs, but the first two are pronounced alike and the third differently. Most English-language dictionaries distinguish between homographs by entering them as separate entry words and by numbering them with small superscripts.

When *homo-* is joined to *phone* (meaning "sound"), we get *homophone:* a word wth the same pronunciation as another but with a different meaning, origin, and, usually, spelling. The words *bore* and *boar* are homophones.

When *homo-* is joined to *nym* (from *onyma*, which gives us *name* as well), we get *homonym:* a word with the same name as another. Because this "same name" can be either spoken or written, or both, *homonym* is often used interchangeably with *homophone* and *homograph.* That is, words pronounced the same but differing in meaning, origin, and, usually, spelling are called either *homophones* or *homonyms.* And, in what some consider loose usage, words spelled the same but differing in meaning, origin, and, sometimes, pronunciation are called either *homographs* or *homonyms.*

abbreviation / acronym

An *abbreviation* is a shortened form of a word or phrase. Abbreviations written with a period at the end, and sometimes in the middle too, are easy to recognize, whether they leave out letters (as in *mt.* for *mountain* or *I.Q.* for *intelligence quotient*) or change letters (*lb.* for *pound* or *no.* for *number*). The trend, however, is to drop the periods in abbreviations, so, for example, *cash on delivery* is now more often abbreviated *COD* or *cod* than *c.o.d.* The exceptions, aside from writers' personal preferences, are mainly titles of courtesy, which are still commonly written with periods in the United States (*Dr., Mrs., Mr.*), though not in Britain.

An *acronym* is a word formed ordinarily from the first, or first few, letters of a series of words; for example, *NATO* (from *North Atlantic Treaty Organization*), *sonar* (from *sound navigation and ranging*), and *Amtrak* (from *American travel track*). As words, acronyms are written without the periods still found in many abbreviations. And acronyms are pronounced as words, not letter by letter as most abbreviations, especially those made up of capital letters, are. For instance, the acronym *AIDS* (from *acquired immune deficiency syndrome*) is said aloud as if it were the plural of *aid.* But the abbreviation *AID* (for *Agency for International Development*) is generally said one letter at a time.

fashion / style

Fashion applies to the prevailing custom in dress, manners, speech, and the like, of a particular place or time. Such a custom is ordinarily established by the dominant sector of society or the leaders in special fields like entertainment, art, literature, and business. Though *style* is often interchangeable with *fashion,* in discriminating use it suggests a distinctive fashion, especially the way of dressing or living that is thought to distinguish people of money and taste. The French word *mode* expresses the same idea but adds the notion of the height of fashion in dress, behavior, and so on, at any particular time. *Vogue* (another French word) stresses the general acceptance or great popularity of a certain fashion. *Fad* emphasizes the impulsive enthusiasm with which a fashion is taken up for a short time, while *rage* and *craze* call attention to an intense, sometimes irrational enthusiasm for a passing fashion.

American plan / European plan

Hotels typically charge guests according to two different rate systems. The system in which the price covers room, service (cleaning, maintenance, and so on), and meals is called the *American plan,* and the system in which the price covers rooms and service but not meals is called the *European plan.* To Americans used to paying separately for their meals when they stay in U.S. hotels, this traditional distinction seems backward.

a la carte / table d'hôte

How diners are charged for a meal varies from place to place, but, wherever the restaurant or hotel dining room, several French phrases are likely to enter into the scheme. *A la carte* (literally "by the bill of fare") means that each item on the menu has a separate price. So, to avoid a surprise at the end of the meal, many people who order a la carte begin by toting up the prices of all the dishes that appeal to them, from appetizer through dessert. On the other hand, *table d'hôte* (literally "table of the host") means that a complete meal whose courses are specified on the menu will be served for a set price. *Prix fixe* ("fixed price"), whose meaning is the same, is becoming popular with upscale American restaurants, which advertise, say, "New Year's Eve suppers: $75, *prix fixe.*" Of the three terms, only *prix fixe* is not sufficiently Anglicized to shed its italics in print.

dinner / supper

Breakfast, everyone agrees, is the first meal of the day. The very word suggests breaking the fast begun the night before. However, when it comes to the names of the other two meals that family members often share, agreement is far from unanimous. Many people regard *dinner* as the chief meal of the day, whether it is eaten in the early evening or around noon. Others insist that the midday meal, especially a light one, is *lunch* and that a large meal eaten in the early evening is *dinner.* Others go along with this description of lunch, but substitute *supper* for *dinner.* (*Supper* applies, as well, to a late, usually light, evening meal such as one eaten after a theater performance. And sometimes also to a small meal eaten just before bedtime, though this is more likely to be called a *snack.*)

boiling / simmering

As anyone who has set foot in a kitchen knows, boiling water for tea is not only less complicated than roasting a pheasant but it is done in a different way. Cooking methods can be divided into four general groups, depending on how the heat is applied to the food.

First, cooking with water or a similar liquid is done mainly in these ways:

Boiling, or maintaining the heat so that bubbles constantly break on the surface. The boiling point of water is 212°F (100°C) at sea level. Nowadays a *solar cooker,* a simple, low-cost device employing focused sunshine, is sometimes used in place of the traditional pot for cooking foods such as rice and cereal and for boiling water.

Parboiling, or boiling the food until it is partly cooked. This step is often in preparation for further cooking. Some beans, for example, are parboiled, then baked.

Simmering, or cooking the food gently in a liquid maintained at or just below the boiling point. As, say, broth is simmered, tiny bubbles form and break before they reach the surface, usually producing a low, murmuring sound.

Stewing, or simmering the food slowly for a long time, usually in a covered pan, with just enough liquid to produce steam. Tough cuts of meat and certain fruits and vegetables are often stewed. Poultry, veal, or lamb that is cut up, stewed, and served in a sauce of its own gravy is said to be *fricasseed.* For most kinds of stewing, a *Dutch oven,* a heavy, deep metal or enamelware pot with a tight-fitting lid, is appropriate. So is a *Crock-Pot,* a trademarked electric cooker consisting of an earthenware pot inside a container with a heating element that maintains a steady low temperature.

Poaching, or cooking the food either in water or another liquid at or below the simmering point or in a small receptacle placed over boiling water. This method is often used for cooking fish in a special stock or cooking an egg without its shell.

Steaming, or cooking the food in moist heat created by boiling water. In *steam-baking,* the food is cooked in the oven in a pan placed over a container of hot water. One way to keep food in contact with steam but above the water is to use a *steamer,* a covered saucepan fitted with one or more perforated containers. The process can be speeded up considerably if a *pressure cooker* is used, since this airtight metal container cooks by means of superheated steam under pressure.

Second, dry heat is usually applied in these ways:

Broiling, or exposing the food, especially small cuts of meat, poultry, or fish, to a flame or other direct source of intense heat. With an electric or gas stove, the meat is placed under the top heating unit, or broil element, inside the oven. Over an open fire, the meat, poultry, fish, mushrooms, tomatoes, or other food is placed on the mesh or metal bars of a cooking unit called a *grill, brazier, barbecue,* or *hibachi;* if charcoal is used to fuel the fire, the method is called *charbroiling. Panbroiling* is mainly used for meat, which is cooked uncovered and with little or no fat on the hot surface of a skillet or griddle.

Roasting, or cooking food in an oven (on the rack over the bottom heating unit), over an open fire, with a *rotisserie* (a grill with an electrically turned spit), or in hot embers. This method is used mostly for large pieces of meat, poultry, and ears of corn.

Baking, which, when done in the oven, is the same as roasting. What are different are the two main groups of food we generally speak of as being either roasted or baked. We say, for instance, that a leg of lamb, a standing rib, a suckling pig, and a turkey are roasted and that cakes, cookies, bread, pies, squash, and casseroles are baked. Yet there are some odd crossovers, such as these: ham and fish are baked, not roasted; chestnuts are roasted, not baked; and potatoes are either roasted or baked.

Third, cooking in fat, also called *frying*, usually takes these forms:

Pan-frying, or cooking the food in a shallow skillet with a small amount of fat or oil. Eggs are often pan-fried. A piece of meat or fish may be dredged, or coated, with flour before being browned on each side. In Chinese cooking, *stir-frying* is frying diced or sliced vegetables or meat very quickly in a little oil, while stirring or tossing constantly. This is often done in a special cooking pan known as a *wok,* which has a convex bottom and is generally held steady by a ringlike stand.

Sautéeing, or cooking the food quickly in an open pan. This method is similar to pan-frying except that the food, such as eggs or the thin strips of meat in beef Stroganoff, is either constantly agitated in the pan or flipped several times (as suggested by the French verb *sautée,* meaning "to leap"). Sautéeing is often the first step in further cooking. For instance, large cuts of meat that tend to be tough unless cooked with moist heat may be simmered in a covered pan after being sautéed; this method is sometimes called *pot-roasting,* sometimes *braising.*

Deep-fat frying, or cooking the food in very hot fat or oil that more than covers it. This method, also known as *French-frying,* is used for strips of potatoes, doughnuts, shrimp, and the like.

Fourth, microwave cooking is an ever-more popular way to prepare a variety of foods, from lamb chops à l'orange to peaches with raspberry sauce. Its use in the kitchen, then, is not limited to heating packaged frozen foods bought in a store.

In a *microwave oven,* high-frequency electromagnetic waves, which are similar to radio waves or the signal from a remote-control television tuner, immediately penetrate the food and, by generating internal heat, cook it evenly and quickly. Not surprisingly, this awesome process of taking aim on the molecules of water in food and moving them about so rapidly as to produce heat, yet barely making the oven hot to the touch, has been given a name in American slang: *nuking,* in allusion to an attack with nuclear weapons.

calisthenics / gymnastics

Calisthenics refers both to exercises, such as push-ups and sit-ups, for developing a strong, trim body, and, in a broader sense, to the art of developing bodily strength and gracefulness by such exercises. *Bodybuilding* has to do with developing a strong body by lifting weights and by doing push-ups, sit-ups, and certain other calisthenic exercises. *Body mechanics* applies to exercises intended to improve one's posture, stamina, poise, and the like.

Gymnastics, though sometimes used as the equivalent of *calisthenics,* ordinarily refers to a sport that combines tumbling and acrobatic feats. These are typically done with apparatus such as the parallel bars and the balance beam. Closely related to *gymnastics, acrobatics* generally denotes tricks in tumbling or on the trapeze and tightrope. An acrobat is in fact a skilled gymnast.

aerobic exercise / anaerobic exercise

The difference between two well-known systems of physical conditioning centers on oxygen: its presence in an *aerobic exercise* and its absence in an *anaerobic* one. This distinction can be seen in the Greek-derived elements in the words. *Bio-* means "life," *aero-* means "air," and *a-* (*an-* before a vowel) means "without."

An *aerobic exercise,* or *aerobics,* conditions the heart and lungs by making the body's intake of oxygen more efficient. In jogging, brisk walking, running, dancing, bicycling, and cross-country skiing, for example, oxygen is used to produce new energy so the exercise can be continued over relatively long periods (15 minutes or more). An *anaerobic exercise,* or *anaerobics,* helps improve speed, power, and strength by making the heart work hard to supply the moving body parts with oxygen and food. These activities, which are done in a sudden brief burst of energy, include sprinting, tennis, handball, weight lifting, calisthenics, and downhill skiing.

decathlon / triathlon

The word *athlete* (denoting a person trained in exercises, games, or contests that require physical strength, skill, stamina, speed, and the like) goes back to the Greek *athlos* ("a contest") and *athlon* ("a prize"). No wonder, then, that the names of several athletic contests held today, whether at the Olympic games or elsewhere, have *athlon* as the root, with the number of events indicted by the other word element. For example:

Bi- means "two," so a *biathlon* combines two events: cross-country skiing and rifle marksmanship. Racing against the clock, the skiers must stop at designated points for target shooting.

Tri- means "three," so a *triathlon* is an endurance race combining three consecutive events: swimming, bicycling, and running.

Deca- means "ten," so in a *decathlon* each contestant takes part in ten events, the winner being the one receiving the highest total of points. These are the events: 100-meter dash, long jump, shot-put, high jump, 400-meter dash, 110-meter hurdles, discus throw, pole vault, javelin throw, and 1,500-meter run.

jujitsu / judo

A Japanese system of unarmed combat, *jujitsu* applies knowledge of anatomy and the principle of leverage so as to exploit to one's own advantage an opponent's strength and weight. *Judo* is a form of jujitsu developed as both a sport and as a means of self-defense without the use of weapons. In Japanese, *jujitsu* means, literally, "soft art"; *judo,* "soft way." *Aikido,* also from Japan, uses slightly different holds and circular movements.

149

Of the many other martial arts originating in the Orient, a number now also rank as popular systems of self-defense and as major competitive sports in the United States and Europe, as well as in Japan. The best known is *karate,* developed in ancient Japan and characterized by sharp, quick blows delivered with the hands, elbows, knees, and feet. The literal meaning of the Japanese word is "empty hand." *Kung fu,* from China, is similar to karate but emphasizes circular rather than linear movements, which are suggested by the original Chinese word, meaning, literally, "boxing principles." The Korean *tae kwon do,* which also resembles karate, emphasizes spinning and jumping kicks, especially to the head. In the stylized Japanese swordplay known as *kendo,* opponents use leather-covered bamboo "swords."

Tai chi (*t'ai chi ch'uan* in full) is a series of postures and exercises developed in China both as a system of self-defense and as an aid to meditation. It is characterized by slow, relaxed, circular movements. *Yoga,* though it too involves prescribed postures, controlled breathing, and other exercises, is quite different. Intense concentration and deep meditation are an integral part of this mystic and ascetic Hindu discipline by which one seeks to achieve liberation of the self and union with the supreme spirit or universal soul.

black belt / white belt

An advanced practitioner in the Oriental martial arts, such as judo and karate, is awarded a *black belt* or sash, to be worn with the traditional white, pajamalike costume. A beginner wears a *white belt.* To symbolize advancement through the intermediate levels of training or achievement, belts of other colors are awarded. There being no single belt system, the choice of colors for each level depends mainly on the school. Besides a solid color like brown, green, or blue, a belt may display a combination of colors, such as red and white.

handball / racquetball

Handball is a singles or doubles game played in a court with four walls or against one, two, or three walls or boards. Using a gloved hand, the opposing players hit a small rubber ball against the wall or walls until one player fails to return it to the front wall before its second bounce.

Paddle ball and *racquetball* are essentially the same as handball, except that in paddle ball the players use a short-handled perforated paddle and in racquetball a short-handled strung racket. Despite its similar name, *racquets* is more like the complex old indoor game of court tennis, in which two players or two pairs of players, using rackets, bounce a fabric-covered hollow rubber ball against the walls of a specially constructed court as well as hit over a net.

Squash is the name given to either of two similar games that combine elements of both regular tennis and handball. One of these games (*squash racquets* in full) is played in a four-walled court with a small, long-handled racket and a small rubber ball. The other (*squash tennis* in full) is played in a similar court, but with a larger racket and a larger, livelier ball.

Paddle tennis adds squash to the mix of tennis and handball. An outdoor game, paddle tennis is played with paddles and a rubber ball on a raised platform surrounded by a screen. This explains why it is also called *platform tennis*.

table tennis / Ping-Pong

A kind of miniature tennis, *table tennis* is a game played on a large, rectangular table. A small, hollow celluloid or plastic ball is used instead of a fabric-covered, rubber tennis ball, and short-handled wooden paddles are used instead of tennis rackets. Table tennis is often known by the trademarked name *Ping-Pong*.

baseball / softball

Baseball is a game played by two opposing teams of nine players each on a field with four bases forming a diamond-shaped circuit. During each of the nine innings that constitute a typical game, the teams take turns at bat and in the field. Using a wooden club called a bat, the batters try to hit a hard, rawhide-covered ball and then to round the bases safely. The team with the highest score—that is, the most runs—wins.

Though similar to baseball, *softball* is played on a smaller diamond, with a larger and softer ball. *Stickball*, too, is played much like baseball. However, there are usually only four or five players to a team and these are likely to be children; the field is typically a city street or other small area; and the equipment is almost always improvised, consisting, say, of a broomstick and an ordinary soft rubber ball. In *stoopball*, a game patterned loosely after baseball, each player throws a rubber ball against a step, as of a stoop, or a wall. The rules vary, so base hits might depend on the number of times the ball bounces before it is caught and the thrower might be called out if the fielders catch the rebounding ball on the fly.

football / soccer

Football is any of several games that two teams play with an inflated leather ball on a field with goals at each end, the object being to get the ball across the opponents' goal. The form most closely related to the original is *soccer*, or *association football*. Here the 11 players on each team move a round ball mainly by kicking or by using any part of the body except the hands and arms. In *rugby*, a form of football popular in England, the players (15 to a side) may pass an oval ball laterally or backward, kick it forward, or run with it, but they are not permitted to be in front of it while it is being kicked or carried by a teammate. In U.S. and Canadian *football*, the elaborated form developed from rugby, the oval ball is clearly in the possession of one 11-member team at a time. In advancing the ball, players may run ahead of it under certain circumstances.

ice hockey / field hockey

When used alone, the word *hockey* can refer to either *ice hockey* or *field hockey*, though nowadays *ice hockey* is usually meant. This game is played on an ice rink, with the six members of each opposing team wearing skates. Using a curved stick with a flat blade (a hockey stick), the players try to drive a hard rubber disk (a puck) into their opponents' goal.

Field hockey is played on an outdoor field. On foot, the 11 players on each team use a hockey stick in trying to drive a small leather- or rubber-covered ball into the opponents' goal.

scuba diving / skin diving

The Americanism *scuba* is a blend formed by letters in <u>*se*</u>*lf-*<u>*c*</u>*ontained* <u>*un*</u>*-derwater* <u>*b*</u>*reathing* <u>*a*</u>*pparatus*. In *scuba diving*, one swims and explores underwater, at considerable depth and for a relatively long period. To do so, the swimmer needs scuba gear—special equipment typically consisting of one or two compressed-air tanks strapped to the back and connected by a hose to a mouthpiece. He or she wears a *wet suit* (a closefitting, usually one-piece rubber suit) for warmth and, on each foot, a large, flat, paddlelike rubber device known as a *flipper*, or *swim fin*, to increase the force of the kick.

Skin diving is mainly an underwater sport, though exploration may be very much in the swimmer's mind. Scuba gear and a wet suit are not required, but flippers and a face mask usually are. Swimming, face down, just below the surface of the water, the skin diver is supplied with air by means of a *snorkel*, a breathing tube that extends above the surface.

horseshoes / quoits

During Mikhail Gorbachev's visit to Washington in June 1990, he and President Bush threw a few *horseshoes* at Camp David. In this game the players toss horseshoes, whether real or horseshoe-shaped pieces of metal, at a stake driven into the ground 40 feet (about 12 meters) away. The object is to encircle the stake or come as close to it as possible. *Quoits* is a similar game, except that the players throw rings of rope, plastic, or flattened metal.

billiards / pool

Billiards is, essentially, a game played with small, hard balls on a rectangular table covered with cloth (usually green baize) and having raised, cushioned edges. Using the tip of a long, tapering stick called a *cue,* the players try to strike a certain ball (the cue ball) in such a way as to drive it into one or more of the other balls.

Of the many variations of billiards, Americans are most familiar with *pool,* or *pocket billiards.* Two ordinarily play this game, which requires a table with six pockets. Besides a white cue ball, there are 15 colored and numbered object balls. Each player drives the cue ball against one or more object balls in an attempt to knock as many of these as possible into the pockets. He or she scores points for each pocketed object ball, but loses both points and a turn if the cue ball drops into a pocket or leaves the table.

Eight ball is a form of pool in which a player or side immediately loses the game by inadvertently pocketing the number-8 ball before pocketing all the other assigned object balls. Thus the slang expression *behind the eight ball* to convey the notion of being in an unfavorable position (as in "Losing my wallet just before Christmas put me behind the eight ball").

Snooker, another form of pool, is played with a white cue ball, 15 red object balls, and 6 object balls of different colors, to which various point values are assigned. Each player must pocket a red ball before pocketing a ball of any other color; then, with all the colored balls back on the table, he or she tries to pocket them in the order of their point values. In snookering an opponent, a player leaves a ball between the cue ball and the object ball, thus making a direct shot impossible. The verb *snooker* has taken on several informal and slang senses, including "to thwart or defeat" ("Supporters of Shoeless Joe Jackson feel snookered by a qualification on the Hall of Fame ballot") and "to deceive" ("Many an investor has been snookered by a fast-talking broker").

In *carom billiards,* the table has no pockets and only three balls (a cue ball and two others) are used. Each player tries to strike the cue ball so that it will carom, or bounce, off a cushion or an object ball. In most forms of this game a player scores by successively striking the two object balls.

auction bridge / contract bridge

Bridge, a card game for two pairs of players, has two main forms: *auction* and *contract.* In *auction bridge,* the players bid for the right to say what suit will be trump (that is, whether spades, clubs, hearts, or diamonds will rank highest during the playing of a hand) or to declare no-trump. The extra tricks the declarer wins beyond his or her bid count toward a game. In *contract bridge,* which developed from auction, only the number of tricks named in the contract (the last and highest bid) may be counted toward a game, additional tricks being counted as a bonus score.

Duplicate bridge is not a form of bridge but a way of playing it. For comparative scoring, the same hands are played off again by players who did not hold them originally.

stud poker / draw poker

With endless variations, most of them anathema to serious poker players, *stud* and *draw* are the basic forms of the game. In *stud poker,* each player is ordinarily dealt five cards, the first face down and the others face up, with the betting taking place on each round of open cards dealt. In seven-card stud, the first two cards and usually the last one are dealt face down. In *draw poker,* each player is dealt five cards face down, and may be dealt replacements for any unwanted cards (usually not more than three).

blackjack / twenty-one

The names *blackjack* and *twenty-one* are applied interchangeably to a gambling game in which a player wins by getting cards totaling 21 points or less, while the dealer gets either a smaller total or a total exceeding 21 points.

The Arts: Fine and Otherwise

fine arts / applied arts

The *fine arts*, in one sense of the term, are any of the art forms created principally for aesthetic reasons, to be enjoyed for their own sake. They include drawing, painting, sculpture, ceramics, and, sometimes, architecture, literature, music, drama, and dance. As their name suggests, the *applied arts* are arts that apply aesthetic principles to the design or decoration of useful objects. They include industrial design, which deals with a wide variety of products, from cars and furniture to telephones and posters; bookmaking; illustration; printmaking; and commercial art, which is often taken to mean work commissioned for use in advertising. The distinction between the fine and applied arts is far from precise. A fifteenth-century fruit-offering bowl designed for use at Buddhist altars, for example, may well be displayed at an American fine art museum with some of Picasso's book illustrations in a nearby gallery.

performing arts / plastic arts

The *performing arts*, which include drama, dance, and music, are creative arts that are generally presented before an audience, or group of people assembled for a particular performance. The *plastic arts*, which include sculpture, architecture, painting, and the graphic arts, are also creative arts, but they are usually presented to public view at an exhibition or on permanent display, not in performance. The term *plastic arts* sometimes refers to three-dimensional works such as sculpture and ceramics, as distinguished from drawing and painting, and may also be applied to other works, such as realistic painting, in which three-dimensional effects are created.

A *performance art* is an art form that draws on both the performing arts and the plastic arts. It combines elements of several media, such as painting, film, dance, and drama, in a presentation in which the artist juxtaposes images on various themes and provides a commentary on them.

caricature / burlesque

Broadly comic representations of people, manners, and literary or artistic styles are described in several ways.

Caricature refers to an imitation that deliberately exaggerates or distorts certain distinguishing characteristics. (English borrowed the word from French, which had earlier adapted an Italian word meaning "satirical picture" or, literally, "an overloading.")

Burlesque implies handling a serious subject lightly or flippantly or, conversely, handling a trifling subject with mock seriousness. (The word, another French borrowing, comes from an Italian word related to one meaning a "jest" or "mockery.")

Parody suggests ridiculing a literary or musical work by closely imitating the style, especially so as to point up its peculiarities or affectations, and by distorting the subject matter nonsensically or changing it to something absurdly incongruous. (The word comes, by way of French and Latin, from the Greek for "burlesque song.")

Travesty implies retaining the subject matter but changing the style and language so as to give a grotesquely absurd effect. (The Latin-derived word conveys the notion of dress, attire, or disguise, just as *transvestite* does.)

Satire refers to a literary work in which follies, vices, stupidities, and abuses in life are held up to ridicule and contempt. (By the time French borrowed the word from Latin, it meant "poetic medley," but earlier it had described a dish of various fruits.)

Lampoon refers to a piece of strongly satirical writing that uses broad humor in attacking and ridiculing the faults and weaknesses of an individual. (The word may go back to *lampons,* meaning "Let's guzzle," a frequent refrain in seventeenth-century French drinking songs and satirical poems.)

Spoof suggests a light parody or satire. (The word was originally applied to a game involving hoaxing and nonsense that was invented about 1889 by the British comedian Arthur Roberts.)

comedy / farce

Nowadays a *comedy* is generally considered to be any theatrical or television play or any film that treats characters and situations more or less humorously and has a happy ending.

A *comedy of manners* (also called *drawing-room comedy*) depicts and satirizes the manners, foibles, and customs of fashionable society.

High comedy both appeals to and reflects the life and problems of the upper social classes. It is characterized by a witty, sardonic treatment and often by sophisticated dialogue.

Low comedy achieves its effect not from intellectual appeal, witty dialogue, and characterization but from crude, sometimes violent, action and situation. Slapstick, horseplay, and farce are likely to find a place in low comedy.

A *farce* is, in its own right, an exaggerated comedy based on broadly humorous, highly unlikely situations. The Latin-derived word, which English borrowed from French, means "stuffing," a reference to the fact that early farces were used to fill interludes between acts.

pathos / bathos

Literary criticism distinguishes between *pathos* and *bathos*. Borrowed from a Greek word meaning "suffering, disease, feeling," *pathos* refers to that quality in a character's actions or feelings which evokes sympathy and a sense of sorrow or pity—for example, King Lear's agony as he wanders about the heath in a raging storm. The English poet Alexander Pope (1688–1744), recalling that *bathos* means "depth" in Greek, first applied the word to a writer's abrupt, ludicrous fall from the lofty to the ordinary or trivial. He called his mock-critical treatise *On Bathos, or, Of the Art of Sinking in Poetry*. Nowadays critics apply *bathos* both to that sense of an unintentional anticlimax and to maudlin sentimentality, or a false or overdone pathos that is absurd in its effect. For example, in 1840, when Charles Dickens's novel *The Old Curiosity Shop* was published, many readers were deeply moved by the death of Little Nell, but most of today's readers would probably find the scene bathetic, not pathetic.

western / horse opera

Western sometimes refers to a movie, radio or television play, novel, or similar artistic work that is set in the western United States, especially during the nineteenth-century period of development and expansion of the frontier. Slang terms include *horse opera* and *oater* (from the oats fed to horses).

A *spaghetti western*, though it may be about cowboys in the western United States and may be distributed to theaters throughout this country, is a movie filmed in Italy. Hiring an Italian production crew and one or two Americans to head a cast of Italian actors keeps costs down, even though some English must be dubbed into the soundtrack. *The Good, the Bad, and the Ugly,* a 1967 spaghetti western directed by the Italian Sergio Leone, for instance, helped make the American Clint Eastwood an international superstar.

sequel / prequel

Any literary work, motion picture, or television drama can have a *sequel;* that is, a work which is complete in itself but continues a story begun in an earlier work. For example, John Updike wrote the novels *Rabbit Redux* (1971), *Rabbit Is Rich* (1981), and *Rabbit at Rest* (1990) as sequels to *Rabbit, Run* (1960). Fourteen years after flocking to see *Rocky* in 1976, moviegoers were flocking to see *Rocky V.* When the Kenneth Branagh film version of *Henry V* was released in 1989, a joke making the rounds was that some people did not plan to see it because they were tired of sequels.

A *prequel* is a work that depicts earlier events in a story already told. The film *Indiana Jones and the Temple of Doom,* for instance, was released in 1984 as a prequel to the 1981 film *Raiders of the Lost Ark.* Then, in 1989, the fearless archaeologist's adventures were carried forward in the sequel *Indiana Jones and the Last Crusade.*

debut / première

One sense of *debut,* as either a noun or a verb, has to do with a first public appearance of an actor, singer, or other performer (as in "Plácido Domingo made his debut as a baritone in Mexico in 1957" or "Plácido Domingo debuted as a baritone in Mexico in 1957"). English borrowed the word (also written *début*) from a French verb meaning "to play first, lead off."

Première (or *premiere*), a French adjective meaning "first," also is used as both a noun and a verb in English. It refers to a first performance, showing, or broadcast of a play, movie, concert, or the like ("NBC televised the première of Menotti's *Amahl and the Night Visitors* on Christmas eve, 1951" or "Menotti's *Amahl and the Night Visitors* premièred on NBC television on Christmas eve, 1951").

Oscar / Emmy

Every year, outstanding work in film, the theater, television, and the recording industry is celebrated in the United States. The award ceremonies, which spice public recognition with suspense and entertainment, have themselves become show business rituals, drawing millions of people to their TV sets. Of the large and growing number of such ceremonies, five claim special attention.

The *Oscar* is any of the many statuettes that the Academy of Motion Picture Arts and Sciences awards to professionals in all branches of the filmmaking industry, including acting, screen writing, directing, producing, cinematography, and set designing. The first Oscars were presented in 1929. No one, not even the executive staff of the Academy itself, knows for sure how the nickname *Oscar* came about. One theory is that the name was chosen arbitrarily. Another is that an Academy official, on first seeing the golden figurine, commented, "He reminds me of my Uncle Oscar." And still another is that in 1935, when Bette Davis won her first Oscar for her role in *Dangerous*, she made up the name in honor of her then-husband, Harmon Oscar Nelson.

Broadway's symbol of professional success is the *Antoinette Perry Tony Award,* created in memory of the American director-producer Antoinette Perry (1888–1946) and better known by Perry's nickname, *Tony.* Honoring the year's highest achievers in more than 25 categories of theater production, Tonys are presented jointly by the American Theatre Wing and the League of American Theatres and Producers. These mounted gold medallions show the classical masks of Comedy and Tragedy.

Any of the annual awards for special achievement in Off-Broadway theater productions is called an *Obie* (a blend of the first letters of *off* and *Broadway* + the suffix *-ie*). Winners of these plaques are chosen by critics who write for the New York City newspaper *The Village Voice* and by selected panelists.

To honor exceptional work in television the National Academy of Television Arts and Sciences has its own awards. Any of these statuettes, showing a winged Muse, is called an *Emmy.* Again, the origin of the name is open to question. Some say that it is an altered form of *Immy,* engineering slang for *image-orthicon camera,* and that H. R. Lubcke, an American TV engineer, proposed the name in 1948 in contrast to *Oscar.* Others say that the award was named for the American entertainer Faye Emerson.

The recording industry's most prestigious prize is the *Grammy,* awarded annually by the National Academy of Recording Arts and Sciences in recognition of outstanding records, songs, and performers. This gold statuette is a composite replica of early gramophones, or record players.

Its name combines a shortened form of *gramophone* with *-my*, as in *Emmy*. (The word *gramophone*, though generally retained in Britain, gave way to *phonograph* in the United States.)

drama / play

Drama and *play* both refer to a literary composition in prose or verse that tells a story by means of dialogue and action and is usually intended for performance before an audience, with actors impersonating the characters. (A work that is written mainly to be read, not staged, is called *closet drama;* for example, Shelley's lyrical *Prometheus Unbound*.) *Play* is commonly used for a theatrical work of any kind, while *drama* often designates a composition or performance that is not a comedy. Both words, as well as *comedy*, characterize various types of musicals. Plays collectively are known as *drama* (as in "Elizabethan drama").

tragedy / melodrama

A *tragedy* is a serious drama or play that generally deals with the problems of a central character and leads to an unhappy or disastrous ending. According to Aristotle, the effect of tragic drama on the audience is catharsis; that is, the purifying of the emotions or the relieving of emotional tensions. In ancient Greek tragedy, the protagonist's downfall is caused by a tragic flaw in his or her character or by being caught in a tragic situation. The king in Sophocles's *Oedipus Rex*, for example, brings both his drought-stricken land and himself to near ruin by unwittingly killing his father and marrying his mother. In modern drama, the protagonist is usually brought down by moral weakness, psychological maladjustment, or social pressures. In Arthur Miller's *Death of a Salesman*, for instance, Willy Loman commits suicide because of his deep sense of failure in his life and work as a traveling salesman.

A *tragicomedy* is not a tragedy with moments of comic relief but a play in which tragic and comic elements are combined. It is sometimes described as a tragedy with a happy ending, for although the protagonist goes through experiences that arouse pity, fear, and suspense in the audience, he or she does not die.

Tragedy is not essential to *melodrama*. Indeed, in the early nineteenth century this word was applied to a sensational or romantic play with interspersed songs, an orchestral accompaniment, and a conventional happy ending. Today it generally refers to a drama concerned with exaggerated conflicts and emotions, often violent physical action, and stereotyped characters (the good being very good and the bad very bad).

monologue / soliloquy

Monologue comes from Greek and *soliloquy* from Latin, but both mean "speaking alone." One sense of each word applies to lines in a play in which a character reveals his or her thoughts to the audience or reader but not to the other characters. The character may or may not be directly involved in the action.

Aside and *stage whisper* appear in written plays. Both indicate the dramatic convention in which a participant in the action addresses the audience but is supposedly not overheard by the other actors.

act / scene

In plays and operas, an *act* is the main dramatic unit and a *scene* is a division within an act. Traditionally, the action in a scene is continuous, limited to a single place, and marked by neither the entrance nor the withdrawal of any character. Nowadays, however, such conventions are not rigorously observed. Nor is the once-traditional system of numbering acts in capital Roman numerals and scenes in lowercase Roman numerals ("Act IV, scene iii," for example). And even if a playwright follows such a system, published references to both acts and scenes are often given in Arabic figures ("Act 4, scene 3").

Besides a unit within an act, the word *scene* refers more generally to the setting or locale of the action of a play, opera, film, novel, or other work (as in "The scene of *A Streetcar Named Desire* is the French Quarter of New Orleans"). In filmmaking, *scene* has the special sense of a section of a film, usually consisting of a series of interrelated shots that are made in continuous action.

Broadway / Off-Broadway

Far more than a main street running north and south through New York City, *Broadway* is known throughout the world as a center of commercial theater and entertainment. The area near Times Square, roughly between 41st and 53d streets, is sometimes still called the *Great White Way*, even though many of the brightly lighted marquees have been dimmed. Some of the theaters have been torn down and replaced with parking lots; others have made the climb to the second or third floors of newly erected office buildings.

While also professional, a number of theatrical productions are considered too unconventional, too experimental, or otherwise too limited in their appeal to be successful on "old Broadway." Many of the smaller theaters and the productions they stage are known collectively as

Off-Broadway. For a time Off-Broadway was mainly in Greenwich Village, a section of New York City on the lower west side of Manhattan, but nowadays a number of O.B. theaters are uptown, some right alongside the Great White Way. Highly experimental theatrical productions that are even less commercial and are scattered throughout small halls and cafes in New York City are referred to as *Off-Off-Broadway.*

repertoire / repertory

Repertoire refers to the stock of plays, roles, operas, or musical compositions that a company or a person is familiar with and ready to perform. We might say, for example, "Shirley Verrett's repertoire includes songs by Ernest Chausson" or "Mahler is a staple of today's orchestral repertoire."

In that sense, *repertory* can be substituted for *repertoire.* However, *repertory* refers as well to the system of producing and presenting plays, operas, and other works engaged in by a *repertory theater* (a theater in which a permanent company presents several works for a season, usually alternating them in limited runs), and this is a meaning not shared with *repertoire. Rep* is a clipped form of *repertory theater.*

arena theater / theater-in-the-round

Arena theater and *theater-in-the-round* refer both to a theater in which a central stage is surrounded by seats and to the techniques and methods used there. Such theaters do not have a *proscenium;* that is, the flat surface which separates the stage proper from the audience and includes the arch (called a *proscenium arch*) and the curtain within it.

rating / share

Television and radio networks always follow viewers' habits closely, but several times a year the scrutiny becomes especially intense. During these *sweep periods,* or *sweeps,* national rating services conduct surveys of local stations to find out which programs have the greatest appeal. The results are crucial, because the networks use sweep ratings in setting advertising rates.

Two measurements are particularly important in these statistical samplings. A *rating* is the percentage of sets tuned in to a program, with each rating point representing a certain number of American homes. A *share* is the percentage of sets tuned in to a particular program from among all the sets turned on at the time. So during a sweep one show might be found to have, say, a 7.4 rating with a 19 share, while a competing show has an 8.8 rating with a 20 share.

How well individual television performers go over with viewers is also monitored. A *TV-Q* is a rating of the familiarity and popularity of actors, newscasters, and other television personalities, so a high *Q-rating* is likely to be more helpful than a low one in contract negotiations with a network.

idiot card / idiot board

Just as the slang term *idiot box* puts down television viewers, *idiot board* is less than complimentary to those on the other side of the screen. Like other slang terms such as *idiot card* and *idiot sheet,* as well as the more formal *cue card, idiot board* refers to a cardboard sign or sheet which, unseen by the audience, reminds a television performer what to say, sing, or do next. As its trademarked name suggests, a *TelePrompTer* is also designed to jog the memory of speakers and actors who appear on television. However, this off-camera electronic device unrolls a prepared speech, script, or other material, line by line.

In the theater, actors are cued during a performance not by a visual device but by a person known as a *prompter.* The word *cue,* in this sense, goes back to the sixteenth and seventeenth centuries, when *q.* or *Q.* was written in plays to indicate actors' entrances. The letter was probably an abbreviation of some Latin word, perhaps *cuando* (meaning "when") or *qualis* ("in what manner"). Motion-picture actors who forget their lines are ordinarily not given cues while the cameras are rolling. Instead, the action is likely to be stopped for a quick look at the script.

recital / concert

A *recital* is a musical or dance program that is usually given by one or two soloists, though sometimes by a small ensemble. A *concert* is a program of vocal or instrumental music in which a number of musicians perform in unison, in agreement, together: after all, that is what *in concert* means.

An opera is said to be performed in concert form only if it is presented on stage without scenery, costumes, or action. When an oratorio like Handel's *Messiah* is performed in a concert hall instead of a church, it is also said to be in concert form.

ballet / modern dance

Like *ballet, modern dance* is staged artistic dancing that is performed to music and presents a story, idea, or mood. The gestures and movements of classical ballet are strictly bound to an elaborate formal technique largely devised by choreographers over the years. Those of modern dance, on the other hand, are a more personal expression of the emotions and inner vision of an individual choreographer or performer, or both. Also, modern dance is usually performed without the costumes and scenery that are so much a part of ballet. Yet, today, the two dance forms are having so marked an influence on each other that the differences between them are gradually narrowing.

orchestra / chamber orchestra

The word *orchestra* appears in the names of many ensembles that play "serious," or "classical," music (as distinguished from "popular" music). For example: The Philadelphia Orchestra and the Bath Festival Orchestra. An orchestra that performs mostly symphonic works may add *symphony* to its name. For example: the Boston Symphony Orchestra. Then, in informal usage, *orchestra* may be dropped, as in the Boston Symphony. The Greek-derived word *philharmonic* (*philos*, meaning "loving," + *harmonia*, meaning "harmony") is applied both to a society formed to sponsor a symphony orchestra and to the orchestra receiving such support; for example, the Philharmonic-Symphony Orchestra of New York. Some words in the name may be shifted or dropped, as in the New York Philharmonic.

A modern *symphony orchestra* consists of between 65 and 90 or so musicians. It is generally divided into four sections: strings, woodwinds, brass, and percussion.

Far smaller, a *chamber orchestra* is normally made up of between 18 and 40 members. It usually plays either modern music composed expressly for small ensembles or orchestral works of earlier periods, when orchestras were smaller than they are today (small enough to perform "in camera"—in a room rather than in a concert hall). Despite its name, a full chamber orchestra does not play chamber music, for this is written for even smaller groups. Some of the ensembles that specialize in chamber music are identified by the number of players, or parts; for example, The Beaux Arts Trio and the Amadeus Quartet.

The ensemble known today as a *string orchestra* generally uses only the bowed stringed instruments found in a symphony orchestra (the violin, viola, cello, and double bass). It is sometimes referred to, loosely, as a *chamber orchestra*.

A *band* is a group of musicians who are more likely to play brass, woodwinds, and percussion instruments than the bowed stringed instruments that are the mainstay of a symphony orchestra. This is especially true of a *brass band* or a *marching band*. However, some strings are ordinarily found in other types of bands, including a *symphonic* (or *concert*) *band*, a *jazz band*, and a *dance band*.

brass instrument / woodwind instrument

The large family of wind instruments—that is, instruments whose sound is produced by the musician's blowing into a mouthpiece—is divided into two smaller families. One of these subfamilies consists of *brass instruments;* the other, of *woodwind instruments.*

All *brass instruments* (*brass* or *brasses* for short) are in fact made of brass or some other metal, and all have a cup-shaped mouthpiece which the player presses against the lips to blow. In a modern orchestra the brass section typically comprises the French horn (generally shortened to horn), the trumpet, the trombone, and the tuba. Military and outdoor bands also use brass instruments, including the cornet, the flügelhorn, the euphonium, and the sousaphone.

The chief *woodwind instruments* (or *woodwinds*) in a modern orchestra are the flute, the piccolo (a small flute whose name means "small" or "diminutive" in Italian), the oboe, the English horn, the clarinet, the bass clarinet, the bassoon, and the double bassoon (or contrabassoon). Most of the woodwinds are made of wood and are *reed instruments* (that is, one or two thin strips of cane or some other flexible material called reeds are attached to the mouthpiece, which the player places between the lips to blow). The flute and the piccolo are exceptions on both counts, for not only are these instruments usually made of metal but the player produces the various tones by blowing a stream of air over an opening, or hole.

The saxophone occupies a special place among the wind instruments. Because it has a reed mouthpiece, it is often considered a woodwind. Yet, because it is made of metal, it is also thought of as a brass. In an orchestra the saxophone is therefore sometimes a part of the woodwind section and sometimes a part of the brass section.

harpsichord / clavichord

A *harpsichord* and a *clavichord* are alike in that both are musical instruments with a keyboard, and, as the Latin-derived word *chord* suggests, both have strings. *Harpsi,* which shares a common origin with *harp,* conveys a notion of how the sound is produced on the harpsichord; *clavi,* from the Latin *clavis* ("key"), does the same for the clavichord.

The *harpsichord* is likely to have two separate keyboards. When the keys are pressed, points of leather or quill pluck the strings, producing short, abrupt tones. On the *clavichord,* metal wedges at the ends of the keys strike the strings, producing tones of very limited degrees of loudness or softness. By means of small, felt-covered hammers operated by the keys, the *piano—*

successor to the clavichord—is able to produce an extremely wide range of tones; indeed, *pianoforte,* the earlier name of this instrument, means "soft-loud" in Italian.

violin / fiddle

A *violin* is the smallest and highest-pitched of modern string instruments. Held horizontally under the chin, resting against the collarbone, it is played with a bow.

Informally, both in and outside music circles, a violin is often called a *fiddle,* especially if it is used to play folk music, country music, and the like. *Second fiddle* is the part played by the second violin section of an orchestra or by the second violin of a quartet or other group. By extension, the idiomatic expression *play* (or *be*) *second fiddle* implies having secondary status, as in another person's affection or attention.

double bass / bull fiddle

The largest and the deepest-toned of the stringed instruments is known by several names, including *double bass, bass viol, contrabass, string bass, bass fiddle, bull fiddle,* and simply *bass.* Because of the instrument's great girth and height, most bassists either sit on a high stool or stand. In a jazz band or dance band, the bass is likely to be played pizzicato; that is, the strings are plucked with the finger instead of being bowed. A note produced this way, either loud or soft, lends a short, resonant accent to the music.

absolute music / program music

Absolute music (also called *abstract music* or *pure music*) is music for its own sake. That is, it is concerned solely with such musical elements as structure, melody, harmony, and rhythm. On the other hand, *program music* (also called *descriptive music*) is music meant to depict or suggest a subject outside the music itself, such as a story or scene, or to create a mood.

The distinction centers mainly on the composer's purpose, for the listener's reaction to music is not always predictable. Brahms's Quartet in B-flat Major, op. 67, for example, is undoubtedly absolute music, but who is to say that it might not call up an image of the forests, streams, and hills outside Vienna? And a symphonic poem like Richard Strauss's *Till Eulenspiegel's Merry Pranks,* based on a German folk tale about a young man who is part hero and part mischief-maker, is surely program music. Yet, with its free rondo form and sparkling melodies, *Till* is rich in purely musical ideas.

melody / tune

A *melody* is a succession of musical tones arranged in a rhythmic pattern, with a sense of completion or fulfillment. A *tune*—sometimes said to be an easily remembered, whistleable melody—is in fact arranged like a melody, but it is typically lighter, more popular, and not necessarily complete in itself. An *air* is generally considered to be a song or simple tune.

timbre / tone color

In music, *timbre* (borrowed from the French) and *tone color* are used interchangeably to describe the characteristic quality of sound that distinguishes one voice or musical instrument from another. This quality, which is determined by the harmonics, or overtones, enables even a casual listener to notice the difference between a note played on, say, a flute from the same note played on a violin.

adagio / allegro

To show the rate of speed at which a musical composition or passage is to be performed, composers ordinarily use Italian tempo marks. These are among the most common: slow—*adagio, largo, lento;* moderate—*allegretto, andante, moderato;* fast—*allegro, presto.*

To call for gradual changes in speed, they use other terms such as *ritardando* ("becoming gradually slower") and *accelerando* ("becoming gradually faster").

piano / pianissimo

Of the many musical directions that English has borrowed from Italian, a number apply specifically to *dynamics*—that is, the loudness or softness with which a composition or passage is to be performed. These are the four main indications of the volume of sound: *piano* (meaning "soft"), *pianissimo* ("very soft"), *forte* ("loud"), *fortissimo* ("very loud").

To show further gradations, composers often combine or modify those terms. *Mezzo piano,* for example, means "moderately soft"; *fortepiano,* "loud, then abruptly soft." Or they may use other explicit terms, such as *crescendo* ("gradually louder") and *decrescendo* or *diminuendo* ("gradually softer").

symphony / concerto

When most people think of classical instrumental music, sonatas, symphonies, concertos, and chamber music probably come to mind. Some stop at sonatas, which they see as incorporating the other three musical forms.

A *sonata* is a composition usually for one or two instruments—perhaps the piano alone or another solo instrument, such as the violin, with piano accompaniment. (A composition that gives equal importance to two instruments is called a *duet* or a *duo*, although *duo* is more likely to be applied to the two performers.) The word *sonata* (from the Latin *sonare*, meaning "to sound") originally referred to a piece that was sounded on instruments, as opposed to a *cantata* (from *cantare*, "to sing"), a piece to be sung. Most sonatas are divided into three or four movements, or comparatively independent parts. As a very general rule, those with three movements follow a fast-slow-fast scheme, while those with four insert a dancelike movement after the slow one. A *sonatina* is a short or simplified sonata.

Like the sonata, a *symphony* is a long composition that usually consists of three or four movements; in fact, a symphony is sometimes called a "sonata for the whole orchestra." The word goes back to the Greek *symphōnia* (*syn-*, meaning "together," + *phōnē*, meaning "sound"). So do *sinfonia* and, with an Italian diminutive, *sinfonietta*. A *sinfonia* is any of various early Italian instrumental works, especially a type of overture, as to an opera; a *sinfonietta* is a brief symphony, usually for a small orchestra.

A *concerto* is a composition—again, some say, a sonata—for one or more solo instruments and orchestra, usually in three symphonic movements. Although concertos (or, as they are sometimes called, *concerti*) generally give equal importance to the orchestra and the solo instrument or instruments, solo virtuoso parts do of course focus attention on the individual performer or performers.

Chamber music is a collective term for compositions ordinarily written for between three and eight solo instruments, with one player to a part. (In orchestral music, on the other hand, one part might be assigned to 16 musicians playing a single instrument such as the first or second violin.) The different types of chamber music are identified by the number of players, or parts: three in a *trio;* four in a *quartet;* five in a *quintet;* six in a *sextet;* seven in a *septet;* eight in an *octet;* nine in a *nonet.* The structure of certain chamber-music works so closely resembles that of the sonata, with its three of four movements, that a string quartet, for example, is sometimes called a "sonata for four strings."

Sonatas, symphonies, concertos, and some chamber works have in common the *sonata form,* which is most likely to appear in the first movement. This musical structure generally consists of an exposition, or presentation of the main theme or themes, in two distinct keys; a development, which expands on any or all of the themes presented in the exposition; and a recapitulation, which, in restating the previously presented themes, returns to the original key or tonality. These three sections may be followed by a coda, or concluding passage. Although the sonata form is not strictly limited to the first movement of musical works, it is often called a *first-movement form*. And, because the first movement of many sonatas is marked *allegro* (a musical direction meaning "fast"), the sonata form is also called a *sonata-allegro form*.

Whether in sonatas, symphonies, concertos, or some chamber music, the sonata cycle has often included forms of instrumental music that are also independent compositions. For example:

A *rondo* is a lively piece whose principal theme is stated three or more times in the same key, interposed with subordinate themes. It has frequently been used as the last movement in the four-movement sonata cycle. English borrowed the word *rondo* from Italian, which in turn had taken it from the French *rondeau,* meaning "round."

A *minuet* is a slow, stately dance, in 3/4 time, that was introduced in France in the seventeenth century. It was later carried into the sonata, where it has usually served as the third movement. The French word *menuet* originally meant "minute, tiny," in allusion to the short steps of the dance.

A *scherzo,* a lively, playful composition, usually in 3/4 time, has often taken the place of a third-movement minuet. In Italian *scherzo* means "a jest, sport."

symphonic poem / tone poem

The terms *symphonic poem* and *tone poem* are used interchangeably to designate a musical composition for symphony orchestra that is based on a historical, literary, pictorial, or other nonmusical subject. Such works, which are usually in one fairly long movement, are considered program music, as distinguished from absolute music. The titles of many symphonic poems describe the subjects, or "programs," that are developed in the stories or mood pictures; for example, Modest Mussorgsky's *A Night on Bald Mountain*, Richard Strauss's *Don Quixote*, and Charles Ives's *Three Places in New England.*

oratorio / cantata

An *oratorio* is a long dramatic composition, on a religious or serious theme, for solo voices, chorus, and orchestra. It is presented in a concert hall or church, without stage action, scenery, or costumes. The word *oratorio,* meaning "small chapel" in Italian, goes back to the sixteenth century, when such music was performed at the Oratory of Saint Philip Neri, in Rome. Two hundred years later, Handel composed the *Messiah*, which, with its Hallelujah Chorus, is not only the composer's most popular work but one of the world's best-loved oratorios.

Derived from the Latin verb *cantare*, meaning "to sing," the word *cantata* embodies the notion of the human voice. Like an oratorio, a *cantata* is a composition for solo singers and chorus, often with instrumental accompaniment, that serves as the setting for a story to be sung but not acted. But a cantata is typically shorter than an oratorio, and whereas an oratorio usually has an elaborate plot centering on a biblical subject, a cantata may have either a religious or a secular text, with little or no plot. Most of the 300 or so cantatas that Johann Sebastian Bach composed in the early eighteenth century have religious themes. Today's religious cantatas have been compared to small-scale oratorios; the secular ones, to short operas presented as concerts. Cantatas composed in the twentieth century include Béla Bartók's *Cantata profana* (for tenor, baritone, chorus, and orchestra) and Arthur Honegger's *Une Cantate de Noël* (for baritone, mixed chorus, children's chorus, organ, and orchestra).

A *mass* is a musical setting for certain parts of the Roman Catholic Eucharistic rite that consists of prayers and ceremonies centered on the consecration of bread and wine as a real though mystical reenactment of the sacrifice of Christ on the cross. The name for both the religious service and the music comes from the Latin *missa*, one of the words said by the priest in dismissing the congregation: *ite, missa est (contio)*. Bach's Mass in B Minor and Beethoven's Mass op. 123 (*Missa solemnis*) rank among the masterpieces of the form. Leonard Bernstein's Mass, composed in 1971, is also based on the Roman Catholic rite, but, besides singers, choruses, and instrumentalists, it calls for actors and dancers.

opera / grand opera

An *opera* is a play having all or most of its text set to music. Operas are generally performed not only with orchestral accompaniment but also with elaborate costumes and scenery. The word *opera*, like *opus*, comes from a Latin word meaning "a work" or "labor." In fact, the plural of *opus*, which is often applied to any of the musical works of a composer numbered in order of composition or publication, is both *opera* and *opuses*.

Grand opera refers to operas whose plots are generally serious, even tragic, and which are sung throughout. Opera lovers seldom tire of grand operas such as Verdi's *Rigoletto* and Puccini's *Madama Butterfly*.

A variation on the traditional operatic form is the *music drama*. This name was first applied to Wagner's later operas—particularly the four that make up *The Ring of the Nibelung*—in which the music and the story develop together in a continuous flow.

An *opéra comique* is an opera that has some spoken dialogue and typically deals with a serious subject. Bizet's *Carmen* exemplifies this kind of opera.

A *comic opera* is an opera on a light, sentimental subject, with humorous situations, a story that ends happily, and, usually, some spoken dialogue. Mozart's *Cosi fan tutte* and Rossini's *Barber of Seville* are among the best-known comic operas. More farcical types of comic opera are the *opéra bouffe* (French) and the *opera buffa* (Italian).

An *operetta* (the diminutive of *opera* in Italian) is a light, amusing opera that usually includes some spoken dialogue and dancing, as well as singing. Johann Strauss's *Die Fledermaus*, Arthur Sullivan's *Pirates of Penzance*, and Victor Herbert's *Naughty Marietta* are well-known operettas. The term *light opera* is sometimes used in place of *operetta*.

An outgrowth of the operetta, the theatrical or film production known as a *musical* develops its story line through dialogue and an integrated musical score featuring songs and dances in a popular idiom. It is likely to be elaborately costumed and staged. Widely acclaimed musicals include *Show Boat, Oklahoma!, My Fair Lady,* and *A Chorus Line*. The full names of this form, which, like *musical* itself, originated in the United States, are, variously, *musical comedy, musical play,* and *musical drama*.

libretto / score

In an opera or musical, the words are called the *libretto*, or *book* (in fact, in Italian *libretto* means "little book"). A written or printed copy of the musical notes to be played and sung is called the *score*. For Gilbert and Sullivan's operettas of the late nineteenth century, for example, Sir William Gilbert was the librettist and Sir Arthur Sullivan was the composer. About a hundred years later, James Lapine wrote the book for the Broadway musical *Into the Woods* and Stephen Sondheim composed the score. (The word *book* refers also to a script for a play.)

In a song, the words are called either *words* or *lyrics*. James Van Heusen, for instance, wrote the music for "Come Fly with Me"; Sammy Cahn, the lyrics, or words.

verse / chorus

Many popular songs open with a *verse*, an introductory section which typically has a free tempo and rhythm and no fixed number of measures, or bars. Next comes the main part, called either the *chorus* or the *refrain*, which traditionally consists of four eight-bar sections.

People who sing or hum a ballad like "Where or When," with music by Richard Rodgers and lyrics by Lorenz Hart, are likely to start with the chorus. Indeed, they may not even know that the song begins with a verse. That is probably why today's composers usually skip the verse and go right to the chorus.

representational art / abstract art

From the bellowing bison painted in a cave in Altamira, Spain, about 15,000 B.C., through Leonardo da Vinci's *Mona Lisa*, to Edward Hopper's *Nighthawks* and Andrew Wyeth's *Christina's World*, painting has been largely concerned with giving recognizable form to objects, figures, and elements in nature. Art that seeks to depict the physical appearance of reality is called *representational art, objective art,* or *figurative art.*

Abstract art (also called *nonobjective art* or *nonfigurative art*) is, in its purest sense, painting or sculpture in which the depiction of real objects is eliminated; that is, the shapes, forms, and colors have no counterparts in nature. Aesthetic content is expressed in line and organization that may be definite and geometric (as in Piet Mondrian's *Composition in White, Black, and Red* and Mark Rothko's *No. 118*) or fluid and amorphous (as in Wassily Kandinsky's *Composition Number Three* and Helen Frankenthaler's *Interior Landscape*).

An umbrella term, *abstract art* encompasses a number of nonrealistic schools or trends, including abstract expressionism and op art. Indeed, not all works considered abstract are entirely devoid of natural objects. *Semiabstract art,* including Pablo Picasso's painting *Harlequin with Violin,* Joseph Stella's painting *Brooklyn Bridge,* and Henry Moore's sculpture *Three Piece Reclining Figure,* present real subjects, but so stylized or broken down into basic forms as to be all but unrecognizable.

baroque / rococo

The *baroque* style of art and architecture, which dominated Europe throughout the seventeenth and first half of the eighteenth centuries, was characterized by drama and intensity, a bold use of ornament and decoration, and curvilinear forms. Even today, something that is gaudily ornate might be described as *baroque.* (English borrowed the word from French, in which it originally meant "irregular"; earlier, the Portuguese word *barroco* was applied to an "imperfect pearl.")

Both an extension of and a reaction to the baroque, the *rococo* style is also marked by profuse and delicate ornamentation, but on a smaller scale and often with more lightness and grace. The rococo flourished in the early eighteenth century. Like *baroque, rococo* is sometimes used nowadays as a slightly disparaging term for, say, an architectural work, a musical composition, or a piece of furniture that is extremely elaborate, even florid and tasteless. (This word, too, came into English from French, in which *rocaille* means "rock work" or "shell work.")

Like the names of most other artistic schools and periods, *baroque* and *rococo* are sometimes capitalized.

impressionism / expressionism

In 1874, in Paris, an art exhibition marked the beginning of *impressionism,* a theory and school of painting exemplified chiefly by Edouard Manet, Claude Monet, Pierre Auguste Renoir, and Edgar Degas. This revolutionary movement wanted, above all, to capture a momentary glimpse of nature, especially to reproduce the changing effects of light by applying paint to a canvas in short strokes of pure color. The term *impressionism* was later extended to literature (for example, the fiction of Virginia Woolf, John Dos Passos, and Stephen Crane and the poetry of imagists like Ezra Pound, Amy Lowell, and Carl Sandburg) and to music (as in the tone poems of Claude Debussy and Maurice Ravel).

If the impressionists sought to restructure reality by rendering scenes from the world around them more subjectively, those who came after them went even further. In the early-twentieth-century movement known as *expressionism* the artist's vision and emotions became all-important. Line, shape, and color that once represented reality were distorted, and symbols, stylization, and other artistic devices gave objective expression to inner experience. Indeed, inner experience was considered the only reality. Prominent expressionist painters included Wassily Kandinsky, Edvard Munch, and Paul Klee. As a literary style, expressionism is perhaps best exemplified by the playwrights August Strindberg, Eugene O'Neill, and Tennessee Williams, although expressionist elements appear as well in the novels of James Joyce and William Faulkner, among others. In music, expressionism reached its height in works of Arnold Schoenberg and Alban Berg.

abstract expressionism / action painting

Though sometimes used interchangeably, *abstract expressionism* and *action painting* refer to slightly different artistic styles. A post–World War II movement that developed from expressionism, *abstract expressionism* freed the artist from the need to represent reality by recognizable objects in the real world. The canvases of Jackson Pollock, Willem de Kooning, Franz Kline, and Robert Motherwell exemplify the creation of nonrepresentational compositions by the spontaneous and self-expressive application of paint.

Action painting is a form of abstract expressionism. Pollock pioneered the use of methods such as the pouring, dripping, or splattering of paint to create bold, fluid, apparently random compositions.

art nouveau / art deco

A late-nineteenth- and early-twentieth-century movement in painting, sculpture, printmaking, architecture, and decorative design, *art nouveau* (literally "new art" in French) got its name from a Paris art gallery (*Maison de l'Art Nouveau*) that carried examples of such art. Exponents of the style, with its exuberant, curvilinear designs patterned largely from nature, included the illustrator Aubrey Beardsley and the craftsman and decorative artist William Morris, in England; the stained-glass designer Louis Comfort Tiffany, in the United States; and the architect Antonio Gaudí, in Spain.

Art deco is a decorative style whose name is drawn from the middle of *Exposition Internationale des Arts Décoratifs et Industriels Modernes,* an exhibition of modern decorative and industrial arts held in Paris in 1925. Distinguished for its streamlined and geometric forms that suggested the sleekness of modern technology, the style reached its high point around 1925. At that time, artists like the Russian-born Erté were displaying their talents in the world of fashion, the theater, and interior decoration. Radio City Music Hall and the Chrysler Building, in New York City, are among the best examples of art deco in architecture.

pop art / op art

In the 1960s the New York art scene was dominated by a style of painting and sculpture that drew its techniques and subject matter largely from commercial art and the mass media. *Pop art* (or *pop*) is representational art that depicts such items of popular culture as comic strips, posters, and brand-name foods. Andy Warhol's canvas filled with Campbell's soup cans came to epitomize the style. Other exponents included Roy Lichtenstein, with his greatly enlarged newspaper comic strips, and Jasper Johns, whose favorites among everyday, banal images are numbers, letters, targets, and maps.

Op art (or *op*) is a style of abstract art that, under the leadership of painters such as Victor Vasarély, gained prominence about the same time as pop art. A clipped form of *optical, op* refers to the extremely complex visual effects, such as the illusion of movement, that are created through the use of two or more different but related systems of shapes and colors. By stimulating a reaction on the retina of the eye, the sharply defined geometric patterns produce a dazzle effect. Nowadays it is not unusual to find op art motifs in textile designs and other forms of decorative art.

watercolor / tempera

Not surprisingly, a water-based paint is used in both a *watercolor* and an *aquarelle* (*aqua* meaning "water" in Latin). The luminous transparency of these paintings comes mainly from the white of the paper, not from white paint. On the other hand, a *gouache*, though a watercolor, is tempered with white and therefore produces an opaque but brilliant effect. Technically, a *tempera* is also a watercolor, since the pigments are dispersed in an emulsion that usually combines egg yolk and water. Yet the soft, glowing color quality of this kind of painting distinguishes it from the other watercolors.

A *wash* is a thin, watery layer of watercolor, applied with an even, sweeping movement of the brush. The term sometimes refers as well to a type of drawing, such as *pen and wash,* in which the main areas of shadow are laid on in washes of dark watercolor. A *wash drawing* is a brush drawing done in one color, the linear elements being enhanced by many washes of transparent watercolor or of India ink, shading from light to dark.

collage / montage

English borrowed the French names for several related techniques for building up the surfaces of artistic compositions and for the works so created.

Collage (meaning "a pasting") refers to an art form in which bits of objects, such as newspaper, cloth, string, pressed flowers, and railway tickets, are pasted together on a canvas or panel in incongruous relationships for their symbolic or suggestive effect.

Decoupage, derived from a verb meaning "to cut out," refers to an art form in which designs or illustrations are cut out of paper or foil, mounted decoratively on a surface, and covered with several coats of varnish or lacquer.

Montage refers to an art form that brings together in a single composition a number of complete or partial photographs or prints. These pictures or parts of pictures are arranged, usually by superimposing one on another, so that they form a blended whole while retaining their identity.

Assemblage refers to an art form that, in its three-dimensionality, is more like a piece of sculpture than a painting. Objects and materials of various sizes and shapes—whether found in nature, manufactured, or produced by the artist—are assembled and arranged as part of a larger work or as a freestanding composition.

engraving / etching

Generally classified among the plastic arts, the *graphic arts* include engraving, etching, lithography, serigraphy, drypoint, and offset. In all of them the final result is a *print*—that is, any of the multiple impressions of a picture or design made from a single block, plate, screen, roll, or other media. The work created by the artist is sometimes called the *original print;* the individual impressions made from it, *proofs.* In another sense, however, a proof is only a trial impression taken before the actual printmaking begins.

Among the printmaking processes that have developed over the years, the four most commonly used by artists today are *relief, intaglio, planography,* and *stencil.*

Relief, the oldest method, is aptly named, because all the nonprinting areas of the block or plate are carved, engraved, or etched away, leaving only the design projecting from the surface. Once the raised design is inked, it is transferred to paper pressed against it, either by hand or in a press. The main types of relief prints are the *woodcut, wood engraving, linocut* (short for *linoleum cut*), and *relief etching.* A *woodcut* and a *wood engraving* are very similar, both being printed from a carved block of wood. However, a woodcut is carved from a block sawn along the grain and has broad, openly cut areas, whereas a wood engraving is carved from an end-grain block and has an image that is generally linear in concept. A *relief etching* is printed from a metal plate on which all but the design has been etched away by acid.

Intaglio is the reverse of relief. As the Italian word (a form of a verb meaning "to cut in, engrave") suggests, the design is carved, incised, etched, or engraved below the surface of a steel, copper, or zinc plate. The metal plate is then inked and wiped clean, leaving ink only within the grooves beneath the surface. With dampened paper laid over it, the plate is taken through a press under high pressure. On being forced into the grooves, the paper picks up the ink. Best known of these prints are the *etching, aquatint, line engraving, drypoint,* and *mezzotint.* In both an *intaglio etching* (as distinguished from a *relief etching*) and an *aquatint,* the design is created by coating the surface of the metal plate with an acid-resistant layer and then bathing it in acid, which eats into the areas laid bare with special needles. Whereas the effect of an etching is linear, that of the aquatint is tonal, somewhat like that of a wash drawing or water-color. (After all, in Latin *aquatint* means "dyed in water.") Instead of having pitted areas and textures bitten into the plate with acid, a *line engraving, drypoint,* and *mezzotint* (or *mezzo*) have their designs directly cut or scratched into the plate with fine, hard needles and other special tools. In general, the engraving produces a clean and sharp linear effect; the drypoint, a softer, more feathery effect; and the mezzotint, which is often used to copy paintings, tonal impressions of light and shade.

Planography, a method of printing from a flat surface, is based on the repulsion between grease and water. The design is applied to the surface with a greasy material, and then water and printing ink are successively applied. The greasy parts, which repel water, absorb the ink, but the wet parts do not. Because stone was the first printing surface, this method is commonly known as *lithography* (*lithos,* meaning "stone" in Greek, + *-graphia,* which Latin borrowed from a Greek word meaning "writing"). Besides stone, metals such as zinc and aluminum are now widely used. Color lithographs require a separate image and printing surface for each color.

The *stencil* method involves perforating or cutting through a thin sheet of material, such as paper or metal, in such a way that when ink or paint is applied to the sheet, the pattern is marked on the surface below. In the ever-more-popular *silk-screen process,* the artist creates each successive color design on a piece of silk or other fine cloth that is stretched on a wooden frame and hinged to a wooden base. After all parts of the design not to be printed have been blocked out by an impermeable film, the paint is forced through the screen onto the paper below. The creation of an artist's original print by the silk-screen process is called *serigraphy,* and a silk-screen print made by the artist personally is called a *serigraph.*

In sorting out the various types of prints, we are apt to have the most trouble keeping the terms *engraving* and *etching* straight. There are two main reasons for this confusion. First, both an engraving and an etching can be produced by two basically opposite printmaking processes: relief and inta-glio. Second, both *engraving* and *etching* sometimes appear as the second element of somewhat ambiguous compound words. For example, *relief etch-ing* and *intaglio etching* convey the notion of process, while *wood engraving* indicates the material and *line engraving* suggests the visual effect.

high relief / low relief

A sculpture in which figures project from the background by half or more than half their full natural depth is known as *high relief*. The Italian term *alto-rilievo* and the variant *alto-relievo* (whose spelling is influenced by that of *relief*) are also used. On the other hand, sculpture in which figures are carved in a flat surface so that they project only a little from the background is commonly known by the French loanword *bas-relief*. Other names for it are *low relief* and the Italian borrowings *basso-relievo* and *basso-rilievo*.

mobile / stabile

A *mobile* is an abstract sculpture whose aim is to depict movement—that is, kinetic rather than static rhythms. The delicately balanced arrangement of rings, rods, wires, flat plates, and the like is suspended by a thin filament and set in motion by slight air currents. A *stabile* is also an abstract sculp-ture. However, instead of being light, flexible, and floating in midair, it is heavy, rigid, and stationary. Both forms were invented by the American sculptor Alexander Calder (1898–1976).

needlework / embroidery

Needlework, as its name suggests, is work done with a needle. Though it may be ordinary sewing, it is more likely to be *fancywork*, or decorative needlework, such as *embroidery*. This ornamenting of fabric with a design is done in several different ways. *Needlepoint*, for example, is embroidery in which woolen threads of various kinds and various weights are worked on canvas, generally for use in upholstery and tapestries. *Crewelwork* (or *crewel*) is embroidery, often on linen or cotton, in which a loosely twisted, fine worsted yarn is stitched into geometric, floral, animal, and many other kinds of patterns. *Cutwork* is open embroidery, usually on linen, in which part of the cloth is cut away from the design.

Crocheting, in which loops of thread or yarn are interwoven by means of a single hooked needle, is another kind of fancywork. So is *knitting* done by hand. Here a pair of eyeless, usually long needles of metal, bone, or plastic, with a blunt point at one or both ends, loop yarn or thread together to make a stretchy fabric or articles of clothing such as sweaters and scarves.

warp / weft

In weaving, the series of parallel threads or yarns that run lengthwise in the loom are called the *warp*. The thread or yarn that the shuttle carries back and forth, across the warp, is called the *weft*, or *woof*. Anyone who has trouble keeping the distinction in mind might replace *weft* with *left* and then picture a left-to-right progression, instead of an up-and-down movement.

All three words, but particularly the combination *warp and woof*, are used figuratively as well, in the sense of a basic material or foundation. One might say, for instance, "Tom Wolfe's novel *The Bonfire of the Vanities* captures the warp and woof of contemporary urban life."

Doric order / Ionic order

In classical architecture, *order* refers to any of several styles of structure, determined chiefly by the type of column, capital, and entablature (the horizontal superstructure, including the frieze and cornice, which rests on the capital). The three best-known orders are the *Doric*, the *Ionic*, and the *Corinthian*.

The *Doric order* is distinguished by a somewhat massive fluted column and simple capital and entablature. It is the only order subdivided into Greek and Roman, the main difference being the absence of a base at the foot of the Greek Doric column (used on the Parthenon, for example).

Lighter and more graceful than the Doric, the *Ionic order* is distinguished mainly by the ornamental scrolls (spiral volutes) on the capital of the fluted column.

The lightest and most ornate of the three, the *Corinthian order* is distinguished by a slender fluted column and by a bell-shaped capital decorated with a design of acanthus leaves. Though developed by the Greeks, it became more popular with the Romans.

In establishing the *Composite order*, the Romans drew largely on the Corinthian and the Ionic. To the scroll-like ornaments of the Ionic capital, for example, they added the acanthus design of the Corinthian. Another Roman order is the *Tuscan*, the only one of the five to be distinguished by smooth (unfluted) columns. This simplicity can be seen, as well, in the unadorned ringlike capital.

building / edifice

A *building* is any fixed structure that has a roof, is supported by columns or walls, and is intended as a shelter for people, animals, or property. A house, a motel, a hospital, a factory, a toolshed, and a stable, then, are buildings, but a tent is not. An *edifice* is a large or stately building. The word is sometimes used figuratively (as in "edifice of democracy"). A *structure* is also an imposing building. This word has special application when the material of construction is being stressed (as in "a steel structure").

story / floor

In architecture, *story* (*storey* in British English) and *floor* are freely interchanged in two senses. First, in reference to the section or horizontal division of a building that extends from the floor to the ceiling or roof directly above it (as in "The apartment house has six stories [floors]"). Second, in reference to all the rooms on the same level of a building ("A fire broke out on the third story [floor]"). Yet certain constructions usually call for one word instead of the other; for example, "a twenty-story (twenty-storied) hotel," but "the view from the top floor." *Flight*, in designating a set of stairs between landings or floors, sometimes but not always takes the place of *story* or *floor*. For example, we might say "The fire broke out three flights (stories, floors) up," but probably not "A fire broke out on the third flight."

The floor or story of a building that is approximately level with the ground is called the *ground floor* ("There is a restaurant on the ground floor"). In the United States this floor is also called the *first floor*. In Britain, however, the *first floor* is the floor above the ground floor—what Americans call the *second floor*. So the *second floor* in Britain is the *third floor* in the States, and so on.

A *mezzanine* (or *mezzanine floor*) is a low-ceilinged floor or story between two main ones, usually immediately above the ground floor and in the form of a balcony projecting only partly over the floor below it. Mezzanines are ordinarily found in hotels, department stores, and other large public buildings, on either side of the Atlantic. When it comes to theaters, American and British usage differ. In American theaters, a mezzanine is generally the first few rows of the balcony, separated from the others by an aisle. In British theaters, it is a room or floor under the stage.

attic / garret

As an architectural term, *attic* designates a low wall or story above the cornice of a classical façade. In everyday usage it refers to the room or space just below the roof of a house. *Garret*, which once meant a "watch-tower," is also used in this second sense, but it is a more literary word than *attic*. We are, for instance, likely to talk about old clothes and toys being kept in an attic but about an artist living in a garret. *Loft* used to refer simply to an attic or atticlike space that is ordinarily not partitioned into rooms and is located immediately below the roof of a house, barn, or other building. American English has added a new sense to the word: any of the upper stories of a warehouse or factory, often more specifically a dwelling place or artist's studio on an upper story of a converted warehouse or factory. *Crawl space*, a term that originated in the United States, refers to an unfinished space, usually under a roof or floor, so small as only to allow access to wiring and plumbing.

basement / cellar

A *basement* is the lowest story, or floor, of a building, under the main one and wholly or partly below the surface of the ground. The basement in a house is often used as living space or as an informally furnished place for relaxation and recreation—what Americans call a *family room*. A structure other than a residence (a department store, for example) may have a basement too; here it is the lowermost floor, entirely underground.

Like a basement, a *cellar* is wholly or partly below the ground level of a building. But this room or group of rooms is ordinarily used only for storage. In a house, fuel (coal or, more likely nowadays, the furnace), food, wine, and unused possessions are likely to be kept here.

steeple / spire

A *steeple* is a tower that rises above the main structure of a church or other building and is usually capped with a tall, pointed structure known as a *spire*. This difference between a steeple and a spire is, however, often overlooked. Sometimes the two words are used interchangeably, and sometimes *steeple* is applied to a church tower and spire taken together.

staircase / stairway

A *staircase* and *stairway* are very much alike in that both consist of a series of stairs designed to permit access from one level of a building to another. Loosely speaking, the words are interchangeable. Technically, however, a *stairway* need not have a handrail or a balustrade, whereas a *staircase* usually does.

banister / balustrade

Any of the small posts that support the upper rail of a railing, as on a staircase, is called a *baluster*. English borrowed this word from the French *balustre*, which in turn had come from the Italian *balaustro* (meaning "pillar"). An earlier related Italian word, *balausta*, and even earlier Latin and Greek words had conveyed the sense of "flower of the wild pomegranate," because of the similarity between a feature of the molded post and the curving calyx of that flower. *Balustrade*, which designates a railing held up by balusters, also came into English from French by way of Italian.

A *banister* (also spelled *bannister*) is a handrail held up by balusters, as along a staircase. The word, which is often taken to mean the supporting balusters as well as the railing, is an altered form of *baluster* itself. The post at the top or bottom of a flight of stairs, supporting the handrail, is called a *newel*, or *newel post*.

step / stoop

Among the many meanings of *step* is "a rest for the foot in climbing, as a stair or the rung of a ladder." The plural form, *steps*, ordinarily refers to a flight of stairs, or a stairway. The Americanism *stoop* designates a small porch or platform with steps and, originally, seats at the entrance to a house. Baltimore, for example, is well known for the white stoops leading up to the front doors of its row houses.

myth / legend

Over the centuries, people throughout the world have been handing down stories from one generation to another. While these traditional narratives differ in form, content, and purpose, most of them are alike in that they started out being transmitted orally, their original authors were unknown, and they took on different versions as they moved from one place to another. In time, many of the old stories found their way into published collections and many others are acknowledged literary creations.

Myths, legends, epics, folk tales, fairy tales, and *fables* are but a small part of the storehouse of learning that we call *folklore* (a word suggested in 1846 by the English antiquary W. J. Thomas to replace *popular antiquities*). Superstitions, sayings, games, songs, nursery rhymes, ballads, and much, much more can be found among the accumulated beliefs, customs, and traditions of ordinary people.

A *myth* often serves to explain some phenomenon of nature, the origin of humankind, or the customs, institutions, religious rites, and beliefs of a people. Among the ways it does so is by telling of supernatural events and the exploits of a gods or heroes. The myth of the Greek Titan Prometheus, for example, is an account of how people got fire.

A *legend*, more than a myth, is popularly believed to have a historical basis, however distorted and unverifiable. Once limited to recounting the miracles of saints, legends have gone on to tell of other incredible acts and wonderful events. In this way they usually embody the spirit of a people. One of the best-known British legends is the story of King Arthur.

An *epic* is a long narrative poem typically centering on the deeds of a traditional or historical hero. Among the most celebrated epics of world literature are the *Iliad* and the *Odyssey*, which, though usually attributed to Homer, were probably the work of many ancient Greek poets who told the stories in many ways over many generations.

A *folk tale* (or *folk story*) and a *fairy tale* (or *fairy story*) are generally thought to fall within the same category of traditional narrative. Though they resemble both the myth and the legend, these timeless stories are more personal than either. They often depict fantastic, even magical, adventures, and they include such supernatural characters as fairies, giants, witches, and talking animals (but not gods or goddesses). Yet the best of them—from "The Three Little Pigs" to "Sleeping Beauty"—manage to bring the feelings and emotions shared by large groups of people down to the level of a single listener or reader.

A *fable* is a very short tale intended to teach a moral lesson. The characters are usually animals that act and talk like people. Aesop's fable "The Grasshopper and the Ant," for example, teaches the need to work hard and be thrifty.

story / narrative

Story applies to a series of connected events, true or fictitious, that is written or told with the intention of entertaining or informing. *Narrative,* a more formal word, refers to the kind of story that recounts happenings. *Tale* is a somewhat elevated or literary term, usually suggesting a simple, leisurely story, more or less loosely organized, especially a fictitious or legendary one. *Anecdote* refers to a short, entertaining account of a single incident, usually personal or biographical.

novel / novella

The imaginative prose narratives that make up fiction can contain any number of words and deal with any subject. After all, the word *fiction*, like *dough*, comes from a Latin verb meaning "to form, mold." Length and the effect of compression or extension on content and style vary, of course, from work to work. Yet literary critics and historians generally agree on certain characteristics and approximate lengths for the most common narrative forms.

The *novel*, the dominant form of prose narrative throughout the world, generally centers on a more or less complex plot or pattern of events in portraying the actions, feelings, and motives of a group of characters. A typical novel runs somewhere between 30,000 and 100,00 words.

Historically, the *novella* is a short prose narrative that usually has a moral and is often satirical (any of the tales in Boccaccio's *Decameron*, for example). Nowadays the word refers simply to a short novel, ranging between, say, 15,000 and 30,000 words.

Though sometimes considered the same as a *novella*, the *novelette* is often regarded as a work that is banal, inferior in quality, and highly commercial. A novel of any length that is based on a film script is called a *novelization*.

The *short story* characteristically develops a single central theme and is limited in both scope and number of characters. Ordinarily containing fewer than 15,000 words, it can be read straight through.

The *short short story* is a short story that is not only brief (generally fewer than 2,000 words) but is likely to have a surprise ending. This form of narrative prose is sometimes known as a *short-short*.

biography / autobiography

A person's life story can take any of several forms. If the account is prepared by someone else, the work is a *biography* (*bio-*, meaning "life," + *-graphy*, meaning "a method of writing"). For example: *George Eliot: A Biography*, by Gordon S. Haight. If the account is prepared by the subject himself or herself, it is an *autobiography* (since *auto-* means "self"). For example: *The Autobiography of Malcolm X*, by Malcolm X. *The Autobiography of Alice B. Toklas* is an intentionally misleading title, for the book is really an autobiography of Gertrude Stein, who wrote it as though the author were Toklas, her secretary and companion.

An autobiography that reveals faults and confidential personal details is sometimes called a *confession* (or *confessions,* as in Thomas De Quincey's *Confessions of an English Opium Eater*). A biography or biographical sketch, usually one written by someone who knew the subject well, is a *memoir* (*Memoirs of the Life of Sir Walter Scott,* by John Gibson Lockhart, the writer's son-in law). *Memoir,* or *memoirs,* is applied also to an autobiography that is objective and anecdotal in emphasis, rather than inward and subjective (*The Memoirs of a Publisher,* by F. N. Doubleday), and to a report or record of important events based on the writer's personal observation or knowledge (*A Memoir of China in Revolution,* by Chester Ronning).

diary / journal

Like other forms of autobiography, a *diary* and a *journal* are concerned with the subject's own experiences. However, instead of reordering and reshaping events in that person's life in recollection, these are typically daily records of happenings, thoughts, and feelings. *Diary* suggests an emphasis on personal detail and insight (*The Diary of a Young Girl,* by Anne Frank, for example), whereas *journal* implies a more objective account of events (*Original Journals of the Lewis and Clark Expedition*). Yet the two words are often used interchangeably, and with good reason. *The Diary of Samuel Pepys,* for instance, goes far beyond revealing details about the author's life and character to present a vivid picture of seventeenth-century London. And, while reporting on his visits to North and South America in 1946 and 1949, the French writer Albert Camus devotes a good part of his *American Journals* to introspection.

stream of consciousness / interior monologue

In his *Principles of Psychology* (1890), the American psychologist and philosopher William James first used *stream of consciousness* in describing individual conscious experience not as separate, disconnected events but as a continuous series of occurrences. The term was soon applied to a narrative technique in which prespeech levels of consciousness are explored as a way of revealing characters' fluid and shifting inner states—their thoughts, perceptions, sensations, feelings, associations, memories, and other mental processes. Writers who use this technique are likely to represent the often disorderly workings of the human mind by experimentation with the unities of time and space, disjointed syntax, and unconventional punctuation and typefaces.

Literary critics do not agree on the precise relationship between *interior monologue* and *stream of consciousness* Some say that interior monologue is the same as stream of consciousness. Others consider interior monologue to be a part of stream of consciousness, especially if the passage represents the unspoken thoughts of a single character caught up in a single event. Others believe that interior monologue, in presenting the psychic content and processes of character at various prespeech levels, is more consciously controlled than stream of consciousness. And still others make other distinctions. Yet most literary critics agree that Molly Bloom's ebb and flow of consciousness, which, without a paragraph break or a mark of punctuation, fills the last 45 pages of James Joyce's novel *Ulysses*, best exemplifies the narrative technique that revolutionized fiction toward the end of the nineteenth century.

simile / metaphor

At one time or another, everybody—not just poets and fiction writers—uses words in a nonliteral or unusual sense to add beauty, vividness, and clarity to what they are saying or writing. They might make up their own figurative language to suit a particular occasion or they might borrow a ready-made expression. The two most common figures of speech are *simile* and *metaphor*.

In a *simile* two things, often dissimilar, are compared through the use of *like* or *as*. One might say, for example, "In a computer store my grandfather is like a baby with a lollipop" or "The latecomers made their way to their seats as unobtrusively as elephants on a rampage." In her poem "A Good Woman Feeling Bad," Maya Angelou says that "persecuting / Blues I've known / Could stalk / Like tigers, break like bone." And in her novel *Lives of Girls and Women*, Alice Munro speaks of "light lying in bands on the tree trunks, gold as the skin of apricots."

A *metaphor* suggests rather than states a comparison. That is, without using *like* or *as*, it refers to something by a word or phrase that is ordinarily applied to something else. For example, in describing a governmental crisis, one might say "The ship of state is listing badly" or, in poking fun at chronic television viewers, one might speak of "a generation of couch potatoes." In his poem "Sailing to Byzantium," William Butler Yeats says, "An aged man is but a paltry thing, / A tattered coat upon a stick."

In a *mixed metaphor* two or more inconsistent metaphors are combined in a single expression, leaving the task of sorting out the images up to the reader or listener. For example, in a memo to his fellow Republicans in the California Assembly, Tom McClintock called the results of a 1990 special election "a tragic milestone in the downward spiral of our caucus."

verse / stanza

Verse has a number of poetry-related senses. For example, it is sometimes used as the equivalent of *poetry* itself (as in "The anthology includes both prose and verse"). It may refer to metrical writing or speaking that, though metered and rhymed in form, is somewhat less than serious in content ("Ogden Nash was a master of light verse"). It is often applied to a particular form of poetic composition, such as free verse. And it often designates a single line of a poem ("The first verse of Robert Penn Warren's 'Mortal Limit' reads: 'I saw the hawk ride updraft in the sunset over Wyoming'").

Stanza ordinarily refers to a group of verses, or lines—traditionally four or more—that make up a division in a poem. Most stanzas have a recurrent pattern not only in the number of verses but also in their meter and rhyme. In some poems, however, the stanzas vary a good deal in the number, length, and rhyme scheme of their verses. The possible patterns of a stanza are virtually limitless in English poetry. This is the first stanza of Warren's "Mortal Limit":

> I saw the hawk ride updraft in the sunset over Wyoming.
> It rose from coniferous darkness, past gray jags
> Of mercilessness, past whiteness, into the gloaming
> Of dream-spectral light above the last purity of snow-snags.

Canto refers to any of the main divisions of a long poem, usually an epic or narrative one. Cantos correspond to the chapters of a book.

blank verse / free verse

One of the commonest metric patterns in English poetry is *iambic pentameter;* that is, a line (or verse) in which each of five feet consists of an unaccented syllable followed by an accented one. For example, these first lines from two poems by William Wordsworth are in iambic pentameter:

> The world is too much with us; late and soon,

and

> There was a Boy: ye knew him well, ye cliffs

The first line is from the sonnet "The World Is Too Much with Us," which is said to be in *rhymed verse* because of the regular recurrence of corresponding sounds, especially at the ends of lines.

> The world is too much with us; late and soon,
> Getting and spending, we lay waste our powers:
> Little we see in Nature that is ours;
> We have given our hearts away, a sordid boon!
> . . . .

However, the second poem, "There Was a Boy," is said to be in *blank verse,* because such rhyme is lacking.

> There was a Boy: ye knew him well, ye cliffs
> And islands of Winander!—many a time,
> At evening, when the earliest stars began
> To move along the edges of the hills,
> Rising or setting, would he stand alone,
> . . . .

Free verse (also known by its French name, *vers libre*) is poetry without obvious and usual patterns of meter, line length, and stanza form, as well as rhyme. This, for instance, is how Mary Cheever's "English 53" begins:

> Standing before you I can only guess
> at what you see. For rare
> moments when you give me back
> a living image, I endure these others
> when your faces slick as glass,
> lit by incredulity, darkened by disgust,
> fuse in one backward mirror
> and I remember
> ghostly grammarians
> . . . .

Nature and Science

flora / fauna

Derived from a Latin word meaning "flowers," *flora* refers both to the plants of a specified region or time and to a descriptive, systematic list of such plants (as in "the flora of Africa"). *Fauna*, a parallel term, refers both to the animals of a specified region or time and to a descriptive, systematic list of such animals (as in "the fauna of the Tertiary Period"). In Roman mythology Flora is the goddess of flowers and Fauna, the counterpart of Faunus, is a goddess of the fields, farming, and animals.

The system of classifying animals is further refined. For example, *avifauna* designates the birds and *piscifauna* the fishes of a specified region or time. In both of these terms *fauna* is combined with another Latin-derived word element, *avis* meaning "bird" and *piscis* meaning "fish."

genus / species

The system of arranging animals and plants into natural, related groups on the basis of some common factor (structure, embryology, or biochemistry, for example) is called *taxonomy*. These are the broad, principal taxonomic groups now in use, in descending order from most inclusive to least inclusive: *kingdom* (as in "the animal kingdom"), *phylum* (in botany, sometimes *division*), *class, order, family, genus*, and *species*.

In print or writing, names in the groups below *kingdom* and above *genus* are ordinarily capitalized but not italicized. For example:

Insects and crustaceans are among the invertebrate animals in the phylum Arthropoda.

Spiders and scorpions are among the arthropods in the class Arachnida.

Cicadas and aphids are among the arachnids in the order Homoptera.

The cicada is among the homopterans of the family Cicadidae.

Both genus and species names are italicized, but whereas the genus name is always capitalized, the species name ordinarily is not (*Desmocerus californicus*, for example).

All the major taxonomic groups have natural subdivisions (*subphylum, subclass, suborder, subfamily, subgenus,* and *subspecies*). A subspecies, for instance, exhibits small but persistent morphological variations from other subdivisions of the same species living in different geographic regions or times. The subspecies name usually follows the species name and, like it, is italicized but not capitalized (*Desmocerus californicus dimorphus,* for example).

endangered species / threatened species

The dodo and the dinosaur may be the best-known animals that have disappeared from the face of the earth, but they are far from the only ones with no living descendants. Moreover, the rate of extinction is expected to rise. Air and water pollution, oil exploration, land clearing, road building, the use of pesticides, hunting, and other human activities are some of the reasons why more and more animals, vertebrate as well as invertebrate, and plants are becoming *extinct species.*

According to the U.S. Endangered Species Act, an *endangered species* is any species or subspecies of fish or wildlife or plant that is in danger of extinction throughout all or a significant portion of its range, whereas a *threatened species* is any species that is likely to become endangered within the foreseeable future. The U.S. Fish and Wildlife Service, in the Department of the Interior, periodically publishes an official List of Endangered and Threatened Wildlife and Plants, giving the common and scientific names of the species, the historic range of their habitats, their status (endangered or threatened), and other information. These are but a few of the approximately 1,000 species on the April 1990 list:

Birds—California and Andean condors (endangered); Florida scrub jay (threatened); ivory-billed woodpecker (endangered)

Mammals—African elephant (threatened); Asian elephant (endangered); giant panda (endangered); jaguar (endangered)

Reptiles—American and Cuban crocodiles (endangered); Galapagos tortoise (endangered); New Mexican ridge-nosed rattlesnake (threatened)

Amphibians—Panamanian golden frog (endangered); San Marcos salamander (threatened); Wyoming toad (endangered)

Fish—Paiute cutthroat trout (threatened); short-nose sturgeon (endangered); snail darter (threatened)

Insects—Kern primrose sphinx moth (threatened); Oregon silverspot butterfly (threatened); Tooth Cave ground beetle (endangered)

Plants—dwarf bear-poppy (endangered); Maguire primrose (threatened); pygmy fringe tree (endangered)

natural selection / survival of the fittest

According to Darwinian theory, all species of plants and animals have developed from earlier forms by the hereditary transmission of slight variations in successive generations. This theory of evolution, propounded by Charles Darwin (1809–1882), further holds that *natural selection* determines which forms will survive. That is, those individuals of a species with characters that help them become adapted to their specific environment tend to leave more progeny and transmit their characters, while those individuals less able to become adapted tend to leave fewer progeny or to die out. So, in the course of generations, there is a progressive tendency in the species to a greater degree of adaptation. A widely used but nontechnical term for *natural selection* is *survival of the fittest*.

dwarf / pygmy

In scientific usage *dwarf* and *pygmy* refer to an individual, whether an animal, plant, or person, that is much smaller than the usual one of its species, sometimes implying that the parts are deformed or not in normal proportion. For example: *dwarf salamander, dwarf Japanese quince, hypothyroid dwarf, pygmy hippopotamus, pygmy owl, pygmyweed*.

In everyday usage *dwarf* and *pygmy*, and *midget* as well, are applied interchangeably to a very small person. A *midget*, however, is generally considered a very small human being of normal form and proportions. *Manikin*, whose suffix *-kin* means "little," may denote a small man. *Pygmy*, written with a capital letter, designates any of several races of small African or Asian peoples described in ancient history and legend, and also a person belonging to any of several modern African and Asian peoples.

The International Anti-Euthanasia Task Force, which is concerned with rights for people with disabilities, advises against the use of *midget* or *dwarf* except in a description of a medical condition. Instead, the organization recommends "person, man, woman, child of short stature."

chromosome / gene

The *cell* is the functional and structural unit of all living organisms. Within the nucleus of each tiny cell are *chromosomes,* microscopic rod-shaped bodies made up mainly of DNA (deoxyribonucleic acid) and protein. Chromosomes are constant in number for each species; each cell in the human body, for example, has 46.

These 23 pairs of human chromosomes, in turn, carry linearly arranged *genes,* which determine hereditary characteristics and transmit them to succeeding generations. Each of the 50,000-plus genes in each cell of the human body, then, is the blueprint for cell construction, specifying such features as color of eyes, height, and susceptibility to certain diseases.

animal / mammal

An *animal* is any living organism other than a plant, bacterium, or virus. Most animals can move about on their own and have specialized sense organs that enable them to react quickly to stimuli. Unlike plants, they do not produce their food from inorganic sources (say, by photosynthesis); instead, they must obtain food already in the form of organic substances.

Animals that have no backbone, or spinal column, are called *invertebrates;* for example, insects and crustaceans (shrimps, crabs, etc.). Animals that have a backbone are called *vertebrates.* The five classes of vertebrates are *fish, amphibians* (frogs, toads, newts, salamanders, etc.), *reptiles* (snakes, lizards, turtles, crocodiles, dinosaurs, etc.), *birds,* and *mammals.* Fish, amphibians, and reptiles are coldblooded; birds and mammals are warmblooded. The main differences between amphibians and reptiles is that amphibians have no scales and usually begin life in the water as tadpoles with gills and only later develop lungs, whereas reptiles have lungs throughout their lives, an entirely bony skeleton, and a body covered with scales or horny plates.

Mammals are the highest class of vertebrates. As the word itself suggests (*mamma* means "breast" in Latin), mammals feed their offspring with milk secreted by the female mammary glands. Instead of producing their young from eggs, like the other vertebrates, most mammals give birth to live young. (Of all the mammals, only the platypus and the spiny anteater lay eggs.) Hair covering all or part of the body and a four-chambered heart are among the other characteristics of mammals.

According to widely accepted classifications, the highest order of mammals is *Primates,* which includes human beings, great apes, monkeys, and lemurs. Aside from a well-developed brain, skills in social organization, and the like, primates are characterized by flexible hands and feet, which are used in grasping objects. Each of the five fingers and toes typically has a flat nail instead of a claw.

Other general types of mammals include the *carnivores,* or fanged, flesh-eating mammals, such as the dog, bear, and lion; the *herbivores,* or plant-eating mammals, such as the cow, giraffe, sheep, and rabbit; the *omnivores,* such as the hog, which eat any sort of food, especially both animal and vegetable food; the *rodents,* or gnawing mammals, such as the rat, mouse, squirrel, and beaver; and the *marsupials,* such as the kangaroo and the opossum, which nurse their incompletely developed offspring in an external abdominal pouch.

group / herd

Group is the basic, general word expressing the simple idea of an assembly of animals. A number of other words are applied to certain groups of animals that feed, live, or move together. For example:

A *pride* is a group of lions.

A *herd* is a group of cattle, sheep, goats, elephants, or similar large animals. A group of goats or sheep is also called a *flock. Drove* refers to cattle, hogs, or sheep that are driven along as a group.

A *pack* is a group of hounds or wolves. Another name for a pack of hounds is *cry.* A pair of hounds or game animals is called a *brace,* and a set of three (that is, a brace and a half) is called a *leash.*

A *flock* is a group not only of goats or sheep but also of birds. A flock made up entirely of geese may be called a *gaggle.* A flock of birds flying together is a *flight.* A *brood* or *clutch* is a group of birds or fowl hatched at one time and cared for together.

A *bevy* is a group of quails or swans, and a *covey* is a group of partridges or quails.

A *swarm* is a group of butterflies, bees, or other insects. A *cloud* is a great number of locusts or gnats close together and in motion.

A *school* is a group of fish, porpoises, whales, or the like. Another name for a group of whales is *gam.* A *pod* is a small group of water animals, especially seals or whales.

larva / pupa

During their development from egg to adult, various animals undergo complex changes in form, structure, or function. In zoology, this more or less sudden physical transformation is known as *metamorphosis,* a word that comes from the Greek (*meta-,* meaning "over," + *morphē,* "form, shape," + *-osis,* "state, condition, action").

The initial, or embryonic, stage is followed by the larval stage. For example, the *larva* of the insect that will one day become a butterfly or moth is known as a caterpillar. Active but still immature, this wormlike form concerns itself mainly with feeding and growing. The larva is next metamorphosed into a *pupa,* which, in the case of a butterfly or moth, is called a chrysalis. On entering this quiescent, nonfeeding stage of development, when many anatomical changes take place, the chrysalis spins a silky or fibrous case (a cocoon) around itself for shelter. Once the body of the larva has been entirely transformed, the adult butterfly or moth emerges from the cocoon.

By a similar process of metamorphosis, a tadpole (or polliwog) is transformed into a frog or toad, a nymph is transformed into a grasshopper, and other animals go through their particular stages of development. The more complete the metamorphosis, the fewer the traces of the larval stage in the adult form.

skin / hide

The general term for the outer covering of an animal's body is *skin.* The layer of fur, hair, or wool that protects the animal and keeps it warm is called a *coat. Hide* refers to the tough skin of certain large animals, such as horses, cows, and elephants. It is tanned, or changed into leather, by soaking in tannin. *Pelt* applies to the skin, especially the untanned skin, of fur-bearing animals, such as minks and foxes.

foot / paw

Foot is the general word for the end part of the leg, on which a person or animal stands or moves. *Paw* refers to the foot of a four-footed animal having claws (sharp, hooked, or curved horny structures, or nails); for example, a dog, cat, or bear. Sometimes an animal is said to have a *talon* instead of a claw, but *talon* is ordinarily used only for birds of prey, such as a falcon or vulture. *Hoof* applies either to the horny covering on the foot of an animal such as a horse, deer, or elephant, or to the entire foot of such an animal.

horn / antler

A *horn* can be anything, besides an ear or a nose, that protrudes naturally from the head of an animal: one of the tentacles of a snail or a tuft of feathers on certain birds, for instance. But the word is generally applied to the hard, unbranched bony projection that grows, in pairs, on the head of various hoofed animals, especially cud-chewing ones like cattle, sheep, and goats. The horns are ordinarily permanent and present in both sexes. Though sometimes called a *horn*, an *antler* refers more strictly to the hard, branched bony growth on the head of a male deer, elk, caribou, or moose. The pair of antlers is shed and renewed every year.

tooth / tusk

A *tooth* is any of a set of hard, bonelike structures set in the jaws of most animals and used for biting, tearing, and chewing. Along with this general, inclusive word are two more specific ones. A *tusk* is a long, pointed, enlarged tooth projecting outside the mouth in certain animals, such as the elephant, wild boar, and walrus, and used either for digging or as a weapon. A *fang* is both a long, hollow tooth through which poisonous snakes inject their venom and a long, sharp tooth with which meat-eating animals like the wolf seize and tear their prey. (People have fangs too, since *fang* is another word for the root of a human tooth.)

snout / muzzle

Snout and *muzzle* are used interchangeably for the projecting part of the head of an animal such as a dog or horse, including the mouth, nose, and jaws. *Proboscis* designates both an elephant's trunk and a long, flexible snout of an animal like a tapir. The word appears in fact in the name of a large Bornean primate, the adult male proboscis monkey having a drooping nose up to 10 centimeters (4 inches) long. The word can also be applied to a person's nose, as the many jokes about Jimmy Durante's proboscis attest.

beak / bill

The horny jaws of a bird, usually projecting to a point, are called a *bill*, a *beak*, or a *nib*. *Beak* is likely to be used for a bird of prey, such as a falcon or vulture. Both *beak* and *bill* are applied, as well, to the protruding mouthpart of various insects, fishes, and other animals. The turtle, for example, is usually said to have a beak and the platypus a bill, but the terms are by no means fixed.

monkey / ape

Monkey is loosely applied to any of a number of hairy jungle animals that spend much of their time in trees. Yet the word is properly limited to certain superfamilies of Old and New World primates (an order of highly developed mammals characterized mainly by flexible hands and feet, each with five digits). Besides a long tail, monkeys typically have a flat, hairless face. Old World monkeys include:

The *baboon*, of Africa and Asia. These large, fierce animals have a short tail, a doglike snout and long teeth, a large head with cheek pouches, and bare calluses on the rump. The male *mandrill*, of West Africa, is marked by blue and scarlet patches on the face and rump.

The *macaque*, of Africa, Asia, and the East Indies. Whether long or short, the tail of these animals is not prehensile; that is, it is not adapted for seizing or grasping, especially by wrapping or folding around the branches of trees. Among the macaques are the *rhesus monkey*, of India, and the *Barbary ape*, of North Africa and Gibraltar. The rhesus is often kept in zoos and is used extensively in biological and medical research. The only surviving wild monkey in Europe, the Barbary ape is so called because of its apelike characteristics, including the lack of a tail.

New World monkeys are typified by a broad, flat nose with nostrils that open to the side, creating a wide, flat septum. Mainly native to South and Central America, they include:

The *marmoset*, a very small monkey with colorful, silky hair. Several South American marmosets, especially a species having black hands and feet, are called *tamarins*.

The *capuchin*, with a nearly bare face and a hoodlike crown of hair. It is named after the long, pointed hood worn by members of the Capuchin branch of the Franciscan religious order.

The *howling monkey*, a large, long-tailed monkey with a loud, howling cry.

The *spider monkey*, with long, spidery limbs, a long, prehensile tail, and a thumb that is either rudimentary or absent.

Although in loose usage the word *ape* refers to any Old or New World monkey, it is properly applied to the Old World primates most closely related to human beings. These animals, like humans, are typified by a nose with the nostrils placed close together and opening to the front.

They have no tail, and their hands and feet make them particularly suited to tree-dwelling, at least part of the time. The family known as the *great apes* includes:

The *gorilla,* of equatorial Africa. The largest and most powerful of the great apes (the adult male weighing up to 225 kilograms, or about 500 pounds), the gorilla is, despite its historical misrepresentation, generally shy, intelligent, and vegetarian.

The *orangutan,* of the swampy, coastal jungles of Borneo and Sumatra. It has shaggy, reddish-brown hair, very long arms, small ears, and a hairless face, and is smaller than the gorilla.

The *chimpanzee,* of equatorial Africa. Somewhat larger than the orangutan but not nearly as large as the gorilla, it is covered with long, black hair and has large, outstanding ears. It is able to walk erect very well and is considered to be the most nearly human of the apes in intelligence. Some captive *chimps,* as chimpanzees are often called informally, are said to have been taught to communicate through sign language or by using a computer.

The *gibbon* too is an ape, though not of the family of great apes. This small, slender, long-armed animal comes from India, southern China, and the East Indies. A *siamang* is a very agile black gibbon of the Malay Peninsula and Sumatra.

cougar / puma

A *cougar* is a large, powerful, tawny cat, with a long, slender body and a long tail. This peculiarly American animal is found from Canada to Patagonia, at the southern end of South America. It has several other common or local names, including *puma,* a word which originated in the South American Indian language known as Quechua and which came into English by way of Spanish; *catamount;* and the Americanisms *mountain lion* and *painter. Panther,* too, is applied to this animal, as well as to a large or fierce leopard.

camel / dromedary

A *camel* is either of two species of large, domesticated cud-chewing animals with a humped back, a long neck, and large, cushioned feet. Mainly because of their unusual strength and their ability to store water and surplus fat as a food reserve in their body, camels are the common beast of burden in Asian and African deserts. One species, ranging from North Africa to India, is the one-humped *Arabian camel*. The *dromedary* is an Arabian camel, especially one trained for fast riding. The other species is the two-humped *Bactrian camel*, which is native to central Asia (Bactria being the name of an ancient country in what is now northeastern Afghanistan). Besides having an additional hump, the Bactrian camel is shorter, heavier, and hairier than the Arabian camel.

llama / alpaca

The *llama*, of the Andean region of South America, is a smaller, humpless member of the camel family. This animal, especially a domesticated species, is used as a beast of burden and as a source of wool, meat, and milk. The *alpaca*, a domesticated llama, is prized for its long, silky brown or black wool. Two forms of the llama are found wild: the woolly, reddish-brown *guanaco* and the small *vicuña*, with soft, shaggy wool. The woolly hair of the alpaca and vicuña, as well as the various fabrics made from it, is known by the names of these animals.

purebred / Thoroughbred

A *purebred* is an animal or plant belonging to a recognized breed with characters maintained through generations of unmixed descent. The noun *Thoroughbred* applies to any of a breed of light horse developed by crossing Arabian and Turkish stallions with English mares and bred primarily for racing. In referring to a horse, dog, or other animal with a recorded or known line of descent, the adjective *thoroughbred* is freely interchanged with *purebred, pedigreed, truebred,* and *well-bred.*

donkey / mule

A *donkey* is a domesticated ass. The *ass*, especially the common wild ass of Africa, is a horselike mammal with long ears and a short mane. A *burro* is also a domesticated ass, but it is more likely to be called a burro instead of a donkey when used as a pack animal in the southwestern United States. A *mule* is the offspring of a donkey and a horse, particularly the offspring of a male donkey (a *jackass*) and a female horse (a *mare*). A *hinny* is the offspring of a female donkey (a *jenny*) and a male horse (a *stallion*). These hybrids are almost always sterile.

pig / hog

Domesticated *pigs* and *hogs* are usually known collectively as *swine,* omnivorous, even-toed hoofed mammals with a bristly coat, a small tail, and an elongated, flexible snout. According to the classification of meat animals in the United States, a *hog* is a domesticated adult swine that, when ready for market, weighs more than 120 pounds (about 54.5 kilograms), whereas a *pig* is an immature swine weighing less.

Most domestic swine are descended from the *wild boar* (*boar* for short) of Europe, Africa, and Asia. This animal, noted for its prominent tusks, has a coarse coat and thin legs. The word *boar* applies also to an uncastrated male swine. A *razorback* is a wild hog, originating from domestic stock of the southern United States, with a slender body, a ridged back, and long legs.

rabbit / hare

Both the *rabbit* and the *hare* belong to the same family of swift mammals having long ears, soft fur, a cleft upper lip, a short tail, and long, powerful hind legs. Yet the two animals differ in several ways. Rabbits are generally smaller than hares, have shorter ears and legs, and run rather than leap. Rabbits live in burrows, while hares live in the open or among rocks, thickets, or other hiding places. Rabbits give birth to blind, naked offspring, while hares produce furry, active young.

A *cottontail* is any of several common North American rabbits with a brownish fur coat but a short, fluffy tail that is white underneath. Cottontails are identified with American woodlands, yet in the classic children's story *The Tale of Peter Rabbit,* by the English writer and illustrator Beatrix Potter, one of Peter's well-behaved sisters is called Cotton-tail. *Bunny* or *bunny rabbit* is a pet name that children use for any rabbit. Though *jack rabbit* combines a clipped form of *jackass* with *rabbit,* this Americanism is popularly applied not to a rabbit but to any of several large North American hares having long, donkeylike ears, as well as strong hind legs.

porcupine / hedgehog

A *porcupine* is a gnawing mammal that has coarse hair mixed with long, stiff, sharp spines that can be raised—and embedded in any predator that comes too close. There are two families of porcupines: the Old World family, whose members live in burrows or in caves in the rocks, and the New World family, whose members live mostly in trees.

A *hedgehog* is a small insect-eating mammal native to the Old World. The animal probably got is name from the fact that it has a hoglike snout and generally lives in a row of closely growing shrubs, bushes, or trees known as a hedge. Hedgehogs resemble porcupines in that they too have a shaggy coat and sharp spines, which bristle and form a defense when the animals curl up. The American porcupine is often, though loosely, called a hedgehog.

woodchuck / groundhog

A *marmot* is any of a large group of thick-bodied, gnawing squirrels with coarse fur and a short, bushy tail. One such marmot, of North America, is commonly called either a *woodchuck* or a *groundhog*. Yet, though these two Americanisms are almost always interchangeable, only *groundhog* is mentioned in connection with a traditional weather prediction. On February 2, according to the tradition, the animal comes out of hibernation; if it sees its shadow, it supposedly returns to its hole for six more weeks of winter. This day is known as Groundhog Day, not Woodchuck Day.

ermine / weasel

Ermine, as applied to the soft, white fur used for women's coats, suggests wealth, fashion, and grand living. On the other hand, with the agile, bushy-tailed animal that feeds on rats, birds, and eggs as the starting point, *weasel* calls to mind a sly, cunning, or sneaky person—not someone invited to join the beautiful people for tea at the Ritz. Yet the ermine, whose white fur is used to make or trim coats, is really a weasel trapped in winter. During the summer the animal's fur turns brown.

mouse / rat

A *mouse* and a *rat* are long-tailed animals belonging to related subfamilies of rodents. Mice are smaller, more timid, more graceful, and cleaner than rats, which live in filthy places and carry such highly contagious diseases as the bubonic plague. The perception of rats as dangerous and unattractive is evident in expressions like "I smell a rat" (suggesting that treachery or chicanery is afoot); in the slang sense of *rat* to designate a sneaky, contemptible person, specifically an informer, a scab, or someone who deserts or betrays a cause (from an old seafarers' superstition that rats leave a doomed ship before it sets sail); and in the slang term *rats!* as an exclamation of disgust, scorn, or disappointment. No such disparagement attaches to expressions like "quiet as a mouse," "poor as a church mouse," and even "when the cat's away the mice will play." In folklore and children's stories centering on animals—from Aesop's "The Lion and the Mouse" to Disney's "Mickey Mouse" to Leo Lionni's *Frederick*—mice are also likely to be portrayed as lively, friendly, intelligent creatures. The few fictional rats that come off rather well include kindly old Walter Rat in Kenneth Grahame's *The Wind in the Willows* and Templeton, the selfish but helpful barnyard rat in E. B. White's *Charlotte's Web.*

The notion of the mouse as friendly and appealing is reinforced by some computer manufacturers. To position a cursor or other object on the display screen of the microcomputer, the user moves a small electronic box about on a pad or the flat surface of a desk. This box, with one or more buttons and a long cord, is known as a mouse. Given the public's sensibilities, calling it a rat would be unthinkable.

dolphin / porpoise

A *dolphin* and a *porpoise* are small-toothed whales. The two fishlike marine mammals resemble each other so closely that in everyday usage the names are often interchanged. However, the dolphin is larger than the porpoise; it is relatively slim and trim, whereas the porpoise is torpedo-shaped; and its snout is typically beaklike, whereas the porpoise's is blunt. Both animals, but especially dolphins, have been the subject of many studies concerning their behavior, intelligence, navigation system, and complex means of communication. Bottlenose dolphins' ability to learn new tricks and their willingness to perform in public make them a favorite at marine parks. Yet none can claim the fame of the porpoise Flipper, whose movie and television career goes back to the 1960s.

seal / sea lion

A *seal* is a marine animal with a doglike head, a torpedo-shaped body, and four webbed feet, or flippers. Seals, which live in cold or temperate waters and usually eat fish, are divided into two families: *eared seals* and *earless seals*. Besides distinct external ears, eared seals have hind limbs that allow them to move about on land. The best-known members of this family are the commercially prized *fur seal*, which has soft, thick underfur, and the *sea lion*, which has no underfur and generally lives in colonies along the coastline of the Pacific Ocean. Earless seals have inconspicuous ears and rudimentary hind limbs. One famous member of this family is the migratory arctic *harp seal*, whose pups have a white, woolly coat. Another is the large, dark-gray *hooded seal* of the North Atlantic, the male having on its head a hoodlike sac that can be inflated.

frog / toad

Frogs and *toads* are both tailless, leaping amphibians that, through the complex process known as metamorphosis, develop from tadpoles. In appearance, the two animals differ mainly in that the frog's skin is smooth and moist while the toad's is rough, warty, and dry. Most frogs are able to live either on land or in water, but toads live in water only during the breeding season—otherwise on moist land. Frogs, as well as toads, lay their eggs in water.

tadpole / polliwog

The larva of certain amphibians, such as frogs and toads, is known as either a *tadpole* or a *polliwog.* This early, free-living, immature form, which lives in water, has gills and a tail. As it matures, the gills are usually lost and legs develop. These interchangeable words may well have a common origin, at least in part. The Middle English *taddepol* comes from *tadde,* meaning "toad," + *poll,* meaning "head"—hence a "toad that seems all head." *Polwygle,* also a Middle English word, probably comes from *poll* + *wigelen,* meaning "to wiggle"—hence a "wiggling head."

The complete physical transformation undergone by a tadpole, or polliwog, as it develops into a frog is known as metamorphosis.

turtle / tortoise

Both a *turtle* and a *tortoise* are reptiles. They have a toothless beak and a soft body encased in a hard shell into which, in most species, the head, tail, and four legs may be withdrawn. Although the terms are properly interchangeable for all species, *turtle* is usually applied to those that live in water, especially the sea, and *tortoise* to those that live on land.

The *terrapin* belongs to a family of North American terrestrial, freshwater, or tidewater turtles. The *diamondback* (*diamondback terrapin* in full), found in coastal salt marshes from Cape Cod to Mexico, is particularly prized for its meat.

alligator / crocodile

There are so many similarities between the *alligator* and the *crocodile* that the differences are not immediately apparent. Both are large, flesh-eating, lizardlike reptiles of the same order (Crocodylia); both have thick, horny skin composed of scales and plates; and both live in and around tropical rivers and marshes. Though both are extremely dangerous, the crocodile is considered more aggressive than the alligator. In appearance, they differ mainly in two ways: the alligator's snout is shorter and blunter than the crocodile's; and the alligator's closed mouth shows no teeth, whereas the crocodile's fourth tooth of the lower jaw (counting from the end of the snout) can be seen to fit into a pocket of the upper jaw. The geographic locations differ too. Alligators are found largely in the coastal plain of the United States, from Texas to North Carolina, and in eastern China; crocodiles, in southern Florida and in Africa south of the Sahara.

The *caiman* and the *gavial* are also crocodilian reptiles. Caimans, which are similar to alligators, live in Central and South America. Gavials, which have a very long, slender snout more like that of the crocodile, live in northern India. The word *gavial* (*false gavial* in full) is also applied to a medium-sized crocodile of Borneo and Sumatra.

lizard / salamander

Although the *lizard* and the *salamander* are often mistaken for one another because of their similar body shape, they are quite different. *Lizards* are small to moderately large reptiles, of the same order of vertebrate animals as snakes. They typically have a long, slender body and tail; four legs, whether well formed or barely visible; a dry scaly skin; and clawed toes. Most species of lizards, which include the chameleon, iguana, Gila monster, and gecko, live in hot, dry regions. In loose usage, the word *lizard* is applied to any of various reptiles or other animals that look somewhat alike, including alligators and even salamanders.

Yet, despite their long lizardlike body and tail, *salamanders* are amphibians, not reptiles. Some live on land; some live in the water; and some, like newts, live both on land and in the water. Nor do all salamanders begin life in the water as gill-breathing tadpoles and later, through metamorphosis, develop into lung-breathing vertebrates; instead, some hatch their young directly from eggs. Unlike lizards, salamanders have a soft, moist skin and no claws. Several, like hellbenders and mud puppies, are edible.

snake / viper

Snake is the general name for any of a limbless suborder of reptiles with an elongated, scaly body, lidless eyes, and a tapering tail. Some, but relatively few, species have a poisonous bite that is harmful or fatal to humans. Garter snakes, green snakes, and water snakes are among the many nonpoisonous snakes found in North America. Nor are all snakes living on other continents poisonous; however, some, like anacondas, boa constrictors, and pythons, crush their prey to death.

Serpent is often applied to any snake but especially to a large or poisonous one. *Sea serpent*, like *sea snake*, designates a family of poisonous snakes living in tropical seas. Ordinarily, however, *sea serpent* refers to any large, unidentified or imaginary serpentlike animal reported to have been seen in the sea. Some people believe, for example, that the Loch Ness monster is a sea serpent that has been living in a Scottish lake since prehistoric times.

Viper, too, frequently replaces the generic *snake* in speech and print. However, it more strictly applies to any of a widespread family of venomous snakes with long fangs attached to the front of a rotating upper jaw. The asp that Cleopatra supposedly clasped to her breast in committing suicide would probably have been the poisonous North African horned viper. The subfamily of vipers known as *pit vipers* have heat-sensitive pits on the sides of the head that enable the snakes to home in on their prey. Pit vipers found in North America include the rattlesnake, copperhead, and water moccasin.

The words *snake, serpent,* and *viper* have similar extended senses drawn from the reptiles' practice of stalking or ambushing their prey and then swallowing it alive. All three suggest malice, spite, and treachery. The phrase *snake in the grass* reinforces the notion of hidden danger or of a treacherous person who is seemingly harmless.

water moccasin / cottonmouth

Rivers and swamps in the southeastern United States are home to the *water moccasin,* a large, poisonous, olive-brown pit viper with horizontal bars. Also called a *cottonmouth* (because of the whitish interior of its mouth), this viper is often confused with various harmless snakes, especially several water snakes.

eagle / condor

The *eagle* and the *condor* have a good deal in common. Both are birds of prey, although the condors are considered vultures—that is, scavengers, feeding chiefly or entirely on the decaying flesh of dead animals—whereas, like hawks and falcons, eagles generally kill their own prey. Both the condor and the eagle are huge birds, the 3-meter (10-foot) wing span of the condor making it the largest bird of prey and that of some species of eagles not being far behind. And species of both birds, including the Andean and California condors and the North American bald eagle, are in danger of extinction. The *bald eagle,* the national bird of the United States, is so called not because it has no feathers on its head but because these feathers are white, just as they are on the neck. A naked head and neck is, however, characteristic of vultures, like the condor and the turkey vulture (or turkey buzzard), whose feathers thus do not become soiled while the birds are feeding on carrion.

crane / stork

A *crane* is any of a family of wading birds with very long legs and neck, and a long, straight bill. The large, white North American *whooping crane,* noted for its long, loud call, is, like a number of other cranes, an endangered species.

In everyday usage, the word *crane* is often applied to any of various unrelated birds, such as the *stork, heron,* and *flamingo,* probably because these too are often seen standing on one leg. Best known among the storks is the European white stork, which nests on rooftops and in trees. It is a symbol of childbirth, parents having told their children over the years that "the stork brought you." Two species of storks are on the endangered list: the Oriental white stork, whose habitats are in China, Japan, Korea, and the Soviet Union, and the wood stork, found in the United States, Mexico, and Central and South America. *Flamingo,* a Portuguese loanword, goes back to the Spanish *flamenco,* meaning, literally, "Flemish," and associated with *flama* ("flame"), because of the bird's bright pink or red feathers.

duck / goose

The many species of *ducks, geese,* and *swans* are known collectively as *waterfowl.* A *duck* is relatively small, with a flat bill, short neck and legs, and webbed feet. The female is called a *duck;* the male, a *drake;* and the young of either sex, a *duckling.*

A *goose* is like a large duck except that its neck is much longer. The word refers especially to the female, *gander* being applied to the male. A young goose is called a *gosling.*

A *swan,* which has a large body, an even longer neck, and, typically, pure white feathers, is a graceful swimmer and strong flier. Neither the male nor the female has a distinguishing name, though a young swan is called a *cygnet.*

parrot / parakeet

A *parrot* is any of a large number of tropical or subtropical birds with a hooked bill, brightly colored feathers, and feet having two toes pointing forward and two backward (making it easier for the birds to grasp food and to hold on to tree branches). A tame parrot is sometimes called a *poll parrot,* a *poll,* or a *polly,* from the name Polly, which, like Molly, is a diminutive of Mary. Anyone who asks "Polly want a cracker?" might well get an answer, or at least a repetition of the question, since many parrots are able to mimic human speech, as well as other birds and mechanical sounds.

A *parakeet*, a small, slender parrot with a long, tapering tail, is particularly popular as a pet. A *lorikeet*, in turn, is a small parakeet. It is so named because its tongue—with a fringed, brushlike tip for feeding on soft fruits and nectar—resembles that of the *lory*, a brightly colored, short-tailed parrot native to Australia and the East Indies. A *budgerigar* (often shortened to *budgie*) is an Australian parakeet having a greenish-yellow body, marked with bright blue on the cheeks and tail feathers, and wings striped with brown. Another small parrot is the *lovebird*, so named because the mates, when kept in a cage, appear to be greatly attached to each other. Lovebirds, most of which are chiefly green or delicate gray, come from Africa, Asia, and South America.

The largest of the parrots is the Central and South American *macaw*, noted for its bright plumage, long tail, and loud, raucous call. Also quite large and noisy is the *cockatoo*, native to Australia and the East Indies. The only parrots with a raised crest, cockatoos usually have predominantly white plumage, often tinged with yellow or pink.

insect / bug

An *insect* is any of an extremely large group of small invertebrate animals that includes butterflies, grasshoppers, ants, bees, beetles, cockroaches, flies, and mosquitoes. Most insects undergo the complex physical transformation known as metamorphosis. As adults, true insects have a body divided into a head, thorax, and abdomen; three pairs of jointed legs; and, usually, two pairs of membranous wings. In popular usage, the word *insect* is applied to any small arthropod, whether winged or wingless, such as a spider, centipede, or mite.

A *bug* (or *true bug*) is any of a special group of insects, characterized by beaklike sucking mouthparts and partly membranous forewings thickened toward the base. Water bugs, squash bugs, and bedbugs are this kind of bug. The word *bug* often refers also to any small insect, especially if regarded as a pest; for example, a louse, cockroach, or scorpion. In another sense, this one informal, *bug* is used as the equivalent of *germ* as a disease-causing microorganism.

butterfly / moth

In the last stage of their metamorphosis a *butterfly* and a *moth* emerge from a cocoon, to begin life as an adult insect. Both have a sucking mouthpart, a slender body, ropelike antennae, and four scaly wings. However, moths are typically smaller than butterflies, their wings are usually not as brightly colored, and the tips of their antennae are simple or feathery rather than knobbed. Most butterflies fly from flower to flower by day, feeding on nectar, whereas most moths do so by night.

bee / wasp

A *bee* is any of a very large family of broad-bodied, four-winged, hairy insects having biting as well as sucking mouthparts and legs especially adapted for gathering pollen and nectar. Most bees have painful stings. Although many bees are solitary, some live in organized colonies where each member performs specific tasks for the common welfare. The *honeybee*, or common hive bee, and the yellow-and-black *bumblebee* are particularly noted for their social habits. The honey that bees make as food from the nectar of flowers is stored in a structure of six-sided wax cells known as a honeycomb. Researchers eager to produce a highly efficient honeybee developed a vicious hybrid in Brazil. After escaping from a Brazilian breeding experiment in 1957, this South American bee, known as the *killer bee* or *Africanized honeybee*, spread northward throughout much of the continent. In October 1990 the first identified swarm in the United States was trapped in Texas, near the Mexican border. Measures were immediately put into effect to destroy the invaders, which threaten not only to cut the production of honey but also to devastate farmers who depend on honeybees to pollinate their fruit and vegetable crops.

A *wasp*, also belonging to a large family of flying insects, resembles the bee in some ways. The female has a vicious sting that can be used repeatedly. Like bees, some wasps are solitary while others are social. The *mud daubers*, for example, are solitary wasps that build cells of hard, caked mud for their larvae. Best known among the social wasps are the *hornet* and the *yellow jacket*, which build papery hanging nests whose cells contain the larvae. These complex communities are made up of males, females, and workers. Intruders are savagely attacked: thus the expression *mad as a hornet*.

dragonfly / darning needle

A *dragonfly* is a large insect that has narrow, transparent, net-veined wings and feeds mostly on flies, mosquitoes, and other smaller insects while in flight. Because its long, thin body resembles a needle used in mending, say, socks, a dragonfly is known also as a *darning needle* and a *devil's darning needle* (even though it is harmless to people). A *damselfly*, a slow-flying, usually brightly colored dragonfly, is distinguished by its habit of holding its long wings vertically when at rest.

firefly / glowworm

A *firefly* (also called a *lightning bug* or *lightning beetle*) is any of a family of nocturnal beetles having a long, soft body and, on the underside of the abdomen, a special organ that produces flashes of light of various colors. The winged males emit the flashes while in flight; the wingless females do so from the ground. The name *glowworm* is applied to both the female and the larva of the firefly.

grasshopper / locust

The name *grasshopper* is often applied to several kinds of leaping, plant-eating insects which generally undergo incomplete metamorphosis; that is, the larval stage partially carries over to the adult form. Most species have large chewing mouthparts, powerful hind legs adapted for jumping, and narrow, hard forewings that cover membranous hind wings. Usually only the males produce the sounds associated with these insects.

Among the so-called short-horned grasshoppers, the *locust* is well known for the devastation it occasionally causes. Traveling in swarms so large that they blacken the countryside, migratory locusts destroy nearly all vegetation in the areas they visit. Best known in the family of long-horned grasshoppers is the *katydid,* whose name is echoic of the shrill sound the male makes by rubbing together highly developed organs on the forewings. The *cricket,* too, has a name suggestive of the sound produced by the male, in this case a creaking or chirping sound. Related to grasshoppers, crickets belong to any of various families of generally dark-colored, leaping insects that typically have long antennae.

Though often associated with grasshoppers, the *cicada* is a large, flylike insect of an order that includes aphids, mealybugs, and other insects especially destructive to plants. The male cicada makes a loud, shrill sound by vibrating a special organ on its undersurface. The *periodical cicada,* better known as the *seventeen-year locust,* lives underground as a larva for from 13 to 17 years before emerging as an adult to live in the open for a brief period.

termite / ant

At first glance, a *termite* is often mistaken for an *ant.* One reason is that both insects are often found in large colonies. Another is that both are so small that their physical differences are barely visible. Yet the *ant* is more closely related to the wasp, bee, and other highly specialized insects that undergo complete metamorphosis. Ants, which are found in all parts of the world, are black, brown, or red. They have a biting, sucking mouth; a waistlike division between thorax and abdomen; and, when winged, four membranous wings. Their complex social organization centers on workers, males, and a queen. Often scavengers with a taste for sugary foods, ants tend to become household pests.

A *termite* is a social insect that does not undergo complete metamorphosis; in other words, the adult form shows traces of the larval stage. For instance, in the soft, pale body there is no clear division between thorax and abdomen. Termites are found in the temperate zones and especially in the tropics. They live in large colonies composed of winged forms that mate and wingless workers and soldiers that are usually sterile or immature. Because they feed on wood, termites can be very destructive to trees and wooden buildings.

shrimp / prawn

The main differences between a *shrimp* and a *prawn* are that the prawn is larger and lives in both fresh and salt water, whereas the shrimp is found mainly in the sea. Both, though, are relatively small, slender, long-tailed, and 10-legged invertebrate animals. As the name of the subphylum to which they belong—Crustacea—suggests, they have a hard crust or shell. Other characteristics of crustaceans are that they usually live in the water, though some live on land, and they breathe through gills.

lobster / crayfish

As crustaceans, like shrimp, prawns, crabs, and a number of similar invertebrate animals, *lobsters* and *crayfish* (or *crawfish*) have a hard outer shell, they usually live in the water, and they breathe through gills. The lobster, however, lives in the sea, while the crayfish lives in fresh water. Besides, the lobster is larger, and the powerful pincers formed by the first pair of its 10 legs are noticeably unequal. Both shellfish are highly prized as food.

plant / bush

The plant (or vegetable) kingdom is, like the animal or mineral kingdom, one of the three great divisions into which all natural objects have been classified. As a living organism, a *plant* resembles an animal. Yet it differs in several important ways, mainly in being confined to one place, in having rigid cell walls and no specialized sense organs, and in being able, usually through photosynthesis, to produce its own food from inorganic sources.

A low, woody perennial plant with several permanent stems instead of a single one is called either a *shrub* or a *bush*. In everyday usage, *shrub* seems to be the more general word and *bush* the more specific. We are, for example, apt to say "a flowering shrub" but "a lilac bush," and to describe a bramble as "a prickly shrub of the rose family" but call the shrub itself a bramblebush.

Another common use of the word *plant* is in reference to a young tree or shrub ready to be put into other soil for growth to maturity. That is, *plant, slip, cutting,* and sometimes *set* are freely interchanged. A *houseplant* is an indoor plant used primarily for decoration.

deciduous plant / evergreen plant

The adjective *deciduous* comes from a Latin verb meaning "to fall off." In botany it is applied to a plant that sheds all its leaves every year. The maple tree and the grape vine, for example, are *deciduous plants.* On the other hand, an *evergreen plant* (*evergreen* for short) has leaves that are green all year. Most cone-bearing trees, such as the pine and cedar, and many broad-leaved plants, including some rhododendrons, are evergreens.

annual / perennial

A plant that reaches maturity and completes its life cycle in one growing season is called an *annual.* Zinnias, marigolds, and flax, for example, die after producing flowers and seed for the first time. A plant whose life cycle lasts more than two years—that is, one which produces flowers and seed from the same root structure year after year—is called a *perennial.* Irises, orchids, and carnations are among the perennials. In between is a *biennial,* which lasts two years, usually producing flowers and seed during the second growing season. Winter wheat, for instance, is planted in the fall and ripens the following spring or summer. Some plants fall into more than one category, depending on the climate where they are grown.

blossom / bloom

A *bud* is a small swelling or projection on a plant, from which will develop a shoot (a sprout, twig, or other new growth), a cluster of leaves, or what is called interchangeably a *blossom, bloom,* or *flower.* The word *bud* applies also to a partly opened blossom, bloom, or flower, whose petals, which are likely to be showy and colorful, have not yet fully emerged.

Blossom, bloom, and *flower* are freely substituted for one another in reference to flowers collectively (as in "Have you ever seen as many blossoms [blooms, flowers] on a rose bush?"). The three words are interchangeable also in reference to the state or time of flowering ("The azaleas are already in blossom [bloom, flower]"). Yet in certain contexts one word is more common than another. For example, *blossom* is apt to be used if qualified by the name of a plant which bears edible fruit. That is, we might speak of "cherry blossoms," but probably not "cherry blooms" or "cherry flowers."

leaf / blade

Leaf is the general word for any of the flat, thin, expanded organs, usually green, that grow laterally from the stem or twig of a plant. *Blade* applies especially to a leaf of grass, and *frond* to a leaf of either a fern or a palm.

Leaves get their green color from chlorophyll, a plant pigment essential to photosynthesis (the chemical process by which carbon dioxide and water are converted into organic substances, especially sugars, by means of sunlight). The leaves of some trees and other plants change color in autumn not because of frost, as many people believe, but because the chlorophyll begins to break down with age and is partly replaced by red, yellow, and purple pigments.

woods / forest

A *wood* (or, usually, *woods*) is any thick growth of trees. A *grove* is a small wood or group of trees without underbrush. A *forest* is a large wood; that is, a thick growth of trees and underbrush covering an extensive tract of land. A *jungle* is land covered with a dense growth of trees, thick underbrush, tall vegetation, vines, and the like. Jungles are typically found in tropical regions and are inhabited by predatory animals.

All these words, except *grove*, are often used metaphorically. For example: Someone who is "out of the woods" is, in informal usage, out of difficulty or danger. Someone who "can't see the forest for the trees" is unable to pick out the essentials from the mass of surrounding details. And someone who spends hours driving in heavy traffic is likely to moan, "It's a jungle out there."

sequoia / redwood

Probably the world's tallest living trees, and among the oldest, belong to the genus *Sequoia* (named in honor of Sequoyah, a noted Cherokee scholar and leader who lived from about 1760 to 1843). Only two species of the true sequoias are alive today: the *redwood*, which is found in coastal regions of California and southern Oregon, and the *giant sequoia*, which prefers the higher altitudes of the Sierra Nevada. Many of these mammoth evergreens grow to about 300 feet (about 91 meters) or more. They typically have huge trunks; thick, fire-resistant bark; enduring, soft wood; small cones; and needlelike leaves.

211

The common names of these trees are often interchanged. The *giant sequoia* is known also as a *big tree*, a *California big tree*, or a *redwood*. And the *redwood* is known also as a *California redwood*, a *coast redwood*, or a *sequoia*.

succulent / cactus

Derived from a Latin word meaning "juice," *succulent* describes many things that are not dry, from "succulent pork" to "a succulent novel." It is also a botanical term, applied, as both a noun and an adjective, to a wide variety of plants that have thick, fleshy tissues for storing water. The thick-leaved jade plant is a succulent. So is the tropical American desert agave, or century plant. And so is the *cactus*, which is any desert plant, native to the New World, that typically has a fleshy stem, reduced or spinelike leaves, and often showy flowers. Some cactuses, like the one popularly called the "old man cactus," are small enough to fit on kitchen windowsills; others, like the giant saguaro, dominate the barren landscape of the southwestern United States and northern Mexico. In short, all cactuses are succulents, but not all succulents are cactuses.

skin / rind

The covering on certain fruits and vegetables is ordinarily known as a *skin*, especially if, as on grapes, peaches, carrots, and potatoes, it is thin and tight. *Rind*, on the other hand, usually refers to the thick, hard or tough covering on fruits such as oranges, grapefruit, and watermelons. This general distinction does not apply to all fruits and vegetables, for the thick, tough covering on, say, bananas and avocados is called a *skin*, not a *rind*. Once removed, either skin or rind is usually known as a *peel*: an orange peel or a potato peel, for example.

Both *hull* and *husk* are applied to the dry outer covering of certain fruits, grains, and seeds. The leaves that enclose an ear of corn, for instance, are usually known as the *husk*. But the husk of a grain, the pod of a pea, and the shell of a nut may each be called a *hull*.

seed / stone

Flowering plants typically produce an embryo which has both a protective coat and stored food and which, under the proper conditions, can develop into a new plant. This fertilized and mature ovule is called a *seed*, as in "watermelon seed," "mustard seed," or "sesame seed." Loosely, *seed* is applied to any part of a plant—a bulb, tuber, and the like—from which a new plant can grow: "a potato seed," for instance.

One of several small seeds of a fruit like the apple, pear, or orange is often called a *pip* (short for *pippin*, which comes from an Old French word meaning "seed"). The single stonelike seed of a fruit like the date is called, appropriately, a *stone*. A *pit* is the hard stone that contains the seed of the apricot, cherry, plum, peach, and most other fruits classified as drupes, or stone fruit.

avocado / alligator pear

Probably because an *avocado* is often used in a salad, along with lettuce, onions, and the like, many people consider it a vegetable. However, this product of the tropical avocado tree—with a thick, yellowish-green-to-purplish-black skin; pear shape; buttery flesh; and single large seed—is a fruit. Some varieties of avocado have a rough skin resembling that of an alligator, so the fruit is known also as an *alligator pear*.

plum / prune

Plums and *prunes* have a good deal in common. In the everyday speech of the ancient Romans both fruits were called *pruna*, and *Prunus* is the genus to which the plum belongs. A *plum* is the fruit of any of various small trees of the rose family, called plums or plum trees. It has a smooth skin that is generally dark bluish-red or reddish-purple, somewhat tart flesh, and a flattened stone at the center. It is eaten raw and used in cooking. *Prune* is the name commonly given to a plum that has been dried for eating. Yet a prune is also any of several varieties of plum that are grown in many parts of the world.

When it comes to their extended senses, however, the two words are quite different. In American slang, a *prune* is a dull or otherwise unpleasant person, whereas a *plum* is something choice or desirable; specifically, a well-paying job requiring little work.

raisin / currant

A *raisin* is any of various kinds of sweet grapes that have been dried. Some raisins are seedless from the start, while others have their seeds removed. Though generally eaten raw, raisins are sometimes used in cooking (especially sauces) and in baking (for instance, raisin bread, raisin pie, and plum pudding, which, despite its name, is no longer made with plums).

A *currant* is the raisin of a small, seedless grape used in cooking. It is also—as when used in jams and jellies—the small, sour red, white, or black berry of several species of hardy shrubs.

filbert / hazelnut

Many trees and the fruits they bear have the same names (apple, mango, and so on). It is therefore not surprising that the edible nut of a filbert, a genus of the birch family, is also called a *filbert*. This word, which English probably borrowed from Norman French, goes back to St. Philibert, whose feast was celebrated in the nutting season. Other names for both tree and fruit are *hazel*, and the fruit is commonly known as a *hazelnut* as well.

latitude / longitude

To pinpoint locations on the earth's surface, geographers and others use the words *latitude* and *longitude* in connection with various imaginary lines drawn on that surface. The lines of latitude, called *parallels,* circle the earth in an east-west direction, parallel to the *equator,* which has all of its points equally distant from both the North and South Poles. The lines of longitude, called *meridians,* circle the earth in a north-south direction, passing through the two poles and points in between. The *prime meridian* passes through Greenwich, England, in connecting both poles.

Latitude is the distance north or south from the equator, measured in degrees, minutes, and seconds (1 minute being the 60th part of a degree of an arc and 1 second being the 60th part of a minute). The equator is at 0° latitude, the North Pole is at 90° north latitude, and the South Pole is at 90° south latitude. So Minneapolis, at about 45° north latitude, is roughly halfway between the equator and the North Pole. The two parallels of latitude known as the Tropic of Cancer and the Tropic of Capricorn are 23°27' north and 23°27' south of the equator, respectively, marking the northern and southern boundaries of the Tropics.

Longitude is the distance east or west, measured as an arc of the equator between the meridian passing through a particular place and the prime meridian, which is at 0°. The longitudes of all other points are measured in degrees east or west of Greenwich, from 0° to 180°. Berlin, for instance, is at about 20° east latitude, and Peoria, Illinois, at about 90° west latitude.

Arctic Circle / polar circle

Polar circle and *Arctic Circle* are used interchangeably for the imaginary circle that is parallel to the equator and about 66°34'north of it. And *polar circle* and *Antarctic Circle* are used interchangeably for the similar imaginary circle that is the same distance south of the equator. So unless the reader or listener can tell from the context which of the two circles is meant, the term *polar circle* is apt to be ambiguous.

horse latitudes / doldrums

The *horse latitudes* are oceanic belts that encircle the earth at approximately 30° to 35° north and south latitudes. Calms, light wind, high barometric pressure, and hot, dry weather characterize these regions, which are said to be so named because, while dead in the water for a long time, sailing vessels transporting horses to the West Indies often had to throw some of the animals overboard because of water shortages.

Doldrums refers to equatorial ocean regions also noted for dead calms and light, fluctuating breezes. These climatic effects are caused by the meeting of two sets of trade winds, blowing steadily toward the equator from the northeast in the tropics north of the equator and from the southeast in the tropics south of the equator. Yet the term, which may go back to a native English word meaning "dull" with the influence of *tantrum*, is more likely to be used in its nonnautical senses: low spirits, or a dull, gloomy, listless feeling, and also a state of sluggishness or complete inactivity. We might, for example, complain about being in the doldrums or talk about the economic doldrums following World War II.

ocean / sea

Ocean comes from a word the ancient Greeks used for "the outer sea," which they thought of as a great river lying beyond the Mediterranean and flowing around the earth. Today *ocean* refers, first, to the great body of salt water that covers about 71 percent of the earth's surface (as in "The ocean is the earth's thermostat, cooling the atmosphere in summer and warming it in winter"). And, second, it refers to any of the four principal geographic divisions of that immense body of water (the Atlantic, Pacific, Indian, or Arctic, each called an ocean in its own right).

Sea generally denotes either a large body of salt water wholly or partly enclosed by land (the Red Sea, the Irish Sea) or a large body of fresh water (the Sea of Galilee). However, in scientific as well as everyday usage, *sea* is freely interchanged with *ocean* in the sense of the continuous body of salt water covering the greater part of the earth's surface, as in "studies of the ocean (sea) floor." Both words are mixed and matched in phrases like "an oceanfront (seafront) hotel," "a seagoing (oceangoing) vessel," and "an ocean (sea) breeze." And both are used metaphorically to suggest vastness or very great amounts, as in "drowning in a sea (ocean) of debt." Yet each word has its particular ways of joining with others to express thought, so it would go against the grain of the language to substitute one for the other indiscriminately. For example: *ocean basin, ocean liner, ocean sunfish,* but *seafood, sea gull, sea change.*

shore / coast

Shore is the general word for an edge of land directly bordering on the sea or ocean, a lake, a river, or other body of water. For example: Columbus reached the shores of Cuba and Hispaniola in 1492. Chicago rises on the southern shore of Lake Michigan. Great civilizations have flourished on the shores of the Nile.

Coast is limited to land along a sea or ocean. So while one can apply *shore* and *coast* interchangeably to Chile's westernmost region, bordering the Pacific, one is not apt to say that Chicago rises on the southern coast of Lake Michigan or that great civilizations have flourished on the coasts of the Nile. The informal Americanism *Gold Coast* is an exception, for it designates a district where rich people live, especially along the shore of a lake (as in "Chicago's Gold Coast"). Another informal American usage is *the Coast*, meaning specifically "the Pacific coast." So a New York producer might say, "I'm taking the red-eye to the Coast," whereas a Los Angeles producer might say, "We'll finish filming on the east coast" (or, more likely, "back East").

Beach applies to a nearly level stretch of pebbles and sand on a shore, whether the stretch is along Copacabana, in Rio, or along the shore of Lake Wallenpaupack, in the Poconos of Pennsylvania. *Strand* is a poetic word for shore or beach, especially one at the edge of a sea or ocean. *Bank* applies to rising or steep land at the edge of a stream or river.

river / stream

River refers to a large amount of fresh water that flows naturally into an ocean, a lake, or another river. *Stream, brook, creek,* and *rivulet* are often applied interchangeably to any small river. Yet these words and several other related ones have their own shades of meaning. Besides suggesting a small river flowing in a channel or along a similar course, *stream* denotes a strong, steady current in water, whether a larger river or the ocean; for example, the Gulf Stream. *Creek* commonly refers to a small stream. *Brook*, popular in place names (Stonybrook, Meadowbrook, Brook Park, and so on), is, like *rivulet* and *rill*, a somewhat literary term.

In this comparison, *run* suggests a small, swift river. The Americanism *branch* refers either to one of the streams into which a river or large creek may divide, usually near the mouth, or to a large tributary flowing into a river. Particularly in the South, the word implies a small stream, such as a brook, rivulet, or run, that usually flows into a creek. So to Americans the term *branch water* is both water from a small stream or brook and water, especially ordinary tap water, used for mixing with whiskey or other liquor.

glacier / iceberg

A *glacier* is a large mass of ice and snow that forms in areas where the rate of snowfall is always greater than the rate at which the snow melts. It moves slowly outward from the center of the accumulation or down a mountain until it melts or breaks away. During the Pleistocene Epoch, between 1.8 million and 10,000 years ago, continental glaciers covered much of northern North America and northwestern Europe. Like *glacial, glacé,* and even *cold, glacier* is believed to stem from an Indo-European word form meaning "to freeze."

An *iceberg,* such as the one that sank the *Titanic* in 1912, is a great mass of ice broken off from a glacier and floating in the sea. The word *iceberg* (*berg* for short), is of Scandinavian origin, *isbjerg* meaning "ice mountain" in Danish. Several interrelated terms with *ice* as the first element further define glaciers and icebergs. *Ice cap* and *ice field,* for instance, denote an extensive mass of thick ice, generally in a highland area, which may feed valley glaciers about its borders. In another sense, *ice field,* like *ice floe,* applies to an extensive area of floating sea ice, specifically an area 8 or more kilometers (5 or more miles) across. Yet *ice floe* refers, as well, to a single piece, large or small, of floating sea ice. *Ice shelf* designates a thick mass of glacial ice which extends along a polar shore, often resting on the bottom near the shore with the seaward edge afloat, and which may protrude hundreds of kilometers out to sea. *Ice sheet* refers to a thick layer of ice covering an extensive area for a long period, as in the geologic time period popularly known as the *ice age.*

lava / magma

Lava is the name given either to molten rock issuing from a volcano or to such rock when solidified by cooling. This molten rock originates deep within the earth, where it is called *magma.* When magma cools and solidifies, it becomes *igneous rock,* of which lava is one type. Other, very different varieties of igneous rock result when magma cools more slowly beneath the surface of the earth. Most of the solid matter making up our planet is in fact igneous rock or derived from it. Like *ignite* and *ignition, igneous* comes from a Latin word meaning "a fire." Another name for this kind of rock—*pyrogenic rock*—also conveys the notion of extreme heat or fire.

stalactite / stalagmite

Both derived from a Greek word meaning "to drop or drip," *stalactite* and *stalagmite* refer to mineral deposits formed in caves by dripping water. As the mineral-rich water trickling from the roof of a cave evaporates, it leaves behind icicle-shaped stalactites that grow downward from the roof. Similarly, cone-shaped stalagmites slowly build up on the floor of the cave, often from the continual dripping of the stalactites above. An easy way to keep the distinction in mind is to associate *stalactite* with *tight*, as in "hold tight" to keep from falling down.

big-bang theory / steady-state theory

Cosmology, the scientific study of the form, content, organization, and evolution of the universe, has produced many theories and hypotheses over the centuries. According to the *big-bang theory*, the expansion of the universe began with a gigantic explosion of primordial matter between 10 and 20 billion years ago, and eventually the galaxies, stars, planets, and everything else in that universe may come crashing together again (the big crunch). The *steady-state theory*, whose supporters are dwindling, holds that the universe has neither a beginning nor an end and that new matter is continuously being created, thus keeping the average density of the expanding universe constant.

star / nova

To most people a *star* is any of the luminous celestial objects seen as points of light in the sky. Astronomers are more precise: to them a star is a self-luminous celestial body having continuous nuclear reactions that send radiation (including light) and subatomic particles in all directions. The sun is a typical star.

In suggesting a first appearance, the word *nova* (meaning "new" in Latin) is misleading, for the type of star it designates is not new but variable. It is an existing star that suddenly increases in brightness by a factor of 100 or more, and then decreases in brightness over a period of months to years. *Supernova*, however, is an accurate description of a nova that suddenly explodes into dazzling brilliance; indeed, for a short time a supernova may shine as brightly as its entire galaxy.

A *neutron star* is a small but extremely dense collapsed star composed almost entirely of neutrons. Such a star is believed to be at the center of a *pulsar*, a spinning celestial object that emits electromagnetic radiation, especially radio waves, at short and very regular intervals. Another starlike celestial object that emits radio waves and light is a *quasar* (the word being derived from *quasi-stellar radio source*), also known as a *quasi-stellar object*. Quasars, which are thought to be the ancient, exploding origins of new galaxies, are perhaps the most distant and oldest observable objects in the universe.

asteroid / planetoid

An *asteroid* is any of the thousands of small planets ranging from 1,000 kilometers (621 miles) to less than 1 kilometer (0.62 mile) in diameter, with orbits usually between those of the planets Mars and Jupiter. The word comes from *astēr,* meaning "star" in Greek, + *-oid,* meaning "something resembling." Such a minor planet used to be called a *planetoid.*

meteor / meteorite

Outer space is populated by many small, fast-moving solid chunks of matter. While in this interplanetary flight, such a piece of extraterrestrial rock is called a *meteoroid.* If it enters the earth's atmosphere, its white-hot tail glowing across the night sky, it becomes a *meteor* (also called a *shooting star,* a *falling star,* or a *fireball*). And if, instead of burning up in the earth's atmosphere as most meteors do, it plunges to earth as a mass of metal or stone, it becomes a *meteorite.* In loose usage, however, the word *meteor* is applied to all three: a meteoroid, a meteor, and a meteorite.

Meteorology is not concerned with the study of meteors, even though the word shares the Greek root *meteōra* (meaning "things in the air"). The term refers both to the science of the atmosphere and atmospheric phenomena and to the study of weather, including weather forecasting.

red giant / white dwarf

In one system of classification, in which numbers and letters are replaced by descriptive names, astronomers convey a great deal of information about the age, size, mass, and chemical composition of stars. They group the stars in five categories, according to their luminosity, or total amount of radiant energy emitted per second: *supergiants, bright giants, giants, subgiants,* and *dwarfs.* A *giant,* or *giant star,* for example, is a star that is at least 30 times larger and more than 100 times as luminous as the sun. A *dwarf,* or *dwarf star,* such as the sun, is a star of relatively small size or mass and low luminosity.

Color designations add to the fairy-tale quality of this scientific classification. Red stars being the coolest and blue-white stars the hottest, a *red giant* is an aging star whose core has cooled off and whose outer regions have expanded enormously. Even without a telescope, stargazers can see the redness of Betelgeuse, in the constellation Orion. A *white dwarf* is even further along in the process of stellar evolution, having heated up, contracted, and collapsed under the gravity of its tightly compressed core. A faint white dwarf is a companion star to Procyon, one of the brightest stars in the sky.

The distinctions are by no means sharp. So, along with the well-known red giants and white dwarfs, there are *red dwarfs, white* and *blue-white giants, yellow dwarfs* (like the sun), and *black dwarfs* (burnt-out cinders). In 1989, astronomers claimed to have discovered a region of *brown dwarfs*—objects somewhere between planets and stars, which shine dimly before shrinking away.

black hole / white hole

Today's astronomers do a lot of speculating about two related but very different hypothetical objects: a *black hole* and a *white hole*. Most of them believe that a *black hole* is the invisible remains of a collapsed star, with an intense gravitational field from which neither light nor matter can escape. They hypothesize that a *white hole*, on the other hand, does not trap matter and energy, but instead is an exit port for matter and energy taken into a black hole. Besides possibly spilling out black holes, white holes may explain quasars. The existence of black holes is widely assumed on the basis of astronomical observations; the reality of white holes is far more conjectural.

atmosphere / stratosphere

The *atmosphere*, called *air* in everyday usage, is a gaseous envelope that surrounds the earth and rotates with it, kept in place by gravity. As the atmosphere extends outward into interplanetary space, it undergoes changes in temperature, chemical composition, density, and other features. Taking these changes into account, meteorologists and space scientists have divided the atmosphere into five interconnected layers, with transition zones between them.

The *troposphere*, the layer immediately above the earth's surface, extends from sea level outward to about 11 km (about 7 miles). Only in the lower few miles of this layer can humans breathe and live naturally and comfortably. This is where what we call weather occurs, and, owing to the large amount of water vapor, there are many clouds. The temperature, like the air pressure, generally decreases with increasing height. Propeller-driven aircraft and commercial jets are at home in the troposphere.

The *stratosphere*, at an altitude of about 11 to 50 km (about 7 to 30 miles), is not as dense as the troposphere, it contains less water vapor, and its temperature rises with increasing altitude. At the lower levels, several bands of high-velocity winds called *jet streams* move from west to east around the earth. The *ozone layer* (at about 25 km, or 15 miles) absorbs much of the harmful ultraviolet radiation from the sun. Supersonic airliners, military jets, and rockets make their way into the stratosphere.

The *mesosphere,* at an altitude of about 50 to 80 km (about 30 to 50 miles), is the coldest layer of the atmosphere. Because it is beyond the reach of aircraft, scientists rely mainly on large helium balloons, rockets, and spacecraft for information about the composition of its gases. Low-altitude auroras are known to originate here.

The *thermosphere* extends from about 80 to 300 km (about 50 to 185 miles). Largely because of powerful energy from the sun and other kinds of radiation, the temperature rises dramatically with increasing altitude. Its lower levels coincide with the beginning of the *ionosphere,* which extends outward to the undefined regions of the atmosphere. Ultraviolet wavelengths of the sun's radiation are so intense in the ionosphere that they split molecules and atoms into their component parts, creating ionized, or electrified, air. Meteors burn up, and atomic particles striking and exciting atoms produce northern and southern lights. Radio waves are reflected back to earth; and noctilucent ("night-shining") clouds reflect twilight to the earth long after sunset or long before sunrise, a phenomenon called *airglow.*

The *exosphere,* the outmost portion of the atmosphere, begins at an altitude of about 300 km (about 185 miles) and gradually fades into interplanetary space. It is made up of a hot layer of hydrogen and helium atoms. ICBMs (intercontinental ballistic missiles) are designed to pass through the exosphere before seeking their targets on earth. And most artificial satellites spend their useful lives in this atmospheric region and in the upper part of the thermosphere.

In *atmosphere* and the names of the five layers, the Greek-derived *sphere* is combined with a descriptive word element: *atmos* (a Greek word for "vapor"); *tropo-* (from the Greek *tropos,* meaning "a changing"); *strato-* (from the Latin *stratum,* "a covering or blanket"); *meso-* (from the Greek *mesos,* "middle"); *thermo-* (from the Greek *thermē,* "heat"); and *exo-* (from the Greek *exō,* "without, beyond").

stratus cloud / cumulus cloud

A *cloud* is a visible mass of tiny, condensed water droplets or ice crystals suspended in the atmosphere. Traditionally, clouds have been grouped in these four categories:

Stratus, a type of gray cloud found at low altitudes and consisting of a uniform layer of water droplets and sometimes ice crystals.

Cumulus, a type of bright, billowy cloud with a dark, flat base, developing vertically through all cloud levels and consisting mostly of water droplets. A round mass of cumulus clouds appearing before a thunderstorm is called a *thunderhead.*

Cirrus, a type of white cloud found at high altitudes, resembling a wispy filament and consisting of ice crystals.

Nimbus, a type of rain-producing cloud.

The basic characteristics of those clouds are carried over to the four larger groups, or families, in which clouds are commonly classified today:

A (high clouds, above 6,000 meters, or 20,000 feet): *cirrus; cirrostratus,* a thin, whitish cloud consisting of ice crystals; *cirrocumulus,* a white cloud resembling a small puff, flake, or streak and consisting of ice crystals and water droplets. Cirrostratus clouds often produce *halo phenomena;* that is, rings of light that seem to encircle the sun, moon, or other luminous bodies, as a result of refraction of light through ice crystals in the atmosphere. A sky covered with rows of small, fleecy, cirrocumulus clouds is called a *mackerel sky,* because it calls to mind the streaks on the back of such a fish.

B (intermediate clouds, between 2,000 and 6,000 meters, or between 6,500 and 20,000 feet): *altostratus,* a gray or bluish cloud consisting of a thick, dense, extensive layer of ice crystals and water droplets and often causing light precipitation; *altocumulus,* a white or gray cloud resembling a sharply defined, wavy patch and consisting of water droplets. Like those of the cirrocumulus type, altocumulus clouds produce mackerel skies.

C (low clouds, below 2,000 meters, or 6,500 feet): *stratus; stratocumulus,* a white or gray cloud consisting of large, smooth or patchy layers of water droplets and possibly some hail or snow; *nimbostratus,* an extensive gray cloud consisting of dense, dark layers of water droplets, rain, or snow and obscuring the sun.

D (clouds of great vertical continuity): *cumulus; cumulonimbus,* a cloud developing vertically through all cloud levels, consisting of water droplets, ice crystals, and sometimes hail, and associated with thunder, lightning, and heavy showers.

contrail / vapor trail

When an airplane or rocket passes overhead, especially at a high altitude, it sometimes forms a white cloudlike trail of condensed water vapor. This trail is called either a *contrail* (a blend of the first three letters of *condensation* plus *trail*) or a *vapor trail.*

new moon / blue moon

The moon looks quite different to us at various times during the 29-plus days it takes to complete one revolution around the earth with respect to the sun. We therefore use different terms to describe its phases. In the following descriptions the references to right and left assume a view from the Northern Hemisphere; the view from the Southern Hemisphere would be reversed.

A *new moon* is in the first phase, when the moon is between the earth and sun, with its dark side toward the earth. At this time the moon cannot be seen at all (unless it happens to be exactly in line between the earth and the sun, and in this case it appears as a black disk partly or completely covering the sun in a solar eclipse).

A *waxing crescent moon* is in the second phase, when the moon appears to have one concave edge and one convex edge. At this stage it is the sliver at the right side of the moon that reflects sunlight to the earth.

A *first-quarter moon* is in the third phase, when only the right half of the moon's face reflects sunlight to the earth.

A *waxing gibbous moon* is in the fourth phase, when more than half, but not all, of the moon's face reflects sunlight to the earth. Again, it is the right portion that is lighted. As used here, *waxing* conveys the notion of growing gradually larger, and *gibbous* suggests a swelling or hump.

A *full moon* is in the fifth phase, when the moon is on the side of the earth away from the sun, with its entire face reflecting sunlight to the earth. A full moon in September, at or about the time of the autumnal equinox, is sometimes called a *harvest moon.* The full moon after the harvest moon is called the *hunter's moon.*

A *waning gibbous moon* is in the sixth phase, when more than half but not all of the moon's face reflects sunlight to the earth. This is opposite from the waxing gibbous stage, so now the left portion of the moon is lighted.

A *last-quarter moon* is in the seventh phase, when only the left half of the moon's face reflects sunlight to the earth.

A *waning crescent moon* (also called an *old moon*) is in the eighth phase, when the moon again appears to have one concave edge and one convex edge. This time it is the sliver at the left side of the moon that reflects sunlight to the earth. The next phase is that of the new moon, signaling the start of another lunar month.

Blue moon applies not to a phase of the moon but to its rare bluish tint, caused by dust particles in the upper atmosphere. By extension, the term suggests any infrequent occurrence (as in "Once in a blue moon the IRS pays out money"). Given the lunar cycle, two full moons seldom occur in a single month. When they do, the second one, with no change in color, is known as a blue moon.

solar eclipse / lunar eclipse

Although an *eclipse* can be the partial or total obscuring of any celestial body by another, the word usually suggests two particular kinds to earthlings: a *solar eclipse,* which occurs when the moon passes between the sun and the earth, and a *lunar eclipse,* which occurs when the moon passes through the earth's shadow. Neither kind of eclipse is possible unless the sun, moon, and earth are aligned.

A solar eclipse (also called an *eclipse of the sun*) takes place only during new moon. Although the moon is much smaller than the sun, its closeness to the earth makes it seem large enough to cover all or most of the solar disk with its dark side. During partial eclipses, which occur several times a year, the moon covers only a part of the sun. Total solar eclipses are rarer and can be seen only in places that are in the path of the moon's shadow as it sweeps across the face of the earth.

A lunar eclipse (or *eclipse of the moon*), which occurs two or three times a year, is visible to most people on the side of the earth away from the sun. Because at such times the earth must be between the sun and moon, lunar eclipses occur only during full moon. The red rays of the sun being refracted by the atmosphere of the earth, the moon may take on a burnished copper or faint orange hue while it is eclipsed. Like a solar eclipse, a lunar eclipse can be total or partial. An *annular eclipse,* in which a ring of sunlight can be seen around the disk of the moon, is considered neither total nor partial.

equinox / solstice

The *equinox* is the time when the sun crosses directly above the equator, making night and day of equal length in all parts of the earth. In the Northern Hemisphere the *vernal equinox* occurs about March 21 and the *autumnal equinox* about September 22. The term *equinox* comes from Latin words meaning "equal" and "night," and *vernal* comes from one meaning "belonging to spring."

Solstice, whose first element, *sol,* is related to "the sun," is short for *summer solstice* and *winter solstice.* In the Northern Hemisphere the *summer solstice* occurs when the sun is farthest north of the celestial equator on the celestial sphere, on about June 21. This is therefore the day of the year having the longest period of sunlight. Again in the Northern Hemisphere, the *winter solstice* occurs when the sun is farthest south of the celestial equator on the celestial sphere, on about December 21. So this is the day of the year having the shortest period of sunlight. Both the references to the seasons and the durations of sunlight are, of course, reversed for the Southern Hemisphere.

weather / climate

Weather is the condition of the atmosphere at a particular time and place, as defined by air temperature, barometric pressure, humidity, rainfall, cloudiness, and wind speed. It can therefore change from day to day and even within a single day. Commenting on the "sumptuous variety" of New England weather, Mark Twain noted in 1876, in a speech to the New England Society: "In the spring I have counted one hundred and thirty-six different kinds of weather inside of twenty-four hours."

Climate is weather viewed over the long haul—that is, the prevailing or average weather conditions of a place or region, as determined by the meteorological changes that occur in all seasons during a period of years. Latitude, proximity to continents and oceans, and local geographic features all affect climate. Argentina, for example, is situated in a temperate zone, where winters are ordinarily cool or cold and summers are ordinarily warm or hot. So a Clevelander speaking to an acquaintance in Buenos Aires probably would not ask, "What's the climate like?" Yet on, say, a January day, "What's the weather like?" would be a logical question, for a summer heat wave might have Buenos Aires in its grip. (In a Southern Hemisphere country like Argentina the seasons occur at opposite times of the year from those in a Northern Hemisphere country like the United States.)

thermometer / barometer

A *thermometer* is an instrument for measuring temperatures. It usually consists of a graduated glass tube with a sealed, capillary bore in which mercury, colored alcohol, or another liquid or gas rises or falls as it expands or contracts from changes in temperature. The two elements in this Greek-derived word are *thermo-*, in the sense of "heat," + -*meter*, meaning "a device for measuring."

A *barometer* is an instrument for measuring atmospheric pressures. (*Baro-*, also borrowed from the Greek, means "weight or pressure, especially atmospheric pressure.") A mercury barometer, the most common kind, is an evacuated and graduated glass tube in which a column of mercury rises or falls as the pressure of the atmosphere increases or decreases. Barometers are used in weather forecasting (a rising barometer generally indicates fair weather; a rapidly falling barometer, stormy weather) and in determining height above sea level (atmospheric pressure decreases with increasing altitude).

windchill index / chill factor

It is bad enough to be outside when the temperature is only 15°F (about −9°C), but if the wind is blowing at 30 miles (about 48 kilometers) an hour, it feels like −25°F (about −32°C). This happens because both low temperature and wind cause body surfaces to lose heat, so a combination of cold and wind makes a body feel colder than the actual temperature. A measurement of the cooling effect of a given temperature and a given wind speed is called a *windchill index,* a *windchill factor,* or a *chill factor.* It is only an approximation, since individual bodies vary in size, shape, and metabolic rate.

mist / fog

Fog is a large mass of water vapor condensed to fine particles at or just above the earth's surface, making it difficult or impossible for people to see very far. *Mist* is a similar mass of condensed water vapor, but one that is less thick and obscuring. *Haze* is a collection of particles of fine sand, smoke, dust, and so on, widely scattered in the air, the lack of transparency making distant objects indistinct. *Smog* is a dark, heavy mixture of fog, smoke, and chemical fumes from industrial centers. The word itself is a blend of *sm(oke)* + *(f)og. Smaze* is a mixture of smoke and haze, similar to smog both in appearance and in the way its name was formed.

Mist, fog, and *haze* are often used figuratively to suggest the blurring of a thing, concept, perception, or the like. One might speak, for example, about "penetrating the mist in which the Dark Ages have been enveloped"; "lifting the fog of doubt that settled over the jurors"; or "spending a weekend in a boozy haze."

sleet / hail

Sleet is partly frozen rain, or rain that freezes as it falls. The transparent or translucent pellets of ice produced by this wintertime precipitation are smaller than .5 centimeter (.2 inch) and a good deal firmer than the soft, white, crystalline flakes that fall as snow. The icy coating formed when rain freezes on trees, streets, and the like is also known as sleet. *Hail* is not only a more solid form of precipitation than sleet but it can occur during a thunderstorm at any time of the year. Hailstones, or frozen raindrops, are rounded pieces of ice that ordinarily range between .5 centimeter (.2 inch) and about 8 centimeters (3 inches). Some, however, are as large as grapefruits and heavy enough to break the windshields of cars.

earthquake / temblor

As its two parts indicate, the word *earthquake* refers to a shaking or trembling of the crust of the earth. This violent movement of the earth, caused by underground volcanic forces or by breaking and shifting of rock beneath the surface, has several other names, including *quake, temblor* (a Spanish loanword), and *tremor.* Yet, however popular in everyday usage, *quake* is not limited to this kind of natural disaster on our planet. It might, for example, be a clipped form of *moonquake,* since the surface of the moon is also subject to trembling, which is thought to be caused by internal rock slippage or, possibly, meteorite impact.

tsunami / tidal wave

A *tsunami* (from the Japanese *tsu,* "a harbor," + *nami,* "a wave") is a huge sea wave caused by a great disturbance, usually an earthquake, under an ocean. Rising higher and higher as it approaches the shore, a tsunami (also called a *seismic wave*) can result in death and destruction.

The nontechnical term *tidal wave* is often applied to a tsunami. It more appropriately designates any destructive sea wave that is caused by strong winds. Despite its name, a tidal wave is not related to the tides.

tornado / cyclone

People who live in certain parts of the world take seasonal weather patterns in stride: wind, rain, snow, even blizzards. What makes headlines is the unleashing of intense, often devastatingly or explosively powerful forces of nature. For example:

A *tornado* is a violently whirling column of air, with wind speeds of about 160 to 480 kilometers (100 to 300 miles) per hour, extending downward from a cumulonimbus cloud. Tornados, which develop especially in Australia and the central United States, are almost always seen as rapidly rotating, slender clouds that usually destroy everything along their narrow path. The term *funnel cloud* generally applies to a funnel-shaped cloud hanging below the greater thundercloud mass of a tornado, but sometimes to a tornado that does not touch the ground.

In informal usage, *twister* refers to either a tornado or a cyclone. *Cyclone,* in fact, is loosely applied to any windstorm with a violent, whirling movement, including a tornado or hurricane. Meteorologists, however, consider a *cyclone* to be a system of rotating winds over a vast area, spinning inward to a low-pressure center (counterclockwise in the Northern Hemisphere) and generally causing stormy weather.

A *hurricane* is a violent tropical cyclone usually originating in the West Indies. Winds moving at more than 117 kilometers (72 miles) per hour are often accompanied by torrential rains. Yet winds of hurricane force sometimes occur in the absence of a hurricane system. A *typhoon* is also a violent tropical cyclone, but it originates in the western Pacific, especially in the South China Sea.

A *monsoon* is a seasonal wind of the Indian Ocean and southern Asia, blowing from the southwest between April and October, and from the northeast during the rest of the year. The word is applied also to the season during which this wind blows from the southwest, usually bringing heavy rains. And, in fact, to any wind that either reverses its direction seasonally or blows constantly between land and adjacent water.

contamination / pollution

The verbs *contaminate* and *pollute,* like their corresponding nouns, *contamination* and *pollution,* have to do with making something impure by contact with or addition of some unwholesome substance. For example, water can be said to be either contaminated or polluted by the discharge of sewage and industrial wastes into rivers and lakes without proper treatment. And both *contaminant* and *pollutant* apply to any substance that causes such corruption. So car exhaust fumes can be designated as either air contaminants or air pollutants. Yet when it comes to describing adverse effects on the natural environment, *pollution* is more commonly used than *contamination* nowadays (air pollution, water pollution, noise pollution, and the like). But pesticides seeping into the ground are said to cause food contamination, and nuclear bombs radioactive contamination.

greenhouse effect / global warming

Much as the glass panes of a greenhouse keep the air inside warm, certain gases, including carbon dioxide, methane, oxides of nitrogen, and chlorofluorocarbons (CFCs), trap heat from the sun on the earth's surface. This *greenhouse effect*, many scientists believe, threatens to produce a *global warming* that could lead to the extinction of animal and plant species, rising sea levels, and shifts in wind and rainfall patterns, with disastrous consequences for agriculture and the economy.

A number of proposals have been put forward to reduce emissions of greenhouse gases and thus prevent global warming. They include phasing out CFCs and other polluting chemicals, replacing fossil fuels with cleaner sources of energy, making cars and appliances more fuel-efficient, modifying agricultural practices, and halting the worldwide destruction of forests.

centripetal force / centrifugal force

In studying action-reaction force as applied to circular motion, Isaac Newton, in the early eighteenth century, coined two terms that are still widely used today: *centripetal* and *centrifugal*. Both have their roots in Latin, and both begin with a word element meaning "center." *Centripetal force* is an inward force (*petere*, in Latin, means "to fall, rush at"). That is, the force required to keep an object moving in a circular path tends to pull that object toward the center of the circle. For example, the moon or an artificial satellite speeding around the earth would leave its orbit and fly off into space if it were not for the centripetal force exerted on it by the earth's gravity.

Centrifugal force, the equal and opposite reaction to centripetal force (*fugere*, in Latin, means "to flee"), is the force that the revolving object exerts on the source of the centripetal force; for example, the pull of the moon's gravity on the earth. The effect popularly called "centrifugal force" in the sense of an outward force keeping the revolving object "out there" is not a true force at all: it is an apparent outward force due to the momentum of the object moving in a circular path. If the centripetal force on an object were suddenly removed, the object would not move radially outward, away from the center, as might be expected if a centrifugal force were acting on it. Instead, it would continue moving in a straight line in the direction it was moving at the instant the centripetal force was removed. Nevertheless, the concept of centrifugal force is useful as a convenient way of visualizing and studying effects associated with rotary motion. We might say, for example, that by using centrifugal force, dairy equipment separates cream by throwing it outward from the milk. Similarly, a salad spinner holds the lettuce within a rotating inner container while forcing the water, through holes or slits, into a stationary outer container.

atom / molecule

As early as the fifth century B.C., Democritus and other Greek philosophers were expounding *atomism,* the theory that the universe is made up of tiny, simple, indivisible particles that cannot be destroyed. Indeed, the English word *atom* comes from the Greek *atomos,* meaning "uncut, indivisible." Modern physics, however, has shown that atoms are themselves divisible (mainly into neutrons, protons, and electrons). Yet, even though they are no longer considered the basic component of all matter, atoms continue to occupy an important place in the physical world. An atom is any of the smallest particles of an element (such as oxygen or sodium) that can chemically combine with similar particles of other elements to produce a compound (such as water or sodium chloride).

Molecules are made up of atoms. A molecule is the smallest unit of matter that can exist in the free state and still retain all the properties of the element or compound of which it is a part. The molecules of elements consist of one atom or two or more similar atoms; those of compounds consist of two or more different atoms.

liquid / fluid

A *liquid* is a readily flowing substance that takes on the form of its container but stays the same in volume. It is unlike a solid because its molecules move freely with respect to each other, and it is unlike a gas because its molecules do not expand into a space indefinitely. Water that is neither ice nor vapor is a liquid.

A *fluid* is any substance that can flow, that is able to change shape without separating when under pressure. A fluid can therefore be a liquid like water or motor oil. But it can also be a gas like steam, or a viscous substance like lava issuing from a volcano. So while all liquids are fluids, not all fluids are liquids.

color / shade

A general term, *color* refers to the wavelength composition of light, particularly its visual appearance. Passing white light through a prism produces these colors of the visible spectrum: red, orange, yellow, green, blue, indigo, and violet, each shading into the next. Some people think of the name Roy G. Biv to keep these seven prismatic colors in order. They are of course the same colors that appear in consecutive bands in the rainbow, which is an arc or ring formed in the sky by the refraction, reflection, and dispersion of light in rain or fog.

Shade ordinarily refers to any of the gradations of a color with reference to its degree of darkness (as in "a light shade of green"). *Hue*, often equivalent to *color*, indicates a modification of a basic color ("an orange or reddish hue"). *Tint* applies to a gradation of a color with reference to its degree of whiteness and suggests a paleness or delicacy of color ("pastel tints"). *Tinge* suggests the presence of a small amount of color, usually diffused throughout ("white with a tinge of blue").

primary color / secondary color

Among the seven main colors of the light spectrum (red, orange, yellow, green, blue, indigo, and violet), red, green, and blue are considered *primary colors* because their light beams, when variously combined, can produce any color. When it comes to dyes, pigments, and paints, however, the primary colors are red, yellow, and blue, which, when mixed in various ways, produce the *secondary colors;* for example, orange (a mixture of red and yellow), green (a mixture of blue and yellow), and purple (a mixture of red and blue).

Complementary colors are any pair of colors that, combined in the right intensities, produce white or nearly white light. Black, white, and gray are often called colors, although black results from the complete absorption of light rays, white from the reflection of all the rays that produce color, and gray from an imperfect absorption of all these rays.

The term *black light* refers to invisible ultraviolet or infrared radiation used mainly for fluorescent effects and photography in the dark.

blackout / brownout

A failure in the generation or transmission of electricity can cause a shutdown lasting anywhere from a few minutes to a few days. Such a total loss of power is generally called an *outage* if it occurs in a localized area, and a *blackout* if it is wide-ranging. A *brownout* is a period of low voltage during which lights, though not turned off entirely, are apt to be dimmed.

Some utility companies allow brownouts to occur in order to maintain service during periods of overload.

rust / corrosion

If an implement made of iron or steel (a gardening spade, for instance) is left outdoors for a long time, exposure to air and moisture will coat the metal or alloy with a reddish-brown or reddish-yellow film and eventually wear the metal away. This process, which can also be caused by the action of a chemical agent like salt or acid, is usually called *corrosion* or, especially in everyday speech and writing, *rusting,* and the film formed on corroded metals or alloys is usually called *rust,* though sometimes *corrosion* as well. Most commonly, the film is caused by oxidation, in which oxygen atoms combine with atoms of the metal to produce metallic oxides. The surfaces of many structures, equipment, and objects that either contain or are derived from iron are therefore coated, plated, or given other kinds of preventive treatment. Stainless steel, for example, is a corrosion-resistant alloy containing not only the iron and carbon that customarily go into steel but also chromium and, generally, lesser amounts of other elements.

fission / fusion

Nuclear energy and *atomic energy* refer interchangeably to the energy released from an atom in nuclear reactions or in radioactive decay. Both terms apply particularly to the energy released in *nuclear fission* (also called *atomic fission* or simply *fission*) and *nuclear fusion* (*atomic fusion* or *fusion*).

In *nuclear fission* the nuclei of atoms of such heavy elements as uranium and plutonium are split into two lighter fragments of approximately equal mass. The products together have slightly less mass than the original nucleus, and this difference in mass is converted to energy. As more and more nuclei are broken apart, the nuclear reaction becomes a chain reaction, releasing huge amounts of energy. This is the principle of the atomic bomb.

In *nuclear fusion* the lightweight nuclei of tritium and deuterium atoms are combined (fused) into a nucleus of helium. In this case the helium nucleus has less mass than the original atoms, and the difference, again, is converted to energy. This is the basic process going on in the sun and other stars, and is the principle of the hydrogen bomb.

Once the fission reaction was controlled in nuclear reactors, it was put to use generating electric power. Although the fusion reaction is a cleaner source of energy in that it produces much less dangerous radioactive waste, it has yet to be contained for more than a split second.

atomic bomb / nuclear bomb

The term *nuclear bomb* encompasses two very destructive types of bomb: the *atomic bomb* and the *hydrogen bomb*. The *atomic bomb* (or *atom bomb* or *A-bomb*) was first used in warfare in 1945 by the United States against the Japanese cities of Hiroshima and Nagasaki. Its power results from the immense quantity of energy suddenly released when a very rapid chain reaction of nuclear fission is set off by neutron bombardment in the atoms of a charge of plutonium or uranium. In the *hydrogen bomb* (or *H-bomb* or *thermonuclear bomb*), an initial atomic bomb explosion creates the intense heat and pressure necessary to start nuclear fusion of the heavy isotopes of hydrogen (deuterium and tritium), producing an even greater explosion than is possible with an A-bomb alone.

A small thermonuclear warhead for battlefield use, a *neutron bomb* is designed to use radiation rather than the heat energy released in nuclear fusion. It is intended to disable or kill enemy soldiers without destroying buildings, vehicles, and other nonliving objects. Because it would produce little immediate fallout and relatively short-lived radiation contamination, it is euphemistically called a "clean bomb."

guided missile / ballistic missile

Missilery has come a long way since Germany used jet-propelled *buzz bombs* against Great Britain and other Allied countries during World War II. These small, pilotless planes (also called *robot bombs, robombs,* or *flying bombs*) were steered by a preset guidance system. Nowadays self-propelled pilotless devices, powered either by a rocket engine or by jet propulsion, can not only be launched at faraway targets with pinpoint accuracy but can receive their directional impulses from heat or other electromagnetic waves emanating from the targets themselves.

A *guided missile* is characterized by its ability to change course while in flight. It does so by means of an internal preset control system, remote radio control, or a target-seeking, self-reacting radar or electromagnetic sensing device.

A *ballistic missile* begins its flight like any other self-propelled guided missile. However, after a certain point in its flight, it follows a ballistic trajectory. That is, like a ball thrown through the air, it becomes a free-falling object acted on only by gravitational forces and resistance of the air it passes through. An *ICBM* is an intercontinental ballistic missile. As its name suggests, an *antiballistic missile* is an *antimissile missile* intended to intercept and destroy an approaching ballistic missile.

spacecraft / spaceship

In various forms and for various purposes, more and more vehicles and devices are placed into an orbit about the earth or into a trajectory to another celestial body.

A *spacecraft* is any vehicle capable of traveling through space beyond the earth's atmosphere.

A *spaceship,* also called a *rocket ship,* is a rocket-propelled spacecraft that is designed to be operated by a crew of astronauts.

A *space capsule* is a spacecraft designed to carry animals, instruments, and sometimes people into space and to be recovered on its return to earth.

A *space station* (or *space platform*) is a spacecraft designed to remain in orbit for a long time and to serve, for example, as a research center or as a station from which to launch other spacecraft.

A *space shuttle* is an airplanelike spacecraft designed to travel back and forth, say, between the earth and a space station, transporting personnel and equipment.

Besides being a moon revolving around a larger planet, a *satellite* can be an artificial object placed into an orbit. There, carrying instruments for the collection and transmission of data, it moves mainly under the gravitational influence of a celestial body such as the earth, another planet, or the sun.

UFO / flying saucer

The first letters of the words *unidentified flying object* give us *UFO*. With *-logy* (meaning "science, doctrine, or theory") added, we get *ufology;* and with *-ist* ("a person skilled in or occupied with") added to that, *ufologist.* A UFO is any of a number of unidentified objects or phenomena that, especially from 1947 on, are frequently reported to have been observed or tracked in the sky and variously explained as being atmospheric phenomena, hallucinations, misperceptions of actual objects, and alien spacecraft, among other things. A *flying saucer* is a UFO, especially when thought to be a spacecraft from another planet. The name comes from the saucerlike shape reported in many early UFO sightings.

radar / sonar

Radar is any of several systems or devices that transmit and reflect radio waves. Besides detecting and determining the direction, distance, height, and speed of aircraft and other objects, its uses include detecting storms and mapping. The word *radar* is an acronym: *ra(dio) d(etecting) a(nd) r(anging)*.

Sonar is an apparatus that transmits high-frequency sound waves through water and registers the vibrations reflected from an object. Locating submarines and determining depths are among its uses. The word *sonar* is also an acronym: *so(und) n(avigation) a(nd) r(anging)*.

Animal sonar (or *echolocation*) is the emission of sound waves and the analysis of reflected echoes by an animal to detect or determine the position of objects. Most bats and toothed whales (including dolphins and porpoises), as well as a few other animals, have this ability.

AM / FM

Radio stations transmit high-frequency electromagnetic waves whose modulations correspond to different sounds. When these modulated radio waves reach the receiving instruments, or radios, they are reconverted into air vibrations so that the ear can recognize them as sounds.

Modulation, which adds information to a carrier wave in accordance with the signal to be transmitted, can take several forms. As their names suggest, *amplitude modulation* (better known as *AM*) is the variation of the amplitude of a carrier wave, whereas *frequency modulation* (*FM*) is the variation of the frequency of a carrier wave. The main advantage of AM—its ability to travel over greater distances than FM—is also a disadvantage, because it limits the number of stations in a region that can use the same broadcast frequency. Besides permitting a larger number of stations to use the same frequency at the same time, FM has another advantage over AM: almost complete freedom from static and interference. This means that FM listeners within reasonable range of the transmitter are spared most of the crackling and hissing noises reproduced in radio loudspeakers during AM transmission. It also means that, after having dominated the radio airwaves for many years, AM broadcasters are losing out to the clean stereo sound of FM.

alloy / amalgam

An *alloy* is any of a large number of substances in which two or more metals or a metal and a nonmetal are combined, usually by melting them together. Alloys generally have greater commercial use than pure metals, because they are able to combine the best features of their component elements and even add properties such as hardness, strength, and resistance to corrosion. Brass, for example, is an alloy of copper and zinc; bronze is an alloy of copper and tin; and certain kinds of steel are mainly alloys of iron and carbon. An *amalgam* is an alloy of mercury with another metal or other metals. Dentists, for example, often use silver amalgam in filling teeth.

herbicide / fungicide

To designate a chemical substance or other agent that either kills or checks the growth of something, the suffix *-cide* is often attached to a word or word base. For example: A *herbicide* is used on plants, especially weeds (thus the synonym *weedkiller*). A *fungicide* is used on fungi or their spores. An *insecticide* is used on insects. An *algicide* is used on algae. A *rodenticide* is used on rodents, especially rats and mice. A *larvicide* is used on larvae.

The same suffix indicates that a person or group of people are the victims of a killing, as in *infanticide* or *genocide.*

microcomputer / minicomputer

A *computer* is an electronic machine that, by means of stored instructions and information, performs rapid, often complex calculations, or compiles, correlates, and selects data. In the early 1980s it was fairly easy to distinguish four main types: *microcomputers, minicomputers, mainframe computers,* and *supercomputers.* These constituted a distinct hierarchy of increasing computing power and cost. Although the names have survived, the distinctions have blurred greatly in the computing world of the 1990s. Today's microcomputers costing a few thousand dollars, for example, have as much computing power as mainframes of a decade ago costing millions. In addition, the gaps between the levels have been filled with other machines like *supermicrocomputers, computer workstations, superminicomputers,* and *minisupercomputers.* As the technology continues to evolve, a continuum of machines ranging from shirtpocket personal computers to super-supercomputers will no doubt supplement, and perhaps replace, these:

A *microcomputer* is a very small, relatively inexpensive computer whose central processing unit is a *microprocessor* (a silicon chip containing the basic arithmetic, logic, and control elements for doing calculations, carrying out stored instructions, and performing other processing tasks). Microcomputers, whose other names include *personal computers, desktop computers,* and *home computers,* are generally designed to be used by one person at a time. Typical uses for microcomputers are word processing (production of text documents), desktop publishing (production of more or less elaborately formatted documents, often including both text and graphics), spreadsheets (analysis of numerical data), and databases (storage, organization, and retrieval of information). In the home, microcomputers also do such things as handle household budgeting, balance bank accounts, compute taxes, and provide entertainment in the form of video games. *Workstations* are generally specialized, high-capacity microcomputers oriented toward engineering design and sophisticated publication work. Although each workstation has its own computing capabilities and is used by one person at a time, such machines are usually connected to one another and to a larger computer (a server) through a network.

A *minicomputer* (or *mini*) is more powerful and more expensive than a microcomputer. It is designed to accommodate, say, 20 to 30 users at a time, all performing different functions. Users generally communicate with the minicomputer from a terminal (basically a device with a typewriter keyboard and a video screen) or a personal computer. Minicomputers are used mostly in businesses, universities, and government agencies to support data management functions and scientific and engineering analysis.

A *mainframe computer* is the next step up in size, power, and cost. A mainframe will support hundreds of users on remote terminals at the same time. Mainframe users are typically the same ones as minicomputer users, but on a larger scale. Common uses are accounting, personnel record management, client/customer data management, large-scale data storage, transaction processing, and reservations management. Mainframes are generally kept in separate rooms, both for environmental control (to keep them cool) and for security.

A *supercomputer* is the fastest and most expensive kind of computer. Supercomputers are designed to perform tasks requiring rapid processing of large amounts of data, such as climatic analysis for weather forecasting, cryptography, economic modeling, and the simulation of complex physical phenomena, from the aerodynamics of flight to the evolution of the universe since the big bang. Though relatively few supercomputers are installed (mainly in government agencies and large research facilities), most are available to outside users through time-sharing arrangements.

analog computer / digital computer

Computers are often classified according to the way they process data. An *analog computer* represents data as values of a continuous variable, such as the magnitude of an electric current. A *digital computer* represents data as combinations of discrete states, such as the presence or absence of an electric charge. Digital computers have all but replaced analog computers. Indeed, the term *computer* has come to mean "digital computer" to the point where anyone who means "analog computer" must say so.

This computer terminology is applied to other instruments as well. An *analog watch*, for example, is a watch with hands whose continually changing position represents the passage of time, whereas a *digital watch* has no hands but, by means of its microprocessor, displays the time in discrete intervals as directly readable numerals. Pointing out that the ordinary watch was around long before digitization, some people object to attaching the modifier *analog* to it. They would like to see a watch with a little hand and a big hand on its face continue to be called simply a *watch*, and a watch that digitizes (that is, translates analog data into digital data) called a *digital watch*. Yet English does not ordinarily take such sentimentality into account, at least not for long. When most television programs were broadcast in black and white, for instance, color programs were labeled "color" in TV listings. Nowadays, however, the few black-and-white programs still shown are identified by the abbreviation "b&w."

hardware / software

In computer terminology, *hardware* refers to the physical components or equipment that makes up a computer system, including the *CPU* (*central processing unit*), input/output devices, keyboard, and video screen. *Software* consists of the programs or instructions that tell a computer what to do. Some software is loaded temporarily into the computer from a disk or tape. Programs that are built into a computer's *ROM* (*read-only memory*) chips and therefore cannot be changed by the user are called *firmware*. *Vaporware* is the name given to a product announced by a software publisher far in advance of its release to the public.

bit / byte

A *bit*, the smallest unit of information recognized by a computer, is a single digit (1 or 0) in a binary number system. A string of bits, usually eight, make up a *byte*, which was the basic unit operated on by early microprocessors. Although the word *byte* is an arbitrary formation, *bit* is a blend of the first letter in *binary* + the last two letters in *digit*.

mathematics / arithmetic

Mathematics encompasses a group of sciences that use numbers and symbols in dealing with quantities, magnitudes, and forms, and their relationships, attributes, and the like. Pure mathematics, one of its two main divisions, is concerned with the intrinsic study of mathematical systems, not with solving practical problems. Applied mathematics, on the other hand, puts mathematics to practical use in such areas as physics, engineering, and astronomy. Americans often shorten the word *mathematics* to *math;* the British to *maths.*

Another way to view mathematics is to divide it into branches, such as arithmetic, geometry, calculus, set theory, and so on. *Arithmetic* is the branch that deals with computing by positive, real numbers, specifically by adding, subtracting, multiplying, and dividing. Along with these fundamental operations and the computational skills involved in them, arithmetic deals with a series of abstract laws of mathematics, including, for example, the commutative property of addition, according to which the order in which numbers are added does not affect the sum.

number / numeral

A *number* is a symbol or word, or a group of either of these, showing how many or which one in a series (as in "This book has 240 pages" or "She is fifth in line"). A *numeral* is a figure, letter, or word, or a group of any of these, expressing a number ("She painted the numeral 6 on her T-shirt" or "The ratio included the numerals 5, 15, and 45"). That is, a number is a quantitative idea, whereas a numeral is a symbol used to express that idea.

This distinction, however, is more likely to be made in mathematics texts than in everyday speech and writing. Most people would, for example, freely substitute *number* for *numeral* in the last two examples given above, reserving the word *numeral* for terms like *Roman numeral.*

Arabic numeral / Roman numeral

An *Arabic numeral* is any of the figures 1, 2, 3, 4, 5, 6, 7, 8, 9, and 0. Because counting was originally done on the fingers, each of these ten numerals is known also as a *digit,* from a Latin word meaning "finger" or "toe." The Arabic, or Hindu-Arabic, numeration system, which originated in India, is the one most commonly used today. According to this system, numbers are expressed as so many individual units, tens, hundreds, and higher powers of 10, with a fixed position (relative to an actual or implied decimal point) for the figure that designates how many of each power of 10. In the numeral 5,328, for example, the 5 means 5 thousands, the 3 means 3 hundreds, the 2 means 2 tens, and the 8 means 8 ones.

A *Roman numeral* is a Roman letter used as a numeral in a system in which I = 1, V = 5, X = 10, L = 50, C = 100, D = 500, and M = 1,000. Other numbers are formed from these by adding or subtracting. The value of a symbol following another of the same or greater value is added (for example, III = 3 and XV = 15). The value of a symbol preceding one of greater value is subtracted (IX = 9). And the value of a symbol standing between two of greater value is subtracted from that of the second, the remainder being added to that of the first (XIX = 19). A bar over a numeral indicates multiplication by 1,000; so, for example, $\overline{V}$ = 5,000.

Roman numerals are ordinarily written in capitals, though at times in lowercase letters, as in numbering subdivisions. The introductory pages of some books, for instance, are numbered in lowercase Roman numerals to distinguish them from the Arabic-numbered pages in the body. Acts and scenes of plays and operas are sometimes numbered in Roman numerals and sometimes in Arabic figures.

cardinal number / ordinal number

A *cardinal number* is any number used in counting or in showing how many; for example, three, twenty, 937. An *ordinal number* is any number used to indicate order; for example, third, twentieth, 937th.

average / mean

Numerical facts or data can be assembled, classified, and tabulated in various ways so as to present significant information about a given subject. These are the most commonly used statistical methods by which a single number is made to represent a set, or series, of numbers:

Average refers to the result obtained by dividing a sum by the number of quantities added. For example, if during a given week a family watched television 6 hours on Sunday, 4 hours on Monday, 4 hours on Tuesday, 5 hours on Wednesday, 4 hours on Thursday, 5 hours on Friday, and 7 hours on Saturday, the average number of hours watched per day would be 35 ÷ 7, or 5. (In an extended sense, *average* designates a usual or ordinary kind or quality, as in "It was an average movie.")

Mean generally denotes *arithmetic mean*, which is the same as *average*. But *mean* also designates a particular kind of average: a figure intermediate between two extremes. For example, on a day with a high temperature of 82° and a low of 56°, the mean temperature is 69°, which is 13° lower than 82° and 13° higher than 56°. (Figuratively, *mean* implies moderation or the safe, prudent way between extremes, as in "Let's try to live by the golden mean.")

Median is the middle number in a series arranged in order of size. For example, if students' scores on a given test are 72, 80, 83, 85, and 92, the median score is 83, since there are two items both below and above the 83. But what if the series contains an even number of values—say, 72, 80, 83, 85, 88, and 92—so there is no middle number? In this case the median score is 84, the number midway between the two middle numbers, 83 and 85. (Here the median is, in fact, the mean of the two middle numbers.)

Mode, or *modal value,* is the value that occurs most often in a given series. To go back to the data on the TV-watchers, the mode is 4, because this is the number of hours that the family watched most often during the week. A series can have more than one mode (if two or more values occur the same number of times).

Percentile refers to any of the values in a series dividing the distribution of items in the series into 100 groups of equal frequency. For example, a score in a set of tests is at the 80th percentile if 20 percent of the test scores are higher and 80 percent of the scores are equal or lower. The median, by definition, is the 50th percentile.

Norm implies a standard of performance or achievement as represented by the median or average achievement of a large group. For example, tests in cognitive skills show that children entering inner-city schools from programs such as Head Start usually score above the norm for their age.

metric system / English system

Two principal systems of weights and measures are in use today: the *English system* and the *metric system.* The *English system,* also called the *customary system,* the *traditional system,* or the *U.S. system,* is based on the standard avoirdupois pound and the standard yard. The *metric system* is based on the kilogram and the meter. In the *International System of Units—SI* (from the first letters of the French term *Système Internationale*)—the metric system is augmented by scientific units used in technology. Established conversion factors, widely available in table form, make it possible to convert from one system to another. For example: 1 kilogram equals about 2.205 avoirdupois pounds; 1 meter equals about 3.281 feet; 1 cubic inch equals about 16.387 cubic centimeters; and 1 U.S. gallon equals about 3.785 liters.

Since the nineteenth century, the United States has been moving slowly toward adoption of the metric system, or SI. With the dawn of the space age in the late 1950s, American scientists, educators, and industrial leaders have redoubled their efforts to have the country fall into step with the rest of the world. Indeed, entire industries, such as wine making and car manufacturing, have gone metric; students are introduced to the metric system in the early grades; and technical publications and reference books generally show metric as well as customary units of measure, as do more and more gasoline pumps, highway signs, and temperature readings on printed weather reports. Yet, largely because of the general public's resistance to change, it is still both possible and legal for Americans to use only inches, pounds, degrees Fahrenheit, and other traditional units of measure in virtually all aspects of everyday life.

Fahrenheit / Celsius

Temperature, the degree of hotness or coldness of anything, is usually measured in degrees on a thermometer. *Fahrenheit* (represented by the symbol F) refers to a temperature scale on which 32° is the freezing point and 212° is the boiling point of water. This scale is commonly used in the United States and other countries that have not fully adopted the metric system.

Celsius (represented by the symbol *C*) is applied to a temperature scale on which 0° is the freezing point and 100° is the boiling point of water. This term, which replaces *centigrade,* is included in the International System of Units (SI). Besides being adopted in scientific circles throughout the world, it is gaining general acceptance in the States. Weather reports on television, for example, usually give temperatures in degrees Celsius along with the traditional degrees. This is how to convert a Fahrenheit temperature to Celsius: Subtract 32 from the °F and multiply the difference by five-ninths. And to convert a Celsius temperature to Fahrenheit: Multiply the °C by nine-fifths and add 32.

Kelvin (represented by the symbol *K*) designates a scale of thermodynamic temperature measured from absolute zero (–273.15°C). One kelvin equals 1 degree Celsius.

nautical mile / knot

When we talk about how many nautical miles a ship averages a day, we mean how far it travels, since a *nautical mile* has to do with distance, mainly in navigation. In the United States, since 1959, a nautical mile has been an international unit of linear measure equal to 1 minute of arc of a great circle of the earth, or 1,852 meters (6,076.11549 feet). This standard is useful because of its simple relationship to the degrees and minutes by which latitude and longitude are measured. A nautical mile is slightly longer than a statute (or land) mile: 1.15 statute miles, in fact.

Yet when we talk about how many knots a ship averages, we mean how fast the ship is going, not how far it travels, because a *knot* is a unit of speed of 1 nautical mile an hour. At least, that is technically the nautical meaning of *knot*, whose origin goes back to the knots that were once actually tied at regular intervals in a line used in measuring a ship's speed. In loose usage, however, *knot* and *nautical mile* are often interchanged.

million / billion

It is hard enough to grasp the meaning of very large numbers—in, say, balance-of-trade figures—without having to cope with the different names many of the numbers go by in various English-speaking countries. *Million* is no problem, because the United States, Canada, and Britain agree that a million is a thousand thousands (1 plus 6 zeros, or, in scientific notation, 10^6).

The confusion arises because in the steps up from a million each named quantity is typically multiplied by 1,000 in the United States and Canada and by 1 million in Britain. To Americans and Canadians a *billion* is a thousand millions (1 plus 9 zeros, or 10^9), whereas to the British a *milliard* has traditionally been a thousand millions and a *billion* has been a million millions (1 plus 12 zeros, or 10^{12}). In recent years, however, the American and Canadian sense of *billion* has been gaining acceptance in Britain. So what is an American or a Canadian—or, for that matter, a Briton—to make of, say, a January 1990 London *Times* report that the Ministry of Defence is considering a cut of about 25 percent in the "£20 billion defence budget"?

Americans and Canadians apply the word *trillion* to what the British used to call a billion (1 plus 12 zeros, or 10^{12}). In Britain a trillion is a million million millions (1 plus 18 zeros, or 10^{18}), yet Americans and Canadians call the number so represented a *quintillion*. To the British a quintillion is represented by 1 plus 30 zeros (10^{30}), but Americans and Canadians express this number by *nonillion*—which in Britain is represented by 1 plus 54 zeros (10^{54}). And so the puzzlement goes on, up the ladder.

Yet all three countries agree that a *googol* is represented by 1 plus 100 zeros, or 10^{100}, the American mathematician E. Kasner (1878–1955) having attached this sense to a child's word. *Googolplex* (*googol* + *-plex*, meaning "-fold") refers to the number 1 plus a googol of zeros (or 10 to the power googol). It also refers to any very large but unspecified number, as do several other fanciful coinages modeled on *million*, including *jillion* and *zillion* (as in "They received jillions [zillions] of Christmas cards").

numerator / denominator

In a fraction, the term above or to the left of the line is the *numerator* and the term below or to the right is the *denominator*. For example, in the fraction shown either as $\frac{3}{4}$ or as 3/4, the numerator is 3 and the denominator is 4.

addend / sum

In addition, a number or quantity to be added to another is an *addend* and the result of adding the addends is the *sum*.

minuend / subtrahend

In subtraction, the number or quantity from which another is subtracted is a *minuend*. The number or quantity that is subtracted is the *subtrahend*. And the amount by which one differs from the other is the *difference* or, in the case of a smaller number or quantity being subtracted from a larger one, the *remainder*.

multiplicand / multiplier

In multiplication, the number or quantity to be multiplied by another is the *multiplicand*. The number or quantity by which the multiplicand is multiplied is the *multiplier*. And the result obtained by this operation is the *product*. The word *factor* is applied as well to either the multiplicand or the multiplier, or both. For example, 3 and 5 are factors of 15.

dividend / divisor

In division, the number or quantity to be divided is the *dividend*. The number or quantity by which the dividend is divided is the *divisor*. And the result obtained by this operation is the *quotient*.

circumference / diameter

A *circle* is a plane figure bounded by a single curved line, every point of which is equally distant from the point at the center of the figure. The *circumference* is the line bounding the circle; it is sometimes described as its length. An *arc* is any unbroken part of the circumference. The *diameter* is a straight line segment passing through the center of the circle and having its endpoints on the circumference. The *radius* is a straight line segment joining the center of the circle and a point on the circumference. A *chord* is a straight line segment joining any two points on the circumference.

acute angle / right angle

An *angle* is the shape made by two straight lines meeting at a common point (the *vertex*) or by two planes meeting along an edge. Angles are commonly measured in degrees, 360 of which make a full circle. An *acute angle* is an angle that measures more than 0° and less than 90°. A *right angle* is an angle of 90°. An *obtuse angle* is an angle that measures more than 90° and less than 180°. A *straight angle* is an angle of 180°. A *reflex angle* is an angle that measures more than 180° and less than 360°. An *oblique angle* is an angle that is either acute or obtuse, but not a right angle.

equilateral triangle / isosceles triangle

As the name suggests, *triangles* have three angles. These geometric figures are classified mainly according to the relationship of their three sides. In an *equilateral triangle* all three sides are the same length. In an *isosceles triangle* two sides are the same length. In a *scalene triangle* all three sides are of different lengths.

Another way to classify triangles is by the measure of their angles. In a *right triangle* one of the three angles is a right angle. In an *acute triangle* all three angles are acute. In an *obtuse triangle* one of the three angles is obtuse. In an *oblique triangle* there is no right angle.

rhombus / rhomboid

Rhombuses (or *rhombi*) and *rhomboids* are parallelograms; that is, four-sided plane figures in which both pairs of opposite sides are parallel. Like a square, a *rhombus* has all four sides of the same length, but instead of having four right angles, as a square does, it has four oblique angles (that is, angles that are either acute or obtuse). A *rhomboid*, too, has four oblique angles, but only its opposite sides are the same length.

trapezoid / trapezium

Both *trapezoids* and *trapeziums* (or *trapezia*) are quadrilaterals; that is, plane figures having four sides and four angles. According to U.S. and Canadian usage, a *trapezoid* has two sides that are parallel, while a *trapezium* has no parallel sides. British usage attaches the opposite meanings to the two words.

Our Bodies and Medicine

disease / illness

When the body or mind deviates from its normal or healthy state for a reason other than an accident, a number of terms are available to describe the result. Some are used interchangeably, while others discriminate shades of meaning.

Disease may apply generally to any departure from health (as in "Malnutrition leads to many diseases in children"). It may also refer to a particular disorder with a specific cause and characteristic symptoms ("Malaria is an infectious disease").

Illness and *sickness* are by and large interchangeable in references to the state of being unwell ("The shop was closed because of illness [sickness] in the family"). Yet Americans give a slight edge to *sickness*, whereas the British are likely to use *illness* in this sense.

Ailment and *disorder* frequently refer to a chronic, annoying upset of normal function of whatever degree of seriousness ("The cause of her ailment was never discovered" or "The study dealt with sleep disorders"). They both sometimes suggest only a slight or transitory indisposition ("Ships' doctors are used to handling passengers' ailments" or "Wherever travelers go, stomach disorders are apt to follow"). But when it comes to mental health problems, *disorder*, not *ailment*, is likely to be used ("Schizophrenia is a major mental disorder of unknown causes").

Malady, a fairly formal word, conveys the notion of a deep-seated chronic disease, frequently one that is ultimately fatal ("An undisclosed malady took the senator out of the race").

Affection, in medical usage, refers to a disorder of a specific organ or part ("He suffers from an affection of the spleen").

In this comparison, *condition* is ordinarily a neutral word applied to any state of physical or mental health, good or bad ("What's the patient's condition?"). Yet, especially in informal usage, it implies a departure from health or normality and may therefore replace one or more of the other

246

words ("Her lung condition is becoming more serious" or "Stress reaction is a widespread psychoneurotic condition").

disease / syndrome

A *disease* is a particular destructive process in an organ or organism, with a specific cause and a characteristic train of symptoms. As diseases like malaria, scarlet fever, cancer, and pneumonia indicate, the word *disease* need not be part of the name. But it often is, especially when preceded by a proper name; for example: Alzheimer's disease, Parkinson's disease, and Addison's disease.

A *syndrome* is a constellation of symptoms that occur together and characterize a specific disease or condition. Although the word *syndrome* may be part of the medical name, the group of symptoms is usually referred to by the first letters in the words. For example: *AIDS,* an acronym, is the common designation of *acquired immune deficiency syndrome,* a disorder of the body's immune system that results in a variety of infections, some forms of cancer, and other afflictions. *PMS,* an abbreviation, is the common designation of *premenstrual syndrome,* a group of physical and emotional symptoms, such as fluid retention, fatigue, depression, and irritability, which may precede a menstrual period. And *FAS,* another abbreviation, is the common designation of *fetal alcohol syndrome,* a symptom complex related to impairment of the fetuses of women who drink heavily during pregnancy, causing their newborn to suffer from mental retardation, curvature of the spine, or facial abnormalities.

infectious disease / communicable disease

An *infectious disease* is a disease caused by the presence of bacteria, protozoa, viruses, or other parasites in the body. If its causative agent can pass or be carried from one person to another, directly or indirectly, such a disease may also be called a *contagious disease,* a *communicable disease,* a *transmittable disease,* or a *transmissible disease.*

germ / bug

A *microorganism* is an animal or vegetable organism that is too small to be seen except through a microscope and, in some cases, through an even more powerful optical instrument such as an electron microscope. Microscopic and ultramicroscopic organisms are found everywhere and in countless varieties. Although many play a useful role in the cycle of matter, others are extremely harmful. Microorganisms, especially those which cause disease in human beings, are often called *germs, microbes,* and, informally, *bugs.* Three large groups of such microorganisms are particularly well known.

A *protozoan* (*protozoa* in the plural), consisting of a single cell or a number of more or less identical cells, lives in water or as a parasite. An example is the *amoeba,* which causes amebic dysentery, among other diseases. (Although the spelling *ameba* is now standard in scientific usage, both for the word itself and in compounds, the spelling *amoeba* is still clearly preferred in general usage. The plural of *ameba* is *amebas* or *amebae;* of *amoeba,* it is *amoebas* or *amoebae.*)

A *bacterium* (*bacteria* in the plural), typically a one-celled microorganism, occurs in three main forms. The spherical *cocci* (*coccus* in the singular) cause diseases like pneumonia and gonorrhea; the rod-shaped *bacilli* (*bacillus* in the singular), diseases like tuberculosis and diphtheria; and the spiral-shaped *spirilla* (*spirillum* in the singular), diseases like syphilis and Lyme disease.

A *virus,* a submicroscopic infective agent, is composed of a protein sheath surrounding a nucleic acid core. Viruses, which can reproduce only within living cells (that is, they cannot grow or reproduce on their own), infect plants and bacteria as well as animals. Measles, influenza, and AIDS are among the diseases they cause in humans.

diagnosis / prognosis

In medicine, a *diagnosis* is a process in which the nature of a diseased condition is determined by examination of the symptoms (as in "a diagnosis of gallstones"). A *prognosis* is a prediction of the probable course of a disease in an individual and the chances of recovery ("The prognosis is good, provided the patient undergoes surgery and follows the prescribed diet").

morbidity / mortality

When we see or hear the word *morbid,* we are apt to think either of something that is gruesome, grisly, or horrible (as in "The article gives all the morbid details of the murder") or of someone who has an unwholesome tendency to dwell on gruesome or gloomy matters ("Being alone all year made her morbid"). But the adjective is also more directly related to sickness and disease, and it is in this sense that the noun *morbidity* is commonly used. A *morbidity rate* (sometimes called a *sick rate*) is the ratio of cases of a particular disease per stated unit of population (usually a hundred thousand or a million people) in a given locality during a given period. It is possible, for example, to calculate monthly AIDS morbidity in New York City or in the country as a whole. Age, sex, income, and other factors can also be taken into account in computing morbidity rates.

Mortality, too, has several meanings, including the ratio of deaths per stated unit of population (ordinarily a thousand people) in a given locality during a given period. *Mortality rates,* or *death rates,* are often broken down by cause and, like morbidity rates, they can be computed by age, sex, income, and other characteristics of the group studied.

mortality table / life table

The notions of dying and living are juxtaposed in *mortality table* and *life table.* These interchangeable terms refer to a statistical table that, based on a sampling of the population, states the percentage of people who live to any given age and the life expectancy at any given age. In projecting risks, premiums, and other variables, life insurance companies are among the businesses that put such tables to use.

incidence / prevalence

As an indication of the cases of a particular disease found in a portion of the population, morbidity can be considered from two points of view. The *incidence* (or *incidence rate*) reflects the number of new cases of that disease occurring during a certain period, while the *prevalence* (or *prevalence rate*) reflects the number of cases of that disease in existence during a certain period. Both rates are usually expressed in terms of sick people, or cases, per thousand individuals at risk.

epidemic / endemic

An *epidemic* is the occurrence of cases of a disease, in a particular community or region, in excess of normal expectancy. In other words, the number of cases indicating the presence of an epidemic (or *epidemic disease*) is relative to the usual frequency of the disease in the same area, among the same population, at the same season of the year. In August 1989, for example, Chicago was hit hard by an unexpected measles epidemic. An epidemic that spreads throughout a whole country or the world is known as a *pandemic.* For example, in the 1918–19 influenza pandemic, some 20 million people died, more than 500,000 of them in the United States alone.

The word *endemic* refers to a disease that is constantly present in a particular community or region. Diarrhea, for example, is said to be endemic, or an endemic disease, in parts of Latin America, especially in children under two years of age.

autopsy / post-mortem

Autopsy, post-mortem (short for *post-mortem examination*), and *necropsy* all refer to an examination and dissection of a cadaver to discover the cause of death, damage done by disease, and the like. Made up of the Greek word elements *auto-* ("self") and *-opsis* ("a sight"), *autopsy* conveys the notion of seeing with one's eyes. In *necropsy, -opsis* is joined to another Greek word element, *necro-* ("death"), so here the sense is that of examining a dead body. (Some words beginning with *necro-* are more common in everyday speech and writing. Newspapers, for instance, publish *necrologies*, or lists of people who have died within a certain period.) In Latin *post-mortem* means, literally, "after death." In extended usage, the word applies to a detailed examination or evaluation of some event just ended (as in "a post-mortem on the World Cup finals").

Biopsy is sometimes confused with *autopsy*, not only because the two words have the same ending but because both refer to a medical examination. A biopsy, however, has to do with a person who is alive, not dead. It is the removal of a bit of living tissue from an organ or other part of the body for microscopic examination, so as to make a diagnosis of a disease or to follow its course.

body / cadaver

Whether dead or alive, the whole physical substance of a person or animal is called a *body*. *Corpse* and the euphemistic *remains* are applied to a dead human body. *Cadaver* refers primarily to a dead human body on whom an autopsy is performed. *Carcass* is used of a dead body of an animal or, contemptuously, of a human being.

brain / mind

The *brain*, a mass of nerve tissue at the upper end of the spinal cord, is the main part of the nervous system. Although brain research is far from complete, there is general agreement on the main characteristics of this organ, also known in anatomy as the *encephalon*: its size (occupying the entire cranium, or cavity enclosed by the skull); its weight (about 3 pounds, or about 1.36 kilograms); its principal parts (cerebrum, cerebellum, and brainstem); and some of the ways it acts as the center of thought and the organ that perceives sensory impulses and regulates motor impulses.

Both *mind* and *soul*, on the other hand, are more elusive. Not only have they not been precisely defined or mapped, but whether they exist at all and, if so, whether they bear any relation to the body are the subject of endless argument. Some consider the *mind* to be a faculty or function of the brain. Others believe that in its detachment from the body the mind is similar to or even identical with the soul. Regardless of its location, the mind is sometimes described as the thinking and perceiving part of consciousness; as intellect or intelligence; as the seat of thought, reasoning, perception, feelings, emotions, desire, and will.

As for the *soul*, this is often regarded as the immortal or spiritual part of a person. Though it lacks physical or material reality, it is credited with the functions of thinking and willing, and hence determining all behavior. In short, it is sometimes said to be the moral or emotional nature of a human being.

The brain, the mind, and the soul, then, cannot easily be placed in separate and distinct compartments.

right brain / left brain

The part of the human brain known as the *cerebrum* is divided into two largely symmetrical hemispheres. Both, researchers have found, are able to handle many specialized tasks. Yet the *right hemisphere* (or, as it is often called, the *right brain*), which controls the left side of the body, is generally considered to be better equipped to perform complex visual and spatial processes. The *left hemisphere* (or *left brain*), which controls the right side of the body, is generally dominant for language functions, whether by speech or writing.

unconscious / subconscious

In psychoanalysis, *the unconscious* is regarded as the sum of all thoughts, memories, impulses, desires, feelings, and the like, of which the individual is not conscious, or aware, but which influence the emotions and behavior. That is, it is the part of one's psyche which comprises repressed material of this nature. In referring to mental processes and reactions, *the subconscious* is similar in that it designates mental activity occurring without conscious perception, or with only slight perception, on the part of the individual. This term, however, is seldom used in psychiatry anymore.

id / ego

In Freudian psychoanalytic theory, the human psyche is said to consist of three parts.

The *id* is the reservoir of the instinctual drives (for food, love, sex, and other basic needs) and the source of psychic energy. It is dominated by the pleasure principle; that is, it automatically adjusts the person's mental activity to secure pleasure, or gratification, and to avoid pain, or unpleasantness. The term *id* is a special use of a Latin word meaning "it."

The *ego* experiences the external world, or reality, through the senses; organizes the thought processes rationally; and governs action. In doing so, it maintains a balance between the impulses of the id, the demands of the environment, and the standards of the superego. The term *ego* comes from a Latin word for the first-person pronoun *I*.

The *superego*, popularly called a person's "conscience," is critical of the self, or ego, and enforces standards of morality or behavior. At an unconscious level, it blocks unacceptable impulses of the id.

artery / vein

In the body's circulatory system, blood flows out of and back into the heart through arteries and veins. An *artery* is any one of the system of thick-walled blood vessels that carry blood from the heart to various parts of the body. A *vein* is a blood vessel through which blood passes from various parts of the body back to the heart. Loosely, the word refers also to any blood vessel. A *capillary* is any of the tiny blood vessels that normally connect the smallest veins and the smallest arteries.

systolic blood pressure / diastolic blood pressure

If told that our blood pressure is, say, "140 over 70," many of us would have little idea what the report means, much less whether the news is good or bad. Each number indicates a pressure that the blood exerts on the walls of the blood vessels. The larger number shows *systolic blood pressure;* that is, the maximum pressure measured during *systole* (the contraction phase of heart action, especially of the ventricles, when the blood is driven onward from the chambers). The smaller number shows *diastolic blood pressure;* that is, the minimum pressure measured during *diastole* (the resting phase of heart action, especially of the ventricles, following each contraction, when the heart muscle relaxes and the chambers fill with blood).

Blood pressure is expressed in millimeters of mercury, usually as a fraction (as in "a blood pressure of 140/70"). Sometimes, however, a whole number is used. If so, the larger value is given ("a blood pressure of 140"). Abnormally high blood pressure, also called *hypertension,* is a serious, almost symptomless condition that, if left untreated, can lead to heart attack, stroke, and other diseases.

red corpuscle / white corpuscle

Among the many substances found in the blood, lymph, and tissues are two kinds of tiny cells, each with a special function: the *red corpuscle* (or *red blood cell* or *erythrocyte*) and the *white corpuscle* (or *white blood cell* or *leukocyte*). Through the hemoglobin they contain, the red corpuscles carry oxygen from the lung to the tissues and carbon dioxide from the tissues to the lungs. Because of their ability to surround and attack bacteria and other microorganisms, the white corpuscles play a major role in defending the body against infection.

low-density lipoprotein / high-density lipoprotein

A *protein* is a complex organic structure essential to the diet. *Cholesterol,* a fatlike substance that is a normal component of the blood, is of concern only when present in excessive amounts. The fatty substance known as a *lipid* is also an important constituent of living cells. Because oil and water do not mix, a lipid is insoluble in water and therefore cannot flow through the blood stream on its own. However, when it is combined with protein, the new "package"—now a *lipoprotein*—can be carried in the blood.

Some lipoproteins are more beneficial than others. A *low-density lipoprotein* (or *LDL*), with its large amount of cholesterol and small amount of protein, tends to be harmful in that, by depositing cholesterol in artery walls, it can lead to atherosclerosis. LDL is therefore sometimes called "bad cholesterol." A *high-density lipoprotein* (or *HDL*), on the other hand, has a large amount of protein and a small amount of cholesterol. Because it helps clear excess cholesterol from the arteries, transporting it from the cells back to the liver for disposal, HDL is sometimes called "good cholesterol."

abdomen / stomach

The part of the body cavity from the chest to the pelvis is called the *abdomen* or—though generally not in formal usage—the *belly*. It contains the liver, stomach, intestines, and other digestive organs. The words *abdomen*, *belly*, and *stomach* are often interchanged, but the substitution of *gut* in this sense is sometimes regarded as indelicate usage. Yet, along with *bowels*, *viscera*, and *entrails*, *guts* is the equivalent of *intestines*.

uterus / womb

The hollow, muscular organ of female mammals in which the ovum is deposited and the embryo and fetus are developed is called either the *uterus* or the *womb*. This word, which originally meant "belly," is often applied to any place or part that holds, envelops, or generates something (as in "the womb of time").

breast / bosom

Breast refers to the front part of the human torso from the shoulders to the abdomen. It also commonly designates either of the female mammary glands. Males have breasts too, though these are usually not as well developed as female breasts. *Bosom*, which refers to the entire human breast, is now generally used in a figurative sense, conveying the notion of the human breast as a source of feeling, a protective, loving enclosure, or the like (as in "the bosom of the family"). It is sometimes used as a euphemism by those who prefer not to mention certain parts of the body and therefore describe a woman as "big-bosomed" instead of "big-breasted." *Bust*, in this context, almost always implies the female breasts and is the conventional term in referring to silhouette or form ("The line in this year's swimsuits emphasizes the bust").

temperature / fever

In everyday speech and writing, *temperature* and *fever* are freely interchanged (as in "Alex was up all night with a temperature [fever]"). In strict usage, however, there is a difference. *Temperature* is simply the degree of hotness or coldness of anything, usually measured on a thermometer. *Fever* is abnormally high body temperature: in humans, over the 98.6°F (37°C) that is considered normal oral temperature in a healthy person.

Pyrexia, from the Greek word *pyr*, meaning "fire," is a medical word for *fever*. This notion is partly implied in the arbitrary coinage *Pyex*, the trademark for a type of glassware that is used for cooking and lab work and is capable of withstanding temperatures up to about 500°C (about 930°F).

change of life / menopause

Most women between the ages of forty and fifty stop menstruating. *Menopause* and *female climacteric* are medical terms for the cessation of menstruation, or cyclic uterine bleeding. This period is popularly known as *change of life.*

malignancy / benignancy

As medical terms, the noun *malignancy* and the adjective *malignant* refer to something dangerous or virulent enough to cause, or be likely to cause, death (as in "The autopsy revealed a malignancy" or "The tumor turned out to be malignant"). In references to something that is not malignant and therefore likely to do little or no harm, the adjective *benign* (or *benignant*) is more common than the noun *benignancy,* especially in nontechnical speech and writing.

heart attack / heart failure

When the blood supply to the heart muscle itself suddenly becomes inadequate, a *heart attack* is likely to occur. Such an acute episode of heart disease is known also as *myocardial infarction*. It may be caused by a *coronary thrombosis* (also called a *coronary occlusion* or simply a *coronary*), in which a clot is formed in a branch of one of the heart arteries, obstructing that artery and, subsequently, damaging the heart muscle. The symptoms of a heart attack include persistent, usually intense pain, accompanied by profuse sweating, pallor, abnormally low blood pressure, shortness of breath, faintness, nausea, and vomiting.

Heart failure occurs when the heart is unable to pump enough blood to maintain an adequate flow to and from the body tissues and organs. There can be more than one cause, including extreme exertion and the improper functioning of organs other than the heart itself. Treatment may include rest, medication, diet, and surgery. One kind of heart failure is *congestive heart failure,* which is caused by excessive fluid in the circulatory system. *Angina pectoris* (often shortened to *angina*) is a condition marked by recurrent pain, usually in the chest and left arm, caused by a sudden decrease of the blood supply to the heart muscle. *Cardiac arrest* is a sudden failure of the heart to pump any blood at all, resulting in a cutoff of the oxygen supply to vital tissues. In an attempt to restart the heart and lungs, the emergency life-saving procedure known as *CPR* (*cardiopulmonary resuscitation*) is often employed.

stroke / apoplexy

A sudden disturbance of the blood supply to parts of the brain can result in coma, followed by paralysis of one side of the body, partial or total loss of the power to use or understand words, convulsions, or death. Such a severe attack is generally called a *stroke* or a *cerebrovascular accident,* the terms *apoplexy* and *apoplectic stroke* being less commonly used nowadays.

The destruction of brain tissue leading to a stroke can have several causes. One is a *cerebral thrombosis,* which occurs when a clot forms in a blood vessel in the brain, preventing the circulation of blood to the blocked area of brain tissue. A similar blockage can occur when a piece of blood clot or other material found elsewhere in the body is released into the blood stream and becomes lodged in a blood vessel supplying a part of the brain. Another cause of destruction of brain tissue is a *cerebral hemorrhage,* which occurs when a ruptured blood vessel causes profuse bleeding into the tissues of the brain.

arteriosclerosis / atherosclerosis

Arteriosclerosis, also known as *hardening of the arteries,* is a disorder characterized by an abnormal thickening and loss of elasticity of the vessel walls. As a result, the blood supply, especially to the brain and legs, may be cut back. Although arteriosclerosis is often present in old age, it can also be caused prematurely by high blood pressure, kidney disease, diabetes, and other health problems.

Atherosclerosis is a form of arteriosclerosis in which nodules of cholesterol, fat, and other substances are deposited on the inner walls of the arteries. The more difficult it is for blood to flow through these narrowed and scarred channels, the greater the likelihood of heart disease and other disorders of the circulatory system.

hyperglycemia / hypoglycemia

With precisely opposite meanings, the prefixes *hyper-* and *hypo-* appear in the names of many diseases or disorders. In this context, *hyper-* means "over, above, more than the normal, excessive," whereas *hypo-* means "under, below, less than the normal, deficient." In *hyperthyroidism,* for example, the activity of the thyroid gland is excessive; in *hypothyroidism,* it is deficient.

The names of a number of paired disorders follow that pattern. *Hyperglycemia* and *hypoglycemia,* for example, both have to do with the level of sugar in the form of glucose in the blood. A *hyperglycemic* has an abnormally high concentration of sugar in the blood; a *hypoglycemic,* an abnormally low concentration.

cancer / carcinoma

Cancer is a general term referring to any of a group of diseases in which the uncontrolled growth of cells disrupts body tissue, metabolism, and other physical processes. *Carcinoma* is applied to a cancerous growth originating in the cellular tissue which covers external body surfaces, such as the skin, or which lines internal surfaces, such as hollow organs and vessels. *Sarcoma* is applied to a cancerous growth mainly in bone, connective tissue, muscle, and blood, or in tissue developed from the mesoderm, particularly in bone or certain muscles. Carcinomas and sarcomas both tend to invade the surrounding tissue and to produce new growths. If unchecked, most cancerous tumors endanger well-being and even life.

black lung disease / brown lung disease

The continued inhalation of certain kinds of dust can lead to chronic diseases of the lungs. Two of them are *black lung disease* (*black lung* for short), which is caused by inhaling coal dust, and *brown lung disease* (*brown lung*), which is caused by inhaling fine textile fibers, especially cotton. In medical terminology, black lung is known as *anthracosis* (*anthrax* being Greek for "coal" + *-osis*, meaning "an abnormal or diseased condition"). And brown lung is known as *byssinosis* (from the Greek word *byssos*, meaning "fine linen or cotton," + the same suffix).

Other lung diseases have names that show which products cause them. For example, *asbestosis* is brought about by inhaling asbestos particles; *silicosis*, by inhaling silica dust; and *tabacosis*, by inhaling tobacco dust. (*Tabaco* and *tabacco* are archaic variants of *tobacco*.)

heatstroke / heat exhaustion

Prolonged exposure to intense heat can cause *heatstroke*. This serious failure of the body's heat-regulation mechanisms is characterized by high fever, dry skin, collapse, and sometimes convulsions or coma. *Sunstroke* (sometimes called *insolation*) is a form of heatstroke, resulting from excessive exposure to one source of intense heat: the sun.

The condition known as either *heat exhaustion* or *heat prostration* is caused by excessive loss of salt and water, usually as the result of overexertion in a hot environment. Its symptoms include dizziness, nausea, low body temperature, muscle cramps, and fainting.

cold / flu

As advertising agencies well know, winter means scratchy throats, runny noses, and achy bones. What neither they nor anyone else knows is precisely what causes any of the infectious diseases that bring on the scratchy throats, runny noses, and achy bones, or how to get rid of them.

A *cold* (often called a *common cold*) is a contagious infection of the respiratory passages, especially of the nose and throat, thought to be caused by many different viruses. Its symptoms include an acute inflammation of the mucous membranes, nasal discharge, watery eyes, a low fever, and a general feeling of discomfort. A *head cold* is a common cold characterized chiefly by congestion of the nasal passages.

Influenza, another highly contagious infection, is caused by any of a large group of viruses. Its chief symptoms are a sore throat, a cough, chills, fever, muscular pain, and weakness. It is sometimes called *grippe* or, more often, shortened to *flu*. The word *flu* is popularly applied as well to any of various respiratory or intestinal infections caused by viruses.

headache / migraine

A continuous pain in the head is commonly called a *headache*. A *migraine* is a type of intense, periodically returning headache that is usually limited to one side of the head and is often accompanied by nausea, vomiting, and visual disorders. A *sick headache* might be either a migraine or any headache accompanied by nausea.

concussion / contusion

A *concussion* is a condition in which some organ, especially the brain, is impaired as a result of a violent blow or impact. A *contusion* is a bruise; that is, an area of body tissue which is injured and discolored, usually as a result of a blow, but in which the skin is not broken.

venereal disease / social disease

A disease such as gonorrhea or syphilis, which is usually transmitted by intercourse with an infected person, is called either a *venereal disease* or, more and more frequently, a *sexually transmitted disease*. Considering these terms distasteful, many people substitute their abbreviations (*VD* and *STD*) or the somewhat old-fashioned *social disease*.

neurosis / psychosis

A *neurosis* (or *psychoneurosis*) is any of various mental or emotional disorders characterized by anxiety, compulsions, phobias, depression, dissociations, and the like. One compulsion, for example, might be kleptomania, an abnormal, persistent impulse to steal that is not prompted by need.

A *psychosis* is any of various major mental disorders in which the personality is very seriously disorganized and contact with reality is usually impaired. Major psychoses are principally of the schizophrenic or manic-depressive type. Organic psychoses are characterized by a pathological organic condition, such as brain damage or disease, or a metabolic disorder. The psychiatric term *psychosis* is often linked with the popular term *insanity*.

insanity / lunacy

Unlike *psychosis*, which designates any of various specialized mental disorders in which the personality is seriously disorganized, *insanity* is not a medical term. Yet in popular usage it refers to the state of being insane, to mental illness or derangement. In law, it refers to any form or degree of mental derangement or unsoundness of mind, either permanent or temporary, that makes a person incapable of what is regarded legally as normal, rational conduct or judgment. Both of these contexts imply that insanity is a mental derangement in one who formerly had mental health.

Luna meaning "the moon" in Latin, *lunacy* originally referred to intermittent insanity that was supposed to change in intensity with the phases of the moon. It later came to suggest simply spells of insanity, and is now most commonly used in its extended sense of "extreme folly" (as in "Driving a moped on the Pennsylvania Turnpike is sheer lunacy").

anorexia / bulimia

Two eating disorders, chiefly among young women, are *anorexia* and *bulimia*. *Anorexia*, which is characterized by an aversion to food and an obsession with weight loss, usually takes the form of self-induced starvation and excessive exercise. *Bulimia*, to the contrary, is characterized by the gorging of large quantities of food followed by purging, as by self-induced vomiting.

combat fatigue / shell shock

Prolonged battle in warfare can lead to a psychological condition characterized by extreme anxiety, irritability, depression, and similar symptoms of stress. This condition was called *shell shock* in World War I and *combat fatigue* in World War II. By the time of the Vietnam War it was known as *stress reaction* or *posttraumatic stress disorder*. Nowadays both of these terms are often applied to a more general response to acute anxiety, caused by any shocking or tragic event, such as the death of a loved one, a natural disaster, or an airplane crash.

sadism / masochism

Sadism is either the getting of sexual pleasure from dominating, mistreating, or hurting one's partner physically or otherwise, or the getting of pleasure from inflicting physical or psychological pain on another or others. The practice is named after the Marquis de Sade (1740–1814), a French soldier and novelist whose writings describe sexual aberrations, especially those involving the infliction of pain. One who indulges in sadism is a *sadist*.

The opposite of sadism, *masochism* is either the getting of sexual pleasure from being dominated, mistreated, or hurt physically or otherwise by one's partner, or the getting of pleasure from suffering physical or psychological pain, inflicted by others or by oneself. This practice is named after Leopold von Sacher-Masoch (1835–1895), an Austrian writer whose stories describe it. One who indulges in masochism is a *masochist*.

Sadomasochism (abbreviated as *S/M* or *S-M*) is the practice of both sadism and masochism. One who derives pleasure, especially sexual pleasure, in this way is a *sadomasochist*.

measles / rubeola

Measles is an acute, infectious, communicable virus disease that occurs most frequently in children who have not been vaccinated. It is characterized mainly by small red spots on the skin, high fever, and nasal discharge. *Rubeola*, which, like *ruby*, comes from a Latin word for "red," is the medical name.

The word *measles* is also applied to various similar but milder diseases. The best known is *rubella*, also called *German measles*. It too produces small red spots on the skin, together with swollen glands, especially at the back of the head and neck.

chickenpox / smallpox

Chickenpox is an acute, contagious viral disease, usually of young children. It is characterized by a slight fever and superficial skin eruptions which, when healed, are only occasionally followed by scars. The medical name, *varicella*, is a diminutive of *variola*, which refers to a more serious group of virus diseases, including *smallpox.* These are marked by prolonged fever, vomiting, and blisterlike elevations on the skin that often do leave pitted scars, or pockmarks.

whooping cough / pertussis

An acute infectious disease that usually affects children, *whooping cough* is characterized by a mucous discharge from the nose and later by short, rapid bursts of coughing that end in a forced intake of breath, or whoop. Its medical name, *pertussis,* comes from the bacillus that causes it. Indeed, *tussis,* a medical term for "cough," appears in the names of a number of over-the-counter cough suppressants, including Pertussin and Robitussin.

poliomyelitis / infantile paralysis

Poliomyelitis (*polio* for short) is an acute viral disease that produces inflammation of the gray matter of the spinal cord. It is accompanied by paralysis of various muscle groups that sometimes atrophy, often with resulting permanent deformities. Because the disease occurs principally in children, it is sometimes called *infantile paralysis.*

Down's syndrome / Mongolism

Mongolism and *Mongolian* (or *Mongoloid*) *idiot* are rarely used anymore in connection with a condition present at birth and characterized by abnormal chromosomes, mental deficiency, a broad face, slanting eyes, and short fingers and toes. The current term for this condition is *Down's syndrome,* named after J. L. H. Down (1828–1896), the British physician who first described it.

crib death / sudden infant death syndrome

Some apparently healthy infants die unexpectedly in their sleep of causes that are unknown but are believed to be related to some faulty mechanism in respiration control. The set of symptoms that characterize this condition is known by the medical name *sudden infant death syndrome,* by the acronym *SIDS,* and by the popular name *crib death.* The full name is not shortened to *sudden death,* however, for this is a sports term (from *sudden-death overtime*) for an extra period added to a tied game that ends as soon as one side scores.

shingles / herpes zoster

Shingles and *zoster* are other names for *herpes zoster,* a viral infection caused by the virus of chickenpox. This acute inflammatory disease affects certain sensory nerves, causing pain and an eruption of blisters on the skin along the route of the nerves infected by the virus.

tetanus / lockjaw

Tetanus is an acute infectious disease that is often fatal. Caused by the specific toxin of a bacillus that usually enters the body through a wound, it is characterized by spasmodic contractions and rigidity of some or all of the voluntary muscles, especially of the jaw, face, and neck. From the earlier term *locked jaw,* tetanus is also called *lockjaw.*

Lou Gehrig's disease / ALS

Amyotrophic lateral sclerosis is a degenerative disease of the nerve cells that control muscular movement. The unwieldy name is better known by the abbreviation *ALS* or as *Lou Gehrig's disease,* after Henry Louis Gehrig, an American baseball player who died of it in 1941.

leprosy / Hansen's disease

Leprosy is also called *Hansen's disease,* after the Norwegian physician A. Hansen (1841–1912), who discovered the bacterium that causes it. This progressive infectious disease not only attacks the skin and nerves, producing nodules, ulcers, and white scaly scabs, but may result in loss of sensation, deformities and the wasting of affected parts, and blindness. Leprosy seems to be communicated only after long and close contact.

rabies / hydrophobia

Rabies is an infectious viral disease of the central nervous system. It is usually transmitted to a person through the bite of an infected animal and is characterized by choking, muscle spasms, an inability to swallow, and, generally, death. Because a rabies sufferer is unable to drink or even stand the sight of water, the disease is also known as *hydrophobia* (from two Greek-derived word elements: *hydro-,* meaning "water," + *-phobia,* meaning "fear").

jaundice / hepatitis

Jaundice is a condition in which the eyeballs, the skin, and the urine become abnormally yellowish as a result of increased amounts of bile pigments in the blood. In popular usage, the word refers to a disease or disorder that is associated with jaundice—for example, *infectious hepatitis* (*hepatitis* for short). This viral disease, which causes inflammation of the liver, is characterized by fever, gastrointestinal distress, and headache, as well as jaundice.

boil / carbuncle

A *boil* (also called a *furuncle*) is an inflamed, painful, pus-filled swelling on the skin, caused by localized infection. A *carbuncle* is a network of boils deep beneath the skin.

cold sore / canker sore

A *cold sore* (also called a *fever blister*) is a viral infection usually caused by type-1 herpes simplex. It is characterized by little blisters that often appear and reappear in or around the mouth during a cold or fever. A *canker sore* (or *canker*) is also likely to occur in the mouth, but this ulcerlike lesion is thought to be caused by a food allergy or emotional stress.

corn / bunion

Since a corn and a bunion are caused by pressure or friction, wearing shoes is a good way to get either or both. A *corn* is a hard, thick, painful growth of skin, especially on a toe. A *bunion*, also accompanied by a thickening of the skin, is an inflammation and swelling of the bursa at the base of the big toe. (A *bursa* is a sac or pouchlike cavity, especially one containing a fluid intended to reduce friction, as between a tendon and bone.)

plaque / tartar

Plaque (or *dental plaque*) is a thin, transparent film on a tooth surface, containing bacteria and other substances. If not removed, it promotes tooth decay. Besides, it is apt to form *tartar* (also called *dental calculus*), which in turn can lead to gum disease and other dental problems. This hard, gritty deposit on the teeth consists of saliva, proteins, food deposits, and various salts such as calcium phosphate.

periodontitis / pyorrhea

Periodontics is the branch of dentistry concerned with diseases of the bone and tissue supporting the teeth. Perhaps best known among these diseases are *periodontitis, gingivitis,* and *pyorrhea. Periodontitis* is an inflammation of the tissues surrounding the root of a tooth. *Gingivitis,* sometimes the result of plaque, is an inflammation of the mucous membrane that encircles the neck of a tooth, causing redness, swelling, and bleeding of the gum. *Pyorrhea* (short for *pyorrhea alveolaris*) is a condition related to but much more serious than the other two in that it involves both gums and tooth sockets. It is characterized by the formation of pus and, usually, by loosening of the teeth.

medicine / medication

Nowadays the word *medicine* often refers to a drug or other substance used in treating disease, healing, or relieving pain. At one time, however, the drug or other substance would have been something like a poison or a love potion used for entirely different purposes. *Medication* has the same meaning as *medicine* does today, but it is more likely to be used by people in the medical profession than by those outside. *Medicament* is a formal equivalent.

drug / psychoactive drug

A *drug* is any substance used as a medicine or as an ingredient in a medicine that kills or inactivates germs or affects any body function or organ. A *psychoactive drug* is a drug, chemical, or the like that has a specific effect on the mind. In the United States, a *controlled substance* is a drug regulated by Title II of the Comprehensive Drug Abuse Prevention and Control Act, commonly known as the Controlled Substances Act (CSA). A *designer drug* is a synthesized analogue of a controlled substance. In order to circumvent existing drug laws, the clandestine manufacturer usually introduces slight variations in the chemical structure of the original, often with profound or unknown effects. In informal usage, *dope* is any drug or narcotic, or such drugs collectively.

Under the CSA, the hundreds of controlled substances that are used—and abused—today fall into five major groups: *narcotics, depressants, stimulants, hallucinogens,* and *cannabis.* Some are prescription drugs turned to nonmedical, illicit uses.

Narcotics, the most effective agents known for the relief of intense pain, are essential in the practice of medicine. Under medical supervision, they are administered orally or by injection. As drugs of abuse, however, they are sniffed, smoked, or self-administered by the more direct routes of subcutaneous (*skin-popping*) and intravenous (*mainlining*) injection. The principal narcotics are *opium; morphine; codeine; heroin* (*horse, smack,* and *junk* in slang); *hydromorphone; meperidine,* or *pethidine;* and *methadone,* which, though designed to control narcotic addiction, has ironically emerged in some metropolitan areas as a major cause of overdose deaths.

Depressants, which lower the rate of activity of the muscles or central nervous system, lend themselves to medical uses as sedatives, hypnotics, and tranquilizers. The principal depressants are *chloral hydrate; barbiturates; benzodiazepines* (two of which are known by the trade names *Valium* and *Librium*); *methaqualone* (whose trade name, *Quaalude,* is sometimes clipped to the slang *lude*); and *glutethimide.* Depressants (*downers* in slang) are usually taken in pill form. *Alcohol,* though available legally and not considered a controlled substance, is also a depressant.

Stimulants (*uppers* in slang) temporarily increase the activity of the central nervous system, making the user feel more alert and active for a time. The two most prevalent stimulants are an accepted part of our culture: *nicotine,* in tobacco products, and *caffeine,* the active ingredient of coffee, tea, and many bottled beverages sold in supermarkets. More potent stimulants, because of their dependence-producing potential, are under the regulatory control of the CSA. *Cocaine* (*coke, flake,* and *snow* in slang), the most potent stimulant of natural origin, is extracted from the leaves of the coca plant. As the hydrochloride salt, it is injected into the vein or, more often nowadays, inhaled into the nostrils (*snorted*). A concentrated form of cocaine base that is smoked is called *freebase* or *crack.* Synthetic stimulants, which are used by prescription mainly to treat certain diseases and to lessen the appetite in dieting, are now popular with chemical abusers, both as pills and in liquid form for injection. They include *amphetamines, phenmetrazine,* and *methylphenidate.* One of the amphetamines that clandestine laboratories are turning out in large quantities for distribution on the illicit market is *methamphetamine* (whose slang names include *speed, crank,* and *crystal*). At the start of the 1990s, a powerful new form of methamphetamine known as *ice* made its way into American cities from the Far East.

Hallucinogens, also known as *psychedelics,* are a group of drugs that cause extreme changes in the conscious mind, such as hallucinations, delusions, and intensification of awareness and sensory perception. They have no medical uses. *LSD* (*lysergic acid diethylamide*), which is called *acid* in slang, is taken orally in the form of tablets, thin squares of gelatin, or

265

impregnated paper. *Mescaline* and *peyote*, which are taken orally as well, are derived mainly from the peyote cactus, although mescaline can also be produced synthetically. (*Mescaline* is not the same as *mescal*, the colorless Mexican liquor distilled from the leaves of maguey plants.) *Phencyclidine*, more commonly known as *PCP* but also sold under at least 50 slang names, including *angel dust, hog, supergrass, killer weed, embalming fluid,* and *rocket fuel,* is taken orally, injected, or applied to leafy material, such as parsley, mint, oregano, or marijuana, and smoked. Laboratory-produced amphetamine variants and phencyclidine analogues, which are smoked, taken orally, or injected, are among the other mind-altering drugs.

Cannabis is a collective term for drugs that are extracted from a species of the hemp plant for their intoxicating and euphoric effects. Three of these substances are currently sold on the U.S. illicit drug market. *Marijuana* (*grass, pot, reefer, weed,* and many other names in slang) is made from the dried leaves and flowering tops of the cannabis plant and is usually smoked in the form of loosely rolled cigarettes (*joints*). *Hashish* (*hash* in slang) consists of the resinous secretions of the cannabis plant that have been dried and compressed into a variety of forms, such as balls, cakes, and cookie-like sheets. *Hashish oil* (*hash oil*) is obtained by repeated extraction of the plant materials so as to produce a powerful psychoactive effect—indeed, a drop or two of this dark, viscous liquid is equal to a single joint of marijuana.

isolation / quarantine

Isolation and *quarantine* are different means for achieving the same end: preventing the spread of a communicable disease. *Isolation* separates an infected person or persons from those who are susceptible or who might spread the disease to others. *Quarantine* isolates or limits the freedom of movement of a person or persons who may have been exposed to a disease so as to prevent contact with those not so exposed. In Italian, from which English borrowed the word, *quarantina* means, literally, "space of 40 days"; and, indeed, a quarantine was originally a 40-day period during which an arriving vessel suspected of carrying a contagious disease was detained in port in strict isolation. Nowadays both quarantine and isolation ordinarily remain in effect for as long as transmission of a particular disease is likely.

vaccination / inoculation

To produce resistance to or protection from a particular infectious disease, a special preparation of modified or killed microorganisms is introduced into the body. This preparation, called a *vaccine,* causes the body to build an immunity to the disease in question. The word *vaccination* was first used to describe the application of smallpox vaccine; however, like *inoculation,* it has come to designate any immunizing procedure that involves the injection of a vaccine. Nowadays *immunization* is often used instead, especially if the vaccine is given by mouth but also if it is injected into the muscle or under the skin. Of the three words, only *vaccination* refers also to a scar on the skin where a vaccine, particularly for smallpox, has been applied.

allergen / antigen

Someone with an *allergy* is hypersensitive to an *allergen*—a substance (pollen, dust, or a food, for instance) or a condition (like heat, cold, or light) which in similar amounts and circumstances would not affect most people whose immune system functions normally. The body's reaction to exposure may take the form of hay fever, asthma, rashes, nausea, and other disorders.

To provide resistance to or protection against allergic attacks, a specific chemical unit called an *antigen* is introduced into the body. When the tissues of the body are invaded by this foreign agent, they produce a specialized protein called an *antibody,* or *immune body,* which, if present in sufficient quantity, neutralizes and thus creates immunity to the specific antigen. This process is known as *desensitization* or *immunization.*

X-ray / ultrasound

Long before *X-rays* began screening luggage at airports, bands of electromagnetic radiation with wavelengths shorter than visible light were widely used in medicine for the study, diagnosis, and treatment of certain organic disorders, especially of internal structures of the body. Over the years, producing images on sensitized films or plates has become highly sophisticated and specialized. For example:

A *mammogram* is an X-ray obtained from mammography, a technique for the detection of cysts or tumors of the breast before they can be seen or felt.

An *echogram,* also called a *sonogram,* is a display or record produced on an oscilloscope by the reflection of ultrasonic waves from tissue. This procedure makes it possible to distinguish abnormal tissue structures from the healthy tissue.

A *CAT scan*, whose name combines the first letters in *computerized axial tomography*, is a noninvasive method for diagnosing disorders of the body, especially of the soft tissues, including the brain. In forming an image, it uses a computerized combination of many tomograms; that is, multiple X-ray photographs are shot in single planes, with the outline of structures in other planes eliminated.

A *PET scan* (from *positron emission tomography*) is another type of tomography used in diagnosing abnormalities. By means of radioactive tracers, it shows the metabolism, say, of glucose, in the body, especially the brain. This type of imaging is also known as a *PETT scan* (from *positron emission transaxial tomography*).

Because of its ability to study the nature and structure of matter, *nuclear magnetic resonance* (*NMR*) is useful in chemical research as well as in medical diagnostics. This computerized technique, often called *magnetic resonance imaging* (*MRI*), measures the signals of various atomic nuclei when placed in a strong magnetic field, where they absorb energy from specific high-frequency radio waves.

mastectomy / lumpectomy

A *mastectomy* is the surgical removal of a breast to treat a cancer. In a *simple mastectomy* only breast tissue is removed, the underlying muscles and nearby lymph nodes being left intact. In a *radical mastectomy*, an entire breast is removed, together with the chest muscles, armpit lymph nodes, and nearby tissues. In a *modified radical mastectomy,* certain large chest muscles and nearby lymph nodes are left in place.

A *lumpectomy* is the surgical removal of a breast tumor with minimal removal of surrounding normal tissue or nearby lymph nodes.

in utero / in vitro

English borrowed *in utero, in vitro,* and *in vivo* from Latin. *In utero* means "in the uterus; unborn" (as in "Drug addiction is often transmitted in utero"). *In vitro* (literally "in glass") describes that which is outside the living organism and artificially maintained, as in a test tube ("The implications of in vitro conception need further study"). *In vivo* has to do with being in the living body of a plant or animal ("Syphilis-causing bacteria are cultivated in vivo in the testicles of rabbits").

birth control / contraception

Birth control is the practice of controlling the number and spacing of children born, specifically through the control of conception. One method of preventing pregnancy is abstaining from intercourse during the woman's probable monthly ovulation period; this is known as the *rhythm method.* Another is *contraception,* the intentional prevention of fertilization of an ovum, mainly through the use of special devices or drugs. Various forms of surgery, for both females and males, are among the other alternatives. However, *abortion,* a deliberate procedure for removing or inducing the expulsion of an embryo or fetus, is not a generally accepted birth-control or family-planning method.

shock treatment / electroconvulsive therapy

Certain mental disorders are treated by applying electric current to the brain or, less often, by injecting drugs, with resulting convulsion or coma. This procedure is commonly called *shock therapy* or *shock treatment.* A form of shock therapy involving the application of electric current is known as *electroshock therapy* or *electroconvulsive therapy* (*ECT* for short).

mercy killing / euthanasia

Euthanasia is a Greek word meaning "a painless, happy death." Today it is rarely used to describe an easy death itself. Instead, it refers to an act or method of causing death painlessly, so as to end suffering. Such a procedure, which some advocate as a way to deal with people dying of incurable, painful diseases, is also called *mercy killing*.

Organizations and Institutions

public school / private school

In the United States, a *public school* is an elementary or secondary school that is part of a system of free schools maintained by public taxes and supervised by local authorities. A *private school*, on the other hand, is one that is not open to, intended for, or controlled by the public. That is, it charges tuition and is operated for profit by an individual or a nongovernmental agency. Americans who read or hear about the educational system in England may be confused, for nowadays an English public school is any of a number of endowed, private boarding schools—Eaton or Harrow, for example—that prepare the students, mainly men, for Oxford, Cambridge, and other established universities.

nursery school / kindergarten

Preschoolers, usually three to five years of age, may attend a *nursery school*, where professionally qualified teachers provide educational experiences, often in cooperation with parents. A *play school* is a nursery school in which play is given more emphasis than teaching. For most children between four and six, formal schooling begins in *kindergarten*. Whether part of an elementary school or a separate school, kindergarten prepares children for first grade by helping them develop basic skills and social behavior through games, exercises, music, simple handicrafts, and the like.

child-care center / day-care center

An increasingly popular facility for the preschool children of working parents is a *child-care center*. Here professionals look after the youngsters while giving them some educational experiences during the day. A *day-care center* does the same, but it also cares for schoolchildren after school or during vacation. Day care is provided to the elderly as well, though more often at a social agency or nursing home than at a separate center.

elementary school / grade school

An *elementary school,* or *grade school,* teaches such basic subjects as reading, writing, arithmetic, history, and science, ordinarily to pupils in kindergarten or in grades 1 through 6. It may go as high as grade 8, but nowadays grades 6 through 8 or 7 and 8 are often considered early secondary education. The term *grammar school* is rarely used anymore, and although *primary school* still is, it is likely to refer to a school for pupils in grades 1 through 3, and sometimes in kindergarten as well.

secondary school / high school

A *secondary school,* which offers instruction in academic or vocational subjects, traditionally begins with grade 9 and ends with grade 12. In the United States, a public secondary school is called a *high school* and a private secondary school that prepares students to enter college is called a *preparatory school,* or *prep school.*

Depending on the school district, formal secondary education can be organized in any of several different ways. For example, grades 10 through 12 might be taught in a *senior high school* (now often shortened to *high school*), and grades 7 through 9 in a *junior high school.* What is known as a *junior-senior high school* in some places might follow that three-three split, or it might assign grades 7 and 8 to junior high and grades 8 through 12 to senior high.

Use of the term *middle school* is far from standardized in educational circles. To some educators and administrators, a middle school is somewhere between an elementary school and a secondary school, consisting of three or four grades variously included in grades 5 through 8. To others, it is an early secondary school, for grades 6 through 8. And to still others, it is a junior high school, for grades 7 and 8. Whatever the level of instruction offered, a middle school is seldom called an *intermediate school* anymore.

day school / boarding school

A *day school* is a private elementary or secondary school whose students live at home and travel to classes daily. A *boarding school,* sometimes called a *residential school,* is also private, but most or all of the students live in dormitories and eat their meals at the school.

junior college / community college

A *junior college,* now often called a *two-year college* because its program ordinarily lasts two years, is a postsecondary educational institution. Some students transfer credit for the courses to a four-year institution. Others take the courses as career training in various fields, receiving an associate degree or a certificate on completion of their studies. They might, for example, be awarded an AA (Associate in, or of, Arts) or an AS (Associate in, or of, Science).

A *community college* is a junior college established to serve a certain community and sponsored by a unit of local government. The program, which normally lasts between one and three years, is more likely to emphasize career training over academic courses. Like a junior college, a community college awards associate degrees.

college / university

Although the word *college* is applied loosely to any institution offering postsecondary education, it has a number of specific meanings. As an institution of higher learning, a college may grant baccalaureate degrees (for example, BA, or Bachelor of Arts, and BS, or Bachelor of Science) after a four-year course of study. Or, like a *junior college* (now often called a *two-year college*), it may grant associate degrees after a two-year course. While some colleges are independent, others are part, perhaps undergraduate divisions, of universities. A college that is a graduate school within a university may grant master's and doctoral degrees in such specialized courses of study as liberal arts, law, medicine, and architecture. Another kind of college is a postsecondary school that offers specialized instruction in some profession or occupation; for example, a secretarial college. (The terms *secretarial college, secretarial school, business college,* and *business school* are sometimes used interchangeably. However, *business school* is more often applied informally to a graduate school of business administration within a university or to an undergraduate college of business administration.)

A *university* is an educational institution of the highest level. In the United States, it typically has one or more undergraduate colleges, together with a program of graduate studies and a number of professional schools. The degrees it confers include the bachelor's, master's, and doctor's.

teachers college / normal school

Nowadays most American teachers receive their four-year college or university training in a *teachers college* or a *college of education*. A *normal school* (the term being based on the French *école normale*) usually offers only a two-year program for training high school graduates to become elementary school teachers.

Annapolis / West Point

The *United States Naval Academy,* a specialized college operated by the Navy to train career officers, is popularly known as *Annapolis* because it is in Annapolis, Maryland. Its counterpart for the training of career officers for the Army is officially called the *United States Military Academy;* unofficially, *West Point,* from its location in West Point, New York.

The federal government operates three similar specialized colleges for preparing career officers: the *United States Air Force Academy,* in Colorado Springs, Colorado; the *United States Coast Guard Academy,* in New London, Connecticut; and the *United States Merchant Marine Academy,* in Kings Point, New York.

continuing education / adult education

Schools, especially at the high school and higher levels, offer special programs for adults who want to continue their education but are not enrolled in regular daytime classes. Career advancement and personal satisfaction are the main reasons for taking these courses, which may or may not carry academic credit toward a college degree. Such a program is likely to be known as *continuing education, adult education,* or *lifelong learning.* Older terms, such as *extension courses, evening school,* and *night school,* are less often used nowadays.

fraternity / sorority

Frater, meaning "brother" in Latin, appears in a number of English words, including *fraternal, fraternize, fratricide,* and *fraternity.* Nowadays *fraternity* generally refers to a Greek-letter college organization; that is, a group of men (or, sometimes, men and women) joined together by common interests or for companionship during their time on campus. In a wider sense, the word is applied to a group of people with the same beliefs, interests, work, and the like (as in "the medical fraternity").

Sorority (from *soror,* meaning "sister") closely parallels *fraternity.* However, in reference both to a Greek-letter college organization and to another group with common interests, the members are taken to be women.

seminar / workshop

The first thing the word *seminar* calls to mind is not apt to be a seed, a seed plot, or a nursery, yet, like *seminary,* it comes from *seminarium,* which means all those things in Latin. Perhaps the notion is not so far-fetched after all, for, whether a group of supervised college students meeting for advanced study or any group engaged in discussion, a seminar promotes the development and growth of ideas. A *workshop* is often considered the same as a seminar, but it is generally an organized meeting or series of meetings at which people gather for intensive study, work, and the exchange of ideas (as in "a writers' workshop").

In ancient Greece a *symposium* was a drinking party at which there was intellectual conversation. Today a symposium is an intellectual conversation at which there is some drinking—at least this is surely the hope of the sponsors of a symposium on, say, the interrelationship between the energy sector and the economy at large.

Colloquium, a more formal word than *symposium*, also implies conversation (this, in fact, is what *colloquium* means in Latin). At a colloquium, as at a symposium or any other specialized conference, scholars or experts in a particular field are invited to present the results of their research and to express their views. Social historians, political scientists, theologians, and art historians, for example, might take part in a colloquium on the Counter-Reformation in Spain.

Peace Corps / VISTA

In 1961 the U.S. government established the *Peace Corps* to help people of underdeveloped areas abroad. Under the program, volunteers skilled in teaching, construction, and other fields spend time living in the places where they provide direct assistance. Three years later the government set up *VISTA* along similar lines, but in this program the volunteers work at improving living conditions of people in impoverished areas of the United States, its possessions, and Puerto Rico. An acronym, *VISTA* is formed by the first letters of *Volunteers in Service to America*. The federal agency known as *ACTION* was established in 1971 to supervise all U.S. government programs and agencies for volunteers.

The *Job Corps* is a different kind of government program. Its purpose is to train underprivileged American youth for employment.

Girl Scouts / Camp Fire Girls

The purpose of the *Girl Scouts of the United States of America* is to give girls from all segments of American life a chance to develop their potential, to make friends, and to become a vital part of their community. Based on ethical values, it is designed to open up a world of opportunity for girls 5 to 17 years of age, working in partnership with adult volunteers. When the organization was founded in 1912, it was called the *Girl Guides*. Today both groups are part of The World Association of Girl Guides and Girl Scouts.

In the States, the girls (called Girl Scouts, or simply Scouts) are divided into five program levels. Daisy Girl Scouts are 5 or 6 years old (or in kindergarten or the first grade). Brownie Girl Scouts—Brownies for short—are between 6 and 8 years old (or in grades 1, 2, and 3). Junior Girl Scouts are between 8 and 11 years old (or in grades 3 through 6). Cadette Girl Scouts are between 11 and 14 years old (or in grades 6 through 9). Senior Girl Scouts are between 14 and 17 years old (or in grades 9 through 12).

The first nonsectarian organization for girls in the United States, *Camp Fire Girls* was established in 1910, shortly after the founding of the Boy Scouts of America. In the mid-1970s the organization formally admitted boys and changed its name to *Camp Fire*. To emphasize this coed policy, in 1988 the national board approved the addition of the tag line *Boys and Girls* to the name. Through its program of informal education, Camp Fire seeks to provide opportunities for boys and girls from preschool through young adulthood "to realize their potential and to function effectively as caring, self-directed individuals, responsible to themselves and others." Improving the conditions in society that affect youth is another purpose of the organization.

Boy Scouts / Cub Scouts

The *Boy Scouts* was founded in England in 1908 as a worldwide boys' organization, with emphasis on character, citizenship, outdoor life, and service to others. The *Boy Scouts of America* was established in 1910 as a division of that organization.

Three of the seven Boy Scout programs admit young women as well as men. Tiger Cubs is a one-year program for boys in the first grade (or 7 years old) and their adult partners. Cub Scouting is a family- and neighborhood-centered program for boys in the second through fifth grades (or between 8 and 10 years old). Boy Scouting is a program for boys who have completed the fifth grade (or are between 11 and 17 years old). Varsity Scouting is a program for young men who have completed the eighth grade (or are between 14 and 17 years old). Career Awareness Exploring, which offers career seminars during school time, is a program for young men and women who are 14 years old and have completed the eighth grade or who are at least 15 but not yet 21 years old. Sea Exploring, which centers on aquatic activities, is a program for young men and women who are 14 years old and have completed the eighth grade or who are at least 15 but not yet 21 years old. Exploring, which, in association with business and community organizations, deals with adult roles and career opportunities, is a program for young men and women who are 14 years old and have completed the eighth grade or who are at least 15 but not yet 21 years old.

jamboree / camporee

In informal usage, the Americanism *jamboree* refers both to a boisterous party or noisy revel and to a gathering or celebration that has planned entertainment. The word applies more specifically to a national or international assembly of Boy Scouts. If the assembly is on the regional or district level, it is called a *camporee* instead. This word, which also originated in American English, is a blend of *camp* + *(jamb)oree*.

museum / art gallery

In Greek mythology, the Muses are the nine goddesses who preside over literature and the arts and sciences. Ancient Greek had a word for the seat of the Muses: *mouseion*, from which the English *museum* is derived. Museums are institutions, buildings, or rooms where artistic, historical, or scientific objects are preserved and exhibited. The word *museum* may appear in the name. For example: the Indiana University Art Museum (Bloomington), The Field Museum of Natural History (Chicago), and the National Air and Space Museum (Washington). And then again it may not. For example: the Pennsylvania Academy of the Fine Arts (Philadelphia), the Frick Collection (New York City), and the Thomas Gilcrease Institute of American History and Art (Tulsa, Oklahoma).

In referring to a collection of paintings, statues, and other works, *gallery* is often interchangeable with *museum*. For example, the Corcoran Gallery of Art, in Washington, has a large collection of American paintings, drawings, and prints from the eighteenth century to the present, as well as European paintings and sculpture, tapestries, and pottery. Yet *gallery* does not share two of its other senses with *museum:* first, any of the display rooms of a museum (as in "six galleries of pre-Columbian sculpture in the museum") and, second, an establishment where original artworks are not only exhibited but also bought and sold.

zoo / menagerie

In cities and towns throughout the world, all sorts of wild animals are brought together in places that replicate their natural habitats as much as possible. These diverse collections allow people not only to study and preserve the animals but also to have fun watching them. A number of English words describe the places where animals are kept for public showing and, often, the collections of animals themselves. The Latin suffix *-arium*, meaning "a place for or connected with," is incorporated in several of these words.

Zoo (short for *zoological garden*) is a general word for a place where wild animals are kept in cages or enclosures. The Greek-derived combining form *zoo-*, meaning "animal, animals," appears in quite a few other words, including *zoology* ("the science, a branch of biology, that deals with animals, their life, structure, growth, and classification").

Menagerie, a French word, means about the same as *zoo*. However, it suggests that some of the animals are strange or exotic, as well as wild. If they are exhibited at, say, a traveling circus rather than in permanent zoolike enclosures, they are probably trained.

Vivarium (*vivus*, meaning "alive, living" in Latin, + *-arium*) applies to an enclosed indoor place for keeping and studying land animals.

Terrarium (*terra*, meaning "the earth" in Latin, + *-arium*) refers to an enclosure in which small land animals are kept. In another sense, the word applies to a glass container enclosing a garden of small plants.

Serpentarium (*serpent* + *-arium*) designates a place where snakes are kept.

Aquarium, the best known of the *-arium* words, attaches this suffix to *aqua* (Latin for "water"). An aquarium is a tank (usually with glass sides) or a pool, bowl, or other receptacle for keeping live water animals and water plants. It may also be a building where such collections are exhibited.

Oceanarium (*ocean* + *-arium*) is a large salt-water aquarium for ocean fish and animals.

Aviary (which goes back to the Latin *avis*, meaning "bird") designates a large cage or building for keeping many birds.

With the suffix *-ary* meaning "a place for" (as in *aviary*), and with *bestia* meaning "beast" in Latin, one might suppose that *bestiary* is another name for a zoo or a similar place for keeping wild animals. But, no. A bestiary is a type of medieval natural history book in which descriptions are combined with moralistic and religious interpretations of actual and mythical animals.

botanical garden / arboretum

A place where collections of plants (including trees, shrubs, and herbs) are kept for scientific study and exhibition is generally known as a *botanical garden*. It is often called an *arboretum* too. (*Arbor* means "tree" in Latin, as can be seen in terms like *Arbor Day*, which designates a tree-planting day observed individually by the states of the United States, usually in spring.)

A *conservatory*, in this comparison, is a glass-enclosed room or building in which the temperature and humidity can be regulated for the cultivation of delicate or out-of-season plants. Other names include *greenhouse* and *hothouse*.

Herbarium, derived from a Latin word meaning "grass," also has to do with plants used for botanical study. But the collection it refers to consists of dried, not living, plants that are classified and mounted. A herbarium can also be a building, room, or case for keeping such a collection.

observatory / planetarium

An *observatory* is either a building equipped for scientific observation, especially such a building with a large telescope for astronomical research, or an institution for such research. For example, the five-domed Palomar Observatory, near San Diego, California, uses a powerful telescope and other sophisticated instruments to monitor the positions, distances, temperatures, and physical properties of planets, stars, and galaxies.

Although some observatories have visitors' galleries, planetariums are built especially to give the public a dazzling, though secondhand, view of the heavens. The word *planetarium*, a blend of *planet* + *(sol)arium* (in allusion to a place exposed to the sun), is applied both to a complex revolving projector and to the domed room or building where the past, present, or future motions of the planets, moons, sun, and other stars are simulated, with accompanying explanations.

amusement park / theme park

An *amusement park* is an outdoor place with refreshment booths dispensing soft drinks, cotton candy, hot dogs, and the like; various rides, usually including a merry-go-round, Ferris wheel, and roller coaster; and other activities designed to entertain the public. A *theme park* is an amusement park built around some central theme, such as a land of fantasy, a future world, a past age, or an aspect of nature.

Millions of people, mostly in families and mostly during the summer, visit amusement and theme parks in many parts of the world. Coney Island, a beach resort in Brooklyn, New York, is the oldest major amusement park in the United States, dating from the mid-nineteenth century. Disneyland, an enormous amusement park in Anaheim, California, encompasses seven theme parks (Adventureland, Bear Country, Fantasyland, Frontierland, New Orleans Square, Tomorrowland, and Main Street, U.S.A.). Among the countless other American theme parks are Universal Studios Florida, which centers on motion pictures and movie making; Sea World (in California, Florida, Ohio, and Texas), which offers a variety of marine-life entertainment; and Six Flags over Texas, which traces the history of the state in light of its various allegiances (to Spain, France, Mexico, the Republic of Texas, the Confederate States of America, and the United States).

company / corporation

A *company* is any organization engaged in business. It can take a number of different forms. The simplest is a proprietorship, or individual proprietorship, in which a single person owns and operates the business, deriving all profits from it and assuming responsibility for its liabilities.

A *partnership* is a business organization created through a contractual agreement between two or more individuals entitled to share in the profits. In a *limited partnership* a *general partner* conducts the day-to-day operations of the business and assumes personal liability for its debts, whereas a *limited partner* (sometimes called a *silent partner*) plays no part in the management of the business and is liable only for his or her capital investment.

Once a company incorporates—in other words, once it becomes a legal entity with a charter granting it perpetual life—it is called a *corporation.* Though separate and distinct from those who own it, a corporation is invested with many of the legal powers given to individuals. It may, for instance, enter into contracts, buy and sell property, and sue and be sued in a court of law. Ownership is easily transferred through the sale of stock, and, thanks to their limited liability, the owners can lose no more than what they invest.

Dow Jones industrial / Fortune 500 company

Industrial is a short way to refer both to an industrial corporation or enterprise and to a stock, bond, or other security issued by such a firm. To keep an eye on short-term financial trends, many people regularly follow indexes of stock prices. The best known of such indexes is the *Dow Jones industrial average*, also called the *Dow Jones industrials*, the *Dow industrials*, and *the Dow*. Named after Charles H. Dow and Edward D. Jones, the American financial statisticians who developed the index in the nineteenth century, the *DJIA* is an average, computed daily, of the prices of 30 selected industrial stocks traded on the New York Stock Exchange (or Big Board). Because these common stocks are issued by some of the largest corporations in the United States, being referred to as "one of the 30 Dow Jones industrials"— as, say, AT & T, General Motors, and Chevron are—indicates membership in an exclusive group.

Another select group of U.S. industrial corporations is called the *Fortune 500*, from the annual listings in *Fortune* magazine. These corporations are considered the 500 largest in terms of net income, total sales, and stock-holders' equity. Although the Fortune 500 is the best-known index of top American corporations, the business magazine also rates the Fortune 100, the Fortune 1,000, and so on.

trust / cartel

A *trust* is a combination of corporations organized for the purpose of gaining a *monopoly;* that is, exclusive control of a commodity or services in a given market. Management of the member corporations is vested in a single board of trustees, who, besides issuing stock certificates to the stock-holders, often set about controlling the market, absorbing or eliminating competition, fixing prices, and so on. The Sherman Antitrust Act of 1890 declared trusts to be illegal in the United States. Some corporations have sought to get around this law by means of a special kind of corporation, the *holding company,* which is permitted to own enough bonds or stocks of other corporations to control their policies. Federal and state legislatures, court decisions, and indifferent law enforcement have helped those corporations achieve their trust objectives.

A *cartel,* which is what Europeans call a trust, is now generally an association of industrialists or business firms concerned with establishing an international monopoly.

A *syndicate,* in this comparison, is a group of bankers or corporations formed to buy large blocks of securities, afterward selling them in small parcels to the public at a profit.

A *corner* is not a group or association. Instead, it is a temporary speculative monopoly of a particular security or commodity for the purpose of artificially raising its market value. Such an arrangement (cornering the market) is illegal in the United States.

not-for-profit institution / nonprofit institution

Today a legally organized group that neither intends nor is intended to earn a profit from its activities is likely to be called a *not-for-profit institution,* though the older qualifier, *nonprofit,* is still used. The wide range of not-for-profit institutions encompasses churches, college- or university-related endowment foundations, medical research organizations, and various cultural, community, health, welfare, and relief agencies. These may be exempt from corporate income taxes, but ordinarily not from other taxes on income-producing property or enterprises.

Private citizens who support qualified not-for-profit institutions may claim a portion of their contributions as tax deductions. To qualify under the tax laws, the corporation, trust, fund, or foundation must, among other things, be created and operated exclusively for religious, charitable, scientific, literary, or educational purposes. It may not, for instance, have a political purpose, as in attempting to influence legislation. This means that someone who donates money to the Red Cross and to the National Organization for Women—both not-for-profit institutions—might be entitled to a tax deduction for the Red Cross contribution but not for the one for NOW.

chamber of commerce / board of trade

A *chamber of commerce,* an association established to further the business interests of the community, is called also a *board of trade* in the United States. The term *board of trade* refers as well to a commodities exchange dealing in grain and other products; for example, the Chicago Board of Trade. In Britain the *Board of Trade* is a governmental department that supervises commerce and industry.

bank / savings bank

A *bank* is an establishment for receiving, keeping, lending, or, sometimes, issuing money, and for facilitating the exchange of funds by checks, notes, and the like. A *savings bank* is a depository financial institution whose principal activity is to accept consumer deposits and make home mortgage loans. A *mutual savings bank* is a savings bank organized for the ownership and benefit of its depositors. A *savings and loan association,* or *S & L,* is a depository financial institution that—traditionally, at least—obtains most of its deposits from consumers and holds most of its assets as home mortgage loans. A *credit union* is a not-for-profit financial institution that is ordinarily formed by employees of a company, members of a labor union, or other group and is operated as a cooperative for pooling savings of members and making loans to them at a low rate of interest. A mutual savings bank, S & L, or credit union is sometimes called a *thrift.* This word, generally used in the plural, is short for *thrift institution.*

Ginnie Mae / Freddie Mac

Investors in the secondary mortgage market are probably familiar with securities called *Ginnie Maes, Fanny Maes,* and *Freddie Macs.* All three are nicknames derived from the initials of government-owned or -sponsored corporations that buy pools of mortgages from private lenders, such as savings and loan associations, and sell interests in them by offering securities to the public. *Ginnie Mae* comes from *GNMA,* which in turn stands for *Government National Mortgage Association,* and *Fannie Mae* (or *May*) comes from *FNMA,* or *Federal National Mortgage Association.* Though less obvious a nickname, *Freddie Mac* comes from *FHLMC,* or *Federal Home Loan Mortgage Corporation.*

craft union / industrial union

American labor unions are commonly divided into craft unions and industrial unions. A *craft union* (also called a *horizontal union*) is a union to which only workers in a certain trade, craft, or occupation can belong. For example, electricians, whether hired by a home-building contractor, a shipyard, or any other employer, are eligible for membership in the same craft union. On the other hand, an *industrial union* (or *vertical union*) is a union to which all workers in a given industry—say, the automobile industry—can belong, regardless of their occupation or trade.

open shop / closed shop

In the context of labor relations, *shop* refers to a place or enterprise where a particular kind of work is done. An *open shop* is a factory, business, or concern that employs workers without regard to whether or not they are members of a labor union with which the employer may have a contract. Not surprisingly, the situation is just the opposite in a *closed shop.* Here the factory, business, or concern operates under a contractual arrangement between a union and the employer by which only members of the union may be employed. *Open shop* and *closed shop* apply also to the policy of employing workers in such a way.

store / shop

A retail establishment where goods are regularly offered for sale is commonly called a *store.* If a single line of goods is sold, the word *store* is often qualified by a descriptive word (as in "grocery store," "hardware store," or "liquor store"). Stores fall into several categories, depending mostly on their retail structure.

A *department store* is a large retail store for the sale of many kinds of goods arranged in departments; for example, appliances, housewares, notions (small, useful articles like needles and thread), luggage, toys, and women's, men's, and children's clothes.

A *general store* is also a retail store where many sorts of merchandise are sold, but not in separate departments. General stores are more often found in small towns than in cities, where, under the pressure of large department stores and a growing number of high-rent shopping centers, they are becoming an endangered species.

A *variety store* is a retail store that, as its name suggests, sells a wide variety of relatively small and inexpensive items. Probably the best known variety store is the *five-and-ten-cent store* (or, as it is often called, a *dime store*). Here the merchandise is ordinarily priced lower than in a department store—though not at five or ten cents, as it was in the late nineteenth century, when F. W. Woolworth opened the first store of this kind.

A *chain store* is a group of retail stores owned by one company. Sears Roebuck and Co., for example, has branches throughout the United States and in many other countries, besides being the world's largest mail-order firm.

An *outlet store* (*outlet* for short) is a retail store that sells defective, damaged, or surplus merchandise at a discount. A *discount store* (or *discount house*) and an *off-price store* also sell goods at less than the regular or list prices; however their merchandise is of a high quality. Many off-price stores or chains specialize in clothing.

A *mom-and-pop store* (or *mom-and-pop stand*) is any small retail business, from a grocery store to a dry cleaner. What sets this kind of establishment apart from the others, aside from its small size, is the fact that it is almost always owned and operated by a single family.

Like a store, a *shop* is a place where certain goods are offered for sale. Most shops, though, are smaller than most stores and they are typically limited to a single line of goods; for example, a dress shop, pastry shop, paint shop, candy shop, closet shop, and camera shop. Some shops are specialized departments in large stores ("the gourmet shop in Macy's"). And some, such as a barbershop and a typewriter repair shop, offer services for sale, whereas most stores do not.

condominium / cooperative

A *condominium* (*condo* for short) is a form of real property ownership in which the purchaser of each unit of an apartment building or in a complex of multiunit dwellings acquires both full title to the unit and an undivided interest in such common elements as the land, lobby, hallways, and elevators. Besides paying maintenance fees for the upkeep of the common elements, condo owners pay real estate taxes on their units, which they are generally free to sell or sublet. A *cooperative* (or *co-op*) is a property in which the residents hold shares and are thus entitled to the exclusive use of their apartments. By a vote of their shares, the members make decisions about the common elements (which are the same as in a condo) and approve the sale of all apartments within the co-op.

motel / bed and breakfast

Though *inn* originally meant "any dwelling or lodging," it has come to refer mainly to an establishment or building that, like a *hotel*, provides lodging and, usually, food and drink for travelers. Yet hotels are likely to be in a town or city, whereas inns are more often found in the country or along a highway.

An inn, then, resembles a motel more than it does a hotel. The word *motel*, a blend of *mo(tor)* + *(ho)tel*, was coined in 1925 by the American architect A. S. Heineman for an inn in San Luis Obispo, California. This kind of establishment, which is intended primarily for those traveling by car and therefore usually allows easy access from each room to a parking space, has a number of other names, including *motor inn, motor court, motor lodge,* and *tourist court.*

A *tourist home* is a private home in which bedrooms are rented to the public, especially to travelers. *Bed and breakfast* is an accommodation, whether at an inn, a tourist home, or another kind of establishment, in which breakfast is included in the price of the room.

The word *hostelry* has an old-fashioned ring, so it is no longer freely interchanged with *inn* or *hotel. Hostel*, however, is still widely used, especially in the term *youth hostel.* This is any of a system of supervised shelters providing cheap lodging on a cooperative basis for young people mainly on bicycle tours and hikes.

hospital / hospice

Related to a Latin word meaning "host, guest," *hospital* and *hospice* originally designated a place of shelter for travelers. In time, *hospital* took on its current sense of an institution that provides medical, surgical, or psychiatric testing and treatment for people who are ill, injured, or pregnant. Besides offering inpatient, outpatient, and emergency care, today's hospitals are often involved with public health programs, research, and medical education. *Hospice*, meanwhile, came to refer to a home for the sick or poor and, as the term is commonly used in the United States, to a homelike facility designed to provide supportive care for terminally ill patients.

A number of other institutions are concerned with certain aspects of health and medicine. For example, a *sanitarium*, in caring for invalids or convalescents, generally makes use of local natural resources, such as mineral springs, or treats a specific disease, such as tuberculosis. In the Latin-derived *sanitarium*, the suffix *-arium* (meaning "a place for or connected with") is attached to *sanitas* ("health"). A *leprosorium* is a hospital or colony for people suffering from leprosy, or Hansen's disease. The word is blend of *lepros(y)* + *(sanit)arium.*

284

grand jury / petit jury

In law, a *jury* is a group of people sworn to hear the evidence and inquire into the facts in a case, and to give a decision based on their findings. A *grand jury* is a special jury of a statutory number of citizens, usually more than 12, that nowadays investigates accusations against people charged with crime. If there is sufficient evidence, the grand jury indicts those people for trial before a *petit jury* (or *trial jury*). This is a jury of 12 or fewer citizens picked to weigh the evidence in, and decide the issues of, a trial in court.

jail / prison

A *jail* is typically a building, though it may be a lockup inside a police station, for the confinement of those who are awaiting trial or who have been convicted of minor offenses (misdemeanors). Local police departments usually administer city jails, and sheriffs' offices usually administer county jails. People convicted of major crimes (felonies) are likely to be confined in a *prison* or *penitentiary*, these words being used interchangeably.

Another type of *penal institution* (the generic term for all places of confinement for those adjudged guilty of a crime) is a *reformatory*, or *house of correction*, where juveniles convicted of lesser offenses are sent for training and discipline intended to reform rather than punish them. A penitentiary for women is sometimes called a *reformatory* as well.

squad / platoon

These are the tactical units into which the forces of the U.S. Army are ordinarily divided, from the smallest to the largest:

A *squad*, led by a noncommissioned officer (usually a staff sergeant), may consist of fewer than 10 members. Its size depends on the type of squad; that is, whether its personnel is drawn from the infantry (soldiers trained and equipped to fight chiefly on foot), the artillery (soldiers specializing in the use of heavy mounted guns), the engineers, or another branch of the Army.

A *platoon*, ordinarily led by a lieutenant, also ranges in size. One platoon, for example, might be composed of three infantry squads (perhaps 38 to 42 soldiers), and another the crew of five tanks.

A *company*, normally commanded by a captain, consists of three or four platoons, so its size varies as well. An artillery unit the same size as an infantry company is called a *battery*, and an armored or air cavalry unit of comparable size is called a *troop*.

A *battalion*, commanded by a lieutenant colonel, is typically made up of five companies, batteries, or troops. An armored or air cavalry unit of equivalent size is called a *squadron*.

A *brigade*, commanded by a colonel, is usually responsible for the tactical operations of two to five battalions, with service and administrative units.

A *division*, commanded by a major general, normally consists of three brigades, or between 12,000 and 18,000 personnel. There are five types of division: infantry, mechanized infantry, airborne, air assault, and armored.

A *corps*, commanded by a lieutenant general, serves as a means of command, control, and support of several divisions (normally two to five). It may have assigned to it a *regiment*, commanded by a colonel and consisting of a headquarters troop, three armored cavalry squadrons, and one air cavalry troop, since regiments are no longer independent tactical units of the U.S. Army.

In addition to these units, the level of command known as *theater operations* is composed of headquarters personnel, two or more corps, and support troops. Its commander is a general.

Green Berets / Special Forces

Small detachments of U.S. Army personnel who train and direct non-U.S. forces in guerrilla operations are called *Special Forces* (*U.S. Army Special Forces* in full). These groups are nicknamed *Green Berets*, from the color of the flat, round caps their members wear.

Weather Bureau / National Weather Service

Americans who wanted to know whether to take an umbrella to work used to phone the *Weather Bureau*. Now the government agency that gathers and compiles data on weather conditions over the United States, as the basis for weather forecasts, is called the *National Weather Service*. This service is part of another government agency, the National Oceanic and Atmospheric Administration (NOAA).

news agency / wire service

News agency is an Americanism for a business organization that supplies news, features, and other information to newspapers, radio and television stations, and other media subscribing to its services. *Wire service* has about the same meaning, except that the organization it designates—The Associated Press (AP), United Press International (UPI), or Reuters, for example—uses wire or, more likely nowadays, electronic means to reach the print and broadcast media. *Syndicate*, in this comparison, applies to an organization, perhaps a single newspaper such as *The New York Times* or a chain of newspapers such as McClatchey, that sells articles, features, comic strips, photographs, and the like for publication by many newspapers or periodicals at or about the same time. *News service* is freely interchanged with *news agency* and *wire service*, as well as with *syndicate* in this sense. The term may also designate a news-gathering and news-disseminating unit within a larger organization; for example, the news service of a university.

Western Church / Latin Church

The term *Western Church* is used mainly in two senses. First, it refers to that part of the Catholic Church which recognizes the pope and follows the Latin Rite—that is, the Roman Catholic Church. Second, and more broadly, it refers to all the Christian churches of Western Europe and America.

In the first sense, *Western Church* is sometimes replaced by *Latin Church* and *Latin Rite*. However, *Latin Rite* applies also to the liturgy and other rites of the Catholic Church as authorized for use in Rome and generally throughout the Western Church.

High Church / Low Church

High Church and *Low Church* are terms used in connection with the Church of England, or, as it is sometimes called, the Anglican Church. *High Church* applies to a conservative party that retains various practices and much of the liturgy of the Roman Catholic Church. *Low Church* applies to a liberal, evangelical party that attaches relatively little importance to traditional rituals and doctrines.

established church / state church

Established church and *state church* both designate a church that is officially recognized by the government and supported as a national institution. For example, Buddhism is the established church of Thailand; Islam, of Iran; Lutheranism, of Sweden; and Roman Catholicism, of Spain.

Established Church (with a capital *c*) is another name for the *Church of England,* or, as it is sometimes called, the *Anglican Church.* With the king or queen as head, this is the church that was officially recognized in the sixteenth century when Henry VIII withdrew allegiance from the bishop of Rome. There is, however, religious freedom in England, just as there is in some other countries that have a state church.

convent / monastery

The general term for a place of religious seclusion, for either men or women, is *cloister,* a word that conveys the notion of retirement from the world. *Convent* was once a general term synonymous with *cloister,* but it is now usually restricted to such a place for women (nuns); indeed, a convent used to be called a *nunnery. Monastery* ordinarily refers to a cloister for men (monks). An *abbey* is a monastery headed by an abbot or a convent headed by an abbess. A *priory,* sometimes a subordinate branch of an abbey, is a monastery headed by a prior or a convent headed by a prioress.

alliance / league

Alliance refers to any association of nations, political parties, or other institutions or groups seeking mutual benefit (as in "President Kennedy's Alliance for Progress, to promote Latin American development"). *League,* often interchangeable with *alliance,* stresses formality of organization and definiteness of purpose in pursuing a common objective ("the League of Arab States"). *Coalition* implies a temporary alliance, sometimes of opposing political parties in a time of emergency ("a Greek coalition cabinet"). In political usage, *confederacy* and *confederation* refer to a combination of independent states for the joint exercise of certain governmental functions, such as defense or customs ("the Southern Confederacy"). *Union* implies a close, permanent alliance and suggests complete unity of purpose and interest ("the Benelux Economic Union").

embassy / legation

An *embassy* is the official residence or offices of an ambassador, the highest-ranking diplomatic representative appointed by one country or government to represent it in another. Ranking just below an embassy in representing a government in a foreign country is a *legation,* the residence or offices of a diplomatic minister. A *consulate,* headed by a government-appointed consul, is also located in a foreign country. Its function is to aid and serve the citizens and business interests of the home country.

FAO / ILO

The alphabet soup served up at the *UN* (*United Nations*) is enriched by a mash of abbreviations and acronyms that stand for other international organizations. The following specialized agencies which, though autonomous, with their own memberships and governing bodies, have a functional relationship or working agreement with the UN:

FAO (*Food and Agriculture Organization,* with headquarters in Rome, Italy)

GATT (*General Agreement on Tariffs and Trade,* Geneva, Switzerland)

IAEA (*International Atomic Energy Agency,* Vienna, Austria)

IBRD (*International Bank for Reconstruction and Development*), which, together with *IDA* (*International Development Association*), constitutes the *World Bank* (Washington, D.C.)

ICAO (*International Civil Aviation Organization,* Montreal, Canada)

IFAD (*International Fund for Agricultural Development,* Rome)

ILO (*International Labor Organization,* Geneva)

IMF (*International Monetary Fund,* Washington)

IMO (*Intergovernmental Maritime Organization,* London, England)

ITU (*International Telecommunications Union,* Geneva)

UNESCO (*United Nations Educational, Scientific and Cultural Organization,* Paris, France)

UNIDO (*United Nations Industrial Development Organization,* Vienna)

UPU (*Universal Postal Union,* Bern, Switzerland)

WHO (*World Health Organization,* Geneva)

WIPO (*World Intellectual Property Organization,* Geneva)

WMO (*World Meteorological Organization,* Geneva)

Besides its six principal organs, including the *ICJ* (*International Court of Justice,* or, as it is commonly called, the *World Court,* in The Hague, Netherlands), the United Nations has established a number of special bodies with responsibility in specific fields. One of these agencies is *UNICEF* (*United Nations Children's Fund,* New York), whose acronym comes from its former name: *United Nations International Children's Emergency Fund.*

These are some of the organizations outside the UN that are often referred to by their abbreviations or acronyms:

ASEAN (*Association of Southeast Asian Nations,* whose central Secretariat is in Jakarta, Indonesia)

CENTO (*Central Treaty Organization,* Ankara, Turkey)

EEC (*European Economic Community,* popularly known as the *Common Market*), which, together with *ECSC* (*European Coal and Steel Community,* Luxembourg) and *EAEC* or *Euraton* (*European Atomic Energy Community*), makes up the *European Community,* or *Communities* (Brussels)

EFTA (*European Free Trade Association,* Geneva)

NATO (*North Atlantic Treaty Organization,* Brussels, Belgium)

OAS (*Organization of American States,* Washington)

OAU (*Organization of African Unity,* Addis Ababa, Ethiopia)

OECD (*Organization for Economic Cooperation and Development,* Paris), which replaced the *OEEC* (*Organization for European Economic Cooperation*)

OPEC (*Organization of Petroleum Exporting Countries,* Vienna)

Appendix 1

Gods and Goddesses in
Greek and Roman Mythology

Role	Name in Greek Mythology	Name in Roman Mythology
Agriculture and fertility	Demeter (goddess)	Ceres (goddess)
Chance or fortune	Tyche (goddess)	Fortuna (goddess)
Changing seasons and growing flowers and fruits		Vertumnus (god)
Dawn	Eos (goddess)	Aurora (goddess)
Death	Thanatos (god)	Mors (god)
Dreams	Morpheus (god)	
Earth	Gaea (goddess)	Tellus (goddess)
Fields, forests, wild animals, flocks, and shepherds	Pan (god)	Faunus (god) Fauna (goddess)
Fire and the forge	Hephaestus (god)	Vulcan (god)
Flowers	Chloris (goddess)	Flora (goddess)
Fruits and fruit trees		Pomona (goddess)
Health	Hygeia (goddess)	
Hearth	Hestia (goddess)	Vesta (goddess)
Law and justice	Themis (goddess)	Justitia (goddess)

Role	Name in Greek Mythology	Name in Roman Mythology
Literature and the arts and sciences	Muses (goddesses): Calliope (eloquence and epic poetry); Clio (history); Erato (erotic lyric poetry); Euterpe (music and lyric poetry); Melpomene (tragedy); Polyhymnia (sacred poetry); Terpsichore (dance); Thalia (comedy and pastoral poetry); Urania (astronomy)	Camenae (nymphs who possess prophetic powers and inhabit springs and fountains; later identified with the Greek Muses)
Love	Eros (god)	Cupid (god, also called Amor)
Love and beauty	Aphrodite (goddess)	Venus (goddess)
Marriage	Hymen (god)	
Medicine and healing	Asclepius (god)	Aesculapius (god)
Memory	Mnemosyne (goddess)	
Messenger of the gods; also the god of science, commerce, eloquence, cleverness, travel, and thievery	Hermes (god)	Mercury (god)
Moon, wild animals, and hunting	Artemis (goddess); earlier, goddess of the moon: Selene	Diana (goddess); earlier, goddess of the moon: Luna

Role	*Name in Greek Mythology*	*Name in Roman Mythology*
Music, poetry, prophecy, and medicine; earlier, the sun	Apollo (god)	Apollo (god, also called Phoebus Apollo)
Night	Nyx (goddess)	Nox (goddess)
Pleasure, charm, and beauty in human life and in nature	Graces (goddesses): Aglaia (brilliance); Euphrosyne (joy); Thalia (bloom)	
Portals and beginnings and endings		Janus (god)
Rainbow	Iris (goddess)	
Reproductive power and fertility	Priapus (god)	Priapus (god)
Retributive justice, or vengeance	Nemesis (goddess)	
Rulers of the gods	Zeus (god, who replaced Cronus)	Jupiter (god, also called Jove; replaced Saturn)
	Hera (goddess; also the goddess of women and marriage)	Juno (goddess; also the goddess of women and marriage)
Sea	Poseidon (god)	Neptune (god)
Sleep	Hypnos (god)	Somnus (god)

Role	Name in Greek Mythology	Name in Roman Mythology
Sorcery and witchcraft; earlier, the moon, earth, and underworld	Hecate (goddess)	Trivia (goddess, whose name means "of the three ways" because, like Hecate, she was worshipped at crossroads)
Strife and discord	Eris (goddess)	Discordia (goddess)
Sun	Helios (god; later identified with Apollo)	Sol (god; later identified with Phoebus Apollo)
Underworld	Hades (god, also called Pluto)	Pluto (god, also called Dis or Orcus)
	Persephone (goddess)	Proserpina (goddess)
Victory	Nike (goddess)	Victoria (goddess)
War	Ares (god)	Mars (god)
		Bellona (goddess)
Wealth	Plutus (god)	
Winds	Aeolus (god)	
Wine and revelry	Dionysus (god, also called Bacchus)	Bacchus (god)
Wisdom, technical skill, and invention	Athena (goddess)	Minerva (goddess)
Youth	Hebe (goddess)	Juventas (goddess)

Appendix 2

Geologic Time Chart

MAIN DIVISIONS OF GEOLOGIC TIME			PRINCIPAL PHYSICAL AND BIOLOGICAL FEATURES
ERAS	PERIODS or SYSTEMS		
		Epochs or Series	
CENOZOIC	QUATERNARY	Holocene 10,000*	Continental glaciers restricted to Antarctica and Greenland; extinction of giant mammals; development and spread of modern human culture.
CENOZOIC	QUATERNARY	Pleistocene 1,800,000	Continental glaciers covered much of N North America & NW Europe; volcanoes along W coast of U.S.; many giant mammals; appearance of modern man late in Pleistocene.
CENOZOIC	TERTIARY	Pliocene 5,000,000	W North America uplifted; much modernization of mammals; first possible apelike humans appeared in Africa.
CENOZOIC	TERTIARY	Miocene 26,000,000	Renewed uplift of Rockies & other mountains; ** great lava flows in W U.S.; mammals began to acquire modern characters; dogs, modern type horses, manlike apes appeared.
CENOZOIC	TERTIARY	Oligocene 38,000,000	Many older types of mammals became extinct; mastodons, first monkeys, and apes appeared.
CENOZOIC	TERTIARY	Eocene 54,000,000	Mountains raised in Rockies, Andes, Alps, & Himalayas; continued expansion of early mammals; primitive horses appeared.
CENOZOIC	TERTIARY	Paleocene 65,000,000	Great development of primitive mammals.
MESOZOIC	CRETACEOUS 136,000,000		Rocky Mountains began to rise; most plants, invertebrate animals, fishes, and birds of modern types; dinosaurs reached maximum development & then became extinct; mammals small & very primitive.
MESOZOIC	JURASSIC 190,000,000		Sierra Nevada Mountains uplifted; conifers & cycads dominant among plants; primitive birds appeared.
MESOZOIC	TRIASSIC 225,000,000		Lava flows in E North America; ferns & cycads dominant among plants; modern corals appeared & some insects of modern types; great expansion of reptiles including earliest dinosaurs.
PALEOZOIC	PERMIAN 280,000,000		Final folding of Appalachians & central European ranges; great glaciers in Southern Hemisphere & reefs in warm northern seas; trees of coal forests declined; ferns abundant; conifers present; first cycads & ammonites appeared; trilobites became extinct; reptiles surpassed amphibians.
PALEOZOIC	CARBONIFEROUS — PENNSYLVANIAN 320,000,000		Mountains grew along E coast of North America & in central Europe; great coal swamp forests flourished in Northern Hemisphere; seed-bearing ferns abundant; cockroaches & first reptiles appeared.
PALEOZOIC	CARBONIFEROUS — MISSISSIPPIAN 345,000,000		Land plants became diversified, including many ancient kinds of trees; crinoids achieved greatest development; sharks of relatively modern types appeared; little evidence of land animals.
PALEOZOIC	DEVONIAN 395,000,000		Mountains raised in New England; land plants evolved rapidly, large trees appeared; brachiopods reached maximum development; many kinds of primitive fishes; first sharks, insects, & amphibians appeared.
PALEOZOIC	SILURIAN 435,000,000		Great mountains formed in NW Europe; first small land plants appeared; corals built reefs in far northern seas; shelled cephalopods abundant; trilobites began decline; first jawed fish appeared.
PALEOZOIC	ORDOVICIAN 500,000,000		Mountains elevated in New England; volcanoes along Atlantic Coast; much limestone deposited in shallow seas; great expansion among marine invertebrate animals, all major groups present; first primitive jawless fish appeared.
PALEOZOIC	CAMBRIAN 570,000,000		Shallow seas covered parts of continents; first abundant record of marine life, esp. trilobites & brachiopods; other fossils rare.
PRECAMBRIAN	LATE PRECAMBRIAN (Algonkian) 2,500,000,000		Metamorphosed sedimentary rocks, lava flows, granite; history complex & obscure; first evidence of life, calcareous algae & invertebrates.
PRECAMBRIAN	EARLY PRECAMBRIAN (Archean) 4,550,000,000		Crust formed on molten earth; crystalline rocks much disturbed; history unknown.

*Figures indicate approximate number of years since the beginning of each division.
**Mountain uplifts generally began near the end of a division.

References

Besides *Webster's New World Dictionary of American English,* Third College Edition, on which I drew heavily for the definitions, synonymies, and etymologies that appear in this book, the following works were particularly helpful to me.

Dictionaries

The Oxford English Dictionary. Compact Edition. Glasgow: Oxford University Press, 1971.

The Random House Dictionary of the English Language. Second Edition, Unabridged. New York: Random House, 1987.

Webster's Third New International Dictionary of the English Language. Springfield, Mass.: Merriam-Webster, 1961.

General References

The Concise Columbia Encyclopedia. Edited by Judith S. Levey and Agnes Greenhall. New York: Columbia University Press, 1983.

Encyclopedia of Associations. 24th ed. Detroit: Gale Research, 1990.

Information Please Almanac, Atlas & Yearbook. Boston: Houghton Mifflin, 1990.

The Lincoln Library of Essential Information. Columbus, Ohio: Frontier, 1972.

The World Almanac and Book of Facts. New York: World Almanac, 1990.

The World Book Encyclopedia. Chicago: World Book, 1990.

Human and Not So Human Beings

Sources of Quotations

The Associated Press Stylebook and Libel Manual. Edited by Christopher W. French. Rev. ed. Reading, Mass.: Addison-Wesley, 1987, pp. 18, 114.

"Bette Davis Dies at 81 of Cancer" (Associated Press story). *San Francisco Chronicle,* October 7, 1989, p. A1.

Gilbert, W. S. *Trial by Jury.* In *The Savoy Operas,* vol. 1. London: Oxford University Press, 1962, p. 11.

The Negro Almanac: A Reference Work on the Afro-American. Compiled and edited by Harry A. Ploski and James Williams. 4th ed. Bronxville, N.Y.: Bellweather, 1983, pp. 95, 110, 140.

"Russoniello Tells Hispanics He Is Sorry." *San Francisco Chronicle,* January 19, 1990, p. B7.

U.S. Department of Commerce, Bureau of the Census. *Your Guide for the 1990 U.S. Census Form.* Washington, D.C.

Other Works Consulted

Oakey, Virginia. *Dictionary of Film and Television Terms.* New York: Harper & Row, Barnes & Noble, 1983.

Walker, David. "An Appeal to Blacks." In *Words That Made American History,* vol. 1. Edited by Richard N. Current, John A. Garraty, and Julius Weinberg. 3d ed. Boston: Little, Brown, 1972.

Weiner, Richard. *Webster's New World Dictionary of Media and Communications.* New York: Simon & Schuster, Webster's New World, 1990.

Here and There

Sources of Quotations

The Associated Press Stylebook and Libel Manual. Edited by Christopher W. French. Rev. ed. Reading, Mass.: Addison-Wesley, 1987, pp. 33, 142.

Cowell, Alan. "Conservatives Take an Early Lead in 3d Greek Election in 10 Months." *The New York Times,* April 9, 1990, p. A2.

James, William. "Lecture 1. The Present Dilemma in Philosophy." In *Pragmatism and Four Essays from "The Meaning of Truth."* Cleveland: World, Meridian, 1955, p. 18.

King, Martin Luther, Jr. "Mountaintop" speech. In Stephen B. Oates, *Let the Trumpet Sound: The Life of Martin Luther King, Jr.* New York: Harper & Row, 1982, p. 486.

The New York Times Manual of Style and Usage: A Desk Book of Guidelines for Writers and Editors. Revised and edited by Lewis Jordan. New York: Times Books, 1976, p. 137.

Whitman, Walt. "By Blue Ontario's Shore." In *Leaves of Grass.* New York: Random House, 1944, p. 397.

Yeats, William Butler. "The Second Coming." In *The Collected Poems of W. B. Yeats.* London: Macmillan, 1950, p. 211.

Other Works Consulted

International Geographic Encyclopedia and Atlas. Boston: Houghton Mifflin, 1979.

Monkhouse, F. J. *A Dictionary of Geography.* 2d ed. Chicago: Aldine, 1970.

The Times Atlas of World History. Rev. ed. London: Times Books, 1984.

Webster's New Geographical Dictionary. Springfield, Mass.: Merriam-Webster, 1984.

Wilcocks, Julie. *Countries and Islands of the World: A Guide to Nomenclature.* London: Clive Bingley, 1981.

Things

Sources of Quotations

The Bookman's Glossary. Edited by Jean Peters. 6th ed., rev. and enl. New York: Bowker, 1983, p. 29.

Dowd, Maureen. "Cuomo and Kennedy, in Capital, Take a Troth to Love." *The New York Times,* June 10, 1990, p. 13.

U.S. Postal Service. *DDM (Domestic Mail Manual),* issue 33. Washington, D.C., December 17, 1989, p. 523.

Other Works Consulted

Alexis Lichine's New Encyclopedia of Wines and Spirits. 3d ed. New York: Knopf, 1984.

Ammer, Christine, and Dean S. Ammer. *Dictionary of Business and Economics.* Rev. and exp. ed. New York: Macmillan, Free Press, 1984.

Code of Federal Regulations: Bureau of Alcohol, Tobacco, and Firearms. Chicago: Commerce Clearing House, 1989.

Diamond, Sidney A. "How to Use a Trademark Properly." *USTA* (The United States Trademark Association) *Executive Newsletter: Trademark Information for Management,* no. 9, 1971.

Dictionary of American Slang. Compiled and edited by Harold Wentworth and Stuart Berg Flexner. New York: Crowell, 1967.

Foods and Nutrition Encyclopedia. Clovis, Calif.: Pegus, 1983.

Grossman, Harold J. *Grossman's Guide to Wines, Beers, and Spirits.* Revised by Harriet Lembeck. 7th ed. New York: Scribner's, 1983.

Hannum, Hurst, and Robert S. Blumberg. *Brandies & Liqueurs of the World.* Garden City, N.Y.: Doubleday, 1976.

How It Works: The Illustrated Encyclopedia of Science and Technology. New York: Marshall Cavendish, 1978.

Macaulay, David. *The Way Things Work.* Boston: Houghton Mifflin, 1988.

The Many Shapes of Golden Grain Pasta. San Leandro, Calif.: Golden Grain Company (a subsidiary of The Quaker Oats Company).

Oglesby, Clarkson H., and R. Gary Hicks. *Highway Engineering.* 4th ed. New York: Wiley, 1982.

Pellaprat, Henri-Paul. *Modern French Culinary Art.* Edited by René Kramer and David White. Cleveland: World, 1966.

Rombauer, Irma S., and Marion Rombauer Becker. *The Joy of Cooking.* Indianapolis: Bobbs-Merrill, 1964.

Sunset Pasta Cook Book. By the Editors of Sunset Books and Sunset Magazine. Menlo Park, Calif.: Lane, 1980.

Wilson, William, and the Editors of *Esquire* Magazine. *Man at His Best: The "Esquire" Guide to Style*. Reading, Mass.: Addison-Wesley, Esquire Press, 1985.

Concepts, Actions, and Other Intangibles

Sources of Quotations

"Angolan Cease-Fire Seen As First Step toward a Settlement." *The New York Times,* June 24, 1989, p. 1.

Black, Henry Campbell. *Black's Legal Dictionary*. 5th ed. St. Paul: West, 1979, pp. 334, 661, 902.

Craig, Alec. *Suppressed Books: A History of the Conception of Literary Obscenity*. Cleveland: World, 1963, pp. 219, 221.

Frost, Robert. Letter to Louis Untermeyer, March 10, 1924. In Elaine Barry, *Robert Frost on Writing*. New Brunswick, N.J.: Rutgers University Press, 1973, pp. 77–78.

The Guide to American Law: Everyone's Legal Encyclopedia, vol. 7. St. Paul: West, 1984, p. 76.

Lewis, Nick. "Court's Test for Obscenity." *The New York Times,* April 8, 1990, p. 17.

McFarlane, Robert C. "Why Cap Is Wrong." *National Review,* June 11, 1990, p. 44.

Montagu, Lady Mary Wortley. "Verses Addressed to the Imitator of the First Satire of the Second Book of Horace." In *The Letters and Works of Lady Mary Wortley Montagu,* vol. 2. Rev. ed. Edited by Lord Wharncliffe, with additions and corrections by W. Moy Thomas. London: George Bell, 1887, p. 481.

Sheridan, Richard Brinsley. *The School for Scandal*. In *A Treasury of the Theatre,* vol. 1 (*World Drama from Aeschylus to Ostrovsky*). Rev. and exp. ed. Edited by John Gassner. New York: Simon & Schuster, 1967, p. 468.

Swift, Jonathan. "A Letter to a Young Gentleman, Lately Enter'd into Holy Orders," January 9, [1721]. In *The Prose Works of Jonathan Swift,* vol. 9. Edited by Herbert Davis. Oxford: Shakespeare Head Press, 1948, p. 65.

Teichmann, Howard. *George S. Kaufman: An Intimate Portrait*. N.Y.: Atheneum, 1972, p. 202.

Other Works Consulted

Congressional Record: Proceedings and Debates of the 101st Congress, First Session, vol. 135, no. 127, Thursday, September 28, 1989.

Downes, John, and Jordan Elliot Goodman. *Barron's Finance and Investment Handbook*. Woodbury, N.Y.: Barron's, 1986.

Hawes, Gene R., and Lynne Salop Hawes. *The Concise Dictionary of Education.* New York: Van Nostrand Reinhold, 1982.

The Oxford Companion to World Sports and Games. Edited by John Arlott. London: Oxford University Press, 1975.

The Reader's Digest Legal Question & Answer Book. Pleasantville, N.Y.: The Reader's Digest Association, 1988.

Shafritz, Jay M.; Richard P. Koeppe; and Elizabeth W. Soper. *The Facts on File Dictionary of Education.* New York: Facts on File, 1988.

Thomsett, Michael C. *Webster's New World Investment and Securities Dictionary.* New York: Simon & Schuster, Webster's New World, 1988.

Webster's Sports Dictionary. Springfield, Mass.: Merriam-Webster, 1976.

The Arts: Fine and Otherwise

Sources of Quotations

Angelou, Maya. "A Good Woman Feeling Bad." In *Shaker, Why Don't You Sing?* New York: Random House, 1983, p. 4.

Cheever, Mary. "English 53." In *The Need for Chocolate and Other Poems.* New York: Stein and Day, 1980, p. 65.

Gunnison, Robert B. "Assembly Seat Loss Has Republicans in Turmoil." *San Francisco Chronicle,* February 2, 1990, p. A28.

Munro, Alice. *Lives of Girls and Women.* New York: McGraw-Hill, 1971, p. 35.

Warren, Robert Penn. "Mortal Limit." In *New and Selected Poems, 1923–1985.* New York: Random House, 1985, p. 6.

Wordsworth, William. "There Was a Boy" and "The World Is Too Much with Us." In *The Complete Poetical Works of Wordsworth.* Cambridge Edition. Boston: Houghton Mifflin, 1932, pp. 111, 349.

Yeats, William Butler. "Sailing to Byzantium." In *The Collected Poems of W. B. Yeats.* London: Macmillan, 1950, p. 217.

Other Works Consulted

Abrams, M. H. *A Glossary of Literary Terms.* New York: Holt, Rinehart and Winston, 1957.

Ammer, Christine. *Harper's Dictionary of Music.* New York: Harper & Row, Barnes & Noble, 1972.

Apel, Willi, and Ralph T. Daniel. *The Harvard Brief Dictionary of Music.* New York: Pocket Books, 1961.

Frye, Northrop; Sheridan Baker; and George Perkins. *The Harper Handbook to Literature.* New York: Harper & Row, 1985.

How It Works: The Illustrated Encyclopedia of Science and Technology. New York: Marshall Cavendish, 1978.

Lemon, Lee T. *A Glossary for the Study of English.* New York: Oxford University Press, 1971.

Mayer, Ralph. *A Dictionary of Art Terms and Techniques.* New York: Harper & Row, Barnes & Noble, 1969.

Rosenthal, Harold, and John Warrack. *The Concise Oxford Dictionary of Opera.* 2d ed. London: Oxford University Press, 1979.

Zigrosser, Carl, and Christa M. Gaehde. *A Guide to the Collecting and Care of Original Prints.* New York: Crown, 1965.

Nature and Science

Sources of Quotations

Adams, James. "Britain Prepares Sweeping Defence Cuts." *The Sunday Times* (London), January 28, 1990, p. A1.

Posner, Michael. "'Gimp' on List of Bad Words" (Reuters story). *San Francisco Chronicle,* December 27, 1989, p. B4.

Other Works Consulted

Bird, John. *The Upper Atmosphere: Threshold of Space.* Washington, D.C.: NASA, 1988.

The Endangered Species Act As Amended by Public Law 97-304 (The Endangered Species Act Amendments of 1982). Washington, D.C.: U.S. Government Printing Office, 1983.

Golden, Frederic. *Quasars, Pulsars, and Black Holes.* New York: Scribner's, 1976.

Jastrow, Robert. *Red Giants and White Dwarfs.* New York: Harper & Row, 1967.

McGraw-Hill Dictionary of Scientific and Technical Terms. Edited by Daniel N. Lapedes. 2d ed. New York: McGraw-Hill, 1978.

Motz, Lloyd. *The Universe: Its Beginning and End.* New York: Scribner's, 1975.

Succulents and Cactus. By the Sunset Editorial Staff, with Jack Kramer. Menlo Park, Calif.: Lane, 1970.

Our Bodies and Medicine

Works Consulted

The American Medical Association Encyclopedia of Medicine. Edited by Charles B. Clayman. New York: Random House, 1989.

Dorland's Illustrated Medical Dictionary. 27th ed. Philadelphia: Saunders, 1988.

The Signet / Mosby Medical Encyclopedia. New York: New American Library, Signet, 1987.

U.S. Department of Justice, Drug Enforcement Administration. *Drugs of Abuse*. Washington, D.C.: U.S. Government Printing Office, 1988.

Organizations and Institutions

Works Consulted

Downes, John, and Jordan Elliot Goodman. *Barron's Finance and Investment Handbook*. Woodbury, N.Y.: Barron's, 1986.

U.S. Department of the Army. *Organization of the United States Army*. Washington, D.C., 1982.

U.S. Master Tax Guide. Chicago: Commerce Clearing House, 1989.

Appendix 1

Works Consulted

The Encyclopedia of Classical Mythology. Englewood Cliffs, N.J.: Prentice-Hall, 1965.

Evans, Bergen. *Dictionary of Mythology, Mainly Classical*. Lincoln, Neb.: Centennial Press, 1970.

Evans, Ivor H. *Brewer's Dictionary of Phrase and Fable*. Centenary Edition. Rev. New York: Harper & Row, 1981.

Grant, Michael, and John Hazel. *Gods and Mortals in Classical Mythology*. Springfield, Mass.: Merriam-Webster, 1973.

Hamilton, Edith. *Mythology*. New York: New American Library, Mentor, 1969.

Tripp, Edward. *Crowell's Handbook of Classical Mythology*. New York: Crowell, 1970.

Appendix 2

Source of Reprinted Material

"Geologic Time Chart." In *Webster's New World Dictionary of American English*. Third College Edition. New York: Simon & Schuster, Webster's New World, 1988, p. 565. Reproduced by permission.

Index of Words